Brad M. McGehee
Chris Miller
Matthew Shepker
Damir Bersinic

Sams
Teach
Yourself

MCSE SQL Server™ 6.5 Administration

IN 14 DAYS

SAMS
PUBLISHING

Sams Teach Yourself
MCSE SQL Server™ 6.5
Administration in 14 Days

Copyright © 1998 by Sams Publishing

International Standard Book Number: 0-672-31312-X

Library of Congress Catalog Number: 98-85198

Printed in the United States of America

First Printing: June, 1998

01   00   99   98   4   3   2   1

Trademarks

Executive Editor
John Kane

Acquisitions Editor
Danielle Bird

Development Editor
Howard A. Jones

Technical Editor
David Besch

Managing Editors
Jodi Jensen
Sarah Kearns

Project Editor
Dana Rhodes Lesh

Copy Editor
Amy Lepore

Indexer
Christine Nelsen

Production
Marcia Deboy
Michael Dietsch
Jennifer Earhart
Cynthia Fields

Overview

Contents

Dedication

As always, to my wonderful wife, Vero.

—Brad M. McGehee

To my wife, Misty, who put up with a lot while I was working on this. Thank you for remembering to do all the little things around the house that I forgot to do.

—Matthew Shepker

Acknowledgments

Thanks to Danielle Bird and Howard A. Jones for their support in preparing this book.

—Brad M. McGehee

About the Authors

Brad M. McGehee

Brad is a full-time computer trainer, specializing in Microsoft Windows NT Server and Microsoft BackOffice products. He is a Microsoft Certified Trainer (MCT), Microsoft Certified Systems Engineer (MCSE), Microsoft Certified Professional + Internet (MCP+I), and Certified NetWare Engineer (CNE). He has passed over 20 Microsoft certification tests and is working to attain his Microsoft Certified Systems Developer (MCSD) certification, among several other industry certifications. After receiving a bachelor's degree in business and economics in 1981, Brad took his first job as a teacher of introductory computer and BASIC programming at a community college. He is the author of four books on computers and over 100 magazine articles and the contributing author of seven additional books on computers. He has also worked for several computer integrators over the years, first becoming involved in networking and relational database management in the middle 1980s. He received his master's degree in business in 1992. Throughout his career, Brad has been a computer consultant, developer, writer, and trainer, switching roles off and on in order to not get too bored with any one task. Currently, Brad lives in Overland Park, KS, with his wife Veronica, who is a network engineer and C++ programmer. He can be reached at `mcgehee@msn.com`.

Chris Miller

Chris Miller is a Microsoft Certified Systems Engineer and Microsoft Certified Solution Developer working for a nationwide wireless telecommunications company as the project lead and database administrator for the team supporting Microsoft Systems Management Server. He provides support for a variety of Microsoft BackOffice products. Prior to that, he worked for a training and consulting company as a systems engineer/database administrator specializing in installation, configuration, and recovery for SQL Server and doing a great deal of database design and analysis. He has consulted and trained on Exchange Server since its release. He currently lives in the Kansas City area with his wife Jennifer and their dog, Dogbert.

Matthew Shepker

Matthew Shepker is a SQL Server consultant and network integrator for Empower Trainers and Consultants in Overland Park, KS. Shepker has been working with SQL Server for over four years in a variety of business applications, including online transaction processing, decision support systems, and other custom software. Shepker is an MCSE and MCT and is now one test away from his MCSD. Shepker currently lives in Overland Park, KS, with his wife, Misty. He can be reached at `mshepker@empower.com`.

Damir Bersinic

Damir Bersinic is president and founder of Bradley Systems Incorporated, an integration and training firm specializing in Microsoft BackOffice and Oracle. He is a Microsoft Certified Trainer and Systems Engineer as well as an Oracle Trainer. His far-ranging experience and breadth of knowledge has helped a number of large organizations, including Corel Corporation, Milkyway Networks Corporation, Corning Glass, the United States Department of the Navy, and Nippon Semiconductor of Japan. Prior to founding Bradley Systems Incorporated, Damir held a number of high-profile positions with Dallas-based Sterling Software. There, he provided consulting and training to clients in Europe, Australia, New Zealand, and North and South America. His areas of expertise include relational database design, Internet technologies, network design, enterprisewide systems integration, and Microsoft BackOffice training, consulting, and integration.

About the Technical Editor

David Besch is currently a senior consultant with Empower Trainers and Consultants, in Overland Park, Kansas. He received a B.S. in Computer Science from the University of Missouri–Rolla in 1993. After graduating, David went to work for the Flesh Company as a senior developer, programming in the languages Pascal and C. He is certified as both an MCP and MCSD. He also holds certifications in Implementing and Administrating SQL Server 6.0, Visual Basic 3.0, Windows NT Workstation and Server 3.51, WOSA, and Networking Essentials. David lives in Olathe, Kansas, with his wife Cheryl and their cat, Blaise.

Introduction

Sams Teach Yourself MCSE SQL Server 6.5 Administration in 14 Days is designed for advanced end users, database administrators, database developers, and network administrators who are considering certification as one of the following:

- Microsoft Certified Systems Engineer (MCSE)
- Microsoft Certified Systems Engineer + Internet (MCSE+I)
- Microsoft Certified Product (MCP) Specialist
- Microsoft Certified Trainer (MCT)

The SQL Server Administration exam (Exam 70-26: System Administration for Microsoft SQL Server 6.5) measures your ability to implement, administer, and troubleshoot Microsoft SQL Server 6.5 and to provide technical support to its users.

Before taking the exam, you should have a comprehensive understanding of SQL Server concepts and procedures. Instead of recalling memorized facts, you should be able to apply your knowledge toward configuring, optimizing, and troubleshooting SQL Server in the real world. This book helps you prepare to take this certification test.

Who Should Read This Book

If you have previous training or experience with SQL Server, you should be able to use this book as your sole study material for the exam. If you are new to SQL Server, you might want to consider additional study information such as SQL Server's paper documentation, SQL Server Books Online, or other technical reference books.

To pass the exam, you don't need to take a class in addition to buying this book. Of course, your own personal study habits will determine whether you need additional study material or want take a preparatory class. Many people who do choose to take a class about SQL Server also purchase this book to help them further review and prepare for the exam.

How This Book Helps You

This Microsoft-approved study guide is designed to make it as easy as possible for you to prepare for the SQL Server Administration exam. It covers all the exam objectives as specified by Microsoft and discusses all the specific skills you need to pass the exam. It also includes helpful hints, tips, real-world examples, exercises, and references to additional study material. Specifically, the book offers the following advantages to help you prepare for the exam:

- *You can master the material in only 14 days.* Sometimes it seems studying can go on forever. To help combat what might seem like a never-ending task, this book prepares you for the certification exam in only 14 days. By limiting the amount of extraneous material, this book enables you to prepare for the exam in a relatively short period of time—studying just several hours a day. You can easily gauge your progress, making it easier for you to see the light at the end of the tunnel. At the end of the book, a comprehensive practice test can help you quickly determine whether you are prepared for the real exam.

- *Important facts are summarized for quick review.* Before each chapter you'll see a section called Test Day Fast Facts. Each Fast Facts section summarizes the most important points of the chapter it precedes. This enables you to single out and focus on the most important information before you begin reading the chapter. Rereading each Fast Facts section before taking the exam is a good review technique.

- *Practice exercises cover test objectives.* At the end of each chapter, you have the opportunity to perform exercises that cover specific exam objectives. It is important to perform these exercises because the certification exam assumes you have hands-on experience with SQL Server. Even if you have used SQL Server before, you still might want to perform the exercises as a comprehensive review.

- *Answers to practice test questions are explained.* At the end of each chapter, you also have the opportunity to take a mini-exam that tests your knowledge of the topics covered on that day. The answer to each question is provided, along with an explanation of why it is correct. This helps you to better understand the answers and to learn how to think like a SQL Server expert.

Day-by-Day Study Outline

The material you need to learn has been divided into 14 chapters. Each chapter is designed to be completed in a single day. Some chapters might take more time to master than others, but you should be able to prepare for the exam in approximately 14 days. It just depends on how much time you have available to study.

The chapters not only cover the specific objectives you need to know for the exam, but they also include important additional information you need to know to be a good SQL Server DBA. The following are the Microsoft exam objectives you will be learning each day.

Day 1: Introduction to SQL Server

- Identify how SQL Server is integrated with Windows NT
- Identify capabilities of SQL Server when used with MAPI

Day 2: Installing SQL Server

- Configure Microsoft Windows NT for SQL Server installations
- Configure SQL Executive to log on as a service
- Load multiple Net-Libraries
- Install client support for network protocols other than named pipes
- Set up support for network clients using various network protocols

Day 3: Configuring SQL Server

- Locate where Windows NT Registry entries for SQL Server are stored
- Configure servers in the enterprise
- Manage servers in the enterprise
- Administer servers in the enterprise
- Configure SQL Server for various memory scenarios
- Install an extended stored procedure

Day 4: Creating and Managing Devices

- Create a device

Day 5: Creating and Managing Databases

- Create a database
- Alter a database
- Create database objects

Day 6: Implementing SQL Server Security

- Set up a security mode
- Identify the effect of integrated security on SQL Server

Day 7: Managing User Accounts

■ Differentiate between a SQL Server login and a SQL Server user

■ Create a login ID

■ Add a database user

■ Add and drop users from a group

Day 8: Managing User Permissions

■ Grant and revoke permissions

■ Predict the outcome of a broken ownership chain

■ Identify system administrator functionality

■ Implement various methods of securing access to data

Day 9: Scheduling Events and Creating Alerts

■ Identify the role of the msdb database

■ Identify the role of SQL Executive service

■ Identify conceptual relationships between the Scheduler service, the msdb database, and the Windows NT event log

■ Set up alerts

■ Schedule tasks

Day 10: Backing Up and Managing SQL Server Data

■ Identify the best uses for the dumping command and the loading command in managing data

■ Identify the functionality of dynamic backup

■ Identify how automatic recovery works

■ Perform a database dump

■ Perform a striped backup

■ Create a dump device

■ Dump a transaction log

■ Identify the best uses for bcp when managing data

Day 11: Restoring SQL Server Data

- Restore a corrupted database
- Re-create a lost device
- Load a database dump

Day 12: SQL Server Replication

- Identify prerequisites for replication
- Identify the appropriate replication scenario to use
- Configure the servers used for setting up replication
- Set up various replication scenarios
- Implement replication
- Schedule a replication event
- Recognize the situations in which you must perform manual synchronization
- Identify the system tables used in replication
- Resolve setup problems
- Resolve fault-tolerance problems and recovery problems

Day 13: Tuning and Optimizing SQL Server

- Identify the benefits of installing the tempdb database in RAM
- Configure the number of worker threads
- Select the appropriate settings for read ahead
- Select the appropriate settings for locks
- Monitor log size
- Tune and monitor physical and logical I/O
- Tune and monitor memory use
- Set database options
- Update statistics

Day 14: Troubleshooting SQL Server

- Locate information relevant to diagnosing a problem
- Resolve network error messages

- Check object integrity
- Investigate a database that is marked suspect
- Cancel a sleeping process

Appendix A: Practice Exam

Appendix A is a comprehensive review examination.

Required Hardware and Software

To successfully prepare for this certification exam, you need hands-on practice with SQL Server. It is extremely difficult to pass the exam without actually having used SQL Server. At the end of each day, you have the opportunity to perform one or more exercises that have been designed specifically to help you master the objectives covered in that chapter. If you perform each exercise, you will be well-prepared to pass the exam.

You might be fortunate enough to have access to SQL Server at your workplace. If so, try to make time to perform all the exercises. You should expect to spend at least one hour on each of the 14 chapters in this book. You might even want to plan some extra time to experiment on your own with SQL Server.

If your company doesn't use SQL Server (or if they do not allow you to practice on a production server or if you prefer to practice at home), you might want to set up SQL Server on your own computer. This will enable you to spend as much time as you need practicing and getting ready for the certification exam. The following two sections describe the hardware and software you need to perform the exercises in this book at home.

Hardware Recommendations

All exercises in this book can be performed on a single computer. You can enhance your learning experience, however, by performing them on a network that has both a SQL Server and another computer to act as a client. The following list describes the minimum hardware requirements for performing the exercises on a single computer. It also contains some specific recommendations. Even if you want to set up two computers to perform the exercises, you still should follow these recommendations for the server. Almost any computer running either Windows 95 or NT Workstation can act as a client, as long as it meets the minimum requirements to run the respective operating system.

- Your computer and peripherals must be on Microsoft's NT Server Hardware Compatibility List (HCL).

- A 486DX2 66-MHz or faster CPU. A Pentium or higher is recommended.

- 16MB RAM, 32MB for the replication exercises. 64MB RAM or higher is recommended.

- At least 500MB of available disk space. 1GB or higher is recommended.

- A VGA or greater video adapter and monitor. An adapter and monitor with 800×600 resolution or higher is recommended.

- A mouse or an equivalent pointing device.

- A CD-ROM drive.

- 3.5-inch 1.44MB floppy disk drive.

- A Network Interface Card. If a network card isn't installed on the computer, you cannot easily load the required NT Server network components. As long as you have a network card, it does not have to be connected to a physical network.

Software Recommendations

Finding the necessary software might be the hardest part of preparing your computer for this book's exercises. Generally, you can go to Microsoft's World Wide Web site at www.microsoft.com and download timed demonstration software, or Microsoft can send you timed demonstration software on CD-ROM for a small fee. This offer varies from time to time and might not always be available. Service packs always can be downloaded for free. I recommend either

- Microsoft NT Server 4.0 with the latest service pack
- Microsoft SQL Server 6.5 with the latest service pack

If you have only one PC and want to load NT Server and SQL Server—but you don't want to replace your current operating system and files—you can always load NT Server on top of your current operating system (if the file partition is FAT) and then dual-boot between your current operating system and NT Server. If you are not familiar with how to dual-boot multiple operating systems on the same computer, check out either Microsoft's *Windows NT Workstation Resource Kit* or its Web site at www.microsoft.com.

Tips for the Exam

As you prepare for the certification exam, keep the following suggestions in mind:

- *Read the entire book.* Some people focus too much on the specific exam objectives provided by Microsoft. Although you need to know these objectives, knowing them is not always enough to pass the test. Microsoft often includes exam questions about material not covered by a specific objective. Therefore, it is important to read each chapter in its entirety. Learn as much as you can about SQL Server and how it fits into an organization.

- *Learn NT Server.* You don't have to be a master NT Server administrator to pass this certification exam, but the more you know, the easier the test will be. If possible, try to get as much hands-on experience as you can with NT Server before taking the exam.

- *Don't try to memorize the material.* If you try to memorize all the material in this book, you will drive yourself crazy. You also will discover it does not help you much on the test. The exam questions don't usually test for rote knowledge. They test your understanding of SQL Server and how it works in a real-world environment. The best strategy when studying is to make sure that you fully understand everything you read. If necessary, read a topic several times until you understand it.

- *Complete all the practice exercises.* The exercises in this book are designed to help you learn the key objectives of the exam. Not every objective on the exam has a corresponding exercise because some of the objectives cannot be performed on a com-puter. The included exercises should be considered an important part of your learning experience. The more hands-on experience you have, the better prepared you will be for the exam.

- *Complete all the practice questions.* Use the questions at the end of each chapter to help you remember key points. Don't try to memorize them, however; you will not see them on the test. The questions are provided to help you review and understand the material, not to prep you for specific exam questions.

When you sit down to take the certification test, keep the following suggestions in mind:

- Be sure to read each question and each answer carefully before selecting an answer. Some potential answers are very similar, and you must read them carefully to recognize the differences.

- Take advantage of the paper and pen you are given to make notes or to draw pictures as necessary.

- Don't forget to answer every question, even though you might not know the correct answer. You usually can eliminate one or two of the answers as obviously incorrect. The more answers you can eliminate, the higher the odds that your guess is correct.

- Although this exam is timed, you should have plenty of time to complete all the questions. If you find that time is running short, don't linger on hard questions. Make a guess and then mark the question so that you can come back to it if you have extra time.

Although the purpose of this book is to prepare you to take and pass the System Administration for Microsoft SQL Server 6.5 certification exam, there are no guarantees. Remember, your objective in preparing for the certification test should not be just to pass the test, but to learn how to be a good SQL Server DBA. The certification test is just a tool to prove to others that you have the knowledge to be a successful DBA—your ultimate goal.

This chapter introduces you to the basics of SQL Server, including SQL Server terminology and architecture. The following are some key facts you'll learn in this chapter:

- SQL Server's many features include a lower cost of ownership, scalability, data replication, network independence, fault tolerance, ANSI-92 SQL support, centralized management, visual administration tools, multiple client support, Internet/intranet connectivity, and tight integration with Microsoft BackOffice.

- SQL Server is tightly integrated with NT Server and takes advantage of many NT Server features.

- The SQL Server Distributed Management Framework (SQL-DMF) serves as the basis for SQL Server's architecture. SQL-DMF is an integrated collection of objects, components, and services that can be used by both DBAs and developers to access SQL Server resources.

- SQL Server is made up of three services. *MSSQLServer*, the SQL database engine, is the only service that has to run. *SQLExecutive* is used to schedule and automate tasks. *MSDTC* only is required when transactions are made to two or more SQL Servers simultaneously.

Day 1

Introduction to SQL Server

Preparing to take the System Administration for Microsoft SQL Server 6.5 certification exam can seem imposing at first. After all, SQL Server 6.5 is a huge product that most people are never able to fully master. Don't let this discourage you, however. The best way to prepare for the certification exam is to break down the information into easily digestible chunks. This is exactly what this book does for you.

This chapter is the first of 14 manageable chunks of information that you can use to prepare for the certification exam. Each chapter is subdivided into smaller chunks of information that you need to be familiar with to pass the test. This chapter covers the following topics:

- Major features of SQL Server 6.5
- SQL Server's integration with NT Server
- SQL Server and relational database terminology
- SQL Server architecture
- SQL Server database objects
- System databases
- System tables
- Other important SQL Server features, such as MAPI

If you are relatively new to SQL Server 6.5, you should study this chapter carefully, perform the recommended exercise, and practice with the review questions. This chapter only covers two test objectives, but it includes many basic building blocks you need to understand before you journey into the more difficult chapters later in the book.

If you are well-versed in SQL Server 6.5, you might want to skim this chapter, focusing only on the two test objectives and any specific topics that might be new to you. However you decide to prepare for the certification test, welcome to the journey.

Objectives

- Identify how SQL Server is integrated with Windows NT
- Identify capabilities of SQL Server when used with MAPI

TEST DAY FAST FACTS

- When SQL Server is installed, four key system databases are created: Master, msdb, model, and tempdb.

- SQL Server databases include these objects: tables, views, indexes, datatypes, defaults, rules, stored procedures, triggers, and constraints.

- SQL Server uses a database device to store databases and transaction logs.

- All SQL Server databases include 18 database catalog tables used to track internal data.

- Microsoft's Messaging Application Programming Interface (MAPI) is built into SQL Server. This means SQL Server has the capability to send and receive email messages, just like any email account.

1.1. Features of SQL Server

SQL Server 6.5 is a powerful, full-featured relational database program that can help businesses of all sizes manage their data. SQL Server 6.5 can be purchased by itself, or it can be purchased as part of Microsoft's BackOffice suite or Microsoft's BackOffice Small Business Server. If you work with large databases, you can purchase the Enterprise Edition of SQL Server that runs under the Enterprise version of NT Server. If you are developer, you can purchase a special developer version that runs under NT Workstation.

Over the years, as Microsoft has improved it, SQL Server has become a leading database when it comes to new, innovative features. The following sections describe some important features of this powerful relational database program.

1.1.1. Lower Cost of Ownership Than Its Competitors'

From any perspective, SQL Server offers a lower total cost of ownership than any of its direct competitors. Hardware costs, server and client license costs, development costs, and on-going management costs are all lower. SQL Server leads the industry with the best price for its performance and the lowest cost per transaction.

1.1.2. Scalable to Meet Enterprisewide Needs

Traditionally, many MIS managers have considered SQL Server to be a lightweight when it comes to managing data. Although this might have been true in the past, it no longer is the case. SQL Server is designed to be scalable—from small to large databases—which makes it a versatile database that can fit the needs of any organization, no matter what size.

1.1.3. Data Replication Support

SQL Server includes an automatic data-replication feature. This feature enables SQL Server data to be replicated to another SQL Server or to any ODBC-compliant database, such as IBM's DB2, Oracle, Informix, Sybase, and even Microsoft Access. Replication can be used to distribute data to remote sites, for load balancing, and to replicate data to a datamart or data warehouse.

1.1.4. Network Independent

Although SQL Server has to run under NT Server, it is network-protocol independent. It can communicate with clients running any operating system that uses industry-standard network protocols, such as Windows NT, Windows 95, Windows for Workgroups, DOS, Novell, Banyan, and UNIX.

1.1.5. Built-in Fault Tolerance

In addition to working with NT Server's built-in fault-tolerant features, SQL Server includes numerous features to make sure mission-critical data is not lost. The new Enterprise version of SQL Server 6.5 even supports Microsoft's Cluster Server for automatic server failover.

1.1.6. Support for ANSI-92 SQL and Extensions

SQL Server is ANSI-92 SQL compliant. Because ANSI-92 SQL has limited functionality, however, SQL Server also includes many extensions to the language, which is called Transact-SQL. SQL programmers will find SQL extensions to be a great benefit when writing client/server applications.

1.1.7. Centralized Management

No matter how many SQL Servers are in your enterprise or where they are located, they all can be managed from one central location. This not only greatly eases the DBA's job, it contributes to SQL Server's overall low total cost of ownership.

1.1.8. Visual Administration Tools

Most SQL Server management tasks can be completed through a GUI interface called the SQL Enterprise Manager. SQL Server also includes a task scheduler that can perform many tasks automatically, such as unattended backups.

1.1.9. Support for Multiple Front Ends (Clients)

Within the context of client/server software, SQL Server is the back end and clients are the front end. SQL Server supports a wide variety of clients that enable users to insert, update, delete, and query data stored in SQL Server databases. SQL Server itself includes a variety of client tools, including MS-Query, ISQL, and ISQL/W. It also works with programs such as Microsoft Excel, Microsoft Access, and Crystal Reports that are able to access data from ODBC-compliant databases. In many cases, organizations write their own custom front end using a development tool such as Microsoft Visual Basic 5 or Microsoft's Visual Studio. This gives organizations the flexibility to create front ends that meet their specific business needs.

1.1.10. Internet/Intranet Connectivity

Organizations are discovering that the public Internet and private intranets provide inexpensive ways to share data. SQL Server easily can share data through Web sites, enabling Web browser users to access data directly from SQL Server databases. In many organizations, developers have decided to standardize Web browsers at the standard client front end because browsers are inexpensive and easy to learn and use. In many ways, it is easier and less expensive to create Web-related applications to access SQL Server data than it is to create a conventional client/server application.

1.1.11. Tight Integration with Microsoft BackOffice

SQL Server not only is tightly integrated with NT Server, but it also is integrated with several Microsoft BackOffice products, including Microsoft Exchange, Microsoft Internet Information Server (IIS), and Microsoft Systems Management Server (SMS). The following is a brief look at how these tools integrate with SQL Server:

- *Microsoft Exchange.* Exchange is Microsoft's enterprise mail server. SQL Server can be set up to send and receive mail messages using Exchange. A user can send a query request to SQL Server through a mail message, for example, and the query results can be emailed back to the user. SQL Server also can send various types of alert messages to DBAs and other users as necessary.

- *Microsoft Internet Information Server.* IIS is Microsoft's enterprise Web server. SQL Server is tightly integrated with IIS in three important ways. First, data from SQL Server automatically can be published as Web pages. This enables users to browse SQL Server data with ordinary Web browsers. Second, users can query information stored in a SQL Server database using a Web browser. The results can be quickly returned to the browser. Third, dynamic Web pages can be created from information stored in a SQL Server database. These pages work well for both Internet and intranet Web sites.

- *Microsoft Systems Management Server.* SMS is a powerful desktop management tool that can perform many tasks, including automatically taking a hardware and software inventory of all desktops and servers connected to a network. SMS requires that SQL Server be the database in which this information is stored. As a result, all inventory information can be accessed like any other data stored in a SQL Server database.

1.2. How SQL Server Is Integrated with NT Server

SQL Server requires NT Server to run, which can be both good and bad. It is good because SQL Server is designed to be tightly integrated with NT Server. This means SQL Server has been optimized to run under NT, which contributes to SQL Server's speed and ease of use. It also can be bad, however, because you cannot use any other operating system to run SQL Server. This is only a problem if you don't want to run

1

NT Server. NT Server is a great operating system for applications, and most people (even if they aren't NT Server fans) are willing to use it to get the many features offered by SQL Server.

NT Server offers many features of which SQL Server can take advantage, including the following:

- *SMP support.* Out of the box, NT Server supports up to 4 CPUs. Under certain circumstances, it can support up to 32 CPUs. NT Server supports true symmetrical processing (SMP), in which the processing load is distributed evenly between the CPUs for greater efficiency. Because SQL Server is a multi-threaded application, it can take advantage of multiple CPUs, and each thread can execute independently of one another. This capability is one of the reasons SQL Server scales so well.

- *Multiple platform support.* NT Server and SQL Server 6.5 not only support Intel CPUs, but they also support DEC Alpha and MIPS CPUs. This gives DBAs the capability to choose the CPU that best matches their needs.

- *Preemptive multitasking.* NT Server includes a scheduling mechanism that controls both the order in which program threads are run and which ones get highest priority. This means any program running on NT Server, including SQL Server, is optimized to run as fast as it possibly can.

- *Reliability.* NT Server's architecture separates operating system programs from application programs. Each program running under NT Server is given its own 2GB of memory space (3GB when using the Enterprise versions of NT Server and SQL Server). This space is separate from all other programs, including the operating system. If one program fails, it shouldn't interfere with other programs or the operating system. This contributes to a stable operating system environment that can run mission-critical SQL Server applications without the fear of unexpected crashes due to software-related problems.

- *Fault tolerance.* NT Server includes it own built-in, software-based fault tolerance (RAID Levels 1 and 5) and supports hardware RAID. NT Server also supports server failover. If one NT Server running SQL Server fails, a backup NT Server running SQL Server can take over automatically. This greatly increases fault tolerance.

- *Central Registry database.* All NT Server configuration information is stored in the NT Server Registry. SQL Server also takes advantage of NT Server's Registry by storing much of its configuration information there.

- *Integrated security.* NT Server offers good security. If implemented properly, NT Server can keep all non-authorized users locked out. SQL Server can take advantage of NT Server's security, which makes it easier for administrators to set up and maintain SQL Server user security.

■ *Background services.* Much of NT Server's power lies in its capability to run applications as background services. SQL Server itself runs as a series of background services.

■ *Performance Monitor counter support.* NT Server provides the necessary APIs to enable anyone to create his own Performance Monitor objects and counters. SQL Server takes advantage of this capability by adding numerous objects and counters that enable the DBA to carefully monitor how SQL Server performs.

■ *Network protocol support.* SQL Server automatically takes advantage of the transport protocols and Interprocess Communications (IPC) mechanisms supported by NT Server. This makes it easier for SQL Server to support multiple clients and network operating systems.

■ *File system and tape backup support.* For maximum security, SQL Server can take advantage of NT Server's NTFS partitions. SQL Server also takes advantage of NT Server's built-in tape backup support to perform dynamic database backups onto tape.

■ *Event logging.* SQL Server takes advantage of NT Server's capability to log information, caution, and warning events. SQL Server can read entries in the NT event log to fire alerts or to run tasks automatically.

■ *SNMP support.* With the help of NT Server's TCP/IP transport protocol and the SNMP service, SQL Server can send SNMP traps to SNMP management workstations such as HP OpenView.

■ *Ease of administration.* NT Server always has been easy to manage because of the many graphics-based administration tools provided by Microsoft. SQL Server not only has many of its own graphics-based management tools, but it also takes advantage of many of NT Server's tools. The major NT Server tools that can be used with SQL Server include NT Server's Event Viewer, User Manager for Domains, Performance Monitor, Control Panel, Registry Editor, Task Manager, and Network Monitor.

1.3. SQL Server Terminology

Microsoft's SQL Server is a client/server relational database system. What exactly is a client/server relational database system? It is easiest to understand when defined in two parts: the *client/server* part and the *relational database system* part.

Client/server, also called *distributing computing*, means that all the data processing of a program does not occur on a single computer as it usually does on mini- or mainframe-based computer systems. Instead, different parts of the program run on more than one computer at the same time. With SQL Server, for example, the database engine—where most of the work is done—resides on a server computer. The other part of the program, the client interface, resides on a client desktop computer. The two components of the client/server system communicate over a network connection.

SQL Server is not limited to the preceding example. Multiple SQL Server databases and thousands of clients can be designed to work together and can scale to any size.

A *relational database system* is a type of database architecture that has been widely adapted by software vendors (including Microsoft for SQL Server). A relational database is divided into multiple tables of data, each of which is further divided into rows (records) and columns (fields). Think of a table as a spreadsheet with rows for records and fields for columns. Most databases have multiple tables.

The following are some other characteristics of relational database systems:

- Almost all modern relational database systems use the SQL language to manipulate data in a database. SQL was developed by IBM in the 1970s and has become an industry standard. Although SQL Server is fully compliant with the latest ANSI-92 SQL standard of the SQL language, SQL Server also extends the language, adding important new features. As a result, the version of SQL included with SQL Server is referred to as Transact-SQL.

- In many ways, a relational database system resembles a high-level programming language. Any type of application can be created within SQL Server to meet an organization's needs.

- Data integrity is critical; otherwise, the data stored by SQL Server is worthless. Relational database systems include many features to help prevent bad data from being introduced into the database.

- The needs of businesses change almost daily, and relational databases are designed to be easily modified.

- Unlike flat-file databases, in which the same data often is repeated in many different records, relational databases exclude most redundant data. This reduces the need for storage space and increases the speed by which data can be accessed.

- Access to data can be limited by the application itself, permitting many levels of security.

SQL Server is a true client/server relational database. It enables enterprises to design a distributed database system to meet their ever-changing informational needs.

1.4. SQL Server Architecture

SQL Server is a complex product. One of the best ways to begin learning about it is to start with an overview of its architecture. After you understand how it is designed, SQL Server is much easier to set up, to use on a day-to-day basis, and to troubleshoot when pesky problems occur.

This section covers the following aspects of SQL Server's architecture:

- The Distributed Management Framework
- The SQL Server database architecture

1.4.1. The Distributed Management Framework

When developers at Microsoft designed SQL Server, they had to meet the needs of two important groups: DBAs and SQL developers. DBAs need to easily and efficiently manage SQL Servers scattered throughout an enterprise. SQL Server developers need to write SQL applications that can access data stored in these same SQL Server databases. These are two very distinct ways of accessing SQL Server.

Although Microsoft has included many tools to help DBAs and developers access SQL Server, it's impossible to anticipate all the needs of both groups. No matter how hard Microsoft developers work to create the ultimate DBA and developer tools, they can't provide everything these two groups could ever need. Microsoft developers, therefore, have decided to provide not only the most common tools used to manage SQL Server and to access data, but also a way for DBAs and developers to work with SQL Server any way they want, even using techniques not available through normal SQL Server tools.

To provide this capability, Microsoft developers created the SQL Server Distributed Management Framework (SQL-DMF), which serves as the basis for SQL Server's architecture. SQL-DMF is best described as an integrated collection of objects, components, and services that can be used by both DBAs and developers to access SQL Server resources and data managed by SQL Server. SQL-DMF can be divided into the following three parts (see Figure 1.1):

Figure 1.1.

The SQL Distributed Management Framework can be divided into three parts.

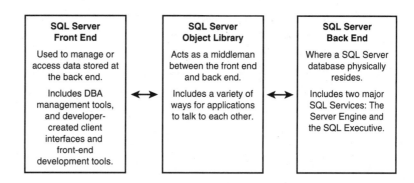

SQL Server Front End	SQL Server Object Library	SQL Server Back End
Used to manage or access data stored at the back end.	Acts as a middleman between the front end and back end.	Where a SQL Server database physically resides.
Includes DBA management tools, and developer-created client interfaces and front-end development tools.	Includes a variety of ways for applications to talk to each other.	Includes two major SQL Services: The Server Engine and the SQL Executive.

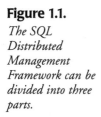

- *SQL Server front end (client).* This part of the framework enables DBAs or developers to access SQL Server resources and data. The most common front-end management tool used by a DBA is the SQL Enterprise Manager. This enables DBAs to easily manage SQL Server. If this tool (or any other management tool included with SQL Server) does not meet all the needs of DBAs, they can create (code) their own front-end management tools to perform whatever tasks are necessary. SQL developers can use off-the-shelf products to manipulate SQL Server data. They also can create (code) their own custom front ends using a wide variety of development tools.

- *SQL Server object library.* The SQL Server Object Library acts as a middle layer between the front end and the back end. It enables any front end to communicate with the back end. In a sense, it acts as an interface or translator.

- *SQL Server back end (server).* The back end is where data is stored, manipulated, and managed. It is made up of two main NT Server services: the SQL Executive service and the SQL Server service. The *SQL Executive service* is responsible for scheduling events; the *SQL Server service* is the SQL database engine used to manipulate data in a database. An additional service, the Distributed Transaction Manager, is discussed later in this chapter.

Before you go any further, pause for a moment and look at the big picture. Previously in this chapter, SQL Server was described as a client/server relational database system. A client/server database is divided into two parts: the client (front end) and the server (back end). The front end is where a user interacts with the data stored by the back end. From a DBA's perspective, the SQL Enterprise Manager is the front end. From a developer's perspective, the front end is any development tool or language used to interact with the back end.

In either situation, the goal is the same—to interact with the back end. The only difference is that a DBA uses one type of front end and a developer uses another. The reason two different front ends are required is that each group wants to perform different tasks. DBAs manage databases; developers access and modify data.

The objective of the SQL-DMF is to enable any type of front end, whether used by DBAs or developers, to communicate with the back end. Another objective of SQL-DMF is to enable people to write their own front-end tools. As long as front-end tools are written to communicate through the SQL Server Object Library components, the front end can communicate with the back end.

Now that you have a basic understanding of the three main framework components, some additional components need to be discussed to show how the framework functions in the real world. Figure 1.2 provides a comprehensive overview of SQL-DMF. The following sections dissect the framework, breaking it down into smaller, more understandable parts.

Figure 1.2.

The SQL Distributed Management Framework can be divided into many components.

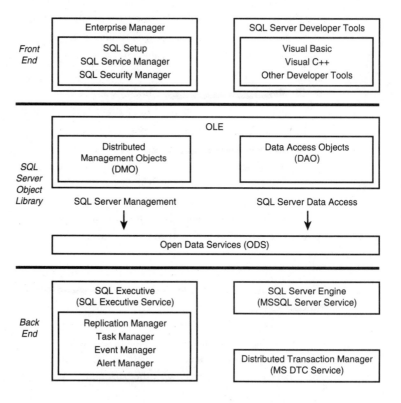

1

1.4.2. SQL Server Front-End Architectural Components

As previously discussed, the front end's purpose is to provide a way to manage and access the data stored at the back end. Although some tasks performed by DBAs and developers overlap, they can be divided into two major types of tasks: data management and data access. The DBA generally is responsible for performing data management tasks such as creating devices and databases, scheduling maintenance tasks, and performing backups. The developer, on the other hand, is responsible for developing front ends that enable end users to access data from a database. This means the front end needs two different parts: the SQL Enterprise Manager (used by DBAs) and the SQL Server Developer Tools (used by developers to create client front ends).

SQL Enterprise Manager and Other Tools

Microsoft includes many tools the DBA can use to manage SQL Server databases. The most powerful and useful tool is the SQL Enterprise Manager. Other available tools include SQL Setup, the SQL Service Manager, and the SQL Security Manager.

SQL Developer Tools

Many front-end development tools can help developers create client front ends that enable users to access data. Although Microsoft offers many, such as Visual Basic and Visual C++, other vendors also provide tools that can be used.

1.4.3. SQL Server Object Library Architectural Components

Unless you are a programmer, you might not be familiar with the components of the middle layer found between the front end and the back end. This middle layer is responsible for providing a common interface between the front end and back end, enabling the two to communicate. Microsoft provides a variety of tools, referred to as the SQL Server Object Library, that enable developers to develop front ends that can communicate with the back end. Developers can choose from several components, which are discussed in the following sections.

OLE

Object linking and embedding (OLE) is an industry-standard programming technology developed by Microsoft for application intercommunications. It not only provides a method for applications to exchange information, but also exposes parts of an application's functionality as objects that can be used by other applications. Microsoft, for example, includes a spelling checker program in its Office suite. This program is designed to check the spelling of words. By its very nature, it provides the functionality of spelling. This functionality can be used by other programs if desired. The same spelling program used by Microsoft Word also can be used by Microsoft Excel, and so on. OLE enables one program to use the functionality of another program.

SQL Server is considered to be an OLE object application (an OLE server) that exposes some of its functionality to other programs. This means other programs can talk directly to SQL Server and can ask it to perform specific tasks. This is how front-end applications can talk to the back end and have it perform specific tasks. If a DBA wants to create a new database using the SQL Enterprise Manager, for example, the DBA's commands, executed from the SQL Enterprise Manager, are passed using OLE to the back end where the database actually is created by the SQL Server service. This means the SQL Server service has exposed part of its functionality (in this case, the capability to create a database) so that another program, the SQL Enterprise Manager, can request that it create a database.

SQL Server's OLE capability can be broken into two parts: distributed management objects and data access objects.

Distributed Management Objects

Distributed management objects (DMO) enable the back end to be managed by front-end applications. It exposes the functionality of all SQL Server management functions as objects, and it enables any OLE-compliant application to use these objects to manage SQL Server and its databases. DMO is used by the SQL Enterprise Manager and other SQL Server management tools to communicate with the back end to manage SQL Server. DMO also enables people to write custom programs to perform SQL Server management tasks.

Data Access Objects

Data access objects (DAO) enable front-end applications to directly access data from a database using open database connectivity (ODBC). Many programming languages, such as Visual Basic, can directly communicate with DAO. This enables data stored by the SQL Server back end to be directly manipulated from an application program. This is how developers create client front ends that are able to access a SQL database.

Open Data Services

Open data services (ODS) is a server-side applications programming interface (API) used to create client/server integration with external application systems and data sources. Developers can use ODS to write applications to distribute SQL Server data to the outside computing environment. Developers can access ODS through client-side programming APIs such as DB-Library and ODBC. This is more of interest to developers than DBAs.

1.4.4. SQL Server Back-End Architectural Components

When most people think of SQL Server, they actually are thinking of SQL Server's back-end components. It's interesting that people never actually see SQL Server because it is composed of two NT services that run in the background. People only see the client front ends. SQL Server's back-end components include two services: the SQL Executive service and the SQL Server service. A third service, the Distributed Transaction Manager, is not a required part of SQL Server, but it fills a special need when two or more SQL services are used together to store distributed data.

The SQL Server Service

The *SQL Server service* (MSSQLServer) is the SQL Server engine. It enables users to query, insert, update, and delete data stored in databases.

The SQL Executive Service

The *SQL Executive service* (SQLExecutive) is used to schedule and automate DBA management tasks, to create alerts that can be sent to a DBA about potential SQL Server problems, and for event auditing. Within the SQL Executive service is a group of managers with specific tasks: Task Manager, Event Manager, Alert Manager, and Replication Manager. These four managers are coordinated by another component called the Scheduler. The following list describes what the four managers do:

- *Task Manager.* This manager causes one or more designated tasks to be carried out when a specific event occurs. Every time the clock hits 1 a.m., for example, a database backup can be made automatically. Designated tasks can be implemented as Transact-SQL statements, scripts, or NT command shell scripts.

- *Event Manager.* This manager writes SQL Server events to the NT Server event viewer log.

- *Alert Manager.* This manager sends one or more designated individuals a message, through either email or a pager, when a specific SQL Server event occurs.

- *Replication Manager.* This manager is used during the replication process to schedule when replication will occur.

The SQL Executive service does not have to be running for the SQL Server service to work. The SQL Executive service only is required if you want to perform specific tasks, such as replicating, creating alerts, or running tasks.

The Distributed Transaction Manager Service

The *Distributed Transaction Manager*, which runs as a service (MSDTC), is not a required SQL Server service. It is used when a SQL Server application modifies data on two or more SQL Servers as part of a single transaction. It guarantees that each data modification on each server will be 100 percent complete on all the servers. In the event of an aborted transaction, any partial modification is rolled back on all the affected servers so the data does not become corrupted.

As you can see, SQL-DMF is quite complex. You just need to remember its three major components—the front end, the SQL Object Library, and the back end—and remember that the front end is used for both administrative and data access at the back end.

1.5. SQL Server Databases and Database Objects

SQL Server can manage one or more databases simultaneously. When you create a SQL Server database (as described in Day 5, "Creating and Managing Databases"), all you are doing is creating an empty database container or shell.

An empty database does not have much value until you populate it with database objects. A *database object* is one of many components that makes up a database, which either contains data or is used to interact with data. Fortunately, for the focus of this book and the SQL Server 6.5 Administration certification exam, you don't have to worry much about how to create database objects. This is the job of the database developer. Even though DBAs don't usually create many database objects, they still should know what they are and how they are used. This section takes a brief look at the following SQL Server database objects:

- Tables
- Views
- Indexes
- Datatypes
- Defaults
- Rules

1

- ■ Stored procedures
- ■ Triggers
- ■ Constraints

1.5.1. Tables

Tables are the most important objects within a database because they are where data is stored. Tables are made up of rows (records) and columns (fields), as shown in Figure 1.3. Databases can include many tables, and each table can have an unlimited number of rows. (Tables are limited only by disk space and performance issues.)

Figure 1.3.

Tables are made up of rows and columns.

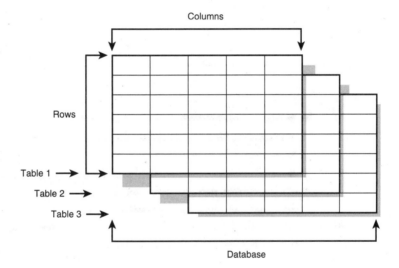

1.5.2. Views

Views, or virtual tables, are created to provide alternative ways to view data stored in tables. Views can display a subset of data from a table, or two or more tables can be linked and combined to create a view (see Figure 1.4). Views themselves do not contain data; they point to selected data and present it visually.

1.5.3. Indexes

Indexes are database objects used to speed up data access. Indexes contain ordered pointers that point to data stored in tables. Like the index in a book, this enables SQL Server to locate data quickly. Without indexes, SQL Server would have to search every row in a table to find a specific piece of data. SQL Server uses two types of indexes: clustered and nonclustered (see Figure 1.5).

Figure 1.4.

Views do not store data; they just present it visually.

staff Table

staff_id	f_name	l_name	title	pager_number	hire_date

PLUS

certification Table

certification	staff_id

EQUALS

View
(Combines columns from the above two tables to create a new virtual table)

staff_id	f_name	l_name	title	pager_number	certification	hire_date

- A *clustered index* forces the rows in a table to be physically stored in sorted order, using one or more columns from the table to sort the rows. A table can have only one clustered index.

- A *nonclustered index* does not physically arrange data; it simply points to the data in a table. The pointers are themselves sorted, which makes it easy to locate data quickly within a table. A table can include an index for every column in the table, although this is uncommon. Generally, only columns that benefit from sorting have indexes.

1.5.4. Datatypes

Datatypes define or describe the type of data that can be entered into a column and how it is stored by SQL Server. A datatype must be specified for each column in a table. If the numeric datatype is specified, for example, the column stores numbers not letters. Datatypes often are used by database designers to prevent people from entering the wrong type of data in a particular column.

1.5.5. Defaults

Defaults are values automatically entered into columns if no values are entered during data entry. Defaults can be assigned to any column in a table. If most business addresses stored in a table are from Kansas, for example, a default of KS can be

1

created for the State column. KS automatically is entered into every newly created row, saving the data entry person a little typing. The default can be overridden whenever necessary.

Figure 1.5.

SQL Server supports clustered and non-clustered indexes.

staff Table Sorted with a Clustered Index

staff_id	f_name	l_name	title	pager_number	hire_date
537	Kristin	Shurley	Tech 1	4823	6-1-95
574	Veronica	Rodriguez	Manager	4887	2-5-95
663	Gail	Jenner	Tech 2	4830	12-1-97
779	Walter	Neil	Tech 2	4811	1-2-95
839	Brett	Marie	Tech 1	4883	4-3-96

In a clustered index, the data is physically sorted. Here, the table is physically sorted by the *staff_id* column.

staff Table

staff_id	f_name	l_name	title	pager_number	hire_date	Physical location
574	Veronica	Rodriguez	Manager	4887	2-5-95	bbb
839	Brett	Marie	Tech 1	4883	4-3-96	ddd
537	Kristin	Shurley	Tech 1	4823	6-1-95	aaa
779	Walter	Neil	Tech 2	4811	1-2-95	ppp
663	Gail	Jenner	Tech 2	4830	12-1-97	nnn

Nonclustered Index

staff_id	pointer
537	aaa
574	bbb
663	nnn
779	ppp
839	ddd

↑
Not a
table
column

A nonclustered index is an object separate from the table. The table remains in the same physical order in which it was created. Above, the nonclustered index is sorted by staff_id. The pointer column points to the physical location in the database where the row is stored, so it can be located quickly.

1.5.6. Rules

Rules are database objects that control what data can be entered in a table. Database designers use rules to prevent bad data from being entered. A rule can be added to a business address table, for example, to verify that addresses entered are proper street addresses. If the data entered is not a proper street address, the data-entry person could be notified with a message.

1.5.7. Stored Procedures

Stored procedures are powerful and flexible database objects that enable you to automate many tasks. They are made up of precompiled Transact-SQL statements that carry out a predetermined task or series of tasks. Transact-SQL developers write stored procedures to automate many data-processing tasks. SQL Server includes many predefined stored procedures, referred to as *system stored procedures*. An example of a system-stored procedure is sp_help. When run, this stored procedure provides information about whatever database object you specified. All built-in stored procedures begin with the characters sp_ and are stored in the Master database. Various stored procedures are described throughout this book.

1.5.8. Triggers

A *trigger* is a special type of stored procedure that executes whenever specific events occur to a table. Triggers can be set up to automatically fire—execute a series of Transact-SQL statements—whenever data in a table is inserted, updated, or deleted. Triggers often are used by Transact-SQL developers to ensure data integrity and to perform other tasks.

1.5.9. Constraints

Constraints are used to enforce data integrity. In many ways, they are similar to datatypes, defaults, rules, and triggers, all of which are also used to enforce data integrity. Constraints, however, are more flexible than these other database objects and are easier to use.

1.6. How SQL Server Stores Data

To manipulate large quantities of data in a reasonable amount of time, SQL Server stores data on physical media in a very specific way. This section discusses how SQL Server allocates storage space and introduces the following terms:

- Device
- SQL Server database
- Transaction log

1.6.1. What Is a Device?

There are two different types of devices: database devices (used to store databases and transaction logs) and dump devices (used to store database backups). This

1

section focuses on database devices. Dump devices are discussed on Day 10, "Backing Up and Managing SQL Server Data."

A *database device* is an NTFS or FAT file stored on physical media such as a hard disk. It is used to preallocate physical storage space to be used by a database or transaction log. A device must be created before a SQL Server database or transaction log can be created. A single device can contain one or more SQL Server databases, and a single SQL Server database can exist on one or more devices. Day 4, "Creating and Managing Devices," discusses devices in more detail.

1.6.2. What Is a Database?

When most people think of a database, they think of a database populated with data and other database objects, ready to be used by end users. This is not the case, however, when a database is created in SQL Server. When a database is first created, it essentially is an empty shell that does not contain any user-created objects. SQL Server allocates space within the database using special data structures called *pages*. After a database shell has been created, it is up to the database developer or DBA to create or add the necessary objects. After the database has been fully populated, only then is it ready to be used by end users. Databases are covered in more detail on Day 5, "Creating and Managing Databases."

1.7. What Is a Transaction Log?

Whenever a database is created using SQL Server, a transaction log automatically is created at the same time. A *transaction log* is a reserved storage area on a device. It automatically records all changes made to database objects before the changes are written to the database. This is an important fault-tolerant feature in SQL Server that helps prevent a database from corruption. Transaction logs also are discussed in more detail in Day 5.

1.8. SQL Server System Databases and Tables

SQL Server manages two types of databases: system and user. *System databases* store data used exclusively by SQL Server to manage both itself and user databases. *User databases* are used to store user data.

When SQL Server is installed on a physical server, it creates a variety of system devices and databases that are integral to SQL Server's operation. The system databases created include Master, model, tempdb, and msdb (see Figure 1.6). One user database, pubs, is included as a sample database. SQL Server uses the information stored in the system databases to operate and manage both itself and the user databases.

Figure 1.6.

SQL Server includes four system databases.

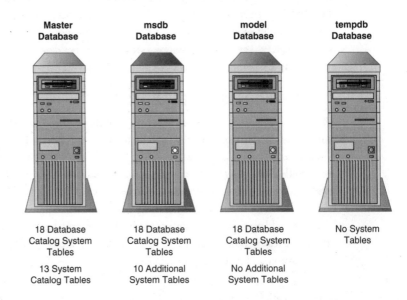

Master Database	msdb Database	model Database	tempdb Database
18 Database Catalog System Tables	18 Database Catalog System Tables	18 Database Catalog System Tables	No System Tables
13 System Catalog Tables	10 Additional System Tables	No Additional System Tables	

Both system and user databases contain system tables. *System tables* store data that tracks information about all SQL Server activities. There are two types of system tables. Every database, whether system or user, includes 18 identical system tables commonly referred to as the *database catalog*. In addition to these common system tables, each system database includes system tables for its own exclusive use. These tables are described in the following sections. All system tables begin with the prefix sys.

After looking at the 18 system tables common to both system and user databases, you will look at the unique system tables of each SQL Server system database.

1.8.1. Database Catalog System Tables

The system tables of the database catalog are used by each database to track information about how it is designed and used. Every database created by SQL Server includes the following 18 database catalog system tables:

- *sysalternates*. Includes one row for every SQL Server user mapped (aliased) to a database user in the database. This enables users to log on to a database using a different name.

- *sysarticles*. Includes information about every article created for replication in this database. Includes information about the base table, publications to which the article belongs, and the article's status.
- *syscolumns*. Includes one row for every column of a table, every column of a view, and every parameter used in a stored procedure in the database.
- *syscomments*. Includes one or more rows containing the SQL definition statements (creation text) for every view, rule, default, trigger, and stored procedure in the database.
- *sysconstraints*. Includes information about all the constraints used in the database.
- *sysdepends*. Includes one row for every table, view, or stored procedure referenced by another view, table, or stored procedure in the database.
- *sysindexes*. Includes one row for every clustered index, nonclustered index, and table without an index. Includes additional rows for each table that stores text or image data in the database.
- *syskeys*. Includes one row for every common, foreign, and primary key used in the database.
- *syslogs*. This is the database's transaction log. It usually is stored on a separate device from the database itself.
- *sysobjects*. Includes one row for every table, view, log, rule, default, trigger, and stored procedure in the database.
- *sysprocedures*. Includes one row for every view, rule, default, trigger, and stored procedure in the database. The information stored is preparsed optimization trees for each object.
- *sysprotects*. Includes information about user permissions for objects in the database.
- *syspublications*. Includes one row for every publication enabled for replication in this database.
- *sysreferences*. Includes one row for every referential integrity constraint used on a column or table in the database.
- *syssegments*. Includes one row for each segment used by the database.
- *syssubscriptions*. Includes one row for every subscription from a subscribing server in the database.
- *systypes*. Includes one row for every default and user-defined datatype used in the database.

- *sysusers*. Includes one row for each user who has permission to access the database.

 Test Tip

Although it might seem overwhelming at first, it's a good idea to learn the purpose of each system table. As a DBA, you need to know them to manage and troubleshoot database problems. You also need to be familiar with them for the certification test.

1.8.2. The Master Database

The Master database is SQL Server's most important database. The information it stores includes available devices and databases, the amount of space allocated to each database, ongoing processes, user accounts, active locks, system error messages, and system stored procedures.

The Master database and its transaction log are stored on the master device (master.dat). The Master database has a default size of 25MB. Because of this database's critical nature, users are not allowed to modify it directly. All changes to the Master database must be made through the SQL Enterprise Manager, Transact-SQL statements, or stored procedures.

 Test Tip

Every time a change made to SQL Server affects the contents of the master database, the master database should immediately be backed up. It's also a good idea to increase the default size of the master database to 40MB or more. This should provide plenty of room for future growth. If the master database grows to exceed its allocated size, it could lock up SQL Server and cause much grief.

In addition to the 18 tables common to all SQL Server databases, the Master database includes the following 13 specialized system tables commonly referred to as the *system catalog* (or data dictionary):

- *syscharsets*. Includes information about the installed character sets.
- *sysconfigures*. Includes system configuration values to be used at the next start-up of SQL Server.
- *syscurconfigs*. Includes current SQL Server configuration values.
- *sysdatabases*. Includes information about databases managed by SQL Server, including database name, owner, and status.

- *sysdevices.* Includes information about database and backup devices.

- *syslanguages.* Includes the installed language sets.

- *syslocks.* Includes information about active locks in all the databases managed by SQL Server.

- *syslogins.* Includes all user account information, including name, password, and configuration information.

- *sysmessages.* Includes all the system error messages available to SQL Server.

- *sysprocesses.* Includes information about all current processes, including process IDs, logon information, and the current status of each logged on user.

- *sysremotelogins.* Includes information about all users logging in from remote SQL Servers.

- *sysservers.* Includes information about the local server and remote servers.

- *sysusages.* Includes information about disk space allocated to every database, including mappings of physical storage areas to individual databases.

1.8.3. The msdb Database

The msdb database is used by the SQL Executive service to schedule alerts, tasks, and replication. It also stores a history of every backup and restore made to every database managed by SQL Server.

The msdb database is stored on the msdbdata device (msdbdata.dat), and its transaction log is stored on the msdblog device (msdblog.dat). The default size of the msdb database is 6MB, and the default size of the msdb transaction log is 2MB.

Every time a change made to SQL Server affects the contents of the msdb database, the msdb database and its transaction log should immediately be backed up. It's also a good idea to increase the default size of the msdb database to 20MB or more and the transaction log to 8MB or more. This should allow both plenty of room for growth.

The msdb database includes the standard 18 system catalog tables, plus the following 10 specialized tables:

- *sysalerts.* Includes information about user-defined alerts.

- *sysbackupdetail.* Includes information about the backup devices used.

- *sysbackuphistory.* Includes a complete history of each time a backup was made of any database managed by SQL Server.
- *syshistory.* Includes a complete history of the success or failure of every scheduled task or alert.
- *sysnotifications.* Includes a list of which operators are associated with which alerts and how the operators are to be alerted.
- *sysoperators.* Includes a list of all the operators to receive alerts from SQL Server, along with contact information.
- *sysrestoredetail.* Includes information about the restore devices used.
- *sysrestorehistory.* Includes a complete history of each time a restore was done on any database managed by SQL Server.
- *sysservermessages.* Includes a list of database and database object error messages.
- *systasks.* Includes information about user-defined tasks.

1.8.4. The model Database

Whenever a new database is created, it always contains the standard 18 system catalog tables previously described. These 18 tables are copied from the model database whenever a new database is created. The sole purpose of the model database is to act as a template for new databases.

Some DBAs and database designers like to modify the model database so that, whenever a new database is created, it also includes these modifications. Examples of common modifications to the model database include adding user-defined datatypes, rules, defaults, and stored procedures. Any change made to the model database automatically is reflected in any new databases created.

The model database is stored on the master device (master.dat) and has a default size of 1MB. As a result, all new databases have this same default size. The model database includes only the 18 system catalog tables.

1.8.5. The tempdb Database

The tempdb database is a shared database used by all SQL Server databases and all database users. It is used to store temporary information, such as sorting information when a temporary index is created during a query on a non-indexed table.

Any temporary tables created as a result of user actions are automatically deleted when the user disconnects from SQL Server. In addition, any temporary tables created in tempdb are deleted every time SQL Server is stopped and restarted.

The tempdb database is located on the master device (master.dat) and has a default size of 2MB. This usually is too small for most applications. It should be increased to meet the demand of the particular applications running on SQL Server.

To increase performance, the tempdb database can be stored in RAM instead of the master device.

1.8.6. The pubs Database

The pubs database is not a system database. It is created during SQL Server's setup, however, and is stored on the master device (master.dat). It includes sample data used in the SQL Server documentation, SQL Server Books Online, and many reference books (including this one). If you don't need this database, it can be deleted.

1.9. Other Important SQL Server Features

This chapter has only just begun to describe the many features of SQL Server and how it works. The material presented so far can be considered core information that all DBAs and developers need to know. In addition to this core data, you need to be aware of several additional features when preparing for the certification test. This section examines the following:

- Queries
- Extended stored procedures
- How MAPI is incorporated with SQL Server

1.9.1. Queries

As you already know, the purpose of a database is to organize data to make it easy to retrieve. The term *query* is used to describe how you retrieve and manipulate data from a database. Queries are Transact-SQL statements, usually run from the SQL Query tool in the Enterprise Manager. Queries also can be run from other user interfaces such as ISQL/W and ISQL.

When a query is run against a database, it is used to return information about the data you are seeking. You might, for example, want to list all customers you do business with in the state of Missouri. Queries also are used to directly manipulate data; they can insert, update, or delete rows in a table. Any time Transact-SQL is used to interact with data in a SQL Server database, a query is being executed. Queries can be run one time, or they can be saved and run over and over.

Although DBAs are not required to be expert query writers, it is important that they learn the basics. Queries are one of the main ways for the DBA to interact with a SQL Server database.

1.9.2. Extended Stored Procedures

Extended stored procedures are not stored procedures, although they sound similar and are executed the same way. An extended stored procedure is a function of a dynamic link library (DLL) that provides the DBA and Transact-SQL developer with additional functionality. SQL Server includes many extended procedures that provide additional administrative functionality. They also can be written by developers to provide functionality not normally available to SQL Server. An example of an extended stored procedure is xp_sendmail, which is used to send mail messages from SQL Server to any MAPI-enabled application. All built-in extended stored procedures begin with the characters xp_.

1.9.3. How MAPI Is Incorporated with SQL Server

The Messaging Application Programming Interface (MAPI) has been built into SQL Server. MAPI is an industry-standard messaging protocol developed by Microsoft. It allows a MAPI-enabled computer program to communicate with another MAPI-enabled mail-based program such as Microsoft Exchange.

SQL Server can take advantage of MAPI in two ways. First, SQL Server can create and send email messages to designated DBAs when specific user-defined events have occurred (such as when a particular database becomes full). Second, SQL developers can include MAPI capability within the SQL Server applications they write. It is possible, for example, to create a SQL Server application that enables a user to send a query to SQL Server through an email message. When SQL Server receives the message, it executes the query and sends the results back to the user through an email message.

MAPI is incorporated into SQL Server through the use of extended stored procedures. These extended stored procedures can either be called automatically from within SQL Server (like when a notification email message is sent) or be used directly by SQL developers when they write SQL Server applications.

Before SQL Server can take advantage of its MAPI capability, however, SQL Mail must first be configured. This is a simple procedure in which you tell SQL Server which email account in your email system you want it to use. Just like any email user, SQL Server must be assigned an email account that it can use to send and receive email messages. SQL Mail is set up using the SQL Server setup program.

If you have never set up SQL Mail before, make sure you do so at least once before taking the certification exam. Practicing its setup can help you better understand how SQL Mail works. The exercise at the end of this chapter shows you how to set up SQL Mail.

1

Lab

Questions

1. You are the Webmaster of an Internet site, and you want to use a relational database to interact with Microsoft's Internet Information Server software. You are considering several database programs, including SQL Server. What are some of the reasons you might choose SQL Server over other relational databases?

    A. SQL Server is scalable.

    B. SQL Server supports dynamic HTML.

    C. SQL Server supports data replication.

    D. SQL Server is network independent.

    E. SQL Server is fault tolerant.

2. You are the IT director of a fast-growing business, and you need to find a relational database to store a datamart. You currently are using NT Server as your primary network operating system. You are considering purchasing SQL Server, but you want to know how well SQL Server is integrated with NT Server. Which of the following are ways in which SQL Server is well integrated with SQL Server?

    A. SQL Server can take advantage of NT Server's capability to do symmetrical processing.

    B. SQL Server can take advantage of NT Server's capability to do preemptive multitasking.

    C. SQL Server can take advantage of NT Server's built-in fault-tolerance features.

    D. SQL Server includes SQL Mail, which enables SQL Server to easily communicate with NT Server's MAPI layer.

    E. SQL Server can store some of its configuration information in NT Server's Registry.

    F. SQL Server can run within NT Server's security environment.

    G. SQL Server can store events in NT Server's event log.

3. Your company has purchased Microsoft BackOffice, but you have yet to load any components other than NT Server. The owner of the business wants to

1

know whether the company can benefit from loading SQL Server. What do you tell her?

    A. You tell your boss that SQL Server is a great database but that, although it is sold as a part of BackOffice, it is a separate program that doesn't gain anything from running with the other BackOffice applications.

    B. You tell your boss that SQL Server is required if SMS is loaded but, other than that, SQL Server probably will not help your business too much.

    C. You tell your boss that, not only is SQL Server a great database program, it is well integrated with Exchange, SMS, and IIS.

    D. You tell your boss that SQL Server integrates well with IIS, but the other BackOffice applications don't integrate well with SQL Server.

4. You are evaluating the possibility of purchasing SQL Server for your organization. One of the most important considerations for choosing a database is whether it supports ANSI-92 SQL. How does SQL Server support the SQL language?

    A. Transact-SQL, the language of SQL Server, does not support ANSI-92 SQL because it does not offer enough development features.

    B. Microsoft-SQL, the language of SQL Server, supports ANSI-92 SQL along with its own proprietary features.

    C. Transact-SQL is a superset of ANSI-92 SQL, and it offers features not offered by ANSI-92 SQL.

    D. ANSI-92 SQL is a superset of Transact-SQL, and it offers features not offered by Transact-SQL.

5. SQL Server can be best described as which of the following? (Select all that apply.)

    A. A client/server database

    B. A relational database

    C. A hierarchical database

    D. A dynamic database

6. As a SQL Server DBA, you have heard a lot about the Distributed Management Framework and what it can do for you. From your perspective, how can you take advantage of the Distributed Management Framework?

A. The Distributed Management Framework is not important to a DBA because it is hidden from view and works invisibly in the background.

B. The Distributed Management Framework is only of benefit to database designers not DBAs.

C. The Distributed Management Framework enables SQL developers to more easily create SQL applications that can be used to run database applications.

D. The Distributed Management Framework enables you to create custom programs that you can use to more effectively manage SQL Server.

7. You are the new DBA of a SQL Server. When you look at NT Server's Control Panel | Services dialog box, you notice the SQLExecutive service is not running. This is strange because users are successfully accessing SQL Server using a custom-designed front-end program. How can users access SQL Server if one of the two key SQL Server services is not running?

A. You must have misread the dialog box. It is impossible for users to access a SQL Server database if the two key SQL Server services are not running.

B. The capability to bypass the SQLExecutive service is a function of the front-end program.

C. SQLExecutive is an optional service. Only the MSSQLServer service is required to run SQL Server.

D. The MSDTC service must be running instead of SQLExecutive.

8. As a new DBA, you are asked to create a new database for a user so that he can store marketing-related information. You create the database as requested and then forget about it. Later, the same user wants to know why he cannot enter any data into the database. What do you tell him?

A. The database must have become corrupt.

B. The user is using ANSI-92 SQL rather than Transact-SQL to create database objects in the database.

C. The user is not using the correct front-end program to access the database.

D. Although you created the database as requested, you did not create any database objects in it. You assumed the user would create the necessary objects to store and manipulate the data, and the user assumed you would create them.

9. A user calls to complain that the database she uses to store her direct mail list is running very slowly. You take a look at the database and notice there are no index objects in the database. What can you do to help speed up database access for the user?

    A. You can add the appropriate clustered and nonclustered indexes to the database.

    B. You can rebuild the database to reclaim unused space.

    C. You cannot do anything to speed up the database other than getting a faster server.

    D. You can add the appropriate primary and foreign keys to the database.

10. You are the DBA of a SQL Server running on a server that is almost out of space. You want to delete any unnecessary files from the server's hard disk to make additional room. Which one of the following databases could you delete without causing any problems?

    A. pubs

    B. Master

    C. msdb

    D. tempdb

11. Your boss wants to be able to send an email to a SQL Server database and have the response automatically returned through email. How do you implement this feature?

    A. This requires two steps. As the DBA, you have to turn on SQL Mail and SQL Mail Query using the SQL Server setup program.

    B. This requires two steps. First, you have to turn on SQL Mail. Second, you have to use an extended procedure to turn on this functionality.

    C. This requires two steps. As the DBA, you can perform the first step of configuring SQL Mail. For the second step, a SQL Server developer has to write an application to incorporate this request.

    D. This is not possible. SQL Server cannot accept email messages. It can only send email messages.

12. As the DBA of a newly installed SQL Server, you set up a SQL Server alert. You configure the alert so that an email message will be sent to you should the alert ever fire. Shortly after you create the alert, it fires but you do not receive

an email message. You have received other email messages in the last few minutes. You also notice the alert created an event in the NT event log. What is the most likely cause of the email message not being sent?

    A. You have not yet set up SQL Mail.

    B. You misconfigured the alert.

    C. The NT event log is not working properly.

    D. Your mail server is not working properly.

Exercise

 This exercise helps to address the following certification exam objective:
    ■ Identify capabilities of SQL Server when used with MAPI

This exercise shows you how to configure SQL Server for SQL Mail. Before beginning this exercise, make sure that SQL Server has been installed correctly; that a MAPI-enabled mail program, such as Microsoft Exchange, has been installed correctly and is available to SQL Server over the network; that an email client has been loaded onto the same server as SQL Server; and that an email account has already been created for SQL Server to send and receive email.

1. Before configuring SQL Mail, you must make sure that whatever service account you are using for the MSSQLServer service has access to the server running the email server program. If you do not, SQL Mail will fail.

2. Make sure that the mail client has been started on the SQL Server and is working properly. Make sure that the mail client is logged on using the email account you created for SQL Mail.

3. From the server running SQL Server, start the SQL Server setup program.

4. Click the Continue button until the Microsoft SQL Server 6.5—Options dialog box opens.

5. Choose the Set Server Options radio button and click the Continue button. This displays the Select Server Options dialog box.

6. From the Select Server Options dialog box, enable the Auto Start Mail Client option.

7. Click the Mail Login button. This displays a new dialog box.

8. Depending on which mail client you use, enter either the name of the mailbox and its password or the name of the mailbox profile.

9. In this same dialog box, if displayed, enable the Copy SQL Mail Configuration From Current User Account option.

10. Click the Continue button. This returns you to the Select Server Options dialog box.

11. To save your new settings and exit SQL Server setup, select the Change Options button. A few seconds after it is selected, a message box displays. Click the Exit to Windows NT button to exit SQL Server setup and return to NT Server.

12. Load the SQL Server Enterprise Manager program so that your SQL Server is displayed. To start the SQL Mail service, right-click the SQL Mail object and choose Start. This starts SQL Mail for the first time. The SQL Mail object turns green to indicate it is running.

SQL Mail is now running and can be used by SQL Server as described earlier in this chapter.

Answers to Questions

1. **A, C, D, E**   SQL offers all these advantages except dynamic HTML. SQL Server does not have any inherent knowledge of dynamic HTML. Like any database, however, SQL Server can act as a database server for a Web server that uses dynamic HTML.

2. **A, B, C, E, F, G**   SQL Server can take advantage of all these NT Server features except MAPI. MAPI is not a core feature of NT Server.

3. **C**   Not only is SQL Server well integrated with NT Server, it also is well integrated with the other major components of BackOffice.

4. **C**   Transact-SQL, the language of SQL Server, is a superset of ANSI-92 SQL. This means that, not only is Transact-SQL able to run ANSI-92 scripts, but it also includes many enhancements that improve ANSI-92 SQL.

5. **A, B**   SQL Server is both a client/server and a relational database.

6. **D**   The Distributed Management Framework enables a programmer to create specialized applications that help you, the DBA, to better manage SQL Server.

7. **C**   SQLExecutive is an optional service, although most DBAs want it running. Without this service, a DBA cannot manage alerts and tasks or perform replication.

8. **D**   When a DBA creates a new database, only a shell database is created. Database objects must first be created in the database before data can be stored there.

9. **A**   Both clustered and nonclustered indexes can be added to tables in a database. These indexes help SQL Server access rows much faster than without them.

10. **A**   The only database you can delete from the list is pubs. This sample database does not need to exist for SQL Server to run. The remaining databases cannot be removed because they are system databases and are required for SQL Server to run.

11. **C**   As the DBA, you can turn on SQL Mail. Such an application, however, requires a custom-written SQL Server application that takes advantage of the `xp_processmail` extended stored procedure. This would probably be written by a SQL Server developer.

12. **A**   Although there could be many reasons for not receiving the email message, only the first of these choices makes sense. SQL Mail probably has not been set up. After it is, the email messages should be sent correctly whenever the alert fires again.

Day 2

Installing SQL Server

At one time or another, all SQL Server DBAs have to install a copy of SQL Server. Installing SQL Server might seem easy, but it's more subtle and complex than most people think. This chapter focuses on how to plan and install SQL Server. It also covers how to upgrade SQL Server version 4.2x or 6.0 to version 6.5, and it discusses how to install and configure the SQL Server administrative client software.

The topics in this chapter are heavily represented on the certification exam, so you should review this chapter carefully. If possible, you should practice installing SQL Server before taking the exam. This chapter provides a comprehensive tutorial that shows you how to install SQL Server. This chapter covers the following topics:

- Required hardware and software to install SQL Server

- How to configure NT Server for a SQL Server installation

- How to create a SQL Server service account

- SQL Server installation and configuration options

- How to install SQL Server

- How to install and configure SQL Server client software

- How to upgrade SQL Server 4.2x and 6.0 to SQL Server 6.5

Objectives

This chapter covers the following material:

- Configure Microsoft Windows NT for SQL Server installations
- Configure SQL Executive to log on as a service
- Load multiple Net-Libraries
- Install client support for network protocols other than named pipes
- Set up support for network clients using various network protocols
- Upgrade SQL Server 4.2x and 6.0 to SQL Server 6.5

2.1. Required Hardware and Software to Install SQL Server

Before you install SQL Server, you must have the correct hardware and software up and running. This means all the hardware must be on Microsoft's NT Hardware Compatibility List (HCL). It also means both the hardware and NT Server must be installed and configured properly. You should verify and thoroughly test the hardware and the NT installation before installing SQL Server. Many problems that can occur during SQL Server installation can be prevented by properly completing these preliminary steps.

This section examines the minimum hardware and software requirements to run SQL Server. It also briefly looks at the network and desktop operating systems with which SQL Server is compatible.

2.1.1. Minimum Hardware and Software Requirements

This section describes the minimum hardware and software requirements to run SQL Server. In the real world, however, you should outfit your SQL Server with the appropriate hardware to meet the needs of your particular SQL Server application. This generally is much greater than the minimum requirements described here. The minimum hardware requirements are just enough for SQL Server to run; they are not enough for a production system. The following minimum hardware requirements apply to the NT Server and NT Workstation editions of SQL Server:

- *CPU.* One Intel 32-bit 80x86-based CPU (such as an 80486 or a Pentium, Pentium MMX, Pentium Pro, or Pentium II), one DEC Alpha AXP CPU, one Power-PC CPU, or one MIPS-based CPU.
- *RAM.* 16MB when replication is not used; 32MB when replication is used.
- *Disk space.* 60MB is required to install a new installation of SQL Server without Books Online; 75MB is required if Books Online also is installed onto the server.
- *CD-ROM.* Only required if installing SQL Server from a CD. SQL Server also can be installed from a network share point.
- *I/O subsystem, display, keyboard, and mouse.* Any NT Server-supported hardware will work.
- *Network card.* Required if running SQL Server on a network. Optional if running stand-alone.
- *File system.* FAT or NTFS.

The following minimum software requirement also applies:

■ *Operating system.* NT Server 3.51 or later is required for the NT Server version. NT Workstation 3.51 or later is required for the NT Workstation version.

> **Note** All server hardware must be on the NT Server Hardware Compatibility List. Although this list is included with your copy of NT Server, it already is out-of-date. To obtain the most recent version, visit Microsoft's Web site at www.microsoft.com.

2

2.1.2. SQL Server-Compatible Network Operating Systems

SQL Server, along with NT, can coexist in virtually any network operating system environment, including the following:

■ Windows NT Workstation 3.51

■ Windows NT Server 3.51

■ Novell NetWare (3.x, 4.x, IntraNetWare)

■ Banyan VINES

■ UNIX

■ DEC PATHWORKS

■ OS/2, LAN Server

The only requirement is that your network support at least one of the following transport protocols:

■ TCP/IP

■ IPX/SPX (NWLink)

■ NetBEUI

2.1.3. SQL Server-Compatible Desktop Operating Systems

SQL Server supports clients running on most desktop operating systems, including the following:

- DOS
- Windows 3.x
- Windows for Workgroups 3.x
- Windows 95 and Windows 98
- NT Workstation
- Novell NetWare Networking Client Software
- Macintosh
- UNIX

It is important to determine which desktop operating systems will be used to access SQL Server because it is important to establish an interprocess communication (IPC) link between the desktop clients and SQL Server. This can accomplished by loading the correct network libraries at both the client and the server, enabling the two to communicate over a network. If a particular desktop operating system does not run any of the network libraries included with SQL Server, that operating system is incompatible with SQL Server. SQL Server network libraries are discussed in more detail later in this chapter.

 Note This certification test focuses on the version of SQL Server that runs on NT Server rather than on NT Workstation. All the advice in this chapter assumes NT Server is used to run SQL Server.

2.2. How to Configure NT Server for a SQL Server Installation

Before loading SQL Server onto NT Server, you must consider several things about NT Server. As you already know, SQL Server and NT Server are closely intertwined. NT Server's configuration can affect how SQL Server works. This section examines NT Server configuration options that can affect how SQL Server functions. The following topics are discussed:

- Selecting an NT Server domain model
- How your NT Server naming scheme affects SQL Server
- Configuring NT Server fault tolerance
- Preparing NT Server for SQL Server backups

- Choosing the NT Server role
- Setting NT Server foreground and background tasking
- Setting NT file caching

2.2.1. Selecting an NT Server Domain Model

NT Server is designed to run under one of four domain models. You can choose from the Single Domain, Master Domain, Multiple Master Domain, and Complete Trust models. A Single Domain consists of one domain that includes both accounts and resources. A Master Domain includes one accounts domain and one or more resource domains. A Multiple Master Domain includes two or more accounts domains and one or more resource domains. A Complete Trust model includes two or more domains that act as both accounts and resource domains; each domain has a two-way trust relationship with all the other domains. This chapter assumes your current NT Server domain model is properly designed and configured with the correct trust relationships.

SQL Server works under virtually any properly designed domain model. Adding SQL Server to the mix generally is not a problem, whether you are adding NT Server to your network for the first time and can choose any model, or you already have an established domain model that meets your needs.

When it comes to the NT Server domain model, two issues affect how SQL Server integrates with NT Server: the SQL Server service account and SQL Server security.

As you might remember from Day 1, "Introduction to SQL Server," SQL Server runs as two major services: the SQL Server service (MSSQLServer) and the SQL Executive service (SQLExecutive). For the SQL Executive service to work properly in most network environments, Microsoft recommends that the service run under a specially created NT Server domain account rather than under the default LocalSystem service account. When SQL Executive is run under a domain account, the service has the capability to cross the network and to communicate with other servers in the network. Creating a SQL Executive service account is discussed in more detail later in this chapter. What you need to consider now is where that service account will be located in regard to your NT Server domain model.

Note

The MSSQLServer service always runs under the LocalSystem account. You do not need to create a special domain account for it.

It is important for the service account to exist in the designated accounts domain of a multiple-domain NT network. (Single-domain networks are not a problem.) A service account should not be created in a resource domain. This is because the same service account must be used by all SQL Servers on the network if they are to communicate with each other. The only way to make sure the same service account is used by all SQL Servers is to create the service account in the NT Server domain's accounts domain.

The second issue you need to consider is security. SQL Server offers three security modes: standard security, integrated security, and mixed security. SQL Server security modes are discussed in more detail on Day 6, "Implementing SQL Server Security," and Day 7, "Managing User Accounts."

Your NT domain design is not relevant to making standard security work. If you choose integrated security or mixed security (which incorporates both integrated and standard security), however, you must consider your NT Server domain model.

The importance of the NT Server domain model to integrated and mixed security is similar to its importance to the SQL Executive service account. For integrated and mixed security to work, the NT user accounts used to access SQL Server must exist in an NT Server domain's accounts domain. They cannot exist in a resource domain.

It is important to understand that, for either integrated or mixed security to be implemented, SQL Server must be installed in a properly designed NT domain, and all the user accounts must be in an accounts domain. If this is the case, either of these security modes will work fine. If your NT domain is not properly designed, however, or if user accounts exist in both accounts and resource domains, you have no choice but to use standard security. This limits your security choices.

2.2.2. How Your NT Server Naming Scheme Affects SQL Server

SQL Server and NT Server use different naming schemes. This can cause a multitude of problems if it's not thought out carefully before SQL Server is installed. SQL Server uses the NetBIOS names of NT Servers as its own names. It also can use NT user accounts as SQL Server login IDs (if integrated or mixed security is used). The main problem is that NT's naming scheme follows different rules than SQL Server's naming scheme. If any of the NT names automatically used by SQL Server do not follow SQL Server's naming scheme, SQL Server does not work as expected.

To prevent problems, the best solution is to enforce SQL Server's naming scheme for all NT computer names and user accounts. This works effectively because SQL

Server's naming scheme is more restrictive than NT's naming scheme. If your current NT network breaks any rules of SQL Server's naming scheme, you should change names that violate these rules before installing SQL Server. The following rules are part of SQL Server's naming scheme:

- Names must not exceed 30 characters.
- Names must not include any spaces.
- Names must begin with a letter or the underline symbol (_).
- After the first letter, characters in names can be any letter or number, or the underline (_), pound (#), or dollar ($) symbols.

2.2.3. Configuring NT Server Fault Tolerance

NT Server includes many fault-tolerant features such as software-based RAID and NTFS partitions. Although these can be added after SQL Server is installed, it is much easier if they are in place beforehand. If you don't plan to use NT Server's built-in software-based RAID—and you instead plan to use hardware-based RAID—you have to make sure the RAID hardware is properly installed before installing SQL Server. In addition, when using hardware-based RAID, you need to make sure any write-back caching supported by your RAID controller is turned off. This feature is not supported by SQL Server.

2.2.4. Preparing NT Server for SQL Server Backups

If you plan to back up your SQL Server data using SQL Server's built-in backup facility, you need to install an NT-supported backup device. This includes loading and configuring the proper backup device driver. Ideally, the hardware and the driver should be installed and tested before installing SQL Server. If they are not installed or configured properly, SQL Server cannot back up your data to a backup device such as tape.

2.2.5. Choosing the NT Server Role

When installing NT Server, you must specify a role. You can choose either primary domain controller (PDC), backup domain controller (BDC), or member server (MS). Although SQL Server can run under any NT Server role, the optimum role is MS. As an MS, NT Server devotes as many of its resources to SQL Server as possible, which makes for a faster SQL Server. Both PDCs and BDCs have a certain amount of overhead due to their participation in client authentication and directory service synchronization. These processes take server resources away from SQL Server.

2.2.6. Setting NT Server Foreground and Background Tasking

By default, after installing NT Server, NT sets the application performance of any foreground application to None. This means your foreground applications get no priority boost over applications running in the background. When SQL Server is in production, you should maintain this setting so SQL Server will get all the CPU cycles it can. When setting up the server and using many foreground applications, however, you might want to temporarily boost the foreground application priority to be more productive. If you make this change, don't forget to return the setting to None when SQL Server is put into production.

2.2.7. Setting NT File Caching

After loading NT Server, but before loading SQL Server, the NT File Caching setting is set to Maximize Throughput for File Sharing. After you load SQL Server, however, the installation process automatically changes this setting to Maximize Throughput for Network Applications. Assuming SQL Server is the only application running on this physical server, leave the setting as Maximize Throughput for Network Applications. This influences how much RAM NT devotes to file caching. The setting Maximize Throughput for Network Applications reduces the amount of RAM dedicated to file caching. The RAM instead is given to the application for use, where it often is more beneficial.

2.3. How to Create a SQL Server Service Account

As previously mentioned in this chapter, SQL Server is made up of two major services: the SQL Server service (MSSQLServer) and the SQL Executive service (SQLExecutive). SQLExecutive is responsible for routine maintenance tasks, such as handling alerts, tasks, events, and replication. MSSQLServer is the SQL Server engine that directly manages databases through Transact-SQL statements.

As NT services, these SQL Server services run continuously in the background, whether or not a user is logged in to NT Server. Like most NT services, the two SQL Server services automatically are started whenever NT Server is rebooted. As NT initializes, it starts all necessary services. As part of the initialization process, every service must log on to NT Server. This is similar to how a user logs on to NT Server to access network resources.

An NT service can log on in two different ways. First, it can log on using NT's built-in LocalSystem account. This is a special security account reserved for NT services. When a service logs on to NT using the LocalSystem account, the service runs under the security context of the physical server on which the service is running. This means the service has permission to operate on the local server, but it cannot interact with the rest of the network. For most NT services, this limitation is not a problem.

Although both SQL Executive and MSSQLService can run under the local security context of a single server, this restricts their capability to communicate with other SQL Servers. This might be adequate for small, single-server SQL Server installation, but when multiple SQL Servers are installed that need to interact, using the LocalSystem account will not work for the SQL Executive service. The MSSQLService always can run under the LocalSystem account.

An NT service also can log on using an NT user account specially created for use by a service. By logging on using a standard NT user account, a service runs under the security context of the domain in which the account is located. This usually is an organization's accounts domain.

To give SQL Executive the greatest flexibility, you should create a special NT Server service account using the User Manager for Domains. (Only a user with administrative privileges can create this account.) The NT service account should be created in the NT accounts domain of your NT Server domain model. This is the domain in which all your NT user accounts reside.

The NT service account should be (but is not required to be) created before SQL Server is installed. You are prompted for the name of the service account during the SQL Server installation process. If you forget to create the account before installing SQL Server, the LocalSystem account can be used instead. After SQL Server is installed, you then can change the startup values of the service under the Services icon in NT's Control Panel.

When creating an NT service account to run SQL Executive, you should configure the account as follows:

- The account must belong to the NT Server's administrators global group that exists in your domain's accounts NT Server domain.
- The Change Password at Next Logon option must not be selected.
- The Password Never Expires option must be selected.

- A password should be assigned to prevent users from logging in to NT using this account. This account also should not be used to log on to NT. It should only be used by the SQL Server services.
- The account must be given the advanced user right Log On as a Service.

Do not make any other changes to the account, such as restricting hours, adding a login script, or restricting the account to specific machines. These changes can prevent the service account from logging on properly.

One of the exercises at the end of this chapter shows you how to create a SQL Server service account.

2.4. SQL Server Installation Options

When it comes time to load SQL Server onto a new physical server, you have the following options:

- Install from a CD
- Install from a network share point
- Install to a remote server

These options are discussed in the following sections, including their pros and cons.

2.4.1. Installing from a CD

The most common way to install SQL Server is from the CD provided by Microsoft. Everything you need to install SQL Server is included on the CD.

The SQL Server distribution CD contains the following folders:

- *I386.* Contains the installation files for Intel CPUs
- *Alpha.* Contains the installation files for Alpha CPUs
- *Mips.* Contains the installation files for MIPS-based CPUs
- *Ppc.* Contains the installation files for Power-PC CPUs
- *Sqlbks65.* Contains SQL Server Books Online
- *Clients.* Contains the SQL Server client software

If you are loading SQL Server onto an Intel-based server, run the setup.exe program located in the i386 folder. If you are loading SQL Server using another CPU type, run the setup.exe program located in the appropriate folder. Although SQL Server Books Online is stored in the sqlbks65 folder, you do not need to install it separately. It can be installed when you run setup.exe.

2.4.2. Installing from a Network Share Point

If you need to install multiple copies of SQL Server—especially if you only have a single copy of the SQL Server CD—you might want to copy the appropriate SQL Server setup files from the CD to a network share point that can be accessed by everyone authorized to install SQL Server.

If you want to create a network share point for installing SQL Server, create a new folder on a file server. Give the folder an appropriate name, such as SQL Setup Files, and copy into it the appropriate folders from the SQL Server CD. If you are only going to install SQL Server onto Intel servers, you only need to copy the i386 and Sqlbks65 folders into your SQL Setup Files folder. After the appropriate files are copied, share the folder and assign the necessary security.

2.4.3. Installing to a Remote Server

Sometimes the physical server on which you want to install SQL Server is not conveniently located. It might be in a server closet on another floor, for example, or even in another building. Although you always have the option to physically go to the server to perform the install, it is not always the most productive use of your time.

SQL Server's install process enables you to push an installation from one NT-based PC to any NT Server on which you want to install SQL Server, no matter where the other server is located. This other server must be accessible through your network, however, and should have a fast LAN connection.

To perform a remote installation of SQL Server, start SQL Server either from the CD or from a network share point. Shortly after you begin the SQL Server setup program (which is explained in more detail later in this chapter), you are asked whether you want to perform a remote installation. All you have to do is enter the name of the other computer and continue the installation. The only difference is that, instead of SQL Server being installed on the local computer, it is installed on the specified remote computer.

2.5. SQL Server Installation and Configuration Options

No matter how you choose to install SQL Server, you first need to consider the following SQL Server installation options. SQL Server setup has many options, and you must carefully consider each as you install SQL Server. After these major issues are covered, a tutorial will show you how to actually install SQL Server. The following sections discuss these options:

- Choosing a licensing mode
- Choosing network protocols
- Choosing a character set
- Choosing a sort order

2.5.1. Choosing a Licensing Mode

As with any Microsoft BackOffice product, you need to select a licensing mode during the installation process. You must tell SQL Server whether you want to use the Per Server or Per Seat client licensing mode.

Per Server licensing means the client licenses are associated with each SQL Server. Each SQL Server throughout the enterprise must have an appropriate number of client licenses for each simultaneous client connection. This is generally the most expensive way to license clients. It should be avoided unless your organization has a single SQL Server.

Per Seat licensing means the client licenses are associated with each client. Each client license has the capability to access as many SQL Servers as necessary simultaneously. This is the least expensive way to license clients in an organization with multiple SQL Servers.

Don't confuse Per Seat client licensing with SQL Server user connections. A single client license is required per physical computer and user, no matter how many user connections a single user might have open.

2.5.2. Choosing Network Protocols

For clients to communicate with SQL Server over a network connection, they must share a common interprocess communication (IPC) mechanism to send network packets back and forth between the client and SQL Server. SQL Server supports several different IPC mechanisms, which are implemented as network libraries in the form of dynamic link libraries (DLL). If both the client and SQL Server do not share a common network library, they cannot communicate.

By default, SQL Server uses the Named Pipes network library. You can, however, add additional network libraries to SQL Server as necessary to support a wide variety of client types. Although SQL Server itself can support multiple network libraries simultaneously, SQL clients do not have this capability. Clients can support only a single network library at a time.

Named Pipes is the only network library automatically installed during the SQL Server installation process. Additional network libraries can be added during the initial installation, or anytime after installation, using the SQL Server setup program.

Before you decide to add network libraries, read about each available network library in SQL Server's Books Online so that you can learn whether it is required. Loading unnecessary network libraries takes away valuable RAM from SQL Server that instead could be used by the SQL Server data cache.

Named Pipes Network Library

Traditionally, NT Server and BackOffice products have used the Named Pipes IPC mechanism to communicate with each other—SQL Server is no exception. When using Names Pipes, SQL Server listens for communications from clients using the *sql_server_name*\pipe\sql\query hidden share, in which *sql_server_name* is the name of the computer on which SQL Server is installed.

All Microsoft-based client operating systems have the capability to communicate with SQL Server using Named Pipes. If all your SQL Server clients are all Microsoft-based, this single network library might be the only one you need to load.

The Named Pipes network library can be removed but only after SQL Server has been installed. Named Pipes is required during the installation process; otherwise installation will fail.

Multi-Protocol Network Library

The Multi-Protocol network library supports remote procedure calls (RPCs). This means SQL Server can use most of the IPC mechanisms supported by NT, including TCP/IP Sockets, NWLink, and Named Pipes. The library also supports Multi-Protocol encryption to protect passwords and data as they move between clients and SQL Server and offers better network performance than Named Pipes and the other network libraries.

The Multi-Protocol network library is more flexible than Named Pipes. As a result, you might want to make it your only network library, assuming all the clients support it. If you do, however, remember not to remove the Named Pipes network protocol until SQL Server has been fully installed.

TCP/IP Sockets Network Library

If your network is 100 percent TCP/IP-based, and if some of the clients accessing SQL Server are UNIX-based, you might want to consider using the TCP/IP Sockets network library. It uses the standard TCP/IP Sockets network API as the IPC mechanism.

If you choose this option, you are prompted to enter the TCP/IP port number SQL Server should use to listen for client communication. The default port is 1433, which is the official port number assigned to SQL Server by the Internet Assigned Number Authority.

NWLink (IPX/SPX) Network Library

If your network is mostly Novell servers and uses the IPX/SPX transport protocol, and if some or all of the clients who will be accessing SQL Server use the Novell SPX protocol exclusively to communicate, you must load the NWLink network library. This network library enables Novell SPX clients to communicate with SQL Server.

If you choose this network library, you are prompted to enter the Novell Bindery Service Name, which is used to register SQL Server on the Novell network. This name generally is the computer name of the SQL Server.

AppleTalk ADSP Network Library

If your network has Apple Macintosh-based clients who will be communicating with SQL Server through AppleTalk, you must install the AppleTalk ADSP network library.

If you select this option, you are prompted for an AppleTalk Service Object Name, which usually is the computer name of the computer running SQL Server.

Banyan VINES Network Library

If any of your network clients running the Banyan VINES Sequenced Packet Protocol (SPP) communicate with SQL Server, you must install the Banyan VINES network library.

The Banyan VINES software for NT first must be installed on NT Server before SQL Server and the Banyan VINES network library are installed.

2.5.3. Choosing a Character Set

A *character set* is a collection of uppercase letters, lowercase letters, numbers, and symbols that is recognized by SQL Server. Traditionally, character sets have 256 characters; this can vary, however, depending on the language supported by the character set. The first 128 characters of each character set supported by SQL Server are identical. The remaining characters can vary significantly from one character set to another.

SQL Server includes many character sets, but only one can be selected at a time. No matter which character set you select, it is critical that the same one be used for both SQL Server and its clients. It also is important for all SQL Servers that need to intercommunicate to use the same character set; otherwise, you might receive unexpected results.

It is important for the correct character set to be chosen during the installation process. Although a character set can be changed later using SQL Server's setup program, changing a character set also requires you to rebuild your databases and reload your data.

By default, SQL Server uses the ISO character set (Code Page 1252). This character set also is known as the ISO-8859-1, Latin 1, or ANSI character set. It is compatible with the Windows and Windows NT operating systems, and it provides the greatest compatibility with most world languages. Unless you have a good reason, you should leave this as the default character set.

Other character sets include the following:

- *Multilingual.* Use this character set when your SQL Server clients are MS-DOS-based and use extended characters.
- *U.S. English.* Although this character set sounds like it might be appropriate, and although it traditionally has been popular in the United States, this character set includes many block graphical characters not used in databases. Only choose this option if you need to maintain backward compatibility with legacy applications.

2.5.4. Choosing a Sort Order

You also must decide which sort order to select. A *sort order* determines how SQL Server resolves queries and sorts data. Different sort orders can produce different output. Notice that the following last names are sorted differently when different sort orders are used.

Dictionary Sort Order, Case-Insensitive
Mcgehee

McGovern

McGovney

Dictionary Sort Order, Case-Sensitive
McGovern

McGovney

Mcgehee

Binary Sort Order
MCGOVNEY

McGovern

mcgehee

As you can see, the sort order you choose can produce unexpected results. You need to choose the correct sort order at SQL Server installation time for two important reasons. First, if you later decide to change the sort order, you have to rebuild your database (using SQL Server setup) and reload your data. Second, all the SQL Servers in your organization that need to intercommunicate also must have the same sort order. Otherwise, unexpected results can occur.

The default sort order for the ISO character set (also a default) is dictionary order, case-insensitive. This produces the kind of results to which you are accustomed. Unless you have a very good reason, this sort order should remain the default.

2.6. How to Install SQL Server

Now that you have reviewed the major SQL Server installation options, you are ready to perform an actual SQL Server installation. This tutorial assumes SQL Server will be loaded from a CD.

1. Log on to NT Server using an account with administrative rights.
2. Make sure that no other programs are running in the foreground, such as NT Event Viewer, Registry Editor, or any other NT administrative tools.

3. Insert the SQL Server CD. Use Explorer to locate the folder on the CD with the correct setup files for your CPU. Double-click the setup.exe program. This launches the setup program and opens the Welcome dialog box (see Figure 2.1).

Figure 2.1.

This is the first of many screens in the SQL Server setup program.

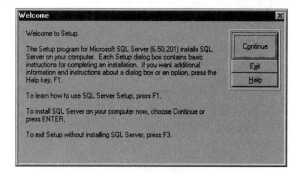

4. Click the Continue button. The Name and Organization dialog box opens.

5. Enter your Name, Company Name, and Product ID. Click the Continue button to open the Licensing Mode dialog box.

6. Choose the appropriate licensing mode based on the information previously provided. Click the Continue button to open the Options dialog box (see Figure 2.2).

Figure 2.2.

The setup program offers various installation options.

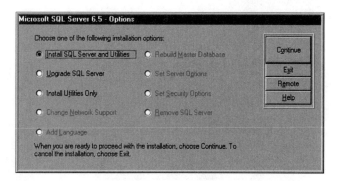

If you are installing SQL Server for the first time on a server, you should choose the Install SQL Server and Utilities option. If you are upgrading an older version of SQL Server, choose Upgrade SQL Server. If you want to install only the SQL Server 32-bit administrative client utilities, choose Install Utilities Only. The latter two options are discussed later in this chapter. If you want to do a remote installation of SQL Server, you can select the Remote button.

7. Select Install SQL Server and Utilities and click the Continue button. This opens the Installation Path dialog box (see Figure 2.3). If the defaults are not appropriate for you, you can select in which drive and folder you want to install SQL Server.

Figure 2.3.

You can select where to install SQL Server.

8. Make the appropriate changes, if any, and click the Continue button. This opens the MASTER Device Creation dialog box (see Figure 2.4).

Figure 2.4.

You must specify the location and size of the MASTER device.

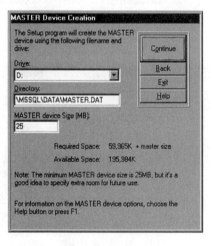

This dialog box offers several choices. You can choose in which drive and folder to install the MASTER device, and you can choose its size. By default, the MASTER device is stored in the \MSSQL\DATA folder and is 25MB in size. Assuming you have the hard disk space, you might want to increase this size to about 50MB, depending on how much you think the MASTER device will grow. The MASTER device holds the Master, model, tempdb, and pubs databases.

9. Enter the appropriate information in the dialog box and click the Continue button. This opens the Books Online dialog box. You can decide to install Books Online entirely on a hard disk, to run Books Online from the CD, or to not install it at all.

10. Click your choice and click the Continue button. This opens the Installation Options dialog box (see Figure 2.5).

Figure 2.5.

The Installation Options dialog box offers many choices, so pay close attention.

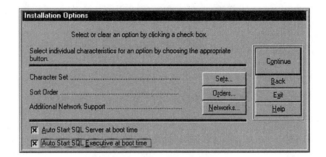

This dialog box is probably the most confusing for new SQL Server users. First you must select the proper Character Set, Sort Order, and Network Support. (Each of these options was previously discussed in the "SQL Server Installation and Configuration Options" section.) To change these options, select the proper button and make the appropriate selections. At the bottom of the dialog box are two additional options: Auto Start SQL Server at Boot Time and Auto Start SQL Executive at Boot Time. By default, these options are not selected. If selected, these options automatically start the MSSQLServer and SQLExecutive services whenever NT Server boots. You should probably select these two options because they will save you from having to start the services manually every time NT Server reboots. If you forget to select these options now, you can select them later using the SQL Server setup program.

11. After you have made the appropriate changes to the dialog box, click the Continue button. This opens the SQL Executive Log On Account dialog box. Enter the name and password of the SQL Server account you created before installing SQL Server.

12. After entering the service account and password, click the Continue button. This ends your part of the installation; the setup program takes over. After 5 to 10 minutes, the setup program informs you the installation is complete.

2.7. How to Install and Configure SQL Server Client Software

After installing SQL Server, you need to think about loading the SQL Server client utilities on desktops used to administer SQL Server. You also might want to load the client utilities on SQL Server developer workstations.

The SQL Server client utilities are the same client utilities you were given a chance to load during SQL Server installation. The advantage of loading them on other workstations is that you can remotely manage SQL Server from any computer, not just from the server itself.

This section covers the following topics:

- SQL Server client utilities
- Client utility hardware and software requirements
- Versions of client software
- How to install the SQL Server client utilities
- How to use the client configuration utility

2.7.1. SQL Server Client Utilities

SQL Server includes a wide variety of client-based tools to manage SQL Server. SQL Server provides the following utilities:

- *SQL Server Enterprise Manager.* If you want to manage SQL Server remotely, installing the SQL Server Enterprise Manager onto your desktop is a must. This program enables the DBA to perform virtually any SQL Server administrative task.

- *ISQL/W.* This utility is used to communicate with SQL Server through Transact-SQL. You should probably load this on most, if not all, remote management workstations. You also might want to load this tool onto SQL Server developers' desktops. It gives developers direct access to SQL Server so that they can run interactive Transact-SQL statements and SQL scripts.

- *SQL Security Manager.* This utility only is used when integrated or mixed security is implemented. It transfers NT user accounts and groups to SQL Server. After NT user accounts have been moved to SQL Server, any authorized NT user account can access SQL Server.

- *SQL Service Manager.* This utility turns SQL Server services off and on. SQL Server services also can be turned off and on from the Control Panel and from the SQL Server Enterprise Manager.
- *SQL Setup.* This is the same setup program you used to load SQL Server. It includes several SQL Server configuration options that only can be performed from this program.
- *SQL Server Performance Monitor.* SQL Server does not actually have its own version of the NT Server Performance Monitor. This item in the SQL Server program group is just a pointer to NT Server's Performance Monitor with a few predefined SQL Server counters.
- *SQL Server Web Assistant.* This wizard shows you how to create Web pages from data stored in a SQL Server database.
- *MS-Query.* This utility enables you to create queries using a GUI-based interface rather than writing them directly in Transact-SQL.
- *SQL Trace.* This utility monitors traffic between SQL Server and clients.
- *Client Configuration Utility.* This utility verifies which DB-Library is installed on a client and selects the network library the client uses to communicate with SQL Server. This tool is discussed later in this chapter.
- bcp. This command-line utility copies data into and out of SQL databases. It is discussed on Day 10, "Backing Up and Managing SQL Server Data."
- isql. This command-line utility is similar to ISQL/W, but it is not GUI-based.
- makepipe *and* readpipe. These two troubleshooting utilities determine whether a client can talk to SQL Server over a network connection. They are discussed on Day 14, "Troubleshooting SQL Server."

Whenever you load any of the SQL Server client administrative utilities, the client support libraries (such as the DB-Library and the various network libraries) also are loaded. These support libraries enable the client software to communicate with SQL Server over a network.

Not all SQL Server client administrative utilities can be run on all desktop operating systems. This is discussed in more detail later in this chapter.

2

2.7.2. Client Utility Hardware and Software Requirements

Just like you need the correct hardware and software to install SQL Server, you also need the correct hardware and software to install the SQL Server client utilities. This section examines the minimum client hardware and software recommendations.

Hardware Requirements

If your client runs NT Server or NT Workstation, make sure that all the hardware is on Microsoft's NT Hardware Compatibility List. If your client runs Windows 95/98, make sure that the hardware is on the appropriate HCLs. The following are the hardware requirements:

- *CPU.* An Intel 32-bit 80386, 80486, or Pentium CPU; an Alpha AXP CPU; or a MIPS-based CPU.

- *RAM.* Depends on the desktop operating system used: 4MB for DOS or Windows 3.x, 8MB on Windows 95/98, or 16MB on NT Server or Workstation.

- *Disk space.* The minimum requirement, if you load all the utilities, is 7MB. If you also load Books Online, you need an additional 15MB.

- *CD-ROM drive.* Only required if you install the client utilities from CD.

Software Requirements

The following are the software requirements for SQL Server client utilities:

- *Desktop operating systems.* DOS and Widows 3.x can be used with 16-bit client utilities. Windows 95/98 can be used with most 32-bit client utilities. NT Server or Workstation 3.51 or later can be used with all 32-bit utilities.

- *Network operating system.* SQL Server client utilities can run under the same network operating systems as SQL Server, including NT Server, Novell, Banyan, and Apple.

2.7.3. Versions of Client Software

Not all client utilities can run under all desktop operating systems. The following is a breakdown of the various client utilities' versions:

32-Bit Client Software

- SQL Enterprise Manger
- ISQL/W, bcp

- SQL Security Manager
- SQL Trace utility
- SQL Server Web Assistant
- MS-Query
- SQL Client Configuration utility

16-Bit Client Software (Windows-Based)

- ISQL/W
- SQL Client Configuration utility
- isql

16-Bit Client Software (DOS-Based)

- isql
- bcp

2.7.4. How to Install the SQL Server Client Utilities

How you install the SQL Server administrative client utilities depends on the desktop operating system into which they are being installed. The different methods are described in the following sections.

How to Install 32-Bit Utilities

To install the 32-bit utilities for NT Server, NT Workstation, and Windows 95/98, use the same setup program used to install SQL Server. Use the following steps to install these 32-bit utilities:

1. Run setup.exe from the folder containing the SQL Server setup files for your CPU platform.
2. Choose Install Utilities Only from the Options dialog box.
3. Select the drive and folder to which you want to install the client utilities.
4. Select which utilities you want to install. You don't have to load all the utilities if you don't need them.
5. Choose whether you also want to load Books Online. Remember that Books Online needs an extra 15MB.

After you make these choices, the utilities are installed, the appropriate program group is created, and the correct DB-Library and network library files are installed. After the client utilities are installed, you can begin using them immediately.

How to Install Windows-Based 16-Bit Utilities

Installing Windows-based 16-bit utilities uses a different setup program. This program is located in the \clients\win16 folder of the SQL Server CD. Use the following steps to install the Windows 16-bit utilities:

1. Run the setup.exe program from the \clients\win16 folder.

2. If you want, change the default folder to which the setup program installs the utilities.

The utilities are installed, the appropriate program group is created, and the default network library is installed. After everything is installed, you can begin using the utilities immediately.

How to Install DOS-Based 16-Bit Utilities

DOS-based 16-bit utilities are not installed using a setup program; they have to be manually installed. The following steps show you how to manually install these utilities:

1. Create a folder on the hard disk of the computer where you want to install the utilities.

2. Manually copy all the files from the \clients\msdos folder of the SQL Server CD to the folder you created on the client computer.

3. If you want, you can add the path of the folder where the client utilities are stored to the autoexec.bat file of the client computer.

4. Before the client utilities can work, you have to load the proper network library. DOS computers load the network library as a TSR program when the client computer first boots. This means you must manually add the name of the proper network library to the autoexec.bat file. Every time the computer boots, the network library will load automatically. Only three Net-Libraries are included—Named Pipes, Novell SPX, and Banyan VINES—and only one can be loaded at a time.

After the autoexec.bat file has been properly modified and the client computer has been rebooted, you can run either of the DOS-based 16-bit utilities: isql or bcp.

2.7.5. How to Use the Client Configuration Utility

The SQL Server Client Configuration utility configures client utilities (except DOS-based utilities) so that they can successfully communicate with a SQL Server. This program should be run only after the client utilities have been loaded, not before. In most cases, you do not have to run this program because the defaults work for most network configurations. If your client software does not communicate with your SQL Server, however, you can use this utility to properly configure the client software so that it can communicate with SQL Server.

This section is divided into four parts. The first part describes how to load the Client Configuration utility. The other three parts describe the options available on the three screens of the configuration utility.

How to Start the Client Configuration Utility

In most cases, the Client Configuration utility was installed with the other client utilities you loaded onto the workstation. If you did not load this utility and now need it, you first must load it as previously described. You then can proceed with the following steps to load this program:

1. If you are working on an NT Server or Workstation, log on using an account with administrative rights. If you are working on a Windows 95/98 desktop, you can log on using any legal user account.

2. Make sure that no other programs are running before you begin. If there are programs open, exit them before continuing.

3. To load the Client Configuration utility, click the Start button, click Programs, and click Microsoft SQL Server (the name of the program group with the utilities). Click Client Configuration Utility.

4. The Microsoft SQL Server Client Configuration Utility dialog box opens (see Figure 2.6). This dialog box includes three tabs that divide its three main options. The three main options are described in the following sections.

DB-Library Configuration

The main purpose of the DB-Library tab is for you to determine whether the most current version of the DB-Library files is installed on the client. Version information is displayed in the Version Statistics part of the screen. You should be using the version that came with SQL Server 6.5 or a later version if the files have since been updated by a service pack or another update.

2

Figure 2.6.

The Client Configuration dialog box.

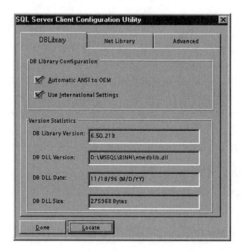

If the current client never has had any version of the client utilities loaded on it before, the only version on the client should be the version loaded when the client utilities were loaded. If you have any older versions of the DB-Library files on the workstation, you should remove them so that they don't get confused with the newer version. This can happen if they are installed in different folders on your computer.

To determine whether there are any older versions of DB-Library files on your computer, click the Locate button. This searches your hard drive, locating the new version and any older versions. If you find any older versions, make a note of their location and delete them using Explorer.

At the top of the DB-Library tab are the DB-Library Configuration options (refer to Figure 2.6). You generally should not change the default settings. The following are the default settings:

- *Automatic ANSI to OEM.* This option, when selected, tells DB-Library to convert characters from the original equipment manufacturer (OEM) to ANSI format when communicating from the client to SQL Server, and to convert characters from ANSI to OEM when communicating from SQL Server to the client. This option often is required because the character set used by SQL Server is different from the one used by the client operating system. This option automatically makes the proper translation of character sets.

  This setting should be selected if the client is running Windows NT or Windows 95/98. If a Windows 3.x client is used, this option should not be selected.

■ *Use International Settings.* This option, when selected, enables DB-Library to get the date, time, and currency format settings from the local operating system instead of using the hard-coded setting. This option should be selected if the client is running Windows NT or Windows 95/98.

Net Library Configuration

The Net Library tab has two sections: Net Library Configuration and Version Statistics (see Figure 2.7). Version Statistics verifies the current version of the network library files. As with DB Library files, you always want the latest version of network library files.

Figure 2.7.

The Net Library configuration options.

When you installed SQL Server, you had to specify one or more network libraries to load. This software is used to make a network connection between SQL Server and client software. Although you can load and run more than one network library at a SQL Server, only one network library can be loaded and active at a time in a client. For a client to communicate over a network with SQL Server, both must be running the same network library. Otherwise, they cannot communicate.

By default, the Named Pipes network library is installed for the client utilities. Assuming Named Pipes also is used at the SQL Server, the client utilities can communicate with SQL Server without any changes. If for some reason you have decided not to run Named Pipes on the SQL Server, you will have to select a network library at the client that matches one of the network libraries running at SQL Server.

If your client operating system is not Windows NT or Windows 95/98, you might have to use another network library, such as the Banyan VINES or NWLink

IPX/SPX network libraries. If this is the case, you also have to make sure these same network libraries run on SQL Server.

Choosing the correct network library can be confusing to many DBAs. At issue is how a client talks over a network with SQL Server. This is difficult because there are so many different possibilities, each with their own way to communicate between a client and server application. The key to choosing the correct network library is to consult with the person developing your SQL Server client/server application. More often than not, that person is writing the application to run over a specific network library. If this is the case, use the network library required to run the application over your network.

Advanced Configuration

You'll rarely need to use the Advanced configuration tab of the Client Configuration Utility (see Figure 2.8). This tab enables you to send special configuration strings to the SQL Server when the client software attempts a connection with it. Unless you are a SQL developer, you probably will never use this option.

Figure 2.8.

The Advanced configuration options.

2.8. How to Upgrade SQL Server 4.2x and 6.0 to SQL Server 6.5

SQL Server 6.5 has been around for a while, so there shouldn't be many SQL Servers that haven't been upgraded. If you still have one or two that haven't been upgraded, you still can upgrade anytime you want.

Older versions of SQL Server can be upgraded in several ways. One way is to use the SQL Server setup program. Another way is to restore older versions of SQL Server databases to a newer version of SQL Server. Both methods get the same results. The method tested on the certification exam, however, is using SQL Server's setup program to perform the upgrade. That method, therefore, is the one discussed in this section.

The following sections shows you how to prepare for the upgrade process, how to perform the upgrade, and how to finish up after performing the upgrade.

2.8.1. Preparing for the Upgrade

Before you perform an upgrade, keep the following points in mind:

- Versions of SQL Server older than 4.2x cannot be upgraded directly to version 6.5.

- The upgrade process must use the same CPU version of the software for both the old and new system. You cannot upgrade across CPU versions.

- Upgrading does not change the sort order. If you want to change the sort order, it must be performed as a separate step after performing the upgrade.

- Upgrading is a one-way process; it cannot be reversed.

Before performing an upgrade, you must prepare the current SQL Server by taking the following steps:

- Make sure that you have good backups of your data before beginning the upgrade process. Should any problems arise during the upgrade, at least you have not lost your data. You will, however, have to reload the older version of SQL Server and restore the data.

- Make sure that the Open Databases configuration option is set high enough. It should be set at a number higher than the total number of databases you will have on the server after it is upgraded. If you are not sure what this number should be, pad your estimate. It can be changed after the upgrade if necessary.

- Run the CHKUPG65 utility on the old databases. This utility is on the SQL Server 6.5 CD. This utility looks for any potential problems that might arise during the upgrade. A report is produced listing the potential problems. You should correct any problems before performing the upgrade.

- If the older SQL Server was involved in replication, make sure to disable it on both the Publisher and Subscriber sides. Make sure the Publisher's database transaction log is empty.

- Make sure any older databases do not have the read-only option set.
- Make sure the Master database has some empty space. If it doesn't, increase its size before upgrading.
- Make sure the system administrator's default database is set to Master.
- Turn off the services on the older version of SQL Server.
- Make sure the hard disk has plenty of free space (at least 50MB).

You are now ready to perform the upgrade.

2.8.2. Performing the Upgrade

Performing the actual upgrade is the easy part. Performing an upgrade is similar to installing SQL Server. The only difference is that, after running the SQL Server setup program, you should choose Upgrade SQL Server rather than Install SQL Server and Utilities.

The upgrade might take a long time, depending on the size of your databases and the speed of your server.

2.8.3. Cleaning Up After the Upgrade

After the upgrade process is complete, you still are not done yet. Your first task is to make new backups of the databases just upgraded. Next, you should test your databases and applications to make sure that they still work as expected. Assuming you fixed any problems discovered by CHKUPG65, you should not have any more problems. After everything tests out okay, you are ready to put your newly upgraded server back into production.

Lab

Questions

1. Your organization wants to begin using SQL Server to manage a new data-mart. To save money, you have been told to install SQL Server on an older server that used to run the NetWare network operating system. Before installing SQL Server onto this older server, what should you do?

   A. Verify that the hardware on the older server is on the NT Server Hardware Compatibility List.

   B. Verify that the hardware on the older server is on the SQL Server Hardware Compatibility List.

   C. Verify that the hardware on the older server is on the Windows 95/98 Hardware Compatibility List. You need to do this because you will be running the SQL Server administrative client utilities on a Windows 95 machine.

   D. You cannot use a server that once ran NetWare to run NT Server and SQL Server.

2. Your skinflint boss want you to spend the least amount of money possible on a new SQL Server. What is the absolute minimum server hardware you can get away with?

   A. 80386 CPU, 16MB RAM, 60MB of free disk space

   B. 80486 CPU, 16MB RAM, 60MB of free disk space

   C. Pentium CPU, 16MB RAM, 60MB of free disk space

   D. Pentium CPU, 32MB RAM, 60MB of free disk space

3. You are running a mixture of NT Server and Novell NetWare in your current network. Currently, all the NT Servers are running as member servers. Your goal is to install SQL Server in your network on at least three additional NT member servers, and you want to use SQL Server's integrated security mode to protect your data. Given your current network design, is this possible?

   A. Yes. As long as member servers are available, SQL Server will run fine as described.

   B. Yes. As long as all your users have user accounts for both NetWare and NT Server, SQL Server will run fine as described.

2

    C. No. SQL Server integrated security will not run in a NetWare environment.

    D. No. SQL Server integrated security will not work properly unless all the NT Servers in the network are moved into a properly designed NT domain.

4. You want to install a SQL Server onto an NT member server. This will be the first SQL Server in your network. The member server onto which SQL Server will be installed currently belongs to a resource domain in an NT Server network that uses the Master Domain model. Before installing SQL Server, you want to create a service account for the SQL Executive service. How and where will you create the service account?

    A. Use the User Manager for Domains to create the account on the local member server.

    B. Use the User Manager for Domains to create the account on the PDC of the resource domain to which the member server belongs.

    C. Use the User Manager for Domains to create the account on the PDC of the accounts domain.

    D. You don't have to use the User Manager for Domains to create any account. The SQL Executive service automatically uses the built-in LocalSystem account.

5. Your current NT network is designed around a Single Domain model. That domain currently includes one PDC, two BDCs, and two member servers. You want to install SQL Server on one of these five NT Servers. Which of the following can be used to optimally run SQL Server?

    A. The PDC only

    B. The PDC or any of the BDCs

    C. The PDC or any of the member servers

    D. Any of the member servers only

    E. Any of the NT Servers

6. You are planning to install SQL Server onto a member server in your NT domain. Currently, your network only runs the TCP/IP transport protocol. You know the Named Pipes network library automatically is installed by SQL Server during the installation process. Is this network library adequate by itself? Or do you need to load additional network libraries?

A. Because you are only using TCP/IP as the transport protocol on the network, the Named Pipes network library must be removed. The TCP/IP network library must be installed instead.

B. Because you are only using TCP/IP as the transport protocol on the network, both Named Pipes and the TCP/IP Net-Libraries must be installed.

C. Only the Multi-Protocol network library has to be installed.

D. Nothing has to be done. The default Named Pipes network library will work fine.

7. You manage a mixed network of NT and NetWare servers. Some of the clients only run Windows 95; others run Windows 3.x using the NetWare redirector (not the Windows redirector). You currently are running the NetBEUI and NWLink protocols on the NT Servers and IPX/SPX on the NetWare servers. You decide to install SQL Server onto a current NT Server running as a member server. Which network libraries must you install when installing SQL Server to enable both the Microsoft and NetWare clients to access data from the SQL Server?

A. Named Pipes only.

B. Named Pipes and Multi-Protocol only.

C. Named Pipes and IPX/SPX only.

D. NetWare clients cannot access SQL Server. As a result, only Named Pipes has to be loaded.

8. When you installed SQL Server, you originally installed both the Named Pipes and the Multi-Protocol network libraries. Over time, you also installed the SQL Server administrative client utilities on a wide variety of clients throughout the network. With this configuration, there was no problem with the clients talking to SQL Server. One day, you decide to optimize SQL Server by removing the Named Pipes network library. You do this because you know the Multi-Protocol network library is more efficient overall than Named Pipes. You also know that the more network libraries are loaded by SQL Server, the more RAM is consumed, RAM that could be better used by SQL Server's data cache. Immediately after you remove the Named Pipes network library, none of the clients can communicate with SQL Server. What did you do wrong?

2

A. You forgot one step. You must also reconfigure each client, using the SQL Server Client Configuration utility to use the Multi-Protocol network library rather than the Named Pipes network library.

B. You forgot to reconfigure the network transport protocol. It must be compatible with whatever network library you choose.

C. You forgot that the Named Pipes network library is mandatory. Instead of removing it, you should have removed the Multi-Protocol network library.

D. You forgot to tell SQL Server to automatically reconfigure all the clients. This can be done through the Network Options dialog box in the Enterprise Manager.

9. You want to remotely manage several SQL Servers from your office. You currently are running Windows 95 as your desktop operating system. You install the 32-bit SQL Server administrative client utilities onto your workstation. After the software is loaded, you realize that the SQL Server Performance Monitor and the SQL Server Service Manager utilities were not loaded. What did you do wrong?

A. You forgot to choose these two utilities when you ran the SQL Server setup program.

B. The two missing utilities are 32-bit programs only. As a result, they will not run under Windows 95.

C. The two missing utilities are based on features only available on NT Server and NT Workstation. As a result, they were not loaded.

D. The two missing utilities require the Multi-Protocol Net-Libraries to work. You have not installed them on SQL Server.

10. You currently have three SQL Servers running version 6.0, and you want to upgrade to 6.5. Although there are many preparatory steps before actually performing the upgrade, which of the following is the most important?

A. Run ScanDisk.

B. Run CHKUPG65.

C. Run DBCC CheckDB.

D. Run SP_CHKUP65.

Exercises

1. Creating a SQL Server Service Account

 Note   This exercise helps to address the following certification exam objectives:

- Configure Microsoft Windows NT for SQL Server installations
- Configure SQL Executive to log on as a service

2

Before SQL Server is installed, you need to create a SQL Executive service account using NT Server's User Manager for Domains. After the account is created, you can instruct the SQL Server setup program to use the account so that, whenever the SQL Executive starts, it automatically logs on using the account. Make sure the account is created in the accounts domain of your NT network. This exercise can be performed on any NT Server running as a PDC or BDC. SQL Server is not used in this exercise.

1. Log on to NT Server as an NT administrator.

2. Start the User Manager for Domains program. This displays the User Manager for Domains main screen.

3. From the menus, select User | New User. This opens the New User dialog box.

4. In the Username box, enter a unique NT username for the SQL Executive service account. Choose a name that makes the function of the account immediately apparent, such as `sql_service` or `sql_account`.

5. The Full Name and Description boxes are optional; you can leave them blank if you prefer. If the account name you specified in step 4 is not self-explanatory, enter more detailed information in these two boxes. Make sure the purpose of this account is very clear.

6. Enter a password in the Password and Confirm Password boxes. The same password must be entered in both boxes. Passwords are limited to 13 characters and are case sensitive. Do not leave these blank. If you do, anyone aware of the account's existence could log on to NT Server and act as an administrator.

7. Deselect User Must Change Password at Next Logon. If you don't remove the check, the SQL Executive service will not start.

8. Check the Password Never Expires option. If you don't add a check here, and if you set the NT Server Accounts Policy to automatically expire passwords

after a designated number of days, the SQL Executive service eventually will fail after the account expires and the service is expired.

9. Leave the other check boxes as they are.

10. Click the Groups button at the bottom of the screen. This opens the Group Memberships dialog box.

11. In this dialog box, add the Domain Administrators global group to this account. To accomplish this, click Domain Admin so that it is highlighted. Click the Add button. This moves the Domain Admin group from the Not Member Of window to the Member Of window. Click OK to save this change and return to the New User dialog box.

12. To create and save this account, click the Add button. The account is saved and a blank New User dialog box opens. To exit this screen, click the Cancel button. This returns you to the main User Manager for Domains screen.

13. Give this account the Log On as a Service advanced user right. To do this, select Policies | User Rights from the menus. This opens the User Rights Policy dialog box.

14. Click the button at the bottom of the screen that says Show Advanced User Rights. If you don't, you will not be able to see or select the Log On as a Service user right in the next step.

15. Click the Right drop-down box and click Log On as a Service. This forces the option to be displayed in the drop-down box.

16. To assign this user right to your SQL Server service account, click the Add button. This opens the Add Users and Groups dialog box.

17. Click the Show Users button. This causes all user accounts, including the SQL Server service account you just created, to be displayed in the list box.

18. Use the scrollbar in the list box to find the SQL Server service account you created. Click it so that it is highlighted.

19. Click the Add button so that your SQL Server service account is displayed in the Add Names box.

20. Click the OK button. The current screen disappears and the Add User and Groups dialog box reappears. In addition, your SQL Server service account now appears in the Grant To box.

21. Click the OK button. This closes the Add Users and Groups dialog box; the User Manger for Domains main screen reappears.

22. To exit the User Manager for Domains program, select User | Exit from the menus. The program is closed.

You have just created a SQL Server service account for use with the SQL Executive service. It is now ready to be used by the SQL Server Setup program.

2. Configuring SQL Server Clients Using the SQL Client Configuration Utility

This exercise helps to address the following certification exam objectives:

■ Install client support for network protocols other than Named Pipes

■ Set up support for network clients using various network protocols

2

This exercise shows you how to identify which network library your SQL Server administrative client software currently is using and how to change it. This exercise can be performed on any computer with the SQL Server administrative client software already loaded, including any SQL Server. If the system you are learning on is a production system, make sure you don't make any actual changes to your current configuration.

1. Log on to the system as an NT Server administrator.

2. Start the SQL Server Client Configuration utility. The SQL Server Client Configuration Utility dialog box opens.

3. This exercise focuses on the network library. Click the Net Library tab so that its screen appears.

4. Notice the drop-down box labeled Default Network. The name you see in this box is the name of the network library currently being used by your client software. It usually will read Named Pipes.

5. To view or change the default network library for this client, click the drop-down box to display the other available Net-Libraries. If you want to change the current default network library, choose it from the drop-down list.

6. When you are finished viewing or changing the network library, you can save your change and exit the program by clicking Done. This saves your changes, if any, and unloads the program.

This exercise showed you how to view and change the default network library for your SQL Server administrative client software.

Answers to Questions

1. **A**   You must verify that the older hardware is on the most current NT Server HCL issued by Microsoft.

2. **B**   This is the recommended minimum to run SQL Server. Although it will work, you won't be very happy with this configuration.

3. **D**   To implement SQL Server integrated security, SQL Server must be running on NT Servers that belong to a properly designed NT Server domain. In addition, all the user accounts must be in a designated accounts domain. A properly designed NT Server domain does not currently exist because all the current NT Servers are member servers. If there's not at least one Primary Domain Controller, there is no domain.

4. **C**   The NT user account used as the service account for the SQL Executive service should always be located in the designated accounts domain of an NT network. This permits any SQL Server, no matter where it is located, to use the same account.

5. **D**   Although SQL Server can run under any of these three NT Server roles, it only runs optimally on member servers. PDCs and BDCs have authentication and replication overhead that take away processing power from SQL Servers. Member servers don't have this overhead.

6. **D**   Although Named Pipes, Multi-Protocol, and the TCP/IP Net-Libraries all work successfully, Named Pipes by itself is all that is absolutely required. Named Pipes must be installed during setup or setup will fail. Named Pipes can be removed later if you want, as long as another network library is installed.

7. **C**   Named Pipes enables Windows 95 clients to communicate with SQL Server. The IPX/SPX network library enables NetWare clients to communicate with SQL Server.

8. **A**   Although SQL Server can have one or more Net-Libraries installed, a client only can have one installed at a time. By default, when the SQL Server administrative client utilities are loaded onto a client, the Named Pipes network library is installed. If you remove the Named Pipes network library from SQL Server, you must manually reconfigure every client to use whatever network library you have chosen to run on SQL Server.

9. **C**   Both the missing utilities use NT-specific features. The SQL Server Performance Monitor is really the NT Server Performance Monitor. The SQL Server Service Manager controls the SQL Server services. Because Windows 95 does not support services, this tool is not loaded onto Windows 95 desktops.

10. **B**   It is important to run CHKUPG65 on the older SQL Server version before upgrading to find potential problems. Although the program itself does not fix any problems, it informs you of them so that you can fix them yourself.

2

TEST DAY FAST FACTS

This chapter shows how to configure SQL Server after the initial installation is complete. The following are some key facts you'll learn in this chapter:

- When SQL Server is installed, it creates new entries in the Registry. These entries are located in `HKEY_LOCAL_MACHINE\SOFTWARE\Microsoft\MSSQLServer`, `HKEY_LOCAL_MACHINE\CurrentControlSet\Services\MSSQLService`, `HKEY_LOCAL_MACHINE\CurrentControlSet\Services\SQLExecutive`, and `HKEY_CURRENT_USER\Software\Microsoft\MSSQLServer`.

- SQL Server services can be turned on, turned off, and paused using these five tools: the SQL Server Service Manager, the SQL Server Enterprise Manager, the NT Server Command Prompt, the Server Manager, and the Services dialog box (which can be reached through the Control Panel).

- All new SQL Servers must first be registered with Enterprise Manager before they can be administered with it.

- Server groups can be created to group like-functioning SQL Servers for administrative purposes.

- SQL Server configuration settings can be set using either the Enterprise Manager or system-stored procedures.

Day 3

Configuring SQL Server

After you install SQL Server, it needs to be tested and configured for your particular application. One of the most important tools used to configure SQL Server for production is the SQL Server Enterprise Manager. It also is a tool you will use on a daily basis to administer SQL Server throughout your enterprise.

If you have ever used the Enterprise Manager, you already know how extensive it is. It is not the goal of this chapter to tell you everything the Enterprise Manager can do. Instead, this chapter helps you understand the basics of the Enterprise Manager, with a special focus on the initial configuration of SQL Server. As you continue through this book, the Enterprise Manager is revisited many times.

If you already have extensive experience with the Enterprise Manager, you might want to skim this chapter and focus only on information that is new to you. If you are new to SQL Server, you should take the time to master the fundamentals in this chapter. The better you understand the fundamentals, the easier it will be to learn the more advanced topics covered later in this book.

This chapter covers the following topics:

- How to verify SQL Server was installed correctly
- How to stop and start SQL Server services

- How to log in to SQL Server
- How to register SQL Server and create server groups
- How to use the SQL Server Enterprise Manager
- How to configure SQL Server for first-time use
- How to install an extended procedure

Objectives

This chapter covers the following material:

- Locate where Windows NT Registry entries for SQL Server are stored
- Configure servers in the enterprise
- Manage servers in the enterprise
- Administer servers in the enterprise
- Configure SQL Server for various memory scenarios
- Install an extended stored procedure

3.1. How to Verify That SQL Server Was Installed Correctly

Before putting SQL Server into production, you need to make sure it was installed correctly by the SQL Server setup program. The installation probably went smoothly, but it never hurts to check. If you understand how SQL Server is installed, you are in a better position to troubleshoot potential problems should they arise later.

This section shows you how SQL Server is installed onto a server. Specifically it covers the following topics:

- How to verify SQL Server file locations
- How to verify SQL Server Registry locations
- How to verify that the SQL services are installed

3.1.1. How to Verify SQL Server File Locations

When you installed SQL Server, you had the opportunity to specify where you wanted the SQL Server program and data files to be located. Most likely, you specified the drive on which the \Mssql was to be located, leaving the \Mssql folder name as is. Although the setup program enables you to name this folder however you want, there's no point in changing this name. If you do, you only make it more difficult for other people to figure out what you have done.

Whatever drive letter or folder name you specified, the SQL Server setup program creates a series of subfolders within the main folder (which is assumed to be \Mssql). Use NT Server Explorer to access that drive or folder and to verify that the following subfolders actually were created:

- *\Mssql\Backup*. Initially, this folder is empty. It is the default location where SQL Server creates backup devices for disk backups. You probably should specify another location for your backups when you perform an actual backup. If you store your backups in this default location, both the original data and the backups are on the same physical hard disk, which is not a good idea.
- *\Mssql\Bin*. This is where the DOS- and Windows-based 16-bit executables and DLLs are stored.
- *\Mssql\Binn*. This is where the 32-bit SQL Server executables and DLLs are stored.

- *\Mssql\Charsets.* All character sets and sort order data are stored here, even though only one is used at a time by SQL Server.

- *\Mssql\Data.* This is the default location for all database devices including the MASTER, MSDB, and MDSBLOG devices, which are used for the SQL Server system databases. Depending how your server is configured, you might want to store your user devices on a separate disk drive or disk array.

- *\Mssql\Install.* This folder contains a variety of miscellaneous files including Books Online (if you loaded it), installation scripts used when SQL Server was installed, and output files (used to diagnose SQL Server setup problems).

- *\Mssql\Log.* This is where SQL stores its log files. All informational, warning, and error messages are stored here. Each time the MSSQLService starts, a new log file is created. Only the six most recent files are kept; the rest are deleted automatically. These files are discussed in more detail on Day 14, "Troubleshooting SQL Server."

- *\Mssql\Repldata.* Initially, this folder is empty. It is used only if you make the current SQL Server a replication distribution server. The distribution database is stored here by default.

- *\Mssql\Snmp.* This folder contains an SNMP (Simple Network Management Protocol) MIB (Management Information Base) file. If this file is installed properly, it enables an SNMP-based management workstation to access SQL Server counters. If you don't plan to use SNMP to manage the SQL Server, this folder can be deleted.

- *\Mssql\Sqlole.* This folder contains sample Visual Basic files. These files can be used to learn more about how to program Visual Basic to work with SQL Server. This folder can be deleted.

- *\Mssql\Symbols.* This folder contains a variety of files that can be used to create stack dumps and traces on SQL Server code. If you don't think you need to do this (which is extremely rare), this folder can be deleted.

After installing SQL Server, take a few minutes to verify that these folders exist. If they don't, you might have to reinstall SQL Server.

3.1.2. How to Verify SQL Server Registry Locations

When SQL Server is installed, it creates several new keys in the NT Registry. You should use the NT Server Registry Editor (regedt32.exe) to verify that they were created (see Figure 3.1). One of the new keys created is HKEY_LOCAL_MACHINE\ SOFTWARE\Microsoft\MSSQLServer.

Figure 3.1.

Use the NT Server Registry Editor to view SQL Server Registry entries.

This key contains configuration information used by SQL Server when the MSSQLService and SQLExecutive services are first started. After these services are started, SQL Server uses information stored in the Master database to store and retrieve configuration information.

The following additional keys are created to store information about the MSSQLService and SQLExecutive services:

```
HKEY_LOCAL_MACHINE\CurrentControlSet\Services\MSSQLService
HKEY_LOCAL_MACHINE\CurrentControlSet\Services\SQLExecutive
```

The preceding keys are used by NT Server to start these services automatically every time NT Server is booted. (This assumes that auto-start for SQL Server has been turned on in SQL Setup.)

You also need to be familiar with the following key, which is used by SQL Server client software:

```
HKEY_CURRENT_USER\Software\Microsoft\MSSQLServer
```

This key stores SQL Server client configuration information and is stored on a user-by-user basis. Whenever you register a SQL Server with the Enterprise Manager, for example, the registration information is stored in this key.

Use the NT Server Registry Editor to make sure these four keys exist. As with any Registry entry, however, you should not make any changes unless you know exactly what you are doing.

3.1.3. How to Verify That the SQL Services Are Installed

If you used the Registry Editor to verify that the two \CurrentControlSet\Services keys were added (one for each main service), you already have verified that the SQL Server services were installed. Another way to verify them—and to make any changes if necessary—is to use the Control Panel | Services option.

To verify that the two services were installed, open the Control Panel and the Services dialog box and scroll through the various services to see if MSSQLServer and SQLExecutive are listed (see Figure 3.2). If they are listed, you know they were installed.

Figure 3.2.

All SQL Server services are configured from the Services dialog box.

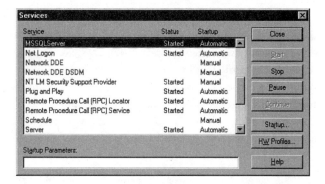

If you want to see how the services were configured by the SQL Server setup program, click one of the services and then click the Startup button. This displays the Service dialog box (see Figure 3.3). You can choose a startup type and select which account is used to start the service.

You can choose from three startup types. If you select Automatic, the service automatically starts each time NT Server is rebooted. If you select Manual, the service does not automatically start when NT Server is rebooted, but you can start the service manually after NT Server boots. If you select Disabled, the service currently cannot be started, either automatically or manually.

Generally, both SQL Server services should be set to Automatic. Although you can change between Automatic and Manual from this screen, you also can perform this task using the Server Options tab in the Server Configuration/Options dialog box (which is discussed in more detail later). In this dialog box, you can change each service's Auto Start status, which is just like the Automatic and Manual options. Auto Start is the same as Automatic and is discussed more later in this chapter.

Figure 3.3.

SQL services can be configured manually from this dialog box.

As mentioned on Day 2, the SQLExecutive service should be started with a SQL Service account rather than the default LocalSystem account. The Service dialog box enables you to verify that the SQLExecutive account is using either a SQL Service account or the LocalSystem account. It also enables you to make any necessary changes. This same task also can be performed from the SQL Server setup program. In the setup program, you also can change the account used by SQLExecutive to start.

3.2. How to Stop and Start SQL Server Services

When you install SQL Server, you usually should specify that you want MSSQLServer and SQLExecutive to auto-start every time NT Server is booted. That way, you won't have to remember to restart the two services every time you restart NT Server.

At times, however, you need to stop and then restart the SQL Server services. This might be because you changed a configuration option that requires you to restart a service for it to take effect. It also could be because a service is not acting correctly, and you want to stop and start the service to see if it fixes the problem. In any event, you need to know how to stop and start the SQL Server services.

There are five different ways to stop and start the SQL Server services. Each method accomplishes exactly the same thing. Most of the time, you can choose whichever method you prefer. At times, however, one or more of the ways might not work depending on your circumstances. The exceptions are discussed in the following sections, in which you will learn how to stop and start the SQL Server services using these methods:

- The SQL Server Service Manager
- The SQL Server Enterprise Manager
- The NT Server command prompt
- The Control Panel | Services dialog box
- The Server Manager

3.2.1. How to Use the SQL Server Service Manager

The SQL Server Service Manager is one of the many SQL Server administrative client utilities that are installed when you load SQL Server (see Figure 3.4). It enables you to start, stop, or pause any SQL Server service.

Figure 3.4.

The SQL Service Manager dialog box enables you to start, stop, and pause SQL Server services.

The following steps show you how to use the SQL Server Service Manager:

1. Log on to NT Server using an administrative account.
2. Start the SQL Server Service Manager. The SQL Service Manager screen displays (refer to Figure 3.4).
3. Select the SQL Server whose services you want to view or change. To do this, click the Server drop-down box. This box should display all the SQL Servers on your network. If it doesn't, enter the server's name in the drop-down box and then click the Connect button to establish a connection to the SQL Server. This feature enables you to remotely manage SQL Servers.

4. Select the SQL Server service you want to view or change. To do this, click the Services drop-down box so the service is displayed.

5. At this point, you can view the current status of the service or you can change it. To stop, pause, or start a service, double-click the action you want to perform. If the SQLExecutive service currently is displayed and is running, for example, the green light will be on. To stop the service, double-click the red light. The green light will go off, the red light will come on, and the message The service is stopping. will appear at the bottom of the screen. After several seconds, the message at the bottom of the screen will change to The service has stopped. To turn the service back on, double-click the green light. The red light will go off, the green light will come on, and the message The service is starting. will appear at the bottom of the screen. After several seconds, the message will change to The service is running.

6. When you are finished, you can close the program by clicking the Close Window icon (the X) in the upper-right corner of the screen.

You can perform these same steps in the SQL Server Service Manager for any of the SQL services.

Note

Although you can pause MSSQLServer, you cannot pause SQLExecutive.

3.2.2. How to Use the SQL Server Enterprise Manager

You have not yet learned how to start or use the Enterprise Manager, so in a sense, this section jumps ahead. Don't worry. Just follow along for now so you learn how to use the Enterprise Manager to stop and start services. Later, after you learn more about the Enterprise Manager, you can try it out.

You can do exactly the same tasks in the Enterprise Manager that you just did in the SQL Server Service Manager. The only difference is that the Enterprise Manager might be more convenient to use, especially if it currently is running (which is common on a DBA's computer). In addition, because most SQL Server configuration is done from the Enterprise Manager, stopping and starting a service to apply a configuration change is handy. About the only time you cannot use the Enterprise Manager to stop and start services is when you are unable to start the Enterprise Manager itself. If this happens, you have to use one of the other three techniques to stop or start SQL Services.

Figure 3.5 shows the Enterprise Manager. In the tree, there is a stoplight by a SQL Server named PDC. Below the stoplight is SQL Executive, and below SQL Executive is the Distributed Transaction Coordinator. Each of these represent a separate SQL Server service. The stoplight represents the MSSQLService, SQL Executive is self-explanatory, and the Distributed Transaction Coordinator is an infrequently used service that manages the posting of transactions to multiple services simultaneously. Your focus here should be only on the first two services.

Figure 3.5.

The Enterprise Manager can be used to stop and start services.

To start, stop, or pause these services, right-click the icon (or the name itself). This opens the window you see to the right of the tree. As you can see, you can start, stop, or pause a service just by selecting the appropriate option. In this case, Start is grayed out because the service already is started. Pause and Stop are the only currently available options.

3.2.3. How to Use the Command Prompt

If you are one of the few people who prefer typing obscure commands at a command prompt rather than clicking buttons in a GUI interface, you will love this feature. Any of the SQL Server services can be started, stopped, or paused from the NT Server command prompt. The commands are as follows:

To Start MSSQLServer or SQLExecutive

```
NET START MSSQLSERVER
NET START SQLEXECUTIVE
```

To Stop MSSQLServer or SQLExecutive

```
NET STOP MSSQLSERVER
NET STOP SQLEXECUTIVE
```

To Pause MSSQLServer

```
NET PAUSE MSSQLSERVER
```

To Restart a Paused MSSQLServer

```
NET CONTINUE MSSQLSERVER
```

Some DBAs find these commands useful because they can be added to BAT files and Transact-SQL scripts to automatically stop and start the SQL Server services.

3.2.4. How to Use the Control Panel

In a previous section, the Services dialog box, reached through the Control Panel, was discussed as a way to verify whether the SQL Server services were loaded (refer to Figure 3.2). This same dialog box also can be used to start, stop, or pause any of the SQL Server services. The following tutorial provides more details about how to use the Control Panel | Services option to start and stop services.

1. Log on to NT Server using an administrative account.

2. From the Start menu, select Settings and then Control Panel. This opens the Control Panel dialog box.

3. Double-click the Services icon. This opens the Services dialog box (refer to Figure 3.2).

4. Scroll through the Service list box until you find either MSSQLServer or SQLExecutive.

5. Click the service you want to stop or start so it is highlighted.

6. To stop the service, click the Stop button. To start the service, click the Start button. To pause the service, click the Pause button. To continue a paused service, click the Continue button.

7. When you are finished, click the Close button.

Any of these options work to start, stop, or pause SQL Server services. Choose the one you find most convenient in the current circumstances.

3.2.5. How to Use the Server Manager

Although there are no questions on the certification exam about using the Server Manager to start and stop services, it still can help you in your job. This section contains a brief explanation of how this NT Server-based administrative tool is used.

Essentially, the Server Manager enables you perform the exact same tasks you can perform using the Control Panel. If you choose File | Services in the Server Manager, you get a dialog box similar to the one you see when you access the Control Panel. The only difference between using the Server Manager and the Control Panel to perform a task is that the Control Panel enables you to stop and start services only on your local computer. The Server Manager, on the other hand, enables you to access NT Servers remotely and to stop and start services remotely. This is an important feature if you manage your SQL Servers remotely.

3

3.3. How to Register SQL Servers and Create Server Groups

If you try to access SQL Server immediately after it is first installed, you have to log in as the system administrator with no password. This is because, by default, SQL Server uses the standard security mode. There is only one login ID available for logging in—the system administrator account (which has no assigned password).

Although most SQL Server administrative client utilities require you to log in each time you start the utility, this is not the case with the Enterprise Manager. The first time you start the Enterprise Manager, you are asked to register any SQL Servers you want to manage with this copy of the Enterprise Manager. Part of the registration process requires you to log in to SQL Server using the system administrator account with no password.

After a SQL Server is registered, the next time you start the Enterprise Manager, you don't have to log in. This is because the process of registering a SQL Server saves the login name and password you entered to your user profile (in the Registry). The advantage is that, if you manage multiple SQL Servers from the Enterprise Manager, you don't have to manually log in to each one each time the Enterprise Manager is started. The downside is that, if you change the system administrator password or change your security mode, you might have to reregister your SQL Servers (at least the ones affected by the change).

The next section shows you how to register a SQL Server. The one that follows it describes what a server group is and how to create one.

3.3.1. How to Register a SQL Server

The following tutorial shows you how to register a SQL Server for the first time. It assumes the copy of the Enterprise Manager you are running is installed on a newly installed SQL Server.

1. Log on to NT Server using an administrative account.

2. Make sure the MSSQLService SQL Server is running. If it isn't, you cannot register your SQL Server with the Enterprise Manager.

3. Start the Enterprise Manager. This opens the Register Server dialog box (see Figure 3.6).

Figure 3.6.

All new SQL Servers must be registered with the Enterprise Manager.

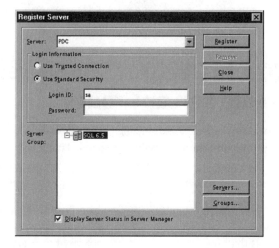

4. In the Server drop-down box, enter the name of the SQL Server you want to register.

5. Make sure the Use Standard Security radio button is selected.

6. In the Login ID box, enter SA and leave the password blank. For now, don't worry about the Server Group. This is discussed in the next section.

7. Click the Register button to register your SQL Server with the Enterprise Manager. The Register Server dialog box remains onscreen, but the Register button grays out.

8. To close the Register Server dialog box, click the Close button. The Enterprise Manager main screen displays, and you can begin using it.

After a SQL Server has been registered with the Enterprise Manager, you have the option to unregister it. To do this, right-click the name of the server from the Enterprise Manager main screen and select Un-Register. When you add a password to the system administrator account, you have to unregister and reregister your SQL Server using the new password.

3.3.2. How to Create a Server Group

When a server is first registered, it automatically is put into a default server group named SQL 6.5. A *server group* is a way to group similarly used SQL Servers. Assume you have four SQL Servers in the marketing department, for example, and six SQL Servers in the production department. You can either place them all in the SQL 6.5 server group, or you can create two server groups: one called marketing and another called production. This way, you can more easily identify which SQL Server does what. This is completely optional, however, and as far as SQL Server is concerned, it means nothing. The following tutorial shows you how to create a server group and how to move a SQL Server from the SQL 6.5 server group to a server group named marketing.

1. Log on to SQL Server using an administrative account.

2. Load the Enterprise Manager. The Enterprise Manager main screen displays.

3. Right-click the SQL 6.5 server group and select New Server Group from the menu. This displays the Manage Server Groups dialog box (see Figure 3.7). The large box at the bottom of this dialog box lists the current server groups. In this case, only the default SQL 6.5 server group exists.

Figure 3.7.

New server groups are created from the Manage Server Groups dialog box.

You can create either top-level groups or subgroups. Rarely will you ever need to create subgroups. You will create a top-level group here.

4. To create a new top-level group, enter the name of the new group in the Name box.

5. Click the Add button to create the new server group. After clicking Add, the dialog box remains onscreen, the Add button grays out, and the new server group is added to the box at the bottom of the dialog box.

6. Click the Close button to close this dialog box.

7. The next step is to move a SQL Server from the SQL 6.5 group to the marketing group. This can be done from the Enterprise Manager main screen. To move a single SQL Server from one server group to another, click the server to be moved, drag it to the new server group, and then release the mouse button. The server is moved from the old server group to the new server group.

You can remove an unused server group by right-clicking it and selecting Remove from the menu.

3.4. How to Use the SQL Server Enterprise Manager

You learned a little about the Enterprise Manager earlier in this chapter, but this section extends your knowledge in a couple important areas. As you might imagine, not everything about the Enterprise Manager is discussed here. Don't worry, you will be seeing a lot more of the Enterprise Manager throughout the rest of this book.

The Enterprise Manager main screen is where you will spend much of your time as a SQL Server DBA (see Figure 3.8).

The main screen is divided into the following sections:

- *The menu bar.* This is your typical Microsoft Windows menu bar. As you learn more about SQL Server, you will rarely use it. Most of the tools you need are available from the tree.

- *The toolbar.* This is your standard toolbar. The icons are hard to figure out, but tool tips are displayed if you move your mouse pointer over an icon.

- *The Server Selection bar.* Two things are possible here. First, you can select which SQL Server you want to administer at this time, assuming you have multiple servers registered with the Enterprise Manager. Just select the one you want to administer from the drop-down box. Second, the icon next to the drop-down box opens the Server Legend. This box tells you what all the obscure icons used by SQL Server mean. If you are new to SQL Server, you might need to refer to this until you learn each icon used by the Enterprise Manager.

Figure 3.8.

The SQL Server Enterprise Manager main screen.

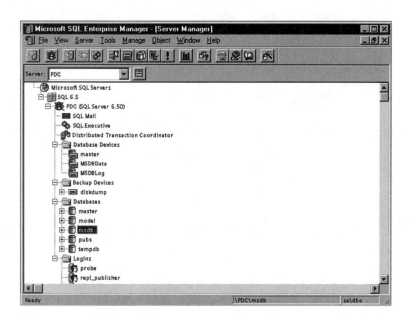

3

- *The tree.* The tree is where you will spend most of your time. It presents a visual overview of all the SQL Servers managed by this copy of the Enterprise Manager. Figure 3.8 showed the tree mostly open. When the Enterprise Manager first is started, most of the tree is closed. It shows you only a high-level view of your SQL Servers. A minus sign (-) means this branch of the tree is open; a plus sign (+) means the branch is closed, but that it can be opened.

  At the top of the tree is a globe with the words Microsoft SQL Servers. This is the very top of the tree. The next level of this tree is the server groups. If you have not created any additional groups, only the default SQL 6.5 server group is at the second level.

  The third level is the SQL Servers themselves. When you open a server group, you see all the SQL Servers that belong to it.

  The fourth level opens individual SQL Servers and shows you their various components, including SQL Mail, SQL Executive, the Distributed Transaction Coordinator, database devices, backup devices, databases, and logins. Components with a plus sign next to them can be opened to even deeper levels of the tree.

Using the tree can be awkward at first, but it's easy to get around after you figure it out. You should experiment with opening all the levels to see what is there.

You can right-click any item in the tree to open a context-sensitive menu that enables you to manipulate that object in the tree. In most cases, this is how you administer SQL Server. If you prefer, however, you can still use the drop-down menu to accomplish most of the same tasks.

> **Note** An important tool in the Enterprise Manager is the SQL Query tool. You can select it from the toolbar or from the drop-down menu (Tools | SQL Query Tool). This tool, which is almost identical to ISQL/W, enables you to enter and execute Transact-SQL statements and stored procedures manually. This tool is not covered on the certification exam, but you still should learn how to use it. You will probably use it to manually manipulate SQL Server. The Enterprise Manager enables you to perform most, but not all, SQL Server administrative tasks. Some tasks are still manual and require you to use Transact-SQL statements or stored procedures. If you have not yet learned how to use the SQL Query tool, take the time now to learn it.

3.5. How to Modify SQL Server's Configuration

After installing SQL Server, you should configure it for first-time use right away. SQL Server has many configuration options, none of which are described here. This section focuses on how to change SQL Server's configuration. Later sections in this chapter—and throughout this book— describe the most common SQL Server configuration options.

SQL Server configuration options can be set in two ways. You can change them using either the Enterprise Manager or a built-in system-stored procedure. Both methods are described in the following tutorial.

The first part of this tutorial shows you how to use the Enterprise Manager to change SQL Server's configuration. The second part shows you how to change the configuration using a stored procedure.

1. Log on to NT Server using an administrative account.
2. Start the Enterprise Manager.

3. Right-click the SQL Server in the tree you want to view or change and choose Configuration from the pop-up menu. This opens the Server Options tab of the Server Configuration/Options dialog box (see Figure 3.9).

Figure 3.9.

The Server Options tab enables you to make changes to SQL Server's configuration.

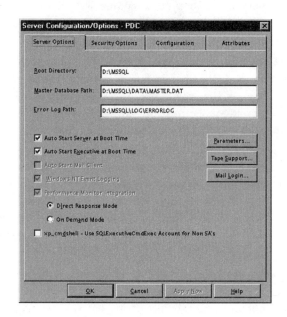

The following is a brief explanation of the available configuration options:

■ *Root Directory.* Specifies where your SQL Server files are located. You're asking for trouble if you want to change these after SQL Server is installed.

■ *Master Database Path.* Specifies where the MASTER database device is stored. If you change this, you also have to change the MSSQLServer startup parameters. (See the Parameters button later in this list.)

■ *Error Log Path.* Specifies where SQL Server log files are stored.

■ *Auto Start Server at Boot Time.* Determines whether MSSQLService is started automatically when NT Server is rebooted.

■ *Auto Start Executive at Boot Time.* Determines whether SQLExecutive is started automatically when NT Server is rebooted.

■ *Auto Start Mail Client.* This option is grayed out and cannot be changed here. It is shown only for reference. It lets you know whether SQL Mail has been set up yet. This option can be set only from the SQL Server setup program.

- *Windows NT Event Logging.* This option is grayed out and cannot be changed here. It is shown only for reference. It determines whether any SQL Server events are logged to NT Server's Event Viewer. If this option is not on, you cannot use SQL alerts (discussed on Day 9, "Scheduling Events and Creating Alerts"). This option can be set only from the SQL Server setup program.

- *Performance Monitor Integration.* This option is grayed out and cannot be changed here. It is shown only for reference, but it does provide some choices. First, this option determines whether NT Server's Performance Monitor tool can be used with SQL Server. This option can be set only from the SQL Server setup program. Assuming you leave this option on (which is a good idea), it works in two different ways. First, the Direct Response Mode (selected by default) means the counters you see in the Performance Monitor are slightly delayed in response. SQL Server's performance, however, is not affected by the monitoring. Second, the On Demand Mode means the Performance Monitor provides up-to-date data. This, however, exacts a slight performance penalty on SQL Server's performance.

- *xp_cmdshell.* If this option is not selected, this extended procedure runs in the security context of SQL Server when run from a client. If this option is selected, the security context is that of the client rather than SQL Server.

- *Parameters.* This option enables you to pass startup parameters to MSSQLService when it is automatically started during NT Server boot-up. One of the parameters tells SQL Server where the MASTER device is located.

- *Tape Support.* Enables you to configure time-out values for any tape device you might be using to back up SQL Server data.

- *Mail Login.* Enables you to change the current mailbox and password used for SQL Mail.

As you might imagine, the explanations of these options could run for many pages. This is enough to get you started, however, and is enough to prepare for the test.

4. Before you exit this dialog box, you need to explore one more tab—the Configuration tab (see Figure 3.10). Select it now.

Figure 3.10.

The Configuration tab enables you to make specific changes to SQL Server's configuration and performance.

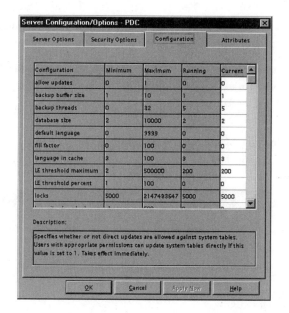

Configuration	Minimum	Maximum	Running	Current
allow updates	0	1	0	0
backup buffer size	1	10	1	1
backup threads	0	32	5	5
database size	2	10000	2	2
default language	0	9999	0	0
fill factor	0	100	0	0
language in cache	3	100	3	3
LE threshold maximum	2	500000	200	200
LE threshold percent	1	100	0	0
locks	5000	2147483647	5000	5000

Description:

Specifies whether or not direct updates are allowed against system tables. Users with appropriate permissions can update system tables directly if this value is set to 1. Takes effect immediately.

This tab offers many configuration options. Some are quite advanced and should be changed only by an experienced DBA. Others are very basic and need to be changed soon after SQL Server is loaded. (Some of the basic options are discussed later in this chapter.)

Scroll through the options. Note that each configuration setting has a minimum and maximum setting. This shows you the acceptable range for each configuration setting. In the Running column, you see the currently displayed setting. The Current column contains the same values as the Running column because the Current column is used to make a change. When you make a change in the Current column, it is not put into effect until MSSQLService is stopped and then restarted.

5. For now, click the OK button to close the Server Configuration/Options dialog box.

Later in this chapter—and throughout this book—the options on these two tabs are explored in more detail. If you change options in these two tabs, they do not take effect until MSSQLService is restarted. This can be done from the Enterprise Manager, as discussed earlier in this chapter.

The rest of this tutorial focuses on how to use a system-stored procedure to change the configuration settings in the Configuration tab of the Server

Configuration/Options dialog box. This part of the tutorial assumes the Enterprise Manager currently is running and the main screen is displayed.

1. Before you can use any stored procedure, you must load a program that enables you to speak directly to SQL Server. Two common methods are to use ISQL/W or to run the SQL Query tool from the Enterprise Manager. In this example, you will use the SQL Query tool.

2. To load the SQL Query tool from the Enterprise Manager, choose Tools I SQL Query Tool. The SQL Query tool displays (see Figure 3.11).

Figure 3.11.

The SQL Query tool directly enters and executes Transact-SQL statements.

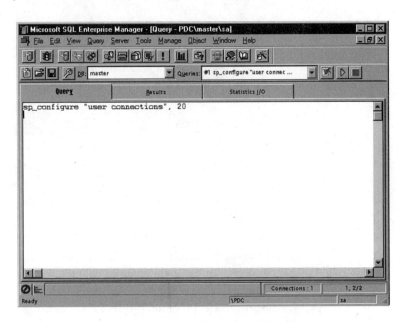

3. The following is the syntax for the `sp_configure` command:

```
sp_configure config_name, config_value
```

In the preceding, `config_name` is the name of the configuration option to be changed, and `config_value` is the new value to be assigned the option.

To find the preceding values, you have to search Books Online or another SQL Server reference.

4. After the command is entered in the Query window of the SQL Query tool (note the first tab at the top of the window), it must be executed. To execute the command, you must choose Query I Execute from the drop-down menu. After you do, you'll see this message in the Results window: Configuration

option changed. Run the RECONFIGURE command to install. This message is telling you to run one more command before you are done.

5. To complete this procedure, first click the Query tab to return to the Query window. Type reconfigure in the window and then execute the command by selecting Query | Execute from the drop-down menu. The results window shows this message: This command did not return data, and it did not return any rows. The change you made has been set, but you still need to perform one more step before the change takes effect.

6. As your last step, you must stop and then restart MSSQLService, as previously discussed in this chapter. At this point, your change goes into effect.

It is much easier to use the Enterprise Manager than to use a system-stored procedure. So why would anyone use a system-stored procedure instead? System-stored procedures are used mostly by DBAs or developers who write their own Transact-SQL scripts to manage SQL Server. Although it is not required to write your own Transact-SQL scripts to perform most SQL Server management tasks, some people prefer them as a management tool.

3.6. How to Configure SQL Server for First-Time Use

This part of the chapter finally provides some specifics. Until now, much of the discussion has been general in nature albeit important to know. After SQL Server is installed, you need to perform a couple configuration tasks immediately. This section shows you how to assign a password to the system administrator account, how to tell SQL Server how much RAM to use and how to allocate it, and how to tell SQL Server how many user connections will be used simultaneously.

3.6.1. Assigning the System Administrator Password

When you first install SQL Server, the only login ID automatically created is the system administrator account, which is not assigned a password. This means anyone who knows anything about SQL Server can log in to your SQL Server and do anything they want. To prevent this, you need to assign a password as quickly as possible after installing SQL Server.

Use the following steps to add a password to the system administrator account:

1. Log on to NT Server using an administrative account.

2. Load the Enterprise Manager. Make sure your SQL Server already has been registered.

3. Expand the SQL Server tree in the Enterprise Manager so you see the Logins folder.

4. Expand the Logins folder to see all the current Login IDs. The system administrator account is in the list.

5. Right-click SA and then select Edit. This opens the Manage Logins dialog box (see Figure 3.12).

Figure 3.12.

The Manage Logins dialog box is used to change the system administrator's password.

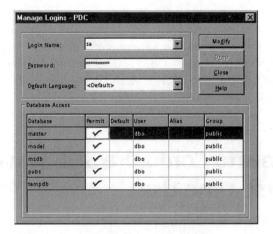

6. The Password box contains a series of asterisks. This does not mean the system administrator account has a password. These are just a filler. To add a password to the system administrator account, enter it in the Password box. The current asterisks are replaced by new asterisks as you enter the new password.

7. After entering the password, click the Modify button. This displays the Confirm Password dialog box. In this dialog box, reenter the password and click the OK button. You now return to the Manage Logins dialog box.

8. Click Close to close the dialog box. You now have added a password to the system administrator account.

9. Although you have finished changing the password, you still have one more step. You have to unregister and then reregister SQL Server. This is because the old registration has the old password (or no password) saved as part of the registration process. You must reregister SQL Server so the new password can be saved as part of the registration information.

3.6.2. Modifying SQL Server's Configuration

You already have learned how to change SQL Server's configuration using either the Enterprise Manager or the sp_configure system-stored procedure. In this section, you learn about three SQL Server settings that should be changed right after installing SQL Server. You already know how to make these changes, so this section focuses on what the settings are and how they should be configured. This section shows you how to set the Memory, Procedure Cache, and User Connections options.

Configuring SQL Server's Memory

Although SQL Server is smart in many ways, it can be dumb in others. Take, for example, the amount of RAM in your SQL Server. Although you might have purchased a server with 256MB of RAM, SQL Server could care less. When you install SQL Server, it examines the amount of RAM in your server and takes one of two actions. If the RAM in the server is 32MB or less, it sets the Memory setting to use only 8MB. If your server has more than 32MB, SQL Server sets the Memory setting to 16MB. These are the only two choices, even if you have a gigabyte of RAM. If your server has more than 32MB of RAM, you need to manually reconfigure the Memory setting so SQL Server can take advantage of all the extra RAM you purchased.

The Memory setting tells SQL Server how much RAM it can use at any one time. If you don't tell SQL Server the RAM exists, SQL Server ignores it. The hard part is to determine how much RAM to allocate to SQL Server. Table 3.1 shows Microsoft's recommendations for the amount of RAM you should allocate to SQL Server. This assumes NT Server is dedicated to SQL Server and is not running other programs.

Table 3.1. Allocating RAM to SQL Server.

RAM in Server	Recommended SQL Server Setting
16MB	4MB
24MB	8MB
32MB	16MB
48MB	28MB
64MB	40MB
128MB	100MB
256MB	216MB
512MB	464MB

These are general recommendations and might not be the optimum Memory setting for your SQL Server and application. To refine these figures, use the Performance Monitor tool to evaluate how your SQL Server is performing. This is discussed on Day 13, "Tuning and Optimizing SQL Server."

When you enter the Memory setting into the Configuration tab of the Server Configuration/Options dialog box, you must enter it in units of 2K (2,048 bytes) pages. Unfortunately, you cannot directly enter the number of megabytes you want to allocate; you must first convert megabytes to 2K pages. To do this, take the number of megabytes and multiple it by 512. This gives you the number of 2K pages—the value you must enter into SQL Server's Memory setting.

Configuring SQL Server's Procedure Cache

SQL Server's procedure cache is a buffer area of memory used to store compiled query trees. Query trees are created the first time a stored procedure is run. By storing this information in a buffer, whenever a stored procedure has to run again, it can run much faster because it does not have to be recompiled. This speeds up SQL Server's performance. In theory, you should have the most commonly stored procedure's query trees in the procedure cache at all times.

The Procedure Cache setting determines how much available RAM is dedicated to its use. Of the RAM dedicated to SQL Server in the Memory setting, a certain amount is dedicated to the overhead of running SQL Server. Any extra RAM from the overhead is divided between SQL Server's data cache and procedure cache. By default, 70 percent is devoted to the data cache and 30 percent goes to the procedure cache. The data cache stores SQL Server data, much like the file cache in NT Server stores data. The larger the data cache, the less time SQL Server has to access a hard disk to get data. This speeds up SQL Server's overall performance.

The problem is that, although the 70/30 ratio is adequate for small amounts of RAM, it is not an appropriate ratio if your server has lots of RAM. Let's say, for example, that the amount of RAM available for the procedure and data cache is 10MB. This means 3MB is dedicated to the procedure cache and 7MB is dedicated to the data cache. Assume 3MB is more than adequate to cache all the stored procedures your SQL Server application uses. If you add more RAM to your SQL Server so that 20MB is available, the procedure cache is allocated 6MB and the data cache is allocated 14MB. The problem is you only need 3MB for your procedure cache, not 6MB. If the 70/30 ratio is not changed, 3MB of RAM is wasted. It's more efficient for SQL Server if this 3MB instead is dedicated to the data cache, where it can be used to hold more data for quick access.

What does this mean to you? If your SQL Server has 64MB or more of RAM, you probably need to adjust the ratio so that the procedure cache does not waste RAM. You cannot easily determine the optimum ratio, however, without extensive testing using the Performance Monitor under a real production environment. Because you don't have good data now, you might want to consider backing off the 30 percent. You can say yes to 20-25 percent now and then, as your system goes into production, use the Performance Monitor to fine-tune your system.

The number you enter into the Procedure Cache setting in the Configuration tab of the Server Configuration/Options dialog box is a percentage. The default is 30. You can change this to another percentage, such as 20 or 25 as a starting point, assuming your server has 64MB of RAM or more.

Configuring SQL Server's User Connections

The final setting you need to adjust soon after installing SQL Server is to increase the number of available user connections. This setting determines how many simultaneous user connections SQL Server can support. This is set by default to 15, which is generally too low for most SQL Server applications. If you try to exceed this figure, you can't. If a 16th user connection is attempted, for example, it is refused by SQL Server.

The hard part about increasing the number of User Connections is that each user connection takes 37KB of RAM, which becomes part of the overhead of SQL Server. This, in effect, takes RAM away from the procedure and data caches. This 37KB is used whether or not an actual user connection has been made. You need to choose a number high enough to allow all the user connections you need, but not high enough to waste RAM.

The best you can do is estimate the number of user connections you think you need and make that your setting. You can monitor user connection usage in the Performance Monitor to determine how close your guess was and adjust the setting accordingly.

3.7. How to Install an Extended Stored Procedure

You might find this topic a little out of place here. Why is knowing how to install an extended stored procedure important? First, it is a test objective; Microsoft expects you to be familiar with the concept. Second, it has to do with configuration, and this chapter is about SQL Server configuration. This is an obscure topic and is a procedure not performed often by the DBA, if at all. In any event, this section discusses what an extended stored procedure is and how you can install one into SQL Server.

3.7.1. What Is an Extended Stored Procedure?

Although an extended stored procedure sounds like a stored procedure, it actually is quite different. A *stored procedure* is a series of precompiled Transact-SQL statements; an *extended stored procedure* is a call to a dynamic link library (DLL) function.

SQL Server has many built-in extended stored procedures. If desired, a developer can write his own DLL that can be accessed using an extended stored procedure from within SQL Server. This is what this section is all about. Extended stored procedures that come with SQL Server already are installed. The only extended stored procedures that need to be installed are those based on custom-written DLLs.

Extended stored procedures start with xp_ and are followed by their name.

3.7.2. Working with Extended Stored Procedures

Before you can install and work with an extended stored procedure, the custom-written DLL must exist. Most DLLs include multiple functions (tasks), and each different function has its own unique name. This means you need to know both the name of the DLL and the name of the function before you can install it as an extended stored procedure in SQL Server. You can obtain this information from the developer of the DLL. Only a system administrator can install an extended stored procedure.

Installing an Extended Stored Procedure

Extended stored procedures can be added to SQL Server's Master database by running a system-stored procedure using the following syntax:

```
sp_addextendedproc function_name, dll_name
```

In the preceding, *function_name* is the name of the function in the DLL. The name of the function becomes the name of the extended stored procedure. In addition, *dll_name* is the name of the DLL.

Removing an Extended Stored Procedure

If you no longer need a custom extended stored procedure, you can remove it from SQL Server using the following syntax:

```
sp_dropextendedproc function_name
```

In the preceding, *function_name* is both the name of the function in the DLL and the name of the extended stored procedure.

Using an Extended Stored Procedure You Have Installed

After an extended stored procedure has been added to SQL Server, it can be used like any of the built-in extended stored procedures. You just need to execute the extended stored procedure like any other Transact-SQL statement. You can do this by running it in either ISQL/W or the SQL Query tool. You might have to enter some parameters if the extended stored procedure requires them.

3

Lab

Questions

1. You have just installed a copy of SQL Server. You start the Enterprise Manager and try to register the new SQL Server for the first time. For some reason, you cannot. Even worse, you cannot even see the SQL Server. It's as if it does not exist. What is the most likely cause of this problem?

   A. The SQL Server setup program did not set up the NT Server Registry entries correctly.

   B. The MSSQLService service has not yet been started.

   C. The SQLExecutive service had not yet been started.

   D. SQL Server's Memory configuration is set incorrectly.

2. Another DBA in your IT department has just installed SQL Server on a new server with multiple disk drives. The other DBA has been called away on an emergency, and it is now your job to verify that the SQL Server installation process went correctly. Using NT Server's Explorer program, you take a quick look at the directory structure on drive C where SQL Server is loaded. You notice \Mssql\Data is empty. You think to yourself that the other DBA must really have goofed up because this is where the MASTER device should be. Even though you know better, you start ISQL/W to try to log in to SQL Server. You expect the connection to fail, but it works. How can SQL Server work if the MASTER device is not in the correct location?

   A. The MASTER device has been moved to another physical drive.

   B. This copy of SQL Server is sharing a MASTER device from another SQL Server.

   C. The MASTER device has been renamed.

   D. Instead of connecting to the new SQL Server, you accidentally connected to another SQL Server that is properly configured.

3. Until recently, SQL Server has been running fine. Whenever you start the Enterprise Manager lately, however, you seem to have a problem. Sometimes everything works fine; other times you can't access your SQL Server through the Enterprise Manager. You also have verified that the two key SQL services have started properly. You suspect that a Registry entry might be corrupted. Using NT Server's Registry Editor, you go hunting through the many keys to

find potential problems. Which of the following keys is most likely to contain a problem that could be responsible for the odd behavior indicated above?

A. `HKEY_LOCAL_MACHINE\SOFTWARE\Microsoft\MSSQLServer`

B. `HKEY_LOCAL_MACHINE\CurrentControlSet\Services\MSSQLService`

C. `HKEY_LOCAL_MACHINE\CurrentControlSet\Services\SQLExecutive`

D. `HKEY_CURRENT_USER\Software\Microsoft\MSSQLServer`

4. You think you are having a problem with the SQLExecutive service. As a possible solution to this problem, you want to stop and then restart the service. Which of the following enables you to stop and then restart this service? (Select all that apply.)

A. The SQL Server Service Manager

B. The Enterprise Manager

C. The NT Server command prompt

D. The Control Panel Services applet

5. You are the DBA of a large SQL Server-based shop. It is your job to administer over 32 SQL Servers, which all are located in the same climate-controlled room. You don't like cold rooms, so you want to manage SQL Server remotely from a single desktop running NT Workstation. Which of the following can help you make your job a bit easier?

A. Create separate local groups to organize the servers by function.

B. Create separate global groups to organize the servers by function.

C. Create separate server groups to organize the servers by function.

D. Create separate security groups to organize the servers by function.

6. Every time your NT Server running SQL Server reboots, both the MSSQLService and SQLExecutive services need to be restarted manually. You are tired of doing this. What is one way to tell these two SQL Server services to start automatically each time NT Server reboots?

A. Turn on Auto Start at Boot Time for both services in the Server Options tab of the Server Configuration/Options dialog box.

B. Reinstall SQL Server. This time remember to turn on Auto Start at Boot Time for both services.

3

    C. Use the SQL Server Service Manager to turn on Auto Start at Boot
       Time for both services.

    D. Use ISQL/W and the appropriate system-stored procedure to turn on
       Auto Start at Boot Time for both services.

7. You want to change a SQL Server configuration option using a system-stored
   procedure rather than using Enterprise Manager. Which of the following is the
   correct syntax for performing this task?

    A. `configure config_value, config_name`

    B. `xp_configure config_name, config_value`

    C. `sp_configure config_value, config_name`

    D. `sp_configure config_name, config_value`

8. Your SQL Server has been running great for the past four months. Like the
   rest of the servers in your company, your SQL Server is located in an open
   office area. As part of your regular routine, you start the Enterprise Manager;
   you cannot, however, log in to the SQL Server. You try to unregister the server
   and reregister it. Although you have no problem unregistering the SQL Server,
   you cannot reregister it. Apparently, SQL Server does not like your password
   when you attempt to register the server as the system administrator. You use
   the default standard security mode, and you are the only person authorized to
   administer SQL Server. What is the most likely cause of this problem?

    A. The Registry has become corrupted.

    B. When you installed SQL Server, you forgot to give the system adminis-
      trator login ID a password. Apparently, someone with SQL Server
      knowledge has accessed it and assigned his own password.

    C. Your NT Server account has expired.

    D. Your system administrator login ID account has expired.

9. Your SQL Server has been running fine for about a year. Lately you've noticed
   it has begun to slow down. You think adding more RAM to the server might
   speed it up, so you decide to double the amount of RAM. Even after doubling
   the amount of RAM, however, the SQL Server is running as slow as ever.
   What is the most likely reason that adding RAM did not speed up SQL
   Server?

A. You forgot to adjust the Memory configuration setting after adding the additional RAM.

B. You forgot to adjust the Stored Procedure Cache configuration setting after adding the additional RAM.

C. You forgot to adjust the Server Memory setting in NT Server's Control Panel System applet.

D. The RAM was installed incorrectly in the server and was not recognized by SQL Server.

10. Your company recently added 10 new people who need to access SQL Server as part of their job. They do not use it all the time, just from time-to-time as their duties demand it. As part of your DBA responsibilities, you purchased 10 additional SQL Server client licenses. The first couple weeks after these people started on the job, everyone who needed to access SQL Server could. Recently, however, you have received calls from many people, old and new, saying that they no longer can access SQL Server. When they try, they get an error message onscreen. What is the most likely cause of this problem?

A. Most likely, the number of SQL Server user licenses is not enough. Perhaps a mistake was made when estimating the number of required licenses.

B. Most likely, SQL Server is running out of memory. The Memory configuration setting must be increased to handle the additional workload.

C. Most likely, the physical server running SQL Server is running out of memory. This problem can be handled by adding more RAM to the server.

D. Most likely, the number of SQL Server User Connections is too low. There might not have been many problems at first because the new people did not access SQL Server much. As they learned more about their jobs and started to access SQL Server more often, however, the user connections finally maxed out. This caused the current problem.

11. Your company's development department recently finished a new SQL Server-based client/server application that performs a critical customer-service task. The application has been tested in the lab, but it has never been in production. The software is installed by a developer onto your SQL Server. When the developer begins to run the application, it fails. The developer is confused. As the DBA, what is one of the first questions you should ask the developer about how the application was designed?

A. Was the application written in ANSI-92-compliant SQL?

B. Was the application written using mostly scripts?

C. Does the application make use of custom-written extended procedures?

D. Does the application use a front end written in Visual Basic?

Exercises

1. Locating SQL Server Registry Entries

Note

This exercise helps to address the following certification exam objective:

■ Locate where Windows NT Registry entries for SQL Server are stored

This exercise assumes SQL Server has been installed onto a copy of NT Server and that you know how to get around the NT Server Registry Editor. You will be examining the four keys used by SQL Server:

1. Log on to NT Server using an account with administrative rights.

2. From the Start menu, select Run. This opens the Run dialog box.

3. In the Run dialog box, enter regedt32 in the Open box and then click the OK button. This loads the NT Registry Editor, now displayed onscreen, with the various keys displayed.

4. Open the HKEY_LOCAL_MACHINE on the Local Machine window.

5. Expand the Software key by double-clicking the plus sign next to it.

6. Expand the Microsoft key by double-clicking the plus sign next to it.

7. Expand the MSSQLServer key by double-clicking the plus sign next to it.

8. Take the time to explore the contents of this key. This is where SQL Server stores general configuration information related to SQL Server.

9. When you are finished exploring this key, reverse the three previous steps by double-clicking the minus sign by each of the keys you opened. The screen should now be as it was in step 5.

10. Expand the System key by double-clicking the plus sign next to it.

11. Expand the CurrentControlSet key by double-clicking the plus sign next to it.

12. Expand the Services key by double-clicking the plus sign next to it. This displays a large list of services.

13. In this large list, look for both the MSSQLService and SQLExecutive keys. Take some time to explore each. These are the settings used by NT Server to control these two SQL Server services.

14. When you are finished exploring, reverse the three previous steps by double-clicking the minus sign by each of the keys you opened. The screen should now be as it was in step 5.

15. To view the last important key, you need to close the HKEY_LOCAL_MACHINE on the Local Machine window.

16. Open the window labeled HKEY_CURRENT_USER on Local Machine so that it displays onscreen.

17. Expand the Software key by double-clicking the plus sign next to it.

18. Expand the Microsoft key by double-clicking the plus sign next to it.

19. Expand the MSSQLServer key by double-clicking the plus sign next to it. This key is used when SQL Server is registered with the Enterprise Manager. Take some time to explore the configuration.

20. You now are done. You can exit the NT Server Registry Editor by selecting Registry | Exit.

2. Viewing Current SQL Server Configuration Settings

Note

This exercise helps to address the following certification exam objectives:

- Configure servers in the enterprise
- Configure SQL Server for various memory scenarios

This exercise shows you how to view the various SQL Server configuration options, specifically the Memory setting:

1. Log on to NT Server with an administrative account.

2. Start the Enterprise Manager. The Enterprise Manager must have properly registered the SQL Server you are examining. If not, register the SQL Server now.

3. Right-click in a SQL Server and then select Configure from the menu. This opens the Server Configuration/Options dialog box.

4. Click the Configuration tab to display the SQL Server's current configuration. Take some time to explore the various settings. If you click any of the options, a brief explanation of the setting displays at the bottom of the screen.

5. Go to the Memory configuration option. Notice the numbers in the Minimum and Maximum columns. This is the amount of RAM, in 2K pages, that legally can be entered. Also notice that the numbers in the Running and Current columns are the same. The Running column shows you the current number of 2K pages SQL Server is using. The Current column always is the same as the Running column until you want to change this setting. All changes are entered into the Running column. After the new setting is saved and SQL Server is restarted, the new figure entered in the Running column goes into effect.

6. When you are finished exploring these options, you can exit by clicking the Cancel button.

Answers to Questions

1. **B**   MSSQLService must be running before SQL Server can be registered with the Enterprise Manager.

2. **A**   The MASTER device can be moved to any physical disk on the server running SQL Server. This option can be made during the setup process. The MASTER device also can be moved after SQL Server is installed, assuming you tell SQL Server where it is.

3. **D**   Whenever you register a SQL Server with the Enterprise Manager, this information is stored in your user profile. Your user profile is represented in the Registry as HKEY_CURRENT_USER\Software\Microsoft\MSSQLServer.

4. **A, B, C, D**   All these possibilities are correct.

5. **C**   By creating server groups using the Enterprise Manager, you can group SQL Servers into function-related groups. This might make it easier for you to remember what each SQL Server does.

6. **A**   Although there are many ways to perform this task, the only way listed here that works is to load the Enterprise Manager, open the Server Options dialog box, and turn on Auto Start at Boot Time for both services.

7. **D**   For performing this task, sp_configure *config_name, config_value* is the correct syntax.

8. **B**   When SQL Server is installed, no password is assigned to the system administrator account. It is frightening how many DBAs never assign a password to the system administrator account. This means anyone with a little SQL Server knowledge can access your mission-critical and confidential data.

9. **A**   SQL Server must be told how much RAM to use. If you add additional RAM without telling SQL Server, SQL Server will not use it.

10. **D**   Each SQL Server can have one or more simultaneous user connections. Should the number of allowed user connections reach the maximum, this prevents others from accessing SQL Server.

11. **C**   Although there could be many reasons for the application to fail, one potential obvious problem is if the application uses any custom-written extended procedures. If it does, these extended procedures first must be installed on the SQL Server on which they will be used. If they aren't, the application will fail.

3

TEST DAY FAST FACTS

This is the first of many chapters in this book that describe the day-to-day tasks most DBAs perform. One of these tasks is to create and manage database devices. The following are some key facts you'll learn in this chapter:

- Two types of devices are used in SQL Server: database devices and backup devices.

- A *database device* is a physical file that resides on a server's hard disk and acts as a preallocated storage area for databases and transaction logs.

- A *backup device*, sometimes referred to as a *dump device*, is used to store backups of databases or transaction logs.

- The Enterprise Manager can be used to view database device information.

- One or more database devices must be created before a database and its transaction log can be created.

- A single device can hold a single database or transaction log, or it can hold multiple databases and transaction logs.

- Devices can be created using either the Enterprise Manager or Transact-SQL.

- When creating a device, it must be assigned both a logical name and a physical name. The *logical name* is how the device is known to

Day 4

Creating and Managing Devices

Many users new to SQL Server find the topic of devices confusing at first. This is because the word *device* is somewhat misleading. It also is because a device's purpose is obscure. This chapter tries to make the subject of devices a littler easier to understand. After you cut through the arcane terminology, you'll find that devices are much easier to understand than you first thought.

Unlike the other chapters in this book, this chapter covers a single test objective. This means today's lesson is a little shorter than most of the others, and you don't have to worry too much about this topic on the test. Although this objective is not heavily covered on the certification test, the material in this chapter provides an important foundation for the following chapter about database creation and management, which *is* heavily covered on the certification test.

If you are already an expert on devices, you can probably just skim this chapter. If you are new to SQL Server, however, you not only need to master this topic, but you should also complete the exercises at the end of this chapter to get some practice under your belt before the test. The following topics are covered in this chapter:

- The definition of a device
- Device creation rules
- How to create a device

- How to increase the size of a device
- How to remove a device

Objective

This chapter covers the following material:

- Create a device

4.1. What Is a Device?

The terminology used in SQL Server can be confusing for new users. First, two types of devices are used in SQL Server—database devices and backup devices—neither of which are physical devices in the sense that people would picture them to be. To make matters worse, these two types of devices are substantially different from each other.

A *database device* is a physical file that resides on a server's hard disk. It acts as a preallocated storage area for databases and transaction logs. In other words, a database device is just an empty file. Why do you need to create database devices? You need to create database devices because a database and its transaction log can be created only on a preexisting device (or devices). They cannot be created from empty space on a hard disk.

The database device helps alleviate the work SQL Server would have to perform if it had to request additional disk storage from the operating system whenever it needed it. Because a device is preallocated disk space, SQL Server does not have to ask the operating system for more space when a database expands. Instead, SQL Server can claim preexisting space from a device, which somewhat speeds up SQL Server's overall performance. The amount of time saved by using a device is not great, but every little bit helps, especially when databases are very large.

Note	Users who hate devices are in luck. The next version of SQL Server, version 7.0, eliminates devices.

A *backup device*, sometimes referred to as a *dump device*, stores backups of databases or transaction logs. Data can be backed up either onto disk or onto a tape device. Day 10, "Backing Up and Managing SQL Server Data," discusses backup devices. This chapter focuses on database devices.

If DBAs and other SQL Server professionals always used the terms *database device* and *backup device*, the two terms usually would not be confused, even though they sound similar. Unfortunately, more often than not, the term *database device* is shortened to *device*. This is what confuses many new SQL Server users. When you hear the word *device*, which type are they talking about? With a little experience, you can figure it out from context.

4.2. Using Enterprise Manager to View Devices

Before you look at how to create new devices, take a moment to learn how to view device information. After you are comfortable with this, you can move on to creating new devices. The following tutorial shows you how to view device-related information using the Enterprise Manager:

1. Log on to NT Server using an administrative account.

2. Start the Enterprise Manager.

3. From the Enterprise Manager's main screen, select a SQL Server and open its folders by clicking the plus sign (+) next to its name. This displays all the folders on this SQL Server.

4. To display all the current devices on this SQL Server, click the plus sign next to the Database Devices folder. This displays all the current devices (see Figure 4.1).

Figure 4.1.

All SQL Server database devices can be viewed in this screen.

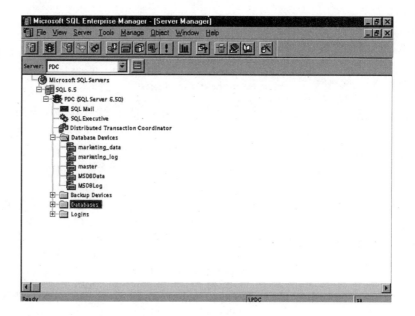

5. For additional information about any devices listed, right-click the device and select Edit from the pop-up menu. This opens the Edit Database Device dialog box (see Figure 4.2).

Figure 4.2.

You can learn about devices in the Edit Database Device dialog box.

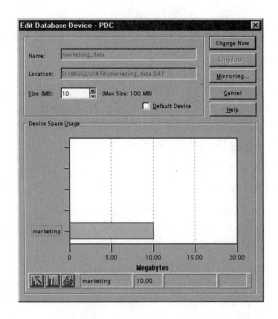

This dialog box can tell you a lot about a particular device. You can find out a device's size (10MB in this example), its logical and physical names (marketing_data and marketing_data.dat), what databases have been stored on it (marketing), and how much free space it has left (none, the marketing database takes up the entire 10MB).

6. Click Cancel to return to the Enterprise Manager's main screen.

7. In addition to this technique for examining devices, the Enterprise Manager can view devices in another way. From the drop-down menu, select Manage | Database Devices. The Manage Database Devices screen opens (see Figure 4.3).

This screen enables you to see all this SQL Server's devices at one time, along with their size and how full they are. Except for the MASTER device, all the devices in this example are full. The dark area in the MASTER device's bar indicates empty space. If you double-click any bars that represent devices, the appropriate Edit Database Device dialog box appears.

8. When finished, you can close this screen by clicking the Close Window icon (X) in the upper-right corner.

Figure 4.3.

All the devices are shown on one screen.

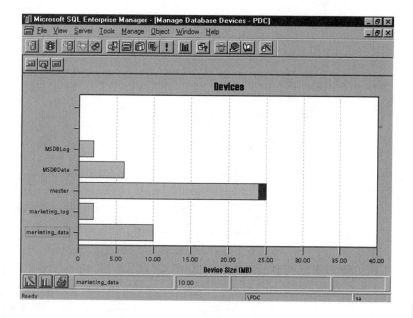

You should become familiar with the various ways you can examine devices. This becomes handy when checking out a new SQL Server for the first time.

4

4.3. How to Create Devices

This section describes how to create database devices. First, you will examine the various rules for creating devices. Pay close attention to this section because some of these rules appear on the certification test in one form or another. You then will learn how to create a new device using both the Enterprise Manager and Transact-SQL. Although you can create a device by using either tool, you need to be familiar with both techniques for the certification test. After you learn how to create devices, you will learn how to increase the size of a device and how to drop a device you no longer need.

4.3.1. Rules for Creating Devices

Devices are easy to create if you keep the following rules in mind:

- Before a new database and transaction log can be created, one or more devices must first be created.

- A single device can hold a single database or transaction log, or it can hold multiple databases and transaction logs. For ease of administration, however, a separate device is created for each database and transaction log.

- Only an sa can create and manage devices. This capability cannot be delegated to anyone else.

- The minimum size of a device is 1MB.

- Whenever a new device is created, the configuration information is stored in the sysdevices table in the Master database.

- When creating a device, it must be assigned a logical name and a physical name. The logical name is how the device is known to SQL Server and the sa. The physical name is how the device is known to the operating system.

- You must adhere to the following rules when creating device logical names:

  - They can range from 1 to 30 characters.

  - The first character of the name must be a letter or one of the following symbols: an underscore (_), an *at* symbol (@), or a pound sign (#).

  - Characters after the first character can include letters, numbers, or the symbols mentioned in the preceding rule.

  - Names must not have any spaces unless the name is surrounded by quotes.

- Device physical names follow the rules of the operating system in use.

- Devices must be created on the local physical server's hard disks. Devices cannot be created on hard disk storage accessed over a network.

- Before creating devices, make sure any hard disk fault-tolerant measures already have been implemented and tested and are ready for use.

- When a device is first created (or any time after a device has been created using the sp_diskdefault system stored procedure), it can be specified as a default device. If a device has been specified as a default device, SQL Server automatically can use it to create a new database if the sa creates a new database and doesn't specify a specific device to use. Default devices are automatically used for databases in alphabetic order by name. When SQL Server is first installed, the MASTER device automatically is a default device. You should change this because you don't want anyone to accidentally create a database on the MASTER device. Sas usually assign a specific database to a specific device because this makes it easier to administer. This means specifying a device as a default device is not required.

■ The size of a device can be increased but not reduced.

■ Always back up the Master database after creating a new device.

4.3.2. How to Create Devices Using the Enterprise Manager

You can create a device any time you want. Most DBAs, however, wait until they need to create a new database before creating a new device. When they are ready, they generally create two devices—one for the database and one for the transaction log. The following tutorial shows you how to create a device by using the Enterprise Manager:

1. Log on to the NT Server using an administrative account.

2. Start the Enterprise Manager.

3. From the Enterprise Manager's main screen, select a SQL Server and open its folder by clicking the plus sign next to its name. This displays various SQL Server folders.

4. Open the Database Devices folder by clicking the plus sign next to it. This displays a list of all the current database devices for this SQL Server.

5. Right-click the Database Devices folder and select New Device from the menu. The New Database Device dialog box opens (see Figure 4.4).

Figure 4.4.

New devices can be created in the New Database Device dialog box.

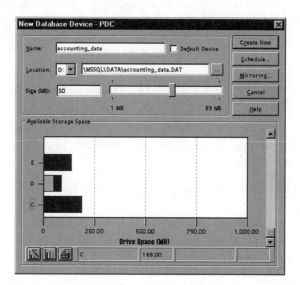

4

6. In the Name box, enter the logical name of the database device. Be sure to follow the logical naming rules previously described.

7. In the Location boxes, select the disk drive, full path name, and physical name of the database device. This information is filled out for you by default. You can leave the default values, or you change them to meet your needs as appropriate.

8. In the Size box, enter the size of the new database device in megabytes. Alternatively, you can drag the slider button to select a size for the new device. The bottom part of the screen is a graphical view of the available storage devices on your computer. It also contains the available free space. Use this as a guide to sizing and locating your devices.

9. When finished, click the Create Now button to create the device. If you don't want to create the device now, you can schedule it for another time by clicking Schedule. Day 9, "Scheduling Events and Creating Alerts," discusses this in more detail.

If you chose Create Now, you will receive a message when the device has successfully been created. This new device will appear with the other devices in the Database Devices folder in the Enterprise Manager's main screen.

When you create a new device, it's a good idea to go ahead and create two devices, one after another. One is used to store a new database; the second is used to store the transaction log for the new database.

4.3.3. How to Create Devices Using Transact-SQL

Although it is easiest to create new devices by using Enterprise Manager, some DBAs find it more convenient to create them manually, using Transact-SQL. If you choose to create a device manually, you can create it from ISQL/W, the SQL Query tool, or another related tool.

The following is the syntax for the DISK INIT Transact-SQL statement:

```
DISK INIT
    NAME = 'logical_name',
    PHYSNAME = 'physical_name',
    VDEVNO = virtual_device_number,
    SIZE = number_of_2K_blocks
```

The preceding syntax contains the following:

logical_name. The logical name assigned to the device.

physical_name. The physical name and location of the physical file that is the device. Includes the full path name.

virtual_device_number. The virtual number is used to uniquely identify the device. Each device must have a unique virtual number from 0 through 255. Device number 0 is reserved for the MASTER device. If you do not know which virtual device numbers already have been used, you find out from the sp_helpdevice system stored procedure. You can assign any virtual device number from 0 through 255 that is not currently being used. When creating a device using the Enterprise Manager, you don't have to specify a virtual device number. It selects an appropriate number for you.

number_of_2KB_blocks. The number of 2KB blocks needed to equal the total space you want allocated to the device. The minimum size is 512 2KB blocks.

The following is an example:

```
DISK INIT
    NAME = 'acct_data',
    PHYSNAME = 'c:\mssql\data\acct_data.dat',
    VDEVNO = 100,
    SIZE = 2560
```

Use the following steps to create a new device using Transact-SQL:

1. Load the SQL Query tool (or a similar tool). Be sure the Query tab is selected.

2. Select the Master database from the DB drop-down menu. New devices must be created from the Master database.

3. Enter the Transact-SQL statement.

4. Execute the statement. The Results window shows the following message:

```
This command did not return data, and it did not return any rows.
```

The device has been created. The new device is not displayed in the Database Devices folder until you refresh the screen by selecting View | Refresh.

4.4. How to Increase the Size of a Device Using the SQL Enterprise Manager

If you need to increase the size of a device to provide more room for a database or transaction log, you can do so at any time using the Enterprise Manager or

Transact-SQL. Although you can increase the size of a device at any time, you can never shrink a device's size. If you discover you've created a device that's too large for your needs, your only choice is to move the database to a smaller device, using Transfer Manager, and then delete the old device. Day 10 discusses the Transfer Manager in more detail.

This section examines the rules for increasing the size of a device and shows you how to accomplish this using both the Enterprise Manager and Transact-SQL.

4.4.1. Rules for Increasing the Size of a Device

Keep the following in mind when increasing the size of a device:

- Only the sa can increase the size of a device.
- Devices can be expanded only to fill the remaining free space of a hard disk. Devices cannot cross hard disks.
- The size of a device can be increased at any time, even if a preexisting database is on the device.
- When you want to increase the size of a device, you must specify the new, final size of the device. Do not specify the amount by which you want to increase the device's size.
- Always back up the Master database after increasing the size of a database.

4.4.2. How to Increase a Device's Size Using Enterprise Manager

1. Log on to NT Server using an administrative account.
2. Start the Enterprise Manager.
3. From the Enterprise Manager's main screen, select a SQL Server and open its folder by clicking the plus sign next to its name. This displays various SQL Server folders.
4. Open the Database Devices folder by clicking the plus sign next to it. This displays a list of all the current database devices for this SQL Server.
5. Right-click the database device you want to increase in size; then select Edit. The Edit Database Device dialog box opens (refer to Figure 4.2).
6. The Size box shows the current size of the device in megabytes. Change this number to the size you want this device to become. If the current size is 4MB, for example, and you want the size to double, change the 4 to an 8 in the Size box.

7. After you have entered the new size, click the Change Now button. The size of the device is increased, and you receive no message telling you what happened. To verify that the device's size was increased, you can right-click the device, select Edit, and view the new size from the Edit Database Device dialog box.

4.4.3. How to Increase the Size of a Device Using Transact-SQL

Just as you can use Transact-SQL to create a new device, you can also use it to increase the size of a device.

The following is the syntax for the DISK RESIZE Transact-SQL statement:

```
DISK RESIZE
    NAME = 'logical_name',
    SIZE = number_of_2K_blocks
```

The preceding syntax contains the following:

logical_name. The logical name assigned to the device.

number_of_2KB_blocks. The number of 2KB blocks needed to equal the total space you want allocated to the device.

The following is an example:

```
DISK RESIZE
    NAME = 'acct_data',
    SIZE = 12560
```

Use the following steps to expand a device by using Transact-SQL:

1. Load the SQL Query tool (or a similar tool). Be sure the Query tab is selected.

2. Select the Master database from the DB drop-down menu.

3. Enter the Transact-SQL statement.

4. Execute the statement. The Results window shows the following message:

This command did not return data, and it did not return any rows.

The device has been expanded. The newly resized device is not reflected in the Server Manager window until it has been refreshed by choosing View | Refresh.

4

4.5. How to Remove Devices

Any time you no longer need a device, you can remove (drop) it to free up space on the server's hard disk. This section examines the rules for dropping devices and shows you how to remove devices using either the Enterprise Manager or a system stored procedure.

4.5.1. Rules for Removing Devices

Keep the following in mind when you remove devices:

- Only an sa can drop a device.
- If you use Enterprise Manager to drop a device that has databases on it, you will be asked whether you want to drop the databases as well. If you answer yes, the Enterprise Manager automatically drops any databases on the device before it drops the device.
- If you want to drop a device using the sp_dropdevice system stored procedure, any databases on the device must first be dropped before the device can be dropped.
- Dropping a device removes it from the sysdevices table in the Master database.
- Dropping a device removes it only from the Master database; it does not automatically delete the physical file. You must delete the file manually, especially if you drop the device using the Enterprise Manager.
- Always back up the Master device after dropping a device.

4.5.2. Dropping a Device Using Enterprise Manager

The following tutorial shows you how to remove a device using the Enterprise Manager. This example assumes no databases are currently on the device.

1. Log on to NT Server using an administrative account.
2. Start the Enterprise Manager.
3. Click the plus sign next to the SQL Server you want to work with to display the server's folders.
4. Click the plus sign next to the Database Devices folder to display all the database devices managed by this SQL Server.
5. Right-click the device you want to remove, and select Delete from the pop-up menu. This displays the Delete Device dialog box, in which you are asked whether you want to delete the device.

6. To delete the device, click Yes. The device is removed, and you receive the message `The database device was successfully deleted.`

7. Click OK to return to the Enterprise Manager's main screen. Although the device has been removed from SQL Server's Master database, you still must delete the physical file that was the device.

8. Use NT Server's Explorer tool to locate and delete the physical file. Be careful not to accidentally delete the wrong file. If you do, you had better hope your backups are current and in good shape.

The only difference between this example, in which the device did not have any databases, and removing a device with databases is that you see an additional screen that lets you know they exist. This forces you to confirm that you really want to delete both the databases and the device in the same step.

4.5.3. Removing a Device Manually

SQL Server includes a special system stored procedure called `sp_dropdevice`, which is used to manually drop a device.

The following is the syntax for the `sp_dropdevice` system stored procedure:

```
sp_dropdevice logical_name [,DELFILE]
```

The preceding syntax contains the following:

> `logical_name`. The logical name assigned to the device.
>
> `DELFILE`. This option tells the stored procedure to automatically delete the physical file after the device is dropped from the Master database. If you don't use this option, you have to manually delete the device file, just as when you use the Enterprise Manager to remove a device.

The following is an example:

```
sp_dropdevice marketing_data, DELFILE
```

Use the following steps to remove a device by using Transact-SQL:

1. Load the SQL Query tool (or a similar tool). Be sure that the Query tab is selected.

2. Select the Master database from the DB drop-down menu.

3. Enter the command.

4. Execute the command. The Results window displays the following message:

```
File: 'D:\MSSQL\DATA\xxxxx.DAT' closed. Device dropped.
(0 row(s) affected) Physical file deleted.
```

Assuming you use the DELFILE option, you are finished removing this device.

If you try this command when a device has one or more pre-existing databases, you receive an error message. If you want to manually delete a device, you must first remove the databases from it. After they are removed, you can manually delete the device.

Lab

Questions

1. As the DBA of a SQL Server, you need to create a new device capable of holding a database that will eventually contain about 20GB of data. The database's transaction log will be placed on a separate device from the database. Your problem is that your server has only four empty 9GB drives. Which device strategy should you follow to find enough space to store this database?

    A. You can map a network drive to another server in your network with a drive big enough to hold the entire 20GB database.

    B. You can create multiple devices on the empty drives that have a cumulative size big enough to hold a single 20GB database.

    C. You can create multiple devices on the empty drives that have a cumulative size of at least 20GB. You then can create separate databases on each device (up to 9GB each) and then combine all the databases to reach the 20GB size.

    D. You can't create a database this large on this server because none of your drives are large enough (20GB) to hold a device capable of holding the entire database.

2. You are the sa of several SQL Servers. You will be on vacation for two weeks and want someone else in your organization to perform routine SQL Server administrative tasks while you are away. You don't, however, want him to have all the power he would have if you let him use the sa account. To prevent this, you create a special login ID that enables him to perform most administrative tasks, but he does not have full sa permissions. After you leave on vacation, your designated assistant is asked by the company's owner to create a new database. Before creating the database, the assistant attempts to create a new device on which to place the database, but this attempt fails. What is the most likely reason for this failure?

    A. Before leaving, the sa forgot to give the assistant the proper rights to create devices.

    B. The assistant has the proper permissions to create the device, but he is not logged in to NT Server as an administrator. Administrative rights are required for any new files to be created on an NT Server.

4

C. The assistant has tried to assign the new device an illegal logical name. If a correct name is used, the device can be created.

D. Only an sa can create a device; this capability cannot be delegated to anyone. The only way for the assistant to create the database as requested is to create it on an existing device.

3. You are the sa of a SQL Server, and you need to create two new devices. One will be used for the database; the other will be used for the transaction log. You decide to assign the names production-data and production-log to the devices. When you attempt to create the first device, you receive an error message. What is the most likely reason for this error message?

A. You are using an illegal device name. You can't use a dash in the name of any device.

B. You are using an illegal device name. Both names are too long and must be shortened.

C. The names are correct, but you don't have permission to create new devices.

D. The names are correct, but you probably have run out of free disk space on your server.

4. You are the sa of a new SQL Server and will be creating a series of new devices so that you can create the necessary production databases. The following is a list of the devices you want to create. Which of the following logical device names will work as given? (Select all that apply.)

A. m

B. _Marketing

C. Marketing_Data

D. Marketing(log)

E. 49ers_data

F. Marketing Data

5. You are the sa of a SQL Server and need to create a new database device that will be used to hold a database of 100MB. You decide to use the Enterprise Manager to create the device. When the New Database Device dialog box opens, you must enter the size of this new database. What value should you specify?

A. 102,400 (in units of KB)

B. 51,200 (in units of 2KB pages)

C. 200 (in units of allocation units)

D. 100 (in units of MB)

6. You are the sa of a SQL Server and need to create a new database device that will be used to hold a database of 10MB. You decide to use Transact-SQL to create the device. When you enter the DISK INIT command, what value should you specify as the size of the new device?

A. 10,240 (in units of KB)

B. 5,120 (in units of 2KB pages)

C. 20 (in units of allocation units)

D. 10 (in units of MB)

7. You have decided to create a new device using Transact-SQL rather than using Enterprise Manager. Which of the following is the correct syntax to create a new device?

A. DISK INIT
```
    NAME = 'acct_data',
    PHYSNAME = 'c:\mssql\data\acct_data.dat',
    VDEVNO = 100,
    SIZE = 5
```

B. DISK INIT
```
    NAME = 'acct_data',
    PHYSNAME = 'c:\mssql\data\acct_data.dat',
    VDEVNO = 100,
    SIZE = 2560
```

C. DISK INIT
```
    NAME = 'acct-data',
    PHYSNAME = 'c:\mssql\data\acct_data.dat',
    VDEVNO = 100,
    SIZE = 2560
```

D. DISK INIT
```
    NAME = 'acct_data',
    PHYSNAME = 'c:\mssql\data\acct_data.dat',
    VDEVNO = 1,
    SIZE = 2560
```

4

8. Currently, you have a 500MB device that is fully occupied by a database. You need to expand the size of the database, so you decide to first expand the device. To leave plenty of room for growth, you decide to increase the size of the device to 1GB. To increase the size of the device, you decide to use the Enterprise Manager. When the Edit Database dialog box opens onscreen, what figure should you enter in the Size box?

   A. 500

   B. 1,000

   C. 256,000

   D. 512,000

9. Currently, you have a 100MB device that is fully occupied by a database. You need to expand the size of the database, so you decide to first expand the device. To leave plenty of room for growth, you decide to increase the size of the device to 500MB. You decide to increase the size of the device using the DISK RESIZE Transact-SQL statement. What value should you enter for the size?

   A. 400

   B. 500

   C. 204,800

   D. 256,000

10. Your SQL Server is almost out of free space. You evaluate the databases on the SQL Server and find out you can delete one because it isn't used anymore. To save time, you decide to remove both the database and the device at the same time using the Enterprise Manager. You delete the device, and it is removed from the Enterprise Manager's main screen. You then use NT Server's Explorer to see how much free space this action generated. You are surprised, however. Even though you deleted the device, no additional free space was generated. What did you do wrong?

   A. The Master database has become corrupt.

   B. You cannot remove a device by using the Enterprise Manager.

   C. You cannot remove a database and its device in the same step.

   D. In addition to removing the database and device, you also must physically remove the device by using Explorer.

Exercises

Note

These exercises help to address the following certification exam objective:

■ Create a device.

1. Creating a Device Using Enterprise Manager

This exercise shows you how to create three new database devices using Enterprise Manager. The devices you create here are used in other exercises in this chapter and the next.

1. From the Enterprise Manager's main screen, select your SQL Server and open its folder by clicking the plus sign. This displays various SQL Server folders.

2. Open the Database Devices folder by clicking the plus sign next to it. This displays a list of all the current database devices for this SQL Server.

3. Right-click the Database Devices folder and select New Device from the menu. The New Database Device dialog box opens.

4. In the Name box, enter sample_dat.

5. In the Location boxes, leave the default values.

6. In the Size box, enter 10.

7. When finished, click the Create Now button to create the device. When the device has been created, you'll see the message: The database device was successfully created. Click the OK button to return to the SQL Server main screen.

8. Repeat these same steps again to create a second device with a logical name of expand_dat and a size of 5MB.

9. Repeat these same steps a third time to create a device with a logical name of delete_dat and a size of 5MB.

10. When finished, return to the SQL Server main screen to see the new devices listed with all the other devices for this SQL Server.

2. Creating a Device Using Transact-SQL

This exercise shows you how to create a new database device using Transact-SQL statements. The device you create will be used in the next chapter.

1. Load the SQL Query tool. Be sure the Query tab is selected.

2. Select the Master database from the DB drop-down menu.

3. Enter the following Transact-SQL statement:

```
DISK INIT
NAME = 'sample_log',
PHYSNAME = 'c:\mssql\data\sample_log.dat',
    VDEVNO = 100,
SIZE = 2048
```

4. Execute the statement. The Results window displays the following message:

```
This command did not return data, and it did not return any rows.
```

The device has been created. The new device is not displayed in the Database Devices folder until you refresh the screen by selecting View | Refresh.

3. Increasing the Size of a Device Using Enterprise Manager

This exercise shows you how to expand the expand_dat device created in the first exercise.

1. If necessary, from the Enterprise Manager's main screen, select your SQL Server and open its folder by clicking the plus sign. This displays various SQL Server folders.

2. If necessary, open the Database Devices folder by clicking the plus sign next to it. This displays a list of all the current database devices for this SQL Server.

3. Right-click the expand_dat device and select Edit from the pop-up menu. This displays the Edit Database Device dialog box.

4. In the Size box, enter 6, which will become this device's new size in megabytes. When using the Enterprise Manager, always enter the new size of the device in megabytes to expand a device.

5. Click the Change Now button. The device immediately is expanded, and you are returned to the Enterprise Manager's main screen.

4. Removing a Device Using Enterprise Manager

This exercise shows you how to remove the expand_dat device you created and expanded in the preceding exercises. You will use both the Enterprise Manager and Explorer to completely remove the device from your server.

1. If necessary, from the Enterprise Manager's main screen, select your SQL Server and open its folder by clicking the plus sign. This displays various SQL Server folders.

2. If necessary, open the Database Devices folder by clicking the plus sign next to it. This displays a list of all the current database devices for this SQL Server.

3. Right-click the expand_dat device and select Delete from the pop-up menu. You'll see the message: `Are you sure you want to delete the device 'expand_dat'?`

4. Click the Yes button, and the device is removed from SQL Server. You are not done yet, however; you need to remove the physical file from your server by using Explorer.

5. Start Explorer and locate the expand_dat.dat device file on your hard disk. When you have found it, delete it. After you finish this step, you will have completely removed the device from your server.

Answers to Questions

1. **B**   A single database can reside on one or more devices, no matter where they are located on the same SQL Server.

2. **D**   The capability to create a device is given only to the sa; it cannot be delegated.

3. **A**   A dash is an illegal character for a device name.

4. **A, B, C**   Device logical names must follow these rules: *1)* They can range from 1 to 30 characters; *2)* The first character of the name must be a letter or one of the following symbols: _, @, or #; *3)* Characters after the first character can include letters, numbers, or the following symbols: _, @, or #; names must not have any spaces, unless the name is surrounded by quotes. This is not recommended.

5. **D**   When creating a new device using the Enterprise Manager, you must specify the size of the device in megabytes.

6. **B**   When creating a new device using `DISK INIT`, you must specify the size of the device in the number of 2KB pages.

7. **B**   Choice A is incorrect because the size of 5 is too small. This is the number of 2KB pages the device is supposed to be, and the minimum size is 512 (1MB). Choice C is incorrect because the logical name contains a hyphen, which is an illegal character. Choice D is incorrect because it specifies a virtual device of 1, which is reserved for the MASTER device.

8. **B**   You must enter the final size of the device in megabytes.

9. **D**   You must enter the final size of the device in 2KB pages.

10. **D**   Although the Enterprise Manager is able to remove both a database and its device at the same time, it can't delete the physical file that makes up the device. This must be done manually.

4

This chapter builds on the preceding chapter about how to
create and manage devices. After
you create a device, you are
ready to create a database and a
transaction log on that device.
The following are some key facts
you'll learn in this chapter:

- Before a SQL Server database or transaction log can
  be created, you first must
  create a device. A single
  device can contain one or
  more SQL Server databases,
  or a single SQL Server database can exist on one or
  more devices.

- A *database* is a preallocated
  portion of a device used to
  store database objects and
  data. In a sense, when you
  create a new database, you
  are creating an empty shell.

- All information in SQL
  Server is stored on a *page*,
  which is the smallest data
  structure used in a database.
  Each page stores 2KB (2,048
  bytes) of information.

- An *extent* is a data structure
  made up of eight contiguous
  pages (8×2KB = 16KB). SQL
  Server automatically allocates an extent whenever a
  new database object, such
  as a table, is created.

- An *allocation unit* is a data
  structure made up of 32
  extents (32×16KB = 512KB),
  or 256 pages. Whenever a
  new database is created,
  space is allocated in multiple
  allocation units of 512KB
  each.

Day 5

Creating and Managing Databases

This chapter discusses the very core of what DBAs do for a living—they create and manage SQL Server databases. The preceding chapter showed you how to create and manage devices. This chapter assumes the appropriate devices have been created and focuses strictly on data-bases.

This chapter demonstrates how to perform most database-related tasks using both the Enterprise Man-ager and system-stored procedures. You should learn how to use both methods as preparation for taking the certification exam. You can never be sure which topics are on the exam, and both Enterprise Manager and stored procedure questions are fair game.

Overall, this chapter should be fairly easy to understand and learn. There is nothing tricky about creating data-bases. If you have extensive experience creating and managing databases, you might want to just skim this chapter, focusing on the objectives or your weaker areas. If you are new to SQL Server, you should study this chapter and complete all the exercises at the end. This will help you understand how to perform all the proce-dures described in this chapter.

This chapter covers the following topics:

- Database storage structures
- How to estimate the size of a database

- The best database creation practices
- How to create a new database
- How to increase and decrease the size of a database
- How to remove a database
- How to create database objects

Objectives

This chapter covers the following material:

- Estimate space requirements
- Create a database
- Alter a database
- Create database objects

5.1. Introduction to Database Storage Structures

To manipulate large quantities of data in a reasonable amount of time, SQL Server stores data on physical media in specific ways. This section introduces the SQL Server database storage architecture and describes the following terms: device, SQL Server database, transaction log, allocation unit, extent, and page.

5.1.1. Databases Can Only Be Created on Preexisting Devices

Even though you learned about devices in the preceding chapter, it doesn't hurt to briefly review exactly what a device is. A database *device* is an NTFS or FAT file stored on physical media, such as a hard disk. It preallocates physical storage space to be used by a database or a transaction log. Before a SQL Server database or transaction log can be created, you must first create a device. A single device can contain one or more SQL Server databases, or a single SQL Server database can exist on one or more devices. A device must be at least the same size as the database being created on top of it.

5.1.2. How SQL Server Stores Data in a Database

A *database* is a preallocated portion of a device used to store database objects and data. When you create a new database, you are creating an empty shell that must first be populated with objects before it can be used.

When a database is created on a device, SQL Server allocates space within the database using special data structures including pages, extents, and allocation units (see Figure 5.1).

What Is a Page?

All information in SQL Server is stored on *pages*, the smallest data structure used in a database. Each page stores 2KB (2,048 bytes) of information. All pages include a 32-byte page header, which leaves 2,016 bytes to store data. The header is used by SQL Server to uniquely identify the data stored on the page. SQL Server uses the following types of pages:

■ *Allocation pages.* Used to control the allocation of pages to tables and indexes within a database.

Figure 5.1.

Databases are made up of pages, extents, and allocation units.

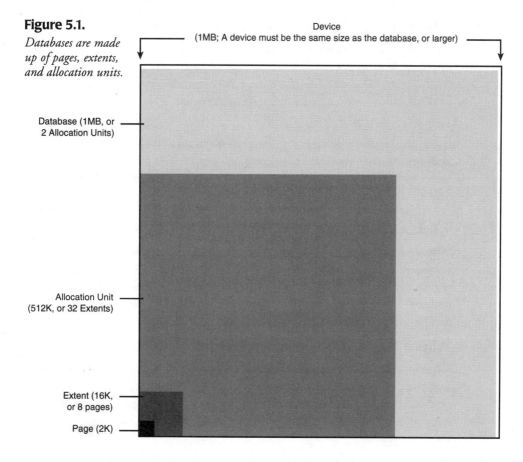

Device
(1MB; A device must be the same size as the database, or larger)

Database (1MB, or 2 Allocation Units)

Allocation Unit (512K, or 32 Extents)

Extent (16K, or 8 pages)

Page (2K)

5

- *Data and log pages.* Used to store database data and transaction log data. Data is stored in data rows on each page. Each page can store up to 256 rows, and the maximum size of any one row is 1,962 bytes. SQL Server does not allow rows to cross pages.

- *Index pages.* Used to store database indexing information.

- *Distribution pages.* Used to store information about the indexes in a database.

- *Text/image pages.* Used to store large amounts of text or binary large objects (BLOBs).

What Is an Extent?

An *extent* is a data structure made up of eight contiguous pages (8×2KB = 16KB). SQL Server automatically allocates an extent whenever a new database object, such as a table, is created. Each extent can include only a single database object.

What Is an Allocation Unit?

An *allocation unit* is a data structure made up of 32 extents (32×16KB = 512KB), or 256 pages. Whenever a new database is created, space is allocated in multiple allocation units of 512KB each. Because a database object takes up at least one extent, a single allocation unit can only contain up to 32 objects.

All SQL Server databases contain these data structures. To keep them all straight, just remember that a database is made up of allocation units, allocation units are made up of extents, and extents are made up of pages. This topic is discussed further in the section "How to Estimate Space Requirements for a Database" later in this chapter.

5.1.3. Understanding Transaction Logs

Whenever a database is created using SQL Server, a transaction log is created at the same time. A *transaction log* is a reserved storage area on a device. It automatically records all changes made to database objects before the changes are written to the database. This is an important fault-tolerant feature of SQL Server that helps prevent databases from becoming corrupted.

Where Transaction Logs Are Created

When a database is created, the location of the device on which to store it must be specified. This also is true for transaction logs. When a database is created, the location of the device used to store the transaction log also must be specified. Although it is possible to store both a database and its transaction log on the same device, it is not recommended.

The following are benefits of creating a transaction log on a separate device from its database:

- The transaction log can be backed up separately from the database.
- Up-to-date recovery is possible in the event of server failure.
- The transaction log does not compete with the database for device space.
- Transaction log space can easily be monitored.
- There is less contention between writes to the database and the transaction log. This can increase SQL Server's performance.

None of the preceding benefits are available if the database and the transaction log occupy the same device.

How Do Transaction Logs Provide Fault Tolerance?

In SQL Server, a *transaction* is a set of operations (Transact-SQL statements that change a database) that are completed at one time, as if they were a single operation. To maintain data integrity, transactions must be completed fully or not performed at all. If a transaction is only partially applied to a database (as the result of a server failure, for example), the database could become corrupt.

SQL Servers use a database's transaction log to prevent incomplete transactions from corrupting data. The following list shows how SQL Server uses a transaction log to prevent data corruption:

1. A user performs a task that modifies an object within the database (on SQL Server).

2. When the transaction begins, a *begin transaction marker* is recorded in the transaction log. This marker is followed by before and after images of the object being changed. The images are followed by a *commit transaction marker.* Every transaction is recorded in the transaction log in this manner.

3. Periodically, a *checkpoint* process occurs. All completed transactions recorded in the transaction log are applied to the database. This process also creates a *checkpoint marker* in the transaction log. This marker is used during the recovery process to determine which transactions have been applied to the database.

4. The transaction log continues to grow, retaining all the transactions, until it is backed up. At that point, the transactions are removed (truncated) to make room for more transactions.

If a server fails after a transaction is entered in the transaction log but before it is applied to the database, or if a server fails at the exact moment when the transaction log is applied to the database, the database does not become corrupted. When the server is brought back up, SQL Server begins a recovery process. It examines the database and the transaction log, looking for transactions that were not applied or that were partially applied but not completed. If transactions in the transaction log were not applied, they are applied at this time (rolled forward). If partial transactions are found that were not completed, they are removed from the database (rolled back). The recovery process is automatic. All the information necessary to maintain a database's integrity is maintained in the transaction log. This capability substantially increases SQL Server's fault tolerance.

5

5.2. How to Estimate Space Requirements for a Database

As a DBA, one of your many tasks is to create new devices and databases, each of which must be a specific size. It is your responsibility to accurately estimate the proper sizes so that you don't waste unnecessary resources or run out of database space. This section shows you how to estimate the size a database should be before creating it.

5.2.1. What You Need to Consider When Estimating the Size of a Database

Many factors affect the final size of a database, and you need to consider them all when estimating database size. The following are some of the most important factors to consider:

- *The size of each row.* Every row is made up of one or more columns of data. These columns contribute to the size of each row. You need to obtain the size of each column from the database developer or by examining each table in the database yourself.

- *The number of rows.* The number of rows in a table might be static or might vary considerably. The database developer can tell you how many rows are expected in each of the tables of the database.

- *The number of tables.* Some databases have a few tables; others have hundreds. You can view the number of tables yourself using the SQL Enterprise Manager.

- *The number of indexes.* Each table can have one or more indexes, which can be either clustered or nonclustered. Each nonclustered index takes up additional space in a database.

- *The size of each index.* The size of an index is determined by the size of the column used for the index, the number of rows in the index, and the index's FILLFACTOR. A FILLFACTOR of 100 means no space is wasted in the index object. A FILLFACTOR of 50 means half the space in an index object is empty space. The larger the FILLFACTOR, the more space is occupied by index objects.

- *The number and size of other database objects.* Databases include many objects such as triggers, views, stored procedures, and others. Some objects, such as stored procedures, can occupy large amounts of space. The database developer should be able to tell you the approximate size of all database objects.

- *The size of the transaction log.* The size of a transaction log can vary widely. It depends on many factors, including how often data is changed in the database. Most transaction logs start at 10 to 25 percent of the database size and are adjusted after the database is put into production and monitored. As a rule of thumb, databases that constantly change need a larger transaction log than databases that rarely change. This is because, with more changes, there are more transactions. A larger transaction log is needed to hold them all. The transaction log's size also is affected by how often it is backed up. The more often it is backed up, the smaller it can be. This is because the backup process truncates the transaction log every time it runs.

- *The projected growth of the database.* Some databases never grow; others grow large amounts every day. To determine an overall projected growth figure, you need growth estimates for each table in the database.

Most of these numbers do not come easily. You need to work closely with the database developer to locate these numbers and to estimate size. When estimating, you should overestimate your storage needs. This usually creates fewer problems than underestimating your storage needs.

You can always increase the size of a database later. If you estimate accurately up front, however, you'll face fewer surprises and your job as DBA will be easier.

5.3. The Best Database Creation Practices

Although SQL Server provides many location options for databases and transaction logs on devices, you should consider the following best practices:

- Before creating a new database, first create two database devices—one for the database and one for the transaction log. Consider adding the word *data* to the logical name of the device used by the database and the word *log* to the device used by the transaction log (for example, marketing_data and marketing_log).
- Don't place more than one database or transaction log on the same device.
- When sizing a database or transaction log, make it the same size as the device it is on.

If you follow these suggestions, your life as a DBA will be much easier.

5

5.4. How to Create Databases

When you create a database, you allocate space on a device to store database objects and data. After the database is created, you (or the database developer) can add the necessary tables, views, indexes, and other objects that make up your database.

When creating a database, you must specify where the transaction log should be located. If you do not specify a device for the transaction log, it is placed on the same device as the database itself. As previously mentioned, it is highly recommended for a database and its transaction log to be placed on separate devices.

Whenever a new database is created, SQL Server uses the model database as a template. The model database, which is automatically created when SQL Server is installed, contains all the system tables necessary to track and manage all the objects stored in a database. The model database is 1MB in size, which means any database you create also must be at least 1MB in size. This assumes that the size of the model database has not been changed. Like any database, the model database can be expanded.

If you want all new databases to have specific objects, database user IDs, or permissions, you can directly modify the model database to include them. After doing so, every new database you create will have these specified features. If the objects you add to the model database increase its size, the default minimum size for all new databases also increases as a result.

5.4.1. Tips for Creating New Databases

When creating new databases, you should keep the following in mind:

- By default, only the system administrator can create a new database. He can, however, delegate this responsibility to others by issuing a specific statement permission. (See Day 8, "Managing User Permissions," for more information.)

- The name you assign to a database must follow the SQL Server naming rules discussed on Day 4, "Creating and Managing Devices."

- All new databases are copies of the model database. This means new databases cannot be any smaller than the current size of the model database.

- Whenever a database is created, a transaction log also is created. By default, a transaction log is created on the same device as the database. If specified during database creation, however, a transaction log can be stored on a separate device. In addition, a transaction log originally created on the same device as the database can be moved at any time to a separate device.

- A single database can be stored on a single device, or it can be spread over multiple devices.

- The size of a database can be either expanded or reduced.

- Whenever a new database is created, SQL Server automatically updates the sysdatabases and sysusages tables in the Master database.

- The For Load option can be set when creating a new database. This option should be selected only if you intend to create a new database and then populate it by restoring a database backup to the new database. Otherwise, you should not choose this option.

5.4.2. How to Create a Database Using the SQL Server Enterprise Manager

Most of the time, you should use the Enterprise Manager to create and manage databases. It's much easier to use the GUI interface than to use arcane Transact-SQL or system-stored procedures. This section shows you how to use the Enterprise Manager to create a new database; the next section shows you how to use Transact-SQL to create a new database.

The following steps show you how to create a database using the Enterprise Manager. This tutorial assumes that SQL Server is properly installed and that preexisting devices exist to create a new database.

1. From the Enterprise Manager's main screen, select a SQL Server and open its folder by clicking the plus sign. This displays various SQL Server folders.

2. Open the Databases folder by clicking the plus sign next to it. This displays a list of all the current databases for this SQL Server (see Figure 5.2).

3. Right-click the Databases folder and select New Database from the menu. The New Database dialog box opens (see Figure 5.3).

4. In the Name box, enter the name of the new database. Make sure that you follow the standard SQL Server naming rules.

5. In the Data Device box, select the appropriate database device from the drop-down list. The available devices are listed at the bottom of the screen, along with the free space available on each device.

5

Figure 5.2.

All SQL Server databases can be viewed from this screen.

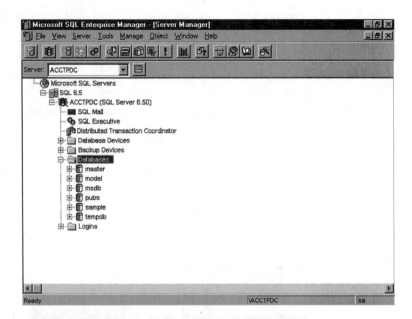

Figure 5.3.

New databases can be created from the New Database dialog box.

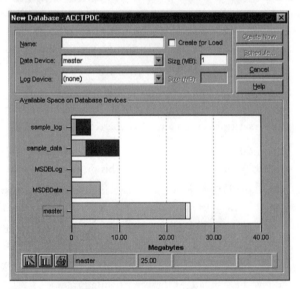

6. In the Size box, enter the size of the new database in megabytes. Because databases must be created in increments of allocation units (512KB), you must enter a number evenly divisible by 512KB.

7. In the Log Device box, select the appropriate database device from the drop-down list. This assumes you want to place the transaction log on a separate device from the database.

8. In the Size box, enter the size of the new transaction log in megabytes.

9. To create the new database now, click the Create Now button. If you prefer to create the database later, you can do so by clicking the Schedule button. Day 9, "Scheduling Events and Creating Alerts," shows you how to schedule the creation of a new database.

If you select Create Now, the database is created immediately. You will not receive feedback from SQL Server about the status of the creation. To verify its creation, you can view the database in the Databases folder of the Enterprise Manager's main screen.

Whenever you create or alter the size of a database, you should document your steps. That way, if you ever need to re-create the database and restore a database backup to it, you can re-create the database following the exact same steps used to create the original database. If these steps are not documented, you might not be able to restore your database from a backup.

5.4.3. How to Create Databases Using Transact-SQL

Creating a database using Transact-SQL requires more work than using the Enterprise Manager. The following is the syntax you enter in the SQL Query tool or ISQL/W to create a new database.

The syntax for the CREATE DATABASE Transact-SQL statement is as follows:

```
CREATE DATABASE database_name
    ON database_device = size, database_device = size, . . .
    LOG ON database_device = size, . . .
```

The preceding syntax contains the following placeholders:

database_name. The name assigned to the new database being created.

database_device. The logical name of the device used to contain the newly created database.

size. The size, in megabytes, of the database or its transaction log.

The following is an example:

```
CREATE DATABASE acct
    ON acct_data = 5
    LOG ON acct_log = 1
```

The following steps show you how to create a database using Transact-SQL:

1. Load the SQL Query tool (or a similar tool). Make sure that the Query tab is selected.

2. Select the Master database from the DB drop-down menu. New databases must be created from the Master database.

3. Enter the appropriate Transact-SQL statement.

4. Execute the statement. The Results window displays the following messages:

```
CREATE DATABASE: allocating x pages on disk 'device_name'
```

and

```
CREATE DATABASE: allocating x pages on disk 'device_name'
```

The database has been created. The new database is not displayed in the Enterprise Manager until the screen has been refreshed by choosing View | Refresh.

5.5. Setting Database Options

After a new database has been created, you can change a variety of database options. These options affect how the database works. They can be changed using the SQL Enterprise Manager or using the sp_dboption stored procedure. Each database's option settings are configured separately from all other databases. The following list describes various database options:

- *Columns Null by Default.* This option determines whether columns in a table are set to NULL or NOT NULL by default. Turning this option on makes SQL Server comply with the ANSI standard for SQL databases. This option is turned off by default.

- *DBO Use Only.* This option configures the database so that only the dbo can access it. If this option is turned on while users are accessing the database, the users are not logged out, but no new users can log in. This option can be used when performing a bcp out from the database to prevent a user from using a table being exported. This option is turned off by default.

- *No Checkpoint on Recovery.* When SQL Server starts, it usually performs an automatic recovery whether one is required or not. This process adds a checkpoint record to the transaction log, which tells SQL Server when the last automatic recovery occurred. This option, which prevents SQL Server from adding a checkpoint record to the transaction log, often is used when a system administrator performs manual online mirroring between production and standby servers. This option is turned off by default.

- *Offline.* This option appears on databases marked for distribution onto removable media. When set to offline, a database cannot be accessed. By default, this option does not appear on databases that have not been prepared for removable media distribution.

- *Published.* This option appears on databases marked for publication in a replication scenario. It indicates that its tables can be published. By default, this option does not appear on a normal database.

- *Read Only.* This option makes a database read-only so that users cannot alter any records in the database. This option is turned off by default.

- *Select Into/Bulk Copy.* This option must be set before any nonlogged operation can be performed on a database. A nonlogged operation bypasses the transaction log and directly alters a database. Examples of nonlogged operations include a fast bcp and the WRITETEXT and SELECT INTO Transact-SQL statements. This option is turned off by default.

- *Single User.* When this option is set, only one user can access the database at a time. This option often is used to prevent users from accessing a database, such as when you run the DBCC SHRINKDB, DBCC CHECKALLOC, or DBCC UPDATEUSAGE commands. This option is turned off by default.

- *Subscribed.* This option appears on databases marked as a subscriber in a replication scenario. It indicates that the database can be subscribed. By default, this option does not appear on a normal database.

- *Truncate Log on Checkpoint.* This option instructs SQL Server to automatically truncate a database's transaction log every time a checkpoint is executed. A transaction log usually is truncated only when it is done manually or when a backup is made of the transaction log. This option sometimes is set when a database is under development, when the possibility exists that the transaction log might become full before it is manually truncated. This option is turned off by default.

Use the following steps to change any of these settings using the SQL Enterprise Manager:

1. From the SQL Enterprise Manager's main screen, select a SQL Server and open its folder by clicking the plus sign. This displays various SQL Server folders.

2. Open the Databases folder by clicking the plus sign next to it. This displays a list of all the current databases for this SQL Server.

3. Right-click the database you want to configure and select Edit. The Edit Database dialog box opens.

4. Click the Options tab at the top of the Edit Database dialog box. This displays the database options. You can change them by clicking the appropriate check box.

5.6. How to Alter the Size of a Database Using the SQL Enterprise Manager

Unlike a device, the size of a database can be increased or decreased. This section shows you how to change the size of a database using either the SQL Enterprise Manager or Transact-SQL.

Use the following steps to increase or decrease the size of a database using the SQL Enterprise Manager:

1. From the SQL Enterprise Manager's Server Manager window, select a SQL Server and open its folder by clicking the plus sign. This displays various SQL Server folders.

2. Open the Databases folder by clicking the plus sign next to it. This displays a list of all the current databases for this SQL Server.

3. Right-click the database you want to change in size and select Edit. The Edit Database dialog box opens (see Figure 5.4).

4. To expand a database, click the Expand button. The Expand Database dialog box opens (see Figure 5.5).

5. From the Data Device drop-down box, select the database device on which you want to expand the database. Enter the number of megabytes by which you want to expand the database. If you want to expand the database by five additional megabytes, for example, enter 5 in the Size box. The bar charts at the bottom of the screen indicate which devices are available and the amount of free space available on each device. This free space can be used for database expansion.

6. If appropriate, from the Log Device drop-down box, select the database device on which you want to expand the transaction log. In the Size box, enter the number of megabytes by which you want to expand the transaction log.

Figure 5.4.

Database size can be changed in the Edit Database dialog box.

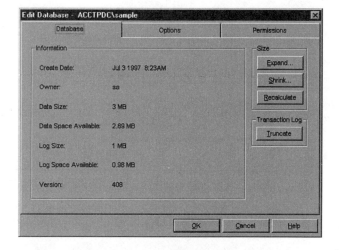

Figure 5.5.

Both a database and its transaction log can be expanded in the Expand Database dialog box.

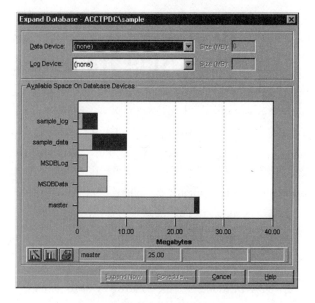

5

7. After you have specified all the appropriate information, click the Expand Now button. The database (and/or transaction log) will increase in size.

8. To shrink the size of a database, click the Shrink button in the Edit Database dialog box.

9. This displays the following message: The database must be set to single-user mode for the duration of this dialog. Continue? When shrinking a database, the database automatically is set to single-user mode. This means

no one can access the database during this process. Click Yes to continue. The Shrink Database dialog box opens (see Figure 5.6).

Figure 5.6.

Database size can be reduced in the Shrink Database dialog box.

10. The Shrink Database dialog box tells the current size of the database and how small you can shrink it. To reduce the size, enter the number of megabytes you want the database to be, without exceeding the minimum possible size.

11. When you are done, click OK. The database automatically shrinks in size.

5.7. How to Change the Size of a Database Using Transact-SQL

To increase the size of a database, use the ALTER DATABASE Transact-SQL statement. To shrink the size of a database, use the DBCC SHRINKDB command.

The syntax for the ALTER DATABASE Transact-SQL statement is as follows:

```
ALTER DATABASE database_name
    On device_name = size, device_name = size, . . .
```

The preceding syntax contains the following placeholders:

database_name. The name of the database to be expanded.

device_name. The logical name of the device where the database is to be expanded.

size. The amount, in megabytes, by which you want to expand the database. If you want to increase the database by 5MB, enter substitute 5 for *size*.

The following is an example:

```
ALTER DATABASE acct
    ON acct_data = 5
```

The syntax for the DBCC SHRINKDB Transact-SQL statement is as follows:

```
DBCC SHRINKDB (database_name, size)
```

The preceding syntax contains the following placeholders:

database_name. The name of the database you want to shrink.

size. The new size, in 2KB pages, that you want the database to be.

The following is an example:

```
DBCC SHRINKDB (acct, 2048)
```

Use the following steps to change the size of a database using Transact-SQL:

1. Load the SQL Query tool (or a similar tool). Make sure that the Query tab is selected.
2. Select the name of the database you want to shrink from the DB drop-down menu. If you want to expand a database, select the Master database instead.
3. Enter the Transact-SQL statement.
4. Execute the statement.

The size of the database is changed. The newly sized device does not display in the Server Manager window until the screen has been refreshed by choosing View | Refresh.

Before you can shrink a database, it must be in single-user mode. You can change this configuration setting using either the Enterprise Manager or the sp_dboption system stored procedure. After you finish shrinking the database, make sure that you remove this setting.

Sometimes you are not able to shrink a database as small as you want. The minimum size, as stated by the SQL Enterprise Manager, might actually be larger than the database actually can be shrunk. If you know a database can be made smaller than the SQL Enterprise Manager indicates, you can use another method to reduce the database's size. Use the Transfer Manager program to copy the database to a new device. This enables you to reclaim lost space. After the database has been copied successfully, the old one can be dropped. Day 10, "Backing Up and Managing SQL Server Data," provides more information about the Transfer Manager.

5

5.8. How to Drop Databases

Whenever you are done using a database, it can be dropped (deleted) from SQL Server. When you drop a database, its transaction log also is dropped. A database can be dropped using either the SQL Enterprise Manager or Transact-SQL (DROP DATABASE).

To drop a database using the SQL Enterprise Manager, right-click the database you want to drop and select Delete. A warning message tells you that the database is about to be deleted. Click Yes to delete the database.

Dropping a database does not automatically drop the device on which it resides. After a database is dropped from a device, the device can be reused. You can create a new database on it, or if you prefer, the device itself can be dropped.

5.9. How to Create Database Objects

Although database objects most often are created by database developers, it is important for DBAs to understand how they are created. The following sections show you how to create several common database objects—tables, views, and indexes—using Transact-SQL statements. You need to know how to create objects for the exam, but you don't need to remember the exact syntax of these examples. The most important thing to remember is the process of how to create objects in a database.

5.9.1. How to Create a Table

After creating a database, the next step usually is to add the necessary tables to store data. Tables are created with the CREATE TABLE Transact-SQL statement. By default, only the system administrator or dbo of a database can create a new table. This task can, however, be granted to others by the system administrator or dbo of the database.

 Note Although most database objects are created using Transact-SQL, most also can be created from within the Enterprise Manager. See SQL Server Books Online for more information about how to create database objects using the Enterprise Manager.

Before you create a table, you need to define its columns (fields). You also need to determine each column's datatype and width. *Datatypes* specify the type of data to be stored in each column, such as text, numbers, dates, and so on. The width specifies how many characters can be entered in a column. SQL Server includes the standard datatypes described in Table 5.1.

Table 5.1. SQL Server datatypes.

Datatype	Transact-SQL Name
Approximate Numbers	`float(n)`, `real`
Binary	`binary(n)`, `varbinary(n)`
Character	`char(n)`, `varchar(n)`
Date & Time	`datetime`, `smalldatetime`
Dollars & Cents	`money`, `smallmoney`
Exact Numbers	`decimal`, `numeric`
Integers	`int`, `smallint`, `tinyint`
Special	`bit`, `timestamp`, `user-defined`
Text & Images	`text`, `image`

n = number of characters

The syntax for the CREATE TABLE Transact-SQL statement is as follows:

```
CREATE TABLE table_name
    ( column_name column_properties,
     . . .
column_name column_properties )
```

The preceding syntax contains the following placeholders:

> `table_name`. The name assigned to the new table being created.
>
> `column_name`. The name of the column.
>
> `column_properties`. The datatype and width of the column.

The following is an example:

```
CREATE TABLE employees
    ( employee_id int,
    f_name char(20),
    l_name char(35),
    title char(25),
    pager_number char(10),
    hire_date smalldatetime )
```

Use the following steps to create a new table object:

1. Load the SQL Query tool (or a similar tool). Make sure that the Query tab is selected.

5

2. From the DB drop-down menu, select the name of the database in which you want to create a new table. Tables must be created in the databases in which they belong.

3. Enter the Transact-SQL statement as given in the preceding example.

4. Execute the statement. The Results window displays this message: This command did not return data, and it did not return any rows. The table was created. This can be verified by opening the Tables folder of the database in which the table was created. If the new table does not immediately appear, you might have to refresh the Tables folder.

5.9.2. How to Create a View

After one or more tables have been created in a database, views can be created using the CREATE VIEW Transact-SQL statement. Views are database objects that enable you to view data from one or more tables in an alternative way you can specify.

Views are not tables and do not include data. They are special objects that enable you to view data in preexisting tables. Views are virtual tables that exist only when displayed.

Views can be used instead of tables to query, view, insert, update, and delete data in tables. Views also can be used to define queries. Instead of entering the same query over and over, for example, a query can be assigned to a view. When that view is displayed, the query automatically runs, and the view displays the results of the query. This includes queries run on a single tables and on multiple tables.

Views can be used to ensure security; they only display data from columns a user is permitted to view. They also can be used to create derived columns, which are often used in calculations. For the most part, view creation is left to the database developer.

The syntax for the CREATE VIEW Transact-SQL statement is as follows:

```
CREATE VIEW view_name
AS
SELECT column_name, . . column_name
FROM table_name
```

The preceding syntax contains the following placeholders:

view_name. The name assigned to the new view being created.

column_name. The name of the column(s) to be included in the view.

table_name. The name of the table on which the view is based.

The following is an example:

```
CREATE VIEW employee_view
AS
SELECT employee_id, f_name, l_name, title, pager_number
From employees
```

Use the following steps to create a view:

1. Load the SQL Query tool (or a similar tool). Make sure that the Query tab is selected.

2. From the DB drop-down menu, select the name of the database in which you want to create the view. Views must be created in the databases in which they belong.

3. Enter the CREATE VIEW Transact-SQL statement as given in the preceding example.

4. Execute the statement. The Results window displays this message: This command did not return data, and it did not return any rows.

The view was created. This can be verified by opening the Views folder of the database in which the view was created. If the new view does not immediately appear, you might have to refresh the Views folder.

5.9.3. How to Create an Index

Most tables in a database need one or more indexes, which are created using the CREATE INDEX Transact-SQL statement. Indexes can enforce the uniqueness of rows in a table and can speed data retrieval during queries. Indexes are database objects, just like tables and views.

SQL Server enables you to create the following two types of indexes:

- A *clustered* index forces the rows in a table to be physically stored in sorted order, using one column from the table to sort the rows. A table can have only one clustered index.

- A *nonclustered index* does not physically arrange data; it simply points to the data in a table. The pointers themselves are sorted, which makes it easy to locate data quickly within a table. A nonclustered index exists as an object separate from the table. Any column of a table can have its own index.

Although most indexes are created by the database developer, the DBA often gets involved after creation because indexes play a significant role in how a database is optimized for speed.

5

The syntax for the CREATE INDEX Transact-SQL statement is as follows:

```
CREATE [UNIQUE] [CLUSTERED¦NONCLUSTERED] INDEX index_name
ON table_name (column_name, . . column_name)
```

The preceding syntax contains the following:

UNIQUE. If used, this specifies that the index being created should be unique. If not used, the index will not be unique.

CLUSTERED¦NONCLUSTERED. Specifies the type of index to be created. Use CLUSTERED to create a clustered index; use NONCLUSTERED to create a nonclustered index. Only one or the other can be used.

index_name. The name assigned to the new index being created.

table_name. The name of the table for which the index is being created.

column_name. The name of the column(s) to be included in the index.

The following is an example:

```
CREATE CLUSTERED INDEX employee_id_idx
ON employees (employee_id)
```

Use the following steps to create an index:

1. Load the SQL Query tool (or a similar tool). Make sure that the Query tab is selected.

2. From the DB drop-down menu, select the name of the database in which you want to create an index. Indexes must be created in the databases in which they belong.

3. Enter the CREATE INDEX Transact-SQL statements as given in the preceding example.

4. Execute the statement. The Results window displays the message: This command did not return data, and it did not return any rows. The index is created.

Before taking the certification exam, you might want to experiment by creating some of these objects to better understand the process.

Lab

Questions

1. As the DBA of a SQL Server, you have been asked to create a new database to store marketing information. From the database developer, you learn that each record will be 1,024 bytes long. Assuming that the database will not include objects other than data tables, how big should you create a database that will eventually hold 250,000 records? Round up to the nearest even megabyte.

   A. 123MB

   B. 245MB

   C. 489MB

   D. 978MB

2. You are the DBA of a SQL Server with very little extra space. Unfortunately, your organization doesn't have the money to purchase additional hard disk space. As a result, any new databases must be sized as accurately as possible so that little or no space is wasted. As part of your calculations to determine the size of a new database, you make these observations: *1)* Your database will include eight stored procedures, each of which will range in size from 18KB to 24KB. *2)* Your database will include two views, each of which will be about 8KB in size. Both views, however, will be able to display about 100MB of data after the database is in production. Based only on the information provided, how much space will be occupied by the eight stored procedures and the two views?

   A. 36KB

   B. 72KB

   C. 144KB

   D. 288KB

3. As the SQL Server DBA, you need to estimate the size of a transaction log. The database developer thinks the database should be 256MB, but he has no idea how to size the transaction log. To help you make an informed decision about the size of the transaction log, which two of the following might you ask the database developer to get a better idea how to proceed with your estimate?

5

    A. Ask whether the database will have many transactions each day or will be used mostly for read-only work.

    B. Ask the developer how mission-critical the database is. This will help you determine how often the transaction log should be backed up. You can back up a transaction log every hour or only once a day, depending on how much data the business can afford to lose.

    C. Ask the developer how many indexes, both clustered and nonclustered, the database will use and how often these indexes should be dropped and re-created.

    D. Ask the developer whether the SQL Server application uses mostly scripts or stored procedures to execute Transact-SQL code.

4. As a SQL Server DBA, you know that estimating the size of new databases is an important part of your job. What are some of the factors you need to consider when estimating the size of any new SQL Server database? (Select all that apply.)

    A. The size of each row

    B. The number of rows

    C. The number of tables

    D. The number of indexes

    E. The size of each index

    F. The number and size of database objects

    G. The size of the transaction log

    H. The projected growth of the database

5. You are a SQL Server consultant and have been asked to help an inexperienced DBA working for one of your clients. After reviewing how the various databases were created, you notice that the DBA created one huge device and placed all the company's databases and transaction logs on that single device. Based on this single observation, which of the following pieces of advice would you give the DBA?

    A. Have the DBA run the Performance Monitor to determine how busy the server is. Assuming the server is not too busy, nothing needs to be done. If the server is a little slow, however, the DBA needs to add RAM to the server.

    B. Recommend that the DBA move the huge device to a RAID Level 5 disk array to increase fault tolerance.

C. Suggest that the DBA create another device on which to place the transaction logs.

D. Recommend that the DBA create new devices so that each database and each transaction log is on its own separate device.

6. You have been hired as the DBA for a company. As one of your first jobs, you decide to create a small database to experiment with. You want to keep it small because you don't want to waste too much hard disk space. You create the database using the Enterprise Manager, but you notice that the smallest size available is 5MB, not the usual 1MB you should be able to make it. What could be causing this problem?

A. The model database is 5MB in size.

B. The Master database is 5MB in size.

C. The size of the default device is 5MB.

D. You must use Transact-SQL, not the Enterprise Manager, to make smaller databases.

7. You need to create a database that can hold 20GB of data. Unfortunately, your server has only four empty hard drives, and each drive can hold only 9GB of data. To create such a large database, what do you have to do?

A. You have to purchase a new drive, one that can hold at least 20GB of data.

B. You have to create multiple devices on the empty drives and create one large database to reside on the multiple devices.

C. You have to create multiple devices on the empty drives and create multiple databases on each device. You then have to link the smaller databases into one larger database.

D. You can format one of the 9GB drives using NTFS and turn on NT Server data compression.

8. Instead of using the Enterprise Manager, you want to use Transact-SQL to create a new database. After the database has been created, you will manually populate it with tables and other objects. Which of the following statements enables you to create a new database that is 5MB in size on one device, with a transaction log of 2MB on another device?

A.

```
CREATE DATABASE marketing
    ON marketing_data = 5
    LOG ON marketing_log = 2
```

B.

```
CREATE DATABASE marketing
    ON marketing_data = 5
    LOG ON marketing_log = 2
    FOR LOAD
```

C.

```
CREATE DATABASE marketing
    ON marketing_data = 2560
    LOG ON marketing_log = 1024
```

D.

```
CREATE DATABASE marketing
    ON marketing_data = 2560
    LOG ON marketing_log = 1024
    FOR LOAD
```

9. As the new DBA of a SQL Server, you run across a database with the Select Into/Bulk Copy and the DBO Use Only options turned on. You know these options are not usually turned on. What is the most likely reason these options are turned on?

   A. Another DBA might be planning to perform a nonlogged operation on this database.

   B. A user accidentally has changed these options because proper security has not been set up on the database.

   C. A database developer might be planning to add a new stored procedure to the database.

   D. Another DBA might be planning to back up the database.

10. You have just been hired as the DBA for a SQL Server that has been around for a year or two. Your first day on the job, as you review how the SQL Server is set up, you notice that one of the databases is 500MB in size but is only about 10 percent full. You ask around and find out the database holds legacy data that is looked up every once in a while, and its size should never increase. Eventually, the database will be replaced by a new database application. Given this information, which of the following actions might you take?

A. To save space, you might want to reduce the size of the device on which the database resides.

B. To save space, you might want to reduce the size of the database using `DBCC SHRINKDB`.

C. To save space, you might want to defragment the database and then compress it using NTFS compression.

D. To save space, you might want to move the database to a smaller hard disk.

11. As the DBA, you need to remove an old database no longer being used. Using the Enterprise Manager, you select the database and drop it. You do not receive an error message, so you assume the database has been dropped successfully. You then use NT Server's Explorer tool to view the folder in which the database was stored. To your surprise, you notice a file that has the same name as the database you dropped. Why wasn't the database dropped as expected?

A. Only a system administrator can drop a database, and you were not logged in as the system administrator for this database.

B. The database was dropped from the Master database, but you must manually delete the database from the hard disk.

C. The database was dropped but you didn't drop the device, which is what you see in Explorer.

D. The Master database has become corrupted, and you need to restore it from a good backup.

5

Exercises

1. Creating a Database Using the SQL Enterprise Manager

This exercise helps to address the following certification exam objective:
- Create a database

This exercise shows you how to create a new database using the SQL Enterprise Manager. You will place the database on the sample_data device and the transaction log on the sample_log device. These devices already exist if you performed the exercises from Day 4. If these devices currently don't exist, you need to create them before beginning this exercise. Day 4 provides information about how to create devices.

1. From the SQL Enterprise Manager's Server Manager window, select a SQL Server and open its folder by clicking the plus sign. This displays various SQL Server folders.

2. Open the Databases folder by clicking the plus sign next to it. This displays a list of all the current databases for this SQL Server.

3. Right-click the Databases folder and select New Database from the menu. The New Database dialog box opens.

4. In the Name box, enter sample1.

5. In the Data Device box, select the sample_data database device from the drop-down list.

6. In the Size box, enter 2.

7. In the Log Device box, select the sample_log database device from the drop-down list.

8. In the Size box, enter 1.

9. To create the new database, click the Create Now button. The database and the transaction log are created immediately. You receive no feedback from SQL Server telling they were created. To verify the creation of the new database, you can view it in the Databases folder of the Server Manager window.

2. Creating a Database Using Transact-SQL

 Note This exercise helps to address the following certification exam objective:
- Create a database

This exercise shows you how to create a new database using Transact-SQL. You will create the database on the sample_data device and its transaction log on the sample_log device. These devices already exist if you performed the exercises from Day 4. If these devices don't currently exist, you need to create them before beginning this exercise. Day 4 provides information about how to create devices.

1. Load the SQL Query tool. Make sure that the Query tab is selected.

2. Select the Master database from the DB drop-down menu.

3. Enter the following Transact-SQL statement:

```
CREATE DATABASE sample2
    ON sample_data = 2
    LOG ON sample_log = 1
```

4. Execute the statement. The Results window displays the following messages:

```
CREATE DATABASE: allocating 1024 pages on disk 'sample_data'
```

and

```
CREATE DATABASE: allocating 512 pages on disk 'sample_log'
```

The database has been created. The new database is not displayed in the Server Manager window until it has been refreshed by choosing View | Refresh.

3. Altering a Database Using the SQL Enterprise Manager

This exercise shows you how to expand by 1MB one of the databases you previously created using the SQL Enterprise Manager.

 Note   This exercise helps to address the following certification exam objective:
■ Alter a database

1. From the SQL Enterprise Manager's Server Manager window, select a SQL Server and open its folder by clicking the plus sign. This displays various SQL Server folders.
2. Open the Databases folder by clicking the plus sign next to it. This displays a list of all the current databases for this SQL Server.
3. Right-click the sample1 database and select Edit. The Edit Database dialog box opens.
4. Click the Expand button. The Expand Database dialog box opens.
5. From the Data Device drop-down box, select the sample_data device. Enter 1 to indicate how much you want to expand the database.
6. After you have specified all the appropriate information, click the Expand Now button. The database is increased in size by 1 megabyte.

5

4. Altering a Database Using Transact-SQL

Note This exercise helps to address the following certification exam objective:
- Alter a database

This exercise shows you how to expand by 1MB one of the databases you previously created using Transact-SQL:

1. Load the SQL Query tool. Make sure that the Query tab is selected.

2. Select Master from the DB drop-down menu.

3. Enter the following Transact-SQL statement:

```
ALTER DATABASE sample2
    ON sample_data = 1
```

4. Execute the statement. The Results window displays this message: `Extending database by 512 pages on disk sample_data`. The size of the database has been changed.

5. Creating Database Objects Using Transact-SQL

Note This exercise helps to address the following certification exam objective:
- Create database objects

This exercise shows you how to create a new table in one of the databases you previously created using Transact-SQL.

1. Load the SQL Query tool. Make sure that the Query tab is selected.

2. Select the sample1 database from the DB drop-down menu.

3. Enter the following Transact-SQL statement:

```
CREATE TABLE employees
    ( staff_id int,
    f_name char(20),
    l_name char(35),
    title char(25),
    pager_number char(10),
    hire_date smalldatetime )
```

4. Execute the statement. The Results window displays this message: This command did not return data, and it did not return any rows. The table was created. This can be verified by opening the Tables folder of the database in which the table was created.

Answers to Questions

1. **C**   Each 1 megabyte of a database contains 512 pages. Although each page is 2,048 bytes, only 2,016 bytes actually is available because of overhead. Because each record will be 1,024 bytes, each data page can contain only one record rather than two. If you divide 250,000 (the number of records) by 512 (the number of pages per megabyte), you get 489MB when rounded up to the nearest megabyte.

2. **D**   Whenever a new database object is created, it always is created in units of extents rather than pages. If a new stored procedure takes only 1KB of actual space, for example, SQL Server always reserves one extent, or 16KB, for the stored procedure—even though the extent will not be full. In addition, SQL Server cannot place more than one object per extent. Given this fact, you can make these calculations: *1)* Because each of the stored procedures is greater than 16KB but less than 32KB, you know each one will take two extents, or a total of 256KB of database space. *2)* Because both views are less than 16KB, you know each one only requires a single extent, or a total of 32KB for the two views. Together, this means you need 288KB of database space for the objects in question.

3. **A, B**   Estimating the appropriate size of a transaction log is never easy. Two of the most important considerations are: *1)* How much it will change each day. The more daily transactions take place, the faster the log fills up. *2)* Each time a transaction log is backed up, it is truncated. If backups are performed often, the log can be smaller. If the log is backed up only occasionally, it needs to be larger.

4. **A, B, C, D, E, F, G, H**   All these responses are correct.

5. **D**   Although not required, it is ideal from an administrative perspective to place each database and its related transaction log on separate devices. Benefits of creating a transaction log on a device separate from its database include the following: *1)* The transaction log can be backed up separately from the database. *2)* Up-to-date recovery is possible in the event of server failure. *3)* The transaction log does not compete with the database for device space. *4)* Transaction log space can easily be monitored. *5)* There is less contention

5

between writes to the database and the transaction log, which can increase SQL Server's performance.

6. **A**   You cannot create a database smaller than the size of the model database. Apparently, someone has increased the size of the model database from its default size of 1MB to 5MB.

7. **B**   A single database can span many devices, even when those devices exist on separate hard disks.

8. **A**   The FOR LOAD option is used only when creating databases that will be restored from a backup. When entering the size of a new database, megabytes are used rather than 2KB pages.

9. **A**   Although these two settings could mean several things, the most likely reason is that someone wants to perform a nonlogged operation on the database and wants to prevent anyone other than the dbo from being in the database until the operation is completed.

10. **B**   Only databases can be reduced in size. After a database is shrunk, you can use the remaining space on the device for other databases. If you prefer, you can move the database to another, smaller device using the Transfer Manager.

11. **C**   Dropping a database is separate from dropping a device. This is why you still can see the device in Explorer. You can drop both a database and a device at the same time by dropping the device using the Enterprise Manager. Whenever a device is dropped using the Enterprise Manager, the device and any databases on the device all are dropped at the same time.

TEST DAY
FAST FACTS

This chapter introduces SQL Server security and provides in-depth coverage of the three security modes: integrated, mixed, and standard. The following are some key facts that you'll learn in this chapter:

- SQL Server supports three security models: integrated, standard, and mixed. Standard is the default, integrated uses Windows NT authentication, and mixed is a combination of both methods.

- Integrated security can be applied only to Windows NT groups.

- Integrated security works only over the RPC network libraries: Named Pipes and Multi-Protocol.

- Standard security works over all supported network libraries.

- Mixed security determines which library the incoming connection is using. If the connection is coming in on Named Pipes or Multi-Protocol, integrated security is used; otherwise, standard security is used.

- Restart SQL Server for changes in the security mode to take effect.

Day 6

Implementing SQL Server Security

This is the first of three chapters examining how SQL Server security works. This chapter provides an overview of the SQL Server security model and then looks at the three security modes: standard, integrated, and mixed. It then focuses on how integrated security affects SQL Server. You'll learn to create user accounts and to manage user groups. You'll also learn to control how users interact with different objects in the database. The next two chapters show you how to create logins, users, and groups and how to secure objects in the database.

Objectives

This chapter covers the following material:

- Set up a security mode.
- Identify the effect of integrated security on SQL Server.

6.1. The SQL Server Security Model

Before discussing SQL Server security modes, you first need some background information about how SQL Server handles user security. Three terms that are often used interchangeably in everyday life have very distinct meanings in SQL Server. These terms are *login*, *user*, and *account*. A login provides a user with access to a server. A login has a password associated with it for security reasons. The definition for each login is stored in the syslogins table in the Master database. Having a login in itself does not give a person access to any server resources. The word *account* is used to reference a Windows NT account created with the User Manager.

A *user* is created in a given database and attached to a login. When a user is created, a login name must be specified to connect the user back to an entry in the Master database. User definitions are stored in the sysusers table in each database on the server. A user does not have a password associated with it but does have permissions to access certain objects. Users get resources; logins don't. A user is a database object.

In this book's exercises so far, you have used the login account sa. The sa login is always attached to the dbo user. Remember that *sa* stands for *system administrator*. The term *dbo* stands for *database owner*. New logins can be created, and then new users can be created. In most cases, a login and a user have the same name associated with them.

When a person wants to log in to SQL Server using ISQL/W, he is prompted to provide a login and a password. By default, the only user login is sa, and its password is blank. After that person has logged in to SQL Server, he has access to every database in which there is a user linked back to his login. Also by default, one database is set as the default database for the login. That database is automatically used when ISQL starts.

6.2. The Three Security Models

SQL Server supports three different security models. These models have to do with how logins are used. Under standard security, the default mode, a person must provide a login and a password to log in. By default, you probably use sa and a blank password.

When a person tries to log in under the integrated security model, SQL Server detects which Windows NT user account is being used to establish the connection and then maps that Windows NT account to a SQL Server account of the same name. The user does not have to provide a password or a login name to be validated;

these are automatically pulled from the environment. SQL Server gets the Windows NT user account information for the login process from the Remote Procedure Call (RPC) connection. This means that, for integrated security to work, the user must be using an RPC connection to log in. The Multi-Protocol and Named Pipes libraries automatically use RPC, so integrated security isn't additional work if either of these libraries is in use between the client and the server.

> **Note**
>
> To establish a connection between client and server using either Named Pipes or Multi-Protocol libraries, one of two conditions must be met. Either the user on the client side must have a valid Windows NT account on the server—an account that the server can validate on its own domain or through any trusted domain—or the server must have the guest account enabled. It usually isn't good practice for the guest account to be enabled, so chances are, if you are using Named Pipes or Multi-Protocol libraries, you already meet all the requirements for using integrated security.

Integrated security has two primary advantages over standard security. The job of a database administrator is to administrate databases, not to manage user accounts. By using integrated security, the management of user accounts is handed back to Windows NT. Also, Windows NT has far more powerful tools for managing user accounts, such as account lockout, password aging, and minimum password lengths. None of these capabilities are present in SQL Server without extensive customization. Examine your Windows NT documentation on user accounts for more information about account restrictions and password management.

Mixed security allows both standard and integrated connections. They are validated based on which network library is used to initiate communications. If a person uses TCP/IP Sockets libraries to log in, for example, she uses standard security; if she uses Named Pipes, however, the connections are validated using the scheme in integrated security. This provides ultimate flexibility to the users.

The type of security mode used is usually determined by the validation model of the network and the communications protocol used between the clients and the server. If the network is primarily a Novell or peer-to-peer network, use the SPX network library and standard security. If you use standard security in this case, it is only necessary to create the logins on SQL Server, not on Windows NT. If the network is primarily a Windows NT network, however, a Windows NT server is probably already validating the users when they log in, so it is less work to use integrated security.

6

By now, you're probably saying to yourself, "Enough already, let's see how this actually works." Now you'll take a look at how to switch security modes and how to link Windows NT accounts to SQL Server logins by using the SQL Security Manager.

6.3. Changing the Security Mode

The security mode can be changed in SQL Server by using either the SQL Server Enterprise Manager or SQL Server Setup. Use the following steps when using the SQL Server Enterprise Manager:

1. Start the SQL Server Enterprise Manager.

2. Verify that the server you want to work on is registered with the Enterprise Manager. If not, use the Register Server option in the Server menu to do so.

3. Expand the server that you want to work on by clicking the plus sign (+) next to the server's name.

4. Click the Server menu, choose SQL Server, and then choose Configure. If you prefer, you can right-click the server name and then choose Configure.

5. Click the Security Options tab, shown in Figure 6.1.

Figure 6.1.

You can choose a security mode on the Security Options tab.

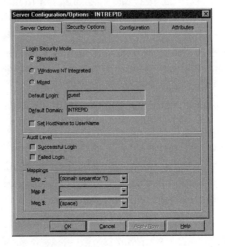

6. The Security Options tab contains three sections. The first section, Login Security Mode, enables you to choose a security mode and provides some other options. The second section, Audit Level, determines whether successful, failed, or both types of login attempts are recorded in the Windows NT Event

log. The third section, Mappings, determines how to substitute for illegal characters in names.

7. In the Login Security Mode box, choose Windows NT Integrated.

8. Verify that the Default Login box still says guest. This SQL Server login is used if a login can't be found to match the Windows NT account.

9. The Default Domain box should contain the name of the domain that contains the bulk of the user accounts using the SQL Server. If SQL Server is running on a standalone server, enter the computer name here.

10. If the Set Hostname to Username option is selected, when utilities such as sp_who or the Current Activity screen in the Enterprise Manager are used, the username is shown in the column reserved for the computer name. It is usually helpful to check this box.

11. In the Audit Level section, choose the type of events that you want to audit. It is helpful to audit failed logins because repeated failed logins are either an intruder or a user that has forgotten his password. Auditing successful logins is good for troubleshooting but tends to fill the log quickly.

12. The Mappings section informs SQL Server how to deal with username characters it otherwise wouldn't know how to deal with. Windows NT, for example, uses the backslash character (\) to delimit domain names from user accounts. When SQL Server encounters a backslash, it replaces it with an underscore (_) by default. When SQL Server encounters a hyphen (-) in a Windows NT username, it replaces it with a hash mark or pound sign (#) by default. When it encounters a space, it replaces it with a dollar sign ($). Changing these mappings is usually unnecessary, but it's important to realize what they do.

13. When all the options are set, click OK to apply the options and to close the dialog box.

14. SQL Server must be restarted for the change to take effect. This can be done by right-clicking the server and choosing Stop. When the server has stopped, right-click the server and choose Start.

6

Use the following steps to perform the same task by using SQL Server Setup:

1. Start SQL Server Setup.

2. Choose Continue twice to skip past the introductory material.

3. Choose Set Security Options and click Continue.

4. At this point, the Security Options dialog box opens, just as it does in SQL Server Enterprise Manager. Follow steps 6 through 13 from the preceding list.

5. Click OK when the options are set; then click Exit to Windows NT.

6. Restart SQL Server for the changes to take effect.

A couple of these steps need to be explained in a little more detail. First, the Default Domain box should contain the name of the domain that most of the user accounts are stored in. This means that if there is a master-domain model, the name of the account domain should go here. If SQL Server is on a standalone server and integrated security is used, the name of the standalone server can be entered in this box. Users from other domains can use the SQL Server, even if they aren't part of the default domain. SQL Server prepends their domain names and the Domain Separator, which is usually an underscore, to their usernames before checking their logins.

The other important section to clarify is Mappings. The Mappings section replaces characters that aren't legal in SQL Server login names with characters that are. Up to three characters can be substituted. The Domain Separator character is the most important of the mapped characters. Remember that all login names are stored in the master.syslogins table. When a person attempts to log in, SQL Server validates the login name provided against this table. When in integrated security mode, the name that SQL Server comes up with for a user is of the format *Domain\Account*. If the domain part of that name is the default domain, SQL Server looks for the account part in the syslogins table. If the domain part is *not* the default domain, SQL Server looks for Domain_Account in the syslogins table. Notice that the underscore is the mapping character for the domain separator. Other mapping characters take care of other problem account names that you might have in your environment, such as hyphenated last names or names with spaces.

Note Remember to restart SQL Server before trying to use integrated security. Changes won't take effect until the server is restarted.

Integrated security is now set up on your server. How do you allow Windows NT users to use your server? Good question. That's the topic of the next section.

6.4. The SQL Server Security Manager

To map Windows NT accounts to your SQL Server, you must use the SQL Server Security Manager. This tool is installed with SQL Server and can be used by an administrator of a server in integrated security mode to set security up for his users. The Security Manager is one of the most frustrating and difficult tools provided with SQL Server, so read this section carefully and watch for the notes that tell you what to avoid.

The Security Manager is used to map all the users of a Windows NT group to a set of SQL Server logins. A nice feature is that it automatically creates the necessary logins for you and offers to create users for you in a specified database. This feature can help you provide all the users in a Windows NT group with access to a database on your server.

The Security Manager contains two levels of privileges. By default, the Security Manager opens in User Privilege mode. In this mode, Windows NT groups can be added to SQL Server. The other mode, System Administrator Privilege, enables you to specify which users will be mapped to the sa login.

By default, when integrated security is turned on, the Windows NT Administrators group is the only group with access to the server. All the accounts in the Administrators group are mapped to the same login, sa. This gives all the administrators the capability to administer the server. As an implementation detail, it might be a good idea to build a new group of SQL Server administrators, add this group, and remove the normal Administrators group. It's not desirable for everyone with an administrator's account to be able to mess up the database.

This tutorial assumes you've set up a Windows NT group using User Manager and that the group has at least one user in it. The following steps show you how to grant access to a Windows NT group by using the Security Manager:

1. Start the SQL Server Security Manager. Connect to the server you want to administer by typing its name in the Server name box, as shown in Figure 6.2.

Figure 6.2.

In the Security Manager login screen, you can enter the server name, login, and password with System Administrator Privilege.

6

2. Verify that the Security Manager is in user mode. The toolbar contains three buttons. The first button, which looks like two cables being connected, enables you to change the server to which you are connected. The next two buttons are toggles, and only one can be pushed down at a time. The first toggle has a picture of a person on it. When this button is down, the Security Manager is in User Privilege mode. The next toggle has a picture of a user and a computer on it. This represents System Administrator Privilege mode.

3. From the Security menu, choose Grant New.

4. The top part of the Grant User Privilege dialog box enables a Windows NT group to be chosen (see Figure 6.3). By default, this contains the names of groups in the local account database. If the SQL Server is a backup domain controller, its domain's groups are listed. To switch to the domain specified in the Default Domain box (you filled this in when setting up integrated security), choose Groups on Default Domain. Choose the group to be added from the list.

Figure 6.3.

Use the Grant User Privilege dialog box to add Windows NT groups to SQL Server.

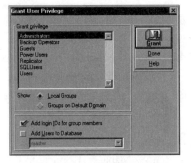

Note

Only groups can be granted access through integrated security. Access can't be given to individual users without first adding them to a group.

5. The bottom part of the dialog box controls what will be done with the accounts in the group specified in the top part. If Add Login IDs for Group Members is checked, every account in the Windows NT group will have a login added for it. If the login already exists, an error is logged, but it continues to process users in the list. If Add Users to Database is checked, corresponding user accounts are added for the logins in the specified database. If users need to be added to multiple databases, run the Security Manager

again, make sure that Add Login IDs is not checked, and then choose the database to add the users to.

6. After all the options are set, click the Grant button. This performs the specified operations. After they are finished, you can view any errors by clicking the Error Detail button.

7. Click Done to acknowledge the status report.

Step 6 mentions that errors might occur during this process. Two types of errors generally occur here. The first is when a login already exists with the same name. This usually occurs when the same group is granted more than once; all the existing logins generate an error. An example of this is shown in Figure 6.4. This does not stop new accounts from being added. It simply notes the error message and moves on. If an account has an illegal character in it (such as an apostrophe) and the character isn't replaced by a mapping, errors can occur. These errors can be fixed by modifying the mapping as necessary to handle the problem.

Figure 6.4.

This status report is shown when there is an attempt to add duplicate logins.

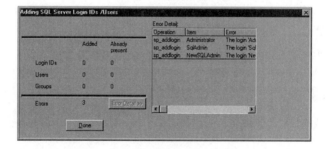

Notice that the status screen where a SQL Server creates the logins contains a counter already present. This counts the number of times a user is added to a database in which a user already exists with the same name. It doesn't count errors for logins that already exist. To check the errors, click the Error Detail button.

6

When a group is granted and the Add Users to Database option is checked, the users are added to the database and placed in a group with the same name as the Windows NT group. Mappings are in effect for the imported group, so if the group name contains illegal characters, substitution occurs according to the mapping specified. A SQL Server group is a database object containing users. This is discussed in more detail on Day 7, "Managing User Accounts."

Sometimes it is necessary to grant more Windows NT accounts the capability to do database administration. The following steps show you how to add accounts with System Administrator Privilege:

1. Start the SQL Server Security Manager.

2. Select the System Administrator Privilege from the toolbar or choose SA Privilege from the View menu.

3. Choose the group and click the Grant button.

System administrator accounts are handled differently than user accounts. Each user has a separate login, whereas all system administrators use the same login ID, sa. As a result, the system administrator groups are dynamic. If an account is added to a Windows NT group that has been granted System Administrator Privilege, that account automatically has the privilege without any additional action. The section "Managing Windows NT Groups and Grants" later in this chapter discusses how this works with user accounts. The sa account is always a member of the group called public. Groups are discussed further on Day 7.

6.4.1. Viewing Account Details

After a Windows NT group is brought into SQL Server, its properties can be viewed in the Security Manager by finding the account and double-clicking it. Use the following steps to find an account:

1. Start the SQL Server Security Manager.

2. From the Security menu, choose Search.

3. Enter the Windows NT account name that you want to view.

4. Click the Search button.

The Search button finds out whether a user has permissions to a server, and it can find all the user objects created for the given Windows NT account. It also displays the full name for the login's corresponding Windows NT account, in the format domain\login, as shown in Figure 6.5. If the login has user privileges, the Account box will say User. If the login has administrative privileges, the box will say Admin. To drop a user, click the Drop button on this screen.

The Search button can also be used to track down orphaned login IDs. An *orphaned login ID* is a login that does not have a Windows NT account associated with it. After you find these logins, they can be dropped using the Drop button in the Search dialog box.

Figure 6.5.

After performing a search, the results are displayed in the dialog box.

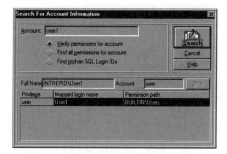

The `repl_publisher` and `repl_subscriber` logins are orphaned. They will always be orphaned. Don't drop these accounts, or you will have trouble getting replication to work.

6.4.2. Managing Windows NT Groups and Grants

When a group is granted access to SQL Server, the group does not become dynamic. This means that as users are added to the Windows NT group, they are not automatically given logins. After adding a user to the Windows NT group, the administrator needs to go back to the Security Manager and use the Grant New option. If a single user account needs to be removed, simply remove it from the Windows NT group. Delete the login by double-clicking the account in the Security Manager and choosing Drop Login. Using the Grant New option doesn't remove the user's login.

6.4.3. Removing Groups

If an entire group needs to be removed from the database, right-click the group and choose Security/Revoke from the menu. There might be error messages for users that either have already had their accounts removed or that aren't present in certain databases. Whenever the Security Manager is used to revoke permissions or to drop logins, it automatically tries to remove a user from every database on the server for each login. This means for each login, it tries to drop a user account in each database. Most of the time, this results in a large number of errors. Sometimes these are even accounted for correctly in the Not Present column of the Revoke Accounts dialog box. A sample status report is shown in Figure 6.6.

6

Figure 6.6.

This figure shows what happens when security is revoked.

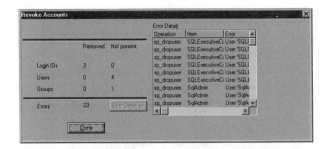

In closing, the Security Manager application performs grants very nicely. Unfortunately, it doesn't maintain groups or handle drops gracefully. This causes more work for the administrator, but it is still significantly less work managing passwords and user accounts by hand.

6.5. The Effect of Integrated Security on SQL Server

A subtitle for this section could be "How does this all work, anyway?" For every other configuration change that you've looked at so far, SQL Server has stored the change in the Master database, usually in the sysconfigures table. Unfortunately, the security mode needs to be determined before the Master database is brought online. Information pertaining to the security mode of SQL Server is stored in the Windows NT Registry with the rest of the startup information needed by SQL Server.

Note

The following is a quote from the Microsoft online knowledge base:

"Before you edit the Registry, make sure you understand how to restore it if a problem occurs. For information about how to do this, view the "Restoring the Registry" Help topic in Regedit.exe or the "Restoring a Registry Key" Help topic in Regedt32.exe."

This is the obligatory message you always see when the Registry is mentioned. Editing the Registry incorrectly is the second fastest way to trash an installation of Windows NT or SQL Server. Be careful, make backups, and, most importantly, don't guess. If you're not sure what something does, leave it alone. (By the way, the fastest way to trash a Windows NT or SQL Server installation is to drop the hardware out of a window.)

The setting for security mode is kept in `HKEY_LOCAL_MACHINE\Software\Microsoft\` `MSSQLServer\MSSQLServer` in the `LoginMode` key. If this is set to 0, standard security is in operation. If it is set to 1, integrated security is used. If it is set to 2, mixed security is used. This key is checked when SQL Server is started, which is why it's important to restart SQL Server after changing the security mode.

When SQL Server starts, it also starts all the configured network libraries. Day 2, "Installing SQL Server," discusses how network libraries are configured. Both the Named Pipes and Multi-Protocol libraries check the `LoginMode` key at startup to see whether they need to check Windows NT security.

At login, the person logging in is always presented with a Login ID and Password dialog box. If integrated security is active, a user can leave both these boxes blank and still be logged in. He can enter a username and password and be logged in. He even can enter garbage and still be logged in. It's fairly foolproof.

6

Lab

Questions

The following are questions to help you review the material in this chapter:

1. An administrator is trying to decide which security model to use. All the people who need access to the SQL Server have Windows NT accounts, and the SQL Server is on a standalone server in the same domain as the user accounts. The clients all use TCP/IP to connect to the server. Which security mode should the administrator choose?

    A. Standard mode.

    B. Integrated mode.

    C. Mixed mode.

    D. Both standard and mixed modes should be used simultaneously.

2. An administrator is trying to decide which security model to use. The people who need access use a variety of network protocols, and the SQL Server is the only Windows NT server on the network. Which mode should the administrator choose?

    A. Standard mode.

    B. Integrated mode.

    C. Mixed mode.

    D. Both standard and integrated modes should be used simultaneously.

3. After configuring his server for integrated security, the administrator begins to get complaints from users who are unable to access the server using their Windows NT logins. Which two of the following are the most likely causes?

    A. The administrator didn't restart the SQL Executive service, which handles all security requests.

    B. The administrator didn't restart the SQL Server service.

    C. The administrator didn't grant any users administrative access to the server.

    D. The administrator hasn't used the Security Manager to map Windows NT accounts to logins.

4. If the default domain is set to KC and a group with a user account named Joe from the STL domain is added to the SQL Server Security Manager, how will the Joe account show up in SQL Server? Assume that the mappings are still set at their defaults.

   A. Joe

   B. STL\Joe

   C. STL_Joe

   D. KC_Joe

5. Which of the following network libraries work(s) with integrated security?

   A. TCP/IP Sockets

   B. SPX

   C. Named Pipes

   D. All of the above

6. Where is information about the security mode kept?

   A. In the Registry

   B. In the master.sysconfigures table

   C. In the event log

   D. In the master.syslogins table

7. The administrator needs both the people using Windows NT accounts and the people using UNIX workstations to be able to access his SQL Server, while minimizing his overhead on managing passwords. Which security mode should be used?

   A. Standard.

   B. Mixed.

   C. Integrated.

   D. Both standard and integrated modes need to be used.

8. After close examination of the Current Activity screen's User Activity tab, the administrator is having difficulty figuring out which users are performing which activity. How can the administrator obtain this data more easily?

6

    A. Use a network protocol analyzer to determine where the packets are coming from.

    B. Use the sp_who stored procedure instead of the User Activity screen.

    C. Examine the Windows NT Event Log for failed and successful logins.

    D. Check the Set HostName to UserName box to make it easier to see which users are performing what tasks.

9. After a group has been granted access to the SQL Server using the Security Manager, the administrator begins to receive calls from new employees who need access to the database. After adding the users to the correct Windows NT group, what does the administrator need to do to provide the new users access to the data on the server?

    A. Nothing, the SQL Server automatically recognizes the new users.

    B. Re-grant the group by using the Security Manager.

    C. Create a new group for each set of new users and grant them all by using the Security Manager.

    D. Delete the group and re-grant it every time the group's account list changes.

10. A user is attempting to attach to a SQL Server using ISQL/W. The server uses integrated security. What can the user enter in the login and password boxes to be correctly validated and to receive access?

    A. His Windows NT account and password.

    B. Nothing, leave the boxes blank.

    C. His Windows NT account and an empty password.

    D. Any of the above will work.

Exercises

These exercises walk you through key procedures outlined in this chapter. They are interdependent: Do them in order, or they won't work.

Note

These exercises help to address the following certification exam objective:

■ Set up a security mode.

1. Setting the Security Mode

In this exercise, you set SQL Server to integrated security mode:

1. Start SQL Server Enterprise Manager.

2. Right-click the server that you want to work with and choose Configure.

3. Choose the Security Options tab; then click Windows NT Integrated for the security mode.

4. Click OK to commit the change.

5. Right-click the server you're working with and choose Stop. Wait a minute or so and then right-click the server you're working with and choose Start.

That's all there is to turning on integrated security. Use the same procedure to turn it off but choose standard in step 3 instead of integrated.

2. Adding Logins with the Security Manager

In this exercise, you add and remove users to and from SQL Server in integrated security mode by using the SQL Security Manager:

1. Start the SQL Server Security Manager.

2. Enter the name of the server that you want to work with and click Connect.

3. Make sure that the SQL Server Security Manager is in User mode by choosing View and selecting User Privilege from the menu.

4. From the Security menu, choose Grant New.

5. Choose a Windows NT group from your domain, preferably one with a small number of members. Click Grant to start the grant process.

6. Click Done when the grant is finished.

7. Click Done again to close the Grant User Privilege dialog box.

8. Choose Security and select Revoke from the menu. Click Yes to revoke the user rights.

9. Click the Error Detail button to view the errors. All the errors are due to users that didn't exist in every database (this should be most of them) and are normal errors. Click Done to close this box.

10. Choose File and select Exit to close the Security Manager.

At this point, you should probably go back and do exercise 1 again. Choose standard security this time so that the exercises in the next chapter will work.

6

Answers to Questions

1. **B**   Because all the users have Windows NT accounts on the network, it doesn't make sense to use the standard or mixed modes.

2. **A**   The users might be using network protocols that don't allow RPC, and they don't have Windows NT accounts already.

3. **B, D**   SQL Executive doesn't have anything to do with integrated security. In addition, there are already administrators because the local Administrators group is mapped in when integrated security is activated.

4. **C**   The backslash character is not legal; it has to be mapped. This eliminates choice B. Because the user isn't in the default domain, his domain must be part of his login. This eliminates choices A and D.

5. **C**   The other library that works is the Multi-Protocol library. TCP/IP Sockets and SPX don't rely on RPC and therefore can't use integrated security.

6. **A**   The information is stored in the Registry.

7. **B**   Only one security mode can be used at a time. Neither standard nor integrated enable all the users in these situations to access the server.

8. **D**   Choice A is more complex than choice D and probably doesn't provide the necessary information anyway. Choice B pulls the same information from the same sources as the User Activity screen. Choice C shows when the users connected and disconnected but not what the users did.

9. **B**   Choice A doesn't work. Choices C and D work but are much more trouble and effort than choice B.

10. **D**   When integrated security is used, it doesn't matter what is entered in the login and password boxes.

TEST DAY FAST FACTS

This chapter discusses managing user accounts. The following are some key facts you'll learn in this chapter:

- Logins are stored in the Master database and are used to authenticate users.

- Users are associated with databases and are used to link logins into a specific database so that they can be granted permissions for that database.

- Each login can be mapped to one or zero users in a database.

- A user belongs to one or two groups. Users always belong to the group *public*. They can belong to one other administator-provided group.

- To remove a user from a group, add the user to the group *public*. That will remove the user's existing group membership.

- The user account called *guest* is used if someone with a login attempts to access a database that she doesn't have a user account in.

- The special user account called dbo, or database owner, is allowed to add and remove users from a database and manage security inside the database.

Day 7

Managing User Accounts

Day 6, "Implementing SQL Server Security," went through the process of choosing a security mode (standard, mixed, or integrated). Now, on Day 7, you're going to examine logins, database users, and techniques for managing these objects. You'll look at what logins and users are and how they interact. Then you'll examine how logins and users can be created using both SQL stored procedures and the Enterprise Manager. Finally, you'll learn about database user groups, including how to add and remove users from groups.

Objectives

This chapter covers the following material:

- Differentiate between a SQL Server login and a SQL Server user
- Create a login ID
- Add a database user
- Add and drop users for a group

TEST DAY
FAST FACTS

- User information is stored in the sysusers table in each database. User information includes all the group information.

- Login information is stored in the syslogins table in the Master database only.

7.1. Users and Logins

In SQL Server, the words *login* and *user* refer to two distinct object types with which a SQL Server interacts. A *login* is a serverwide entity that enables a person to interact with all databases on a server. A *user* is an object linked to one or more logins that provides access rights to a database.

When a user is given a login, he immediately is able to log in to the server. Unless there are users mapped to the login, however, the user can't do very much. A login is similar to a driver's license. It provides the bearer with the authority to drive, but it doesn't provide access to a car.

When a login is mapped to a database user, however, it's like providing the keys to a car. It gives the bearer of a driver's license (a login) the capability to drive one car (a database). One login can be granted access into several databases, just as someone with a driver's license can have keys for several different cars. It doesn't make much sense, however, to give a person with a driver's license multiple sets of keys to the same car. Likewise, a login can be mapped into each database only one time.

Every database has a table called sysusers that contains all the users in the database and all the logins that map to them. Only the Master database contains the syslogins table, which tracks logins and passwords.

7.2. Creating Logins

This chapter, like many others in this book, shows you two different procedures for completing tasks. First you'll learn how to perform a given task using SQL Server stored procedures and Transact-SQL statements. You'll then go through the same process using the SQL Server Enterprise Manager.

It is very simple to create a login in Transact-SQL. The stored procedure to run is `sp_addlogin`. This stored procedure takes up to four parameters, but only the first one is required. The following are the parameters:

- `Login_ID`. This is the login ID to be created. It is the only required argument, and it must be a legal SQL Server object name.
- Password. This is the password for the user. It usually left blank, but it can be set to anything.
- Default database. This is the name of the database used when the login signs on to ISQL or ISQL/W. If no default database is entered, the login defaults to Master.
- Default language. This is the default language for the user.

The following is an example of using this procedure:

```
sp_addlogin "cmiller", "password", "SMS"
```

In this example, a login is created called cmiller, the default database is set to SMS, and the password is set to password. Specifying a default database here does not add the user to the database; it simply defaults the user. If the login is not mapped into the database, the login automatically tries to use the guest user in the default database. If a login attempts to connect to a database it does not have access to, SQL Server attempts to map the login to the guest user. If there is no guest user, the connection attempt is denied. Software such as ISQL/W then attaches the login to the Master database, where there is a guest user.

The sp_addlogin stored procedure inserts records into the syslogins table in the Master database. It also adds the appropriate information into the table, including the login name, the default database, an encrypted version of the password, an identification number called *suid*, and the default language information. The suid is used in the sysusers table of each database to link a user to a login. Both the suid and the login name must be unique.

The following steps show you how to add a user using the SQL Server Enterprise Manager:

1. Start the SQL Server Enterprise Manager.
2. Connect to the server you want to work on by clicking the plus sign to the left of its name.
3. Click the plus sign to the left of the Logins folder. This displays a list of the current logins.
4. Right-click the Logins folder and choose New Login from the pop-up menu. The Manage Logins dialog box opens, as shown in Figure 7.1.
5. Fill in the Login Name and Password boxes.
6. If you want, you can choose a default language from the drop-down box.
7. In the table, you can choose the databases into which the login will be allowed. Simply click in the Permit column next to the database name.
8. To select which database will be the default database for the login, click in the Default column next to the database's name.
9. In the User column, choose the username that will be mapped to the login.

7

Figure 7.1.

Enter a login name and password, click the Add button, and you've created a login.

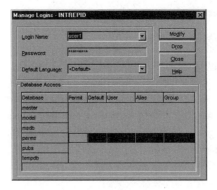

10. Click Add to add the login. If you have specified a password for the user, you are prompted to enter that password again.

Unlike when using Transact-SQL, the Enterprise Manager creates the database user for the login in the default database and in any other database with a check mark in the Permit column. The User and Alias columns are discussed in the next section. Keep in mind that using the Enterprise Manager performs the same tasks and affects the same tables as typing in the Transact-SQL.

7.3. Creating Users and Aliases

Now that a login has been created, how do you map the login to a user? If you're only using the SQL Server Enterprise Manager, you're one step ahead of the game. It's important for you to understand, however, that two distinct steps are happening. First a login is created, and then the login is mapped to a database user.

You can grant a login access to a database in three ways. The first and most commonly used method is to create a new user and map the user to a login. The second method is to create an alias, giving one login the same access privileges as another specified login. Finally, a guest user can be used to provide access to a database. The following sections examine these access methods in more detail.

Note

All the exercises and procedures in this chapter are designed to work with standard security, even though the concepts are the same with integrated security or mixed security. The reason standard security is used is because performing the same exercises using an integrated authentication would require you to log in and out of Windows NT over and over to be authenticated properly.

7.3.1. Adding Users to Databases

Under normal circumstances, each login is mapped to one user in every database the login needs to access, and each user can be traced back to one login. For normal database users, this is the desired state of affairs because it enables database rights and privileges to be set for each user. It also provides maximum flexibility in assigning groups. To add a user to a database using Transact-SQL, use the sp_adduser stored procedure. This procedure takes up to three arguments, but only the first argument is required. The following are the arguments:

- Login ID. The login ID for the user to be mapped.
- User ID. The user ID to be created in the database. If this parameter is omitted, a user with the same name as the login name is added to the database. This is the most common usage.
- Group. The group to which to add the user. Groups are discussed later in this chapter.

The stored procedure operates only on the current database. Make sure to use the database to which you want to add the user prior to executing the stored procedure. The following example adds a user called cmiller—mapped to a login called cmiller—into the current database:

```
Sp_adduser "cmiller"
```

Use the following steps to perform the same operation using the SQL Server Enterprise Manager:

1. Start the Enterprise Manager.
2. Expand the server you want to work on.
3. Expand the database to which you want to add the user.
4. Right-click the Groups/Users folder and choose New User. This opens the Manage Users dialog box, as shown in Figure 7.2.

Figure 7.2.

Use the Manage Users dialog box to add or modify users.

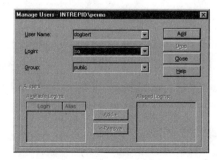

7

5. Enter the name of the user to add and then choose the matching login from the drop-down list.

6. Click Add to add the user to the database.

You now have a new user in the database. You can continue to add users, or you can click Close to close the dialog box.

7.3.2. Aliasing Logins

A login can be aliased to a user. This enables one database user to have multiple logins mapped to it. This also enables privileges to be set one time, which will affect multiple logins. Most commonly, this is used for the special user called *dbo*. The dbo, or database owner, has special rights in each database to perform maintenance and administrative tasks. (These rights are discussed in the next chapter.) The user *sa* always is mapped to the dbo login. Other users, however, can be aliased to the login. This gives them administrative rights over the database without providing login rights to administer the entire SQL Server.

It is important to realize that an alias must be attached to an existing user. A login must be directly mapped to the user using the sp_adduser command. This login can be considered the *owner* of the user. Aliases then can be added to the existing user.

To add an alias using Transact-SQL, use the sp_addalias stored procedure. This procedure takes two arguments, both of which are required.

- Login ID. This is the login ID to be mapped to the database. It is important that the login ID not already be mapped to a user in the current database, either as a created user or as an alias to another user.

- User. This is the name of the user to which to be aliased. This user must already exist in the database.

To alias the login cmiller to the user dbo in the current database, for example, execute the following:

```
Sp_addalias "cmiller", "dbo"
```

For this example to work, the login cmiller cannot be mapped to any users in the current database. The user dbo must exist, which always is the case.

In the SQL Enterprise Manager, aliases are added using the Manage Users dialog box. The following steps show you how to accomplish this.

1. Start the Enterprise Manager.

2. Expand the server you want to work on.

3. Expand the database to which you want to add the user.

4. Right-click the Groups/Users folder and choose New User. This opens the Manager Users dialog box, which is used to manage aliases and to add users.

5. In the User Name drop-down box, choose the user to which to be aliased. This populates the Aliases frame at the bottom of the dialog box.

6. Choose the login to be aliased under Available Logins in the Aliases frame of the dialog box. Click the Add button.

7. Click Modify to confirm the changes.

This is how you add an alias to a user using the Enterprise Manager. Aliases usually are only used for the database owner to provide administrative roles to multiple logins.

7.3.3. System Logins and Users

If you've been following the instructions for creating users and snooping around in system tables, you've probably noticed a few logins and users you didn't create lurking on your server and in your databases. These are the probe, repl_publisher, and repl_subscriber users, as shown in Figure 7.3. The probe login—and its included probe user in the Master database—are used by the system to handle the two-phase commit part of transaction handling. The other logins, repl_publisher and repl_subscriber, are used by the replication services. See Day 12, "SQL Server Replication," for more details.

Figure 7.3.

The Server Manager window contains the repl_publisher, repl_subscriber, and probe users.

7

If you've been experimenting with these concepts as you read, you've probably added a bunch of users and logins to your databases and are wondering "How to I get rid of this mess?" The answer is in the following section.

7.4. Dropping Aliases, Users, and Logins

Now that you've learned how to add logins, users, and aliases, you need to know how to remove them. First you'll learn how to remove aliases and then you'll examine dropping users and logins.

7.4.1. Dropping Aliases

You can drop an alias in two ways. First, you can directly drop the alias using the Transact-SQL stored procedure `sp_dropalias` or by using the SQL Enterprise Manager. Second, you can drop the user to which the alias is attached. Dropping a user automatically drops all aliases associated with that user.

To explicitly drop an alias using Transact-SQL, use the `sp_dropalias` command. The only argument is the login to be removed from the alias. To remove the user cmiller from the dbo alias in the current database, use the following command:

```
Sp_dropalias "cmiller"
```

The login cmiller can only be linked to one user, either directly or by an alias. This completes the job of removing the alias with no ambiguity.

Use the following steps to perform the same task in the Enterprise Manager:

1. Start the Enterprise Manager.
2. Expand the server you want to work on.
3. Expand the database to which you want to add the user.
4. Right-click the Groups/Users folder and choose New User. This opens the Manager Users dialog box, which is used to manage aliases and to add users.
5. In the User Name drop-down box, choose the user to be unaliased. This populates the Aliases frame at the bottom of the dialog box.
6. Choose the login to be unaliased under Aliased Logins in the Aliases frame of the dialog box. Click the Remove button.
7. Click Modify to confirm the changes.

This is how you remove aliases. Remember that alias information is stored in the sysalternates table of each database. Removing the alias deletes the corresponding record in the table. The next section shows you how to remove users.

7.4.2. Dropping Users

Dropping a user removes a login's capability to access a database. Users are dropped when they no longer need access to a database or prior to the corresponding login being dropped. All mapped users must be removed prior to a login being dropped. The database owner cannot be dropped. The database owner can, however, be changed to another login using the sp_changedbowner stored procedure. This takes only one parameter—the login ID of the new owner.

To drop a user in Transact-SQL, use the stored procedure sp_dropuser. This procedure automatically removes any aliases to the user. It then drops the user from the catalog. This procedure takes only one parameter—the username to be dropped. To drop the user cmiller from the current database, use the following command:

```
Sp_dropuser "cmiller"
```

This command checks for aliases in the sysalternates table and removes them. It then removes the entry for the user in sysusers.

Use the following steps to drop users in the SQL Enterprise Manager:

1. Start the Enterprise Manager.
2. Expand the server you want to work on.
3. Expand the database to which you want to add the user.
4. Right-click the Groups/Users folder and choose New User. This opens the Manager Users dialog box.
5. In the User Name drop-down box, choose the user to be dropped. This populates the Aliases frame at the bottom of the dialog box. You can see whether the aliases being removed will cause any problems.
6. Click the Drop button to drop the user.

Alternatively, you can simply right-click the user and choose Delete. This does not provide the opportunity to first view any aliases that might be affected by the drop.

Note

This is a side note for application programmers to keep in mind when dropping users. It is convenient to use the *uid* value in programs and tables to track changes. Although this might seem like a great idea, don't do it. The problem is that numbers in the uid field get reused. After a user is dropped, the next user added picks up the uid of the dropped user. This causes all sorts of misdirection when attempting to tie back an audit trail in the application.

7

7.4.3. Dropping Logins

Dropping logins is similar to dropping users. Much more complex checking must be done, however, to prevent orphaning users in the database. An *orphaned user* is a user that does not have a login mapped to it. Whenever a login is dropped, SQL Server first checks to make sure that the login doesn't exist in any system tables. Depending on which tool you are using, SQL Server either does not remove the login or automatically removes the associated users and aliases.

To remove a user using Transact-SQL, use the `sp_droplogin` stored procedure. This procedure has only one argument—the login to be dropped. If there are users or aliases dependent on the login, SQL Server responds by telling you which databases contain dependent objects and by providing the dependent objects' names. If dependencies exist, you need to go into each database and clear them using `sp_dropuser` or `sp_dropalias`. If the user is the database owner, you need to use `sp_changedbowner` to change ownership to a different login prior to dropping the login.

Use the following steps to drop a login using the SQL Server Enterprise Manager:

1. Start the Enterprise Manager.
2. Expand the server you want to work on.
3. Expand the Logins folder.
4. Find the login to be deleted and double-click it. This opens the Manage Logins dialog box.
5. Review the affected user and alias information and then choose Drop to drop the user. A message box asks to confirm the drop. Choose Yes to drop the login.

Alternatively, you can right-click the login and click the Delete option. This does not provide the opportunity to view the alias and user information prior to deletion.

7.5. How Databases Are Used

When a login attempts to use a database, the sysusers table is accessed to locate a user for the login. If that fails, the sysalternates table is scanned to determine whether the login is aliased to another login in this database. If both these attempts at mapping a login to a user fail, the system attempts to map the login to the guest user (if a guest user exists in the target database). If that fails, the user is denied access.

7.5.1. The Guest User

If a login is not directly mapped or aliased to a user, there still is one other way for a login to access a database. If a user called *guest* exists in the database, the login automatically maps to the guest login and will have all rights and privileges associated with that login. This can be seen as the *fall through* for authentication. It usually is not used because it is better to directly grant users permissions than to allow a guest. To allow the guest account to be used, create a user called Guest. It doesn't need to have a login mapped to it.

7.5.2. Changing the Database Ownership

The *database owner* is a user in the database that owns the objects in the database. Only one user is the database owner, or dbo, but several logins can be aliased to the dbo user. The dbo cannot be dropped. By default, this user is called *dbo*; a user mapped to the login is called *sa*. To change database ownership, you must use the `sp_changedbowner` stored procedure. This stored procedure is the only way to change ownership of a database; there is no analogous procedure in the Enterprise Manager. The stored procedure takes one argument—the login ID of the new owner. That login ID then is mapped to the dbo user.

7.6. Grouping Users

Managing users is a hassle. The biggest hassle is making sure users have access to the data they need but not to the data that is supposed to be out of reach. Fortunately, users tend to work in groups. This means groups of users tend to need the same level of access to the same data. SQL Server provides the capability to assign users into groups. Permissions then can be assigned that will apply to all members of the group.

A group is a database-level object. This means a group consists of users rather than logins. In addition, a user can belong to only one group at a time. Actually, make that two groups. In SQL Server, all users in a database—from the guest account to the database owner—have membership in a group called *public*. A user also can belong to one other, administrator-defined group. A user always is a member of the public group and might be a member of another group.

Let's say, for example, you have a group called Accounting and a group called Managers. If you have a group of managers in the accounting department, these users cannot be placed in both the Accounting and Managers groups. The workaround for this is to create a third group (Accounting Managers, for example) that has the necessary membership and rights these users need to perform their duties.

7

Another use for groups comes with integrated security. When integrated security is used to add a Windows NT group to a database with logins and users in a specific database, a group with the same name is created in each database, and all the users are added to this group by the Security Manager. By leveraging this capability, the database administrator can reduce the amount of work necessary to create groups.

7.6.1. Creating Groups and Adding Users to Groups

As with many other tasks in SQL Server, there are two ways to approach adding groups. You can use either Transact-SQL or the Enterprise Manager. You can add groups using Transact-SQL by using the sp_addgroup stored procedure. This takes one parameter—the name of the group to add. The name must conform to SQL Server naming rules, and the name of the group cannot be the same as the name of a user. To add a user to a group, use the sp_changegroup stored procedure. The sp_changegroup procedure takes two arguments—the name of the group and the name of the user. To remove a user from a group, assign them to the public group.

> **Note**
>
> When using Transact-SQL to interact with users or groups, some interesting shortcuts can be used with names. If the name in question is not a keyword, the name does not need to be placed in quotes because SQL Server will figure out what you mean. If the name is a keyword, you need to use quotation marks. The safe bet is to always use quotation marks around names. This usually doesn't become a problem until you want to assign a user to the public group. The word *public* is a keyword.

The following are some sample statements with a description of what they do:

`sp_addgroup "Accounting"`	Adds a group called Accounting. The quotation marks around the word Accounting are not necessary.
`sp_changegroup "accounting","cmiller"`	Adds the user cmiller to the group accounting. Both the user and the group must exist. It's okay for the users to be in another group first. This yanks them out of any group they are part of and puts them into accounting.

```
sp_changegroup "public","cmiller"
```
Removes the user cmiller from the group accounting by placing him into the group public.

> **Note**
>
> If you're going to use the guest account, make sure to remove it from the public group. Otherwise, any rights defined for public will also work for guest. Usually, a guest should be assigned as few rights as possible.

The following steps show you how to perform these operations in the Enterprise Manager:

1. Start the Enterprise Manager.
2. Expand the server you want to work on.
3. Expand the database to which you want to add the user.
4. Right-click the Groups/Users folder and choose New Group. This opens the Manage Groups dialog box, as shown in Figure 7.4.

Figure 7.4.

The Manage Groups dialog box is used to add and remove groups and to modify membership.

5. Enter a name for the group.
6. Select users to be part of the group. The users are listed in the Users list box. Choose users and click the Add button to add them. Users are shown with the name of their current group in parentheses, such as cmiller(public).
7. After all the users are added, click Add to add the group.

To modify group membership, double-click the group and remove the users. This procedure is similar to the preceding one. This puts the users back into the public group automatically.

7.6.2. Dropping Groups

Groups can be removed from databases similar to how users are removed from databases. The Transact-SQL command is sp_dropgroup. The one catch to performing sp_dropgroup with Transact-SQL is that the group must be empty. All users must be changed to different groups prior to the group being dropped. If you attempt to drop a group with members using sp_dropgroup, this error message displays: `Group has members. It must be empty before it can be dropped.` SQL Server also displays a list of users who are still members. This makes it easy to figure out what needs to be done.

Use the following steps to drop a group using the Enterprise Manager:

1. Start the Enterprise Manager.
2. Expand the server you want to work on.
3. Expand the database to which you want to add the user.
4. Expand the Groups/Users folder.
5. Double-click the group you want to drop.
6. Check to make sure that there aren't any surprises in the list of users and then click Drop. All users in the group automatically are reassigned to the public group, and the group is dropped.

Alternatively, you can right-click on the group and choose Drop. However, this does not give you the opportunity to review the group membership prior to the drop.

7.6.3. Users, Groups, and System Tables

Groups and users are maintained in the sysusers table in every database. The sysusers table has entries for suid, uid, gid, and name. A typical entry for a user includes the suid for the user in the syslogins table; a uid, which is the user's ID in the local database; and a gid, which maps to the group. A gid actually points back to the sysusers table in the uid column. A group is defined as a row in the sysusers table in which the gid equals the uid. For the public group, this means both the gid and the uid are zero. User-defined groups start numbering at uid = 16,384, so it's fairly easy to determine whether an entry is a user or a group based on its uid. The following is an example of the table layout with some groups and users added to it.

suid	uid	gid	name
-16,384	16,384	16,384	Group1
-2	0	0	public
11	1	0	dbo
13	3	16,384	User2

In this example, you can see there are two groups, Group1 and public, because they have a uid equal to a gid. The dbo user has a uid of 1, which always is the case, and a gid of 0, which shows that the dbo user is part of the group public. In addition, the User2 account is part of the group Group1 because of its gid. All the - defined groups have negative numbers assigned to them. These are *int* fields, which have a range of over 4 billion. Using negative numbers for groups, therefore, doesn't impact the number of users you can support until you pass the 2 billion mark.

7.7. Users, Aliases, and System Tables

When a user is added to a database, a new row is inserted into the sysusers table in that database. The sysusers table contains the suid, which links back to the syslogins table; the uid, which is the user ID; a gid, or group ID; and the name of the user. Groups were discussed in the "Grouping Users" section earlier in this chapter.

When an alias is created in a database, the suid of both the login being aliased and the login being aliased to are inserted into the sysalternates table. The sysalternates table contains only suids. If a login has an alias, it actually is mapped to a login that is mapped to the user ID.

7

Lab

The following are some questions and exercises for you to work through. The review questions are similar to questions you'll see on the exam. The exercises take you through the procedures in this chapter with step-by-step instructions so that you can see how everything works.

Questions

1. The administrator is having problems creating an account for his new assistant DBA, Dave. Dave needs to manage two databases on the server, but he should not have rights to all the databases. The server is configured correctly for standard security. How can the administrator best accomplish this task?

   A. Give Dave the password for the sa login.

   B. Create a login for Dave and use db_changeowner to give Dave ownership rights in the appropriate databases.

   C. Create a login for Dave and alias his login to the dbo user in the appropriate databases.

   D. Use the Security Manager to assign Dave the database owner privilege.

2. After a couple weeks, the administrator fires Dave, his assistant DBA. The server is still running with standard security in place. What is the best way for the administrator to remove Dave's access from the server?

   A. Delete Dave's login using the Security Manager.

   B. Use sp_droplogin to drop Dave's login.

   C. Manually edit the syslogins table to remove all traces of Dave.

   D. Use sp_dropalias for each database Dave is aliased in, use sp_dropuser for every database Dave has a user in, and use sp_droplogin to drop Dave's login.

3. The administrator needs to assign a user named Phil to three different groups inside the Accounting database. How can the administrator perform this operation?

   A. Use sp_addusertogroup to add Phil into the groups.

   B. Add Phil to three different Windows NT groups and grant the groups permissions using the Security Manager.

    C. Users can belong to only one group; this cannot be done.

    D. Use sp_changegroup to move Phil into all three groups.

4. The administrator needs to provide all logins with a limited amount of access to a database. What is the best approach for reaching this goal?

    A. Add users for all the logins and assign them access individually.

    B. Add users for all the logins, add the users to a group, and assign access to the group.

    C. Add the Windows NT group Everyone into the access control list for the database files.

    D. Add a user account called Guest and assign access to it as appropriate.

5. Assuming the Guest user exists, which of the following situations would cause a login to access a database using the Guest user?

    A. The login has no assigned user or alias in the target database.

    B. The login has an assigned user but wants to log in as Guest for read-only access.

    C. The login does not have a corresponding Windows NT account.

    D. The login does not have an assigned user in the database, but it is aliased to dbo.

6. The administrator wants to remove a user named Ann from the group Accounting. Which Transact-SQL statement performs this task?

    A. `sp_removegroup "Ann", "Accounting"`

    B. `sp_changegroup "Ann", "Public"`

    C. `sp_removeuserfromgroup "Ann", "Accounting"`

    D. `sp_usergroup "Ann", "Accounting", "Remove"`

7. The administrator needs to remove the group Temps from a database. The group currently has five members that need to be reassigned into the Accounting group. How can the administrator perform this task?

    A. Drop the group using `sp_dropgroup`.

    B. Change the users to new groups using `sp_changegroup` and then drop the group.

7

      C. Drop the users from the database and then drop the group.

      D. Drop the group using `sp_dropgroup` and then reassign the users using `sp_changegroup`.

8. Which database holds the sysusers table?

      A. All user-defined databases have a sysusers table.

      B. All databases have a sysusers table.

      C. The Master database.

      D. The sysusers table is stored in the Windows NT Registry.

9. Which database holds the syslogins table?

      A. All user-defined databases have a syslogins table.

      B. All databases have a syslogins table.

      C. The Master database.

      D. The syslogins table is stored in the Windows NT Registry.

10. The administrator needs to map his sa login to a new user while maintaining its alias to dbo. How can the administrator accomplish this goal?

      A. Use `sp_adduser` to create a new user in the database.

      B. Use `sp_addalias` to map sa to dbo and then use `sp_addalias` to map sa to an existing user account.

      C. This goal cannot be accomplished.

      D. Create a new user using `sp_cloneadmin`.

Exercises

The following exercises assume the server is in standard security mode. If you need help, see Day 6. These exercises are interdependent and must be done in order.

1. Adding Logins

Note

This exercise helps to address the following certification exam objective:
- Create a login ID

In this exercise, you'll add three logins. The first two are added with the SQL Enterprise Manager; the third is added using Transact-SQL.

1. Start the SQL Enterprise Manager.

2. Expand the server you want to work on.

3. Right-click Logins and choose New Login. The Manage Logins dialog box opens.

4. Enter the login name User1 and click Add button.

5. Click in the Login Name box, delete the text User1, and enter User2. Click the Add button.

6. Click the Close button to close the Manage Logins dialog box.

7. Choose Tools | SQL Query Tool from the menu to open a Query window.

8. Execute the following command:

```
sp_addlogin "user3"
```

SQL Server responds with New login created.

9. Type sp_helplogins and click the Execute button to see the list of available logins. User1, User2, and User3 appear in the listing. Close the Query window.

In the next exercise, you'll create users to match these logins.

2. Adding Database Users

 Note This exercise helps to address the following certification exam objective:
■ Add a database user

In this exercise, you'll add users to the pubs database that are linked to the logins created in exercise 1:

1. From the Server Manager window, expand the Databases folder and expand the pubs database.

2. Right-click the Groups/Users folder and choose New User. This opens the Manage Users dialog box.

3. In the User Name field, type User1. In the Login drop-down list, choose User1. Click Add to add User1 to the pubs database mapped to the login User1.

7

4. In the User Name drop-down list, choose dbo. In the Available Logins list box, choose User2. Click Add. This aliases User2 as a database owner. Click Modify to commit the changes.

5. Click Close to close the Manage Users dialog box. Choose Tools I SQL Query Tool to start a SQL Query window.

6. Make sure Pubs is chosen in the Db: drop-down list on the toolbar of the SQL Query window. Enter `sp_adduser User3, User3` and click the Execute button. This adds User3 to the database pubs, mapped to the login User3.

7. Enter `sp_helpuser` and click the Execute button to show the list of available users in the pubs database. User1 and User3 are listed in the first table. The second report shows that you aliased User2 in as dbo. Close the Query window.

In the next exercise, you'll work with groups.

3. Working with Groups

Note | This exercise helps to address the following certification exam objective:
■ Add and drop users for a group

In this exercise, you'll add the users created in exercise 2 to groups in the pubs database:

1. In the Server Manager window, make sure that the correct server is chosen. The Databases folder should be expanded, the pubs database should be expanded, and the Groups/Users folder should be expanded. Right-click the group Public and choose Refresh to ensure that the list of users is up-to-date. Whenever you mix Transact-SQL and the Enterprise Manager, if things don't look quite right, use this feature to synchronize the views. Under the group Public, you should see dbo, User1, and User3.

2. Right-click Groups/Users and click New Group. The Manage Groups dialog box opens.

3. For the name of the group, enter Group1. Choose User1 and User3 and click the Add-> button to add the users to the group. Click the Add button to create the group. Be careful, two different buttons have the word Add on them. Click Close to close the dialog box.

4. You should now see the group Group1 with users User1 and User3 in the pubs database within the Server Manager window. Choose Tools I SQL Query Tool to open a SQL Query window.

5. In the SQL Query window, make sure that the correct database, pubs, is in the drop-down box in the title bar. Type `sp_addgroup group2` and click the Execute button. This adds a new group to the pubs database.

6. Type `sp_changegroup Group2, User1` and click the Execute button. This moves User1 into Group2.

7. Type `sp_dropgroup Group1` and click the Execute button. An error message states that Group1 has members. This is because User3 was forgotten. Move User3 to the new group using `sp_changegroup` and then try to drop Group1 again. SQL Server responds with `Group has been dropped`.

8. Use `sp_changegroup` to move both users into the public group and then drop the group Group2.

Answers to Questions

1. **C**   Choice A provides Dave with system administrator access to the server. Choice B makes Dave the owner, which works but isn't as good as choice C. Choice D won't work because the Security Manager doesn't do anything on servers using integrated security.

2. **D**   Choice A requires integrated security, which isn't running on the server. Choice B won't work as long as user Dave is aliased or has users in any databases. You shouldn't ever edit system tables directly, so choice C is out. Choice D is the most complete answer.

3. **C**   Users only can belong to one group, so none of the other answers work.

4. **D**   Choices A and B both work, but choice D incurs the least administrative overhead. Choice C won't work.

5. **A**   Choice A is the only reason a login maps to the Guest account.

6. **B**   The only way to remove a user from a group is to explicitly assign that user to the Public group.

7. **B**   The group cannot be dropped using `sp_dropgroup` until it has no members, so choices A and D won't work. Choice C is less efficient because the users have to be re-added to the database so that they can be assigned to the Accounting group.

7

8. **B**   All databases have a sysusers table because all databases have distinct mappings of logins to users.

9. **C**   The Master database holds the only copy of logins and passwords.

10. **C**   Each login can map to, at most, one user in each database. Because the login sa already is mapped to dbo, it cannot be mapped to any other user.

Day 8

Managing User Permissions

In the preceding two chapters, you learned how to create logins, users, and groups. You'll now see how that foundation applies to securing your databases. This chapter covers object ownership, statement and object permissions, the process of granting and revoking permissions, and the pitfalls of user-based security.

Objectives

This chapter covers the following material:

- Grant and revoke permissions
- Predict the outcome of a broken ownership chain
- Identify system administrator functionality
- Implement various methods of securing access to data

8.1. Object Ownership

All objects in SQL Server have an object owner, including all databases and database objects. A *database object* is a table, view, stored procedure, rule, user-defined datatype, or default. The owner of an object, by default, is the user who created that object. If the system administrator creates a database, the system administrator login then links to the dbo (database owner) user in the database. If a user creates a table, that user has permissions for that table.

All database objects have owners. The ownership of an object is part of the object's name. Until now, all objects have been owned by the database owner. If you wanted to select the contents of the authors table in the pubs database, you could type `select * from authors`. Now, however, if a user named joe creates a Recipes table in the pubs database, to access that table you need to use a more fully qualified name for that object—joe.Recipes. Any user with the capability to create tables in the database can create a table named Recipes. The database can have joe.Recipes, mary.Recipes, phil.Recipes, and so on. When a user attempts to access an object without qualifying the user, he first attempts to access his own object and then the database owner's object.

The most fully qualified name for an object is `database.owner.object`, as in `pubs.dbo.authors`. As a shortcut, you can specify `pubs..authors`, and the user resolution just mentioned occurs (check for user objects and then check for database owner objects).

Note
> On most production systems, objects are owned by the database owners, and databases are owned by the system administrator. With SQL Server, however, you have to learn how to deal with user ownership of objects.

8.2. Object and Statement Permissions: An Introduction

Permissions are attributes a user account must have to perform certain operations. SQL Server has two different types of permissions. *Object permissions* govern how a user interacts with an object—specifically, whether the user can select, delete, insert, or update rows in a table or can execute a stored procedure. *Statement permissions* cover creation and deletion of objects and backup and recovery of databases. Table

8.1 later in this chapter shows which statements can have permissions granted and how those permissions are set by default.

Certain users in a database are assigned default permissions based on the role they play in the database. There are four categories of users. The first category, system administrators, can create and drop databases and can configure the server. The system administrator always is the owner of the Master database. The second category, database owners, can create and manage objects within a database and can manage the database as a whole. An object owner, the third category, is the owner of a specific object. For a database, the dbo is the object owner. An object owner can grant or revoke permissions on the object and can drop the object. The fourth category, everyone else, is a catchall that includes all the database users that aren't database or object owners.

As you can see, these permissions overlap. The most common configuration is for the system administrator to be the database owner. In this case, the system administrator can create, drop, and manage databases and can manage the server. In addition, because the most common arrangement is for the database owner to own all objects in the database, the system administrator fills the first three categories, leaving ordinary users to fill the fourth.

Note | Every user in a database can create, access, and drop temporary tables, regardless of any statement or object permissions they have.

8.3. Object Permissions

Object permissions govern how users can interact with database objects. There are five different object permissions: Select, Insert, Update, Delete, and Execute. The first four apply to tables and views; Execute applies only to stored procedures. Object permissions are granted using the following Grant statement syntax for object permissions:

```
Grant <permission> on <object> to <user>
```

The preceding syntax contains the following placeholders:

> <permission>. Can be any combination of the permissions valid for that object type. The keyword all can be used instead of specifying all the permissions.

<object>. The object being granted on. This can be a table, a view, a list of columns within a table or view, or a stored procedure.

<user>. A list of one or more users or groups that will be granted the permission.

As just mentioned, permissions can be granted on an entire table or on columns within a table. The following is the syntax for this:

```
<table_name> (<column_list>)
```

In the preceding syntax, `column_list` is the list of column names. The following is an example:

```
Grant all on pubs..authors(au_id, au_lname, au_fname) to public
```

This grants the `public` group rights on the three specified columns in the pubs database. Next, you'll build a database you can use to experiment with permissions.

This tutorial shows you how to set up the database you're going to use to experiment with permissions. The database, Perms, will have a copy of the objects in the pubs database with no permissions set.

1. Open the SQL Enterprise Manager and connect to the server. Make sure that standard security is turned on.

2. Right-click Database Devices and choose New Device. This opens the New Database Device dialog box.

3. Enter `PermsDev` as a name for the device.

4. Choose a disk drive and path for the device.

5. Create a 5MB device by clicking in the Size (MB): box and changing it to `5`.

6. Click Create Now to create the device. You should see the message `The database device was successfully created`. Click OK.

7. Right-click the Databases folder and choose New Database. This opens the New Database dialog box.

8. In the Name box, enter `Perms`.

9. In the Data Device drop-down list, choose PermsDev.

10. Click Create Now. The database is created.

11. Expand the Logins folder. Using the procedures outlined on Day 6, "Implementing SQL Server Security," drop User1, User2, and User3 if they exist.

8

12. Create new users by right-clicking the Logins folder and choosing New Login. Enter the name User1 and click the Permit column next to the Perms database. This automatically creates the user User1 in the database. Click Add and close the dialog box.

13. Repeat step 12 to create User2 and User3.

14. Expand the Databases folder and right-click the pubs database. Choose Transfer.

15. In the Destination area, choose the destination database Perms.

16. Turn off Use Default Scripting Options and click the Scripting Options button. This opens the Transfer Scripting Options dialog box, as shown in Figure 8.1. Turn off all four options in the Security Scripting section of the dialog box. Click OK.

Figure 8.1.

This is how the Scripting Options dialog box should look in step 16.

17. Click Start Transfer to copy the pubs database objects into the Perms database. The Transfer in Progress status window appears and enables you to monitor the status of the transfer. The transfer finishes with this message: Transfer was completed successfully. Click OK and close the Transfer dialog box.

18. Open ISQL/W. Log in as User1. Enter the query Select * from authors. You will receive this error message: SELECT permission denied on object authors, database Perms, owner dbo. Because none of the permissions were transferred from the pubs database to the Perms database, none of the users have permissions to any objects.

19. Open a Query window in the SQL Enterprise Manager. Because the server was registered to use the sa login, all Query windows are logged in as sa. In the Database drop-down list, choose Perms. Execute the same query as in step 18 (Select * from authors). You will receive the contents of the authors table.

Because the system administrator created the Perms database, he owns all objects in the database and has full permissions to all objects.

20. Grant User1 permission to select from the authors table by entering the following command into the SQL Enterprise Manager Query window:

```
Grant select on authors to User1
```

You will receive the following message:

```
The command did not return data, and it did not return any rows.
```

This means it worked.

21. In the ISQL/W program, re-execute the `Select * from authors` query. You will receive the same results as in step 19.

22. From the SQL Enterprise Manager, grant User1 access to the Title_id field in the Titles table by entering the following command:

```
Grant select on Titles(title_id) to User1.
```

23. From ISQL/W, perform the query `Select * from titles`. You will get an error message for every column in the titles table to which User1 does not have access. Perform the query `Select title_id from titles` to see the title IDs.

In this tutorial, you established the base for experimentation with permissions. You also started to see the results of insufficient permissions on objects.

Now that you've seen how permissions are set, you should see how they are revoked. Permissions are revoked using the `Revoke` command's object syntax. The following is the syntax:

```
Revoke <permission> on <object> from <user>
```

The different parameters mean the same thing on both `Grant` and `Revoke` statements. Revoking permissions a user does not have does not cause an error message. You also can grant permissions for a table and then revoke specific columns from the table, if necessary.

8.3.1. Grant Options

If an object owner wants to enable another user to grant permissions on an object, add `with grant option` to the end of the grant statement. The following is an example:

```
Grant select on myauthors to user2 with grant option
```

This enables User2 to grant other users access to the object. User2, however, cannot specify more rights than he has. In this example, User2 can only grant `Select` permissions. When `with grant option` is specified, the user specified must be a user; the user cannot actually be a group. When revoking permissions, if the user being revoked has `grant` options and has granted another user permissions, a standard `Revoke` statement does not remove the permissions. Instead, you should use the following:

```
Revoke <permission> on <object> from <user> with cascade
```

This revokes the user's permissions. Any permissions the user granted to other users also are revoked. Another interesting point to note is the changed behavior of the following statement:

```
Grant all on myauthors to User3
```

With the chaining of grants, the keyword `all` refers to all the permissions the current user has instead of `Select`, `Insert`, `Update`, and `Delete`.

8.3.2. Alternative Syntax

There is an alternative syntax to use with the `Grant` statement. This syntax changes where the column names are in the statement. The new syntax specifies the column names next to the permission being applied instead of next to the table. The following is an example:

```
Grant select(au_id, au_lname, au_fname), update(au_lname, au_fname) on authors to
➥User2
```

This grants User2 the capability to select the three fields but to update only the last two. Previously, this would have been the following two statements:

```
Grant select on authors(au_id, au_lname, au_fname) to User2
Grant update on authors(au_lname, au_fname) to User2
```

These two statements perform what the one statement in the new syntax performs. The following new syntax for a `Revoke` is similar:

```
Revoke select(au_id, au_lname, au_fname), update(au_lname, au_fname) on authors
➥from User2
```

Both forms of `Grant` and `Revoke` are valid, and they can be used interchangeably.

8.4. Ownership Chains

One of the most difficult and complicated concepts in SQL Server security is the ownership chain. At least one question on the exam will cover ownership chains.

When views or stored procedures are built, an ownership chain is created. An *ownership chain* is the list of owners of the dependent objects for a view or stored procedure. When SQL Server checks to see whether a user has permissions to select data from a given view, it checks the user's permissions on the view and then checks the ownership chain.

There are two types of ownership chains. When a view has an *unbroken ownership chain*, all of the objects referenced by the view are owned by the same user. If a user named Sam owns a table and then builds a view on that table, the ownership chain is unbroken.

A *broken ownership chain* occurs when a view relies on objects owned by more than one user. If Sam creates a view on a table belonging to Mary, the ownership chain is broken. There is nothing inherently wrong with broken ownership chains, and any database with multiple users creating views will probably have them. Understanding how permissions work inside an ownership chain is the important part.

> **Note**
>
> This tutorial assumes you completed the previous tutorial. Do not attempt this tutorial if you did not.

This tutorial shows you how to create user-defined objects for different users. It also examines the ownership chain:

1. Open the SQL Enterprise Manager and expand the server on which you want to work.

2. Open the Databases folder, right-click the Perms database, and choose Edit. In the Edit Database dialog box, click Options and enable the Select Into/Bulk Copy option.

3. While still in the Edit Database dialog box, click Permissions. This displays the statement permissions available for the users. Statement permissions are discussed further later in this chapter. For now, check the `Create Table` and `Create View` permissions for User1 (see Figure 8.2). Click OK to commit the changes.

Figure 8.2.

The Edit Database Permissions tab.

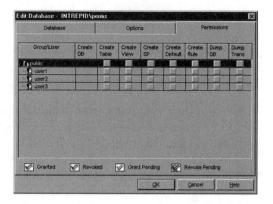

8

4. Open ISQL/W and log in as User1. Enter the following command:

```
Select au_id, au_lname, au_fname into MyAuthors from Authors.
```

This creates a new table, User1.MyAuthors.

5. Create a view on the table MyAuthors, as follows:

```
Create view vMyAuthors as Select * from MyAuthors
```

6. Grant select permission on the view to User2, as follows:

```
Grant Select on vMyAuthors to User2
```

7. Open a new ISQL/W window and log in as User2. Perform the query `Select * from User1.vMyAuthors`, and you get the rows in the view vMyAuthors. Perform the query `Select * from User1.MyAuthors`, and you get a permission denied error.

This tutorial shows a nonbroken ownership chain. Because User1 owns all the tables referenced by vMyAuthors, and because User1 granted access to User2, User2 can perform select queries on the view but not the table. When User2 attempts to access the data in User1.vMyAuthors, SQL Server checks permissions on vMyAuthors and then checks ownership the rest of the way down the chain. If the ownership remains the same—in this case User1 owns the table referenced by vMyAuthors—the permissions aren't checked. Essentially, SQL Server assumes that, because the same user owns the table and the view, the user knows what he is doing and allows access.

The tutorial provides an example of how an ownership chain can be used to control access to data. By providing the view to User2, User1 can grant the capability to select from the view without providing User2 with any knowledge of the underlying tables involved or any direct access to those tables. This is an effective means for providing database security because the owner of the underlying tables always has control over who is accessing the data. Without User1 granting access to the view, User2 cannot access the data. If User1 creates a view on a table to which User2 does not have access, such as a table belonging to the dbo, User2 cannot access the table. ⚹ The key is that permissions only are checked when ownership changes.

In this tutorial, User1 creates a view that relies on both the MyAuthors table and the dbo.Authors table. This creates a broken ownership chain. You'll then learn what can be done to give User2 access to the view.

1. Start ISQL/W and log in as User1.

2. Create a view using the following syntax:

```
create view vJoinedMyAuthors as
    select MyAuthors.au_id, phone
        from authors inner join myauthors
            on MyAuthors.au_id = Authors.au_id
GO
```

3. Grant User2 access to select from the view, as follows:

```
Grant select on vJoinedMyAuthors to User2
```

4. Start another ISQL/W session and log in as User2.

5. In the Query window, use the following query to select data from the vJoinedMyAuthors table:

```
Select * from User1.vJoinedMyAuthors
```

6. This doesn't work. You'll see the following error message:

```
SELECT permission denied on object authors, database Perms, owner dbo
```

SQL Server very nicely provides the name of the object, the database, and the object owner so that the user knows who to call to complain.

7. Start the SQL Server Enterprise Manager, expand the server with which you're working, and open a Query window. Remember, the SQL Server Enterprise Manager logs in as dbo in Perms. Use the following command to give User2 access to run the view:

```
Grant Select on Authors to User2
```

8. From the User2 ISQL/W session, rerun the query. To find out which ISQL/W session you are using, it's easiest to check the title bar of the Query window. It should read `Query - <Server>\Perms\User2`. The query works this time.

Use these steps to grant User2 access to the view. Because the ownership chain changed owners from User1.vJoinedMyAuthors to dbo.Authors, the permissions are checked on the dbo.Authors table. This results in the error message in step 6. After the owner grants permission to the base table, User2 is able to access the view because the permissions check out.

Ownership chains affect stored procedures this same way, as you will see in the Lab exercises at the end of this chapter.

8

8.5. Statement Permissions

Statement permissions grant users the capability to execute certain commands, such as object creation, object drop, and database backup. Statement permissions are tricky in two ways: how they are assigned and defaulted and how they interact with stored procedures.

8.5.1. Statement Permissions, Default Settings, and Who Can Do What

Statement permissions can have the following four roles:

- *System administrator.* The sa account or equivalent
- *Database owner.* The owner of the current database
- *Object owner.* The owner of the current object
- *User.* Anybody that isn't one of the preceding

Any user can fall into any role at any given time. A database owner using a database he doesn't own is just a normal user. A user that owns objects functions as an object owner when accessing those objects. This same user functions as a normal user when accessing other users' objects. The system administrator always is the system administrator, but he can be kept out of databases or objects he doesn't own. He then becomes a normal user.

With these roles in mind, the following are guidelines for figuring out who can do what:

- *Users have ownership of their connection.* This means they can change any properties of the connection, including starting, ending, or aborting transactions and setting variables that determine how the session behaves.
- *An object owner always can manage his objects.* Any object owner, including a database owner, can use Grant or Revoke statements to control who accesses his objects. An object owner can create indexes or triggers on his tables. A database owner can manage his database by changing its size or by backing it

up. An object owner also can drop his objects. The capability to manage an object is nontransferable.

- *An object owner can enable other users to create subobjects.* In other words, the system administrator can enable a user to create a database. That user then becomes the database owner. The database owner, in turn, can enable any user in his database to create other objects, such as tables, stored procedures, or views.

- *Everyone has access to tempdb.* Tempdb is used transparently by many queries, especially when ORDER BY is specified. All users must have access to create and destroy data in tempdb.

This describes, in general, the rules used to come up with Table 8.1. To get through the exam, you need to either know these rules or memorize this table.

Table 8.1. Statement permissions.

Statement	Default User	Transferable?
Create Database	sa	Yes
Alter Database	sa/dbo	Yes
Disk Init/Reinit/Refit	sa	No
Disk Mirror/Unmirror/Remirror	sa	No
Shutdown	sa	No
Kill	sa	No
Reconfigure	sa	No
Dump Database/Transaction	dbo	Yes
Load Database/Transaction	dbo	No
SetUser	dbo	No
Checkpoint	dbo	No
Grant/Revoke (statement)	dbo	No
Create Default Procedure/Rule/Table/View	dbo	Yes
Create Index/Trigger	Object owner	No
Drop Any Object	Object owner	No
Insert/Update/Delete	Object owner	Yes
Execute	Object owner	Yes

Statement	Default User	Transferable?
Grant/Revoke (object)	Object owner	Yes
Truncate Table	Object owner	No
Update Statistics	Object owner	No
UpdateText/WriteText/ReadText	Object owner	Yes
References	Object owner	Yes
Begin/Commit/Rollback/Save Transaction	Any	N/A
Set	Any	N/A
Print/Raiserror	Any	N/A

Now that you've learned about statement permissions, the next section examines how to assign them.

8.5.2. Granting Statement Permissions

Statement permissions are granted using the Grant command, just like object permissions. The following is the Grant command syntax for statement permissions:

```
Grant <statement> to <user>
```

The following is an example:

```
Grant create table to User1
```

This grants to User1 the permissions to create tables in the current database. In the SQL Enterprise Manager, use database properties to change permissions, as outlined in the preceding tutorial and as shown earlier in Figure 8.2.

8.5.3. Statement Permissions and Ownership Chains

*Permissions are not evaluated the same way on statements as on objects. If a stored procedure created by the dbo dumps a transaction log, for example, and if the creator grants Execute permissions on that procedure to a normal user, then SQL Server reports a permissions error when the user executes the stored procedure. The error is DUMP TRANSACTION permission denied, database Perms, owner dbo. If the permissions were evaluated as they are for objects, the user would be able to execute the stored procedure because the dbo owns the stored procedure and he granted access to the user.

In addition, if someone without Dump Transaction rights attempts to create a procedure that dumps the transaction log, the Create Procedure statement fails.

8.6. Permissions and System Tables

Changes in the permissions to access an object or to execute a statement are stored in the sysprotects table in the current database. It isn't necessary to know all the values or columns in the sysprotects table for the exam. You do, however, need to know how it works and what it does. The sysprotects table looks like Table 8.2.

Table 8.2. The sysprotects table.

ID	UID	Action	ProtectType	Columns	Grantor
1	0	193	205	0x01	1
0	3	198	205	(null)	1

The ID field is the object ID of the object affected. UID is the person granted to, and Grantor is the person that executed the grant statement. The Action field is derived from the following list:

26	REFERENCES
193	SELECT
195	INSERT
196	DELETE
197	UPDATE
198	CREATE TABLE
203	CREATE DATABASE
207	CREATE VIEW
222	CREATE PROCEDURE
224	EXECUTE
228	DUMP DATABASE
233	CREATE DEFAULT
235	DUMP TRANSACTION
236	CREATE RULE

The ProtectType column in Table 8.2 specifies what action is done, as follows:

204	GRANT_W_GRANT
205	GRANT
206	REVOKE

The GRANT_W_GRANT permission in Table 8.2 means the user specified in UID can grant permissions on the object in ID. The Columns field determines which columns are granted as a bitmask. If the first, second, and third columns are granted, for example, the value is 0x7 (binary 111 = hex 7). If the value is 0x0, all columns are granted. If it is null, the action granted doesn't have a column associated with it, such as Create Table.

In Table 8.2, the object with ID of 1 (sysobjects) has been granted (ProtectType 205) to UID 0 (the group Public) with the Select permission (Action 193). In the second row, the user with ID 3, which happens to be User1, is granted Create Table privileges. Notice in the second row that the Object ID is 0, and the Columns field is set to null.

8.7. The System Administrator Login

Throughout this chapter, there has been information about how the system administrator interacts with SQL Server. The system administrator account can do anything within a database. The system administrator account is directly responsible for the following:

- Creating logins
- Creating devices
- Configuring the server
- Allowing database creation

In addition, the system administrator can do the following:

- Operate on any table regardless of ownership or permissions
- Take ownership of databases
- Drop databases
- Stop the server
- Stop individual processes from running on a server

All the preceding options have been discussed except the first (operate on any table regardless of ownership or permissions), which will be discussed now.

The Setuser command enables the system administrator or any dbo to impersonate another user in the current database. This usually is used to create objects for a user with the user's ownership. It also can be used to recover data after a user leaves the company or to assimilate user data into dbo-owned tables. The command is used as follows:

```
Setuser <username> [with NoReset]
```

In the preceding, <username> represents the user to be impersonated. When the administrator's tasks are complete, execute Setuser with no options to become the system administrator again. If the NoReset option is used, then after Setuser takes effect, the administrator cannot resume being the administrator without disconnecting from the server.

If the sa login is used to attach to a database, the system administrator has dbo permissions in the database and can access any data in any table, regardless of ownership or permissions granted to the dbo. In other words, the sa login is above all security. If a database owner who is not the system administrator needs to access data in a user table to which he has not been granted, the Setuser command is used.

8.8. How to Implement Object Security

Now that you know how permissions on objects and statements work, you're probably wondering how everything is implemented. A bewildering amount of flexibility is provided by the combination of grants, ownerships, and ownership chains. How can an administrator keep track of it all? Two models are used to create and track security. In the Single Owner model, all objects in the database are owned by the dbo, who grants and revokes all privileges directly. In the Multiple Owner model, users can create tables and manage data on their own. Both models have strengths and weaknesses.

In the Single Owner model, one database owner owns all objects in the database and controls all grants. This is the more commonly used and least complex of the two models. There are no broken ownership chains because one user owns all the objects. Developers can create and destroy stored procedures, but when they are placed into production, the database owner recompiles them and grants them execution rights. This requires the dbo to know what rights go where, but it requires little education in the user community about object ownership. The advantages of the Single Owner model are the amount of control the dbo has on the database and the lack of complexity. The downside is that the dbo has to track all changes to object permissions and deal with them.

8

When multiple users own objects, the dbo takes the more passive role in adding and removing users and assigning capabilities to create objects. The users are responsible for creating and controlling objects. For a trained user base that understands how databases work (and specifically, how SQL Server works), this is a reasonable choice. The advantage of this method is it reduces the responsibilities of the dbo. The downside is the level of user education necessary to overcome issues such as broken ownership chains.

In some unique cases, the Single Owner model is used in conjunction with the Multiple Owner model. In some database designs, it is desirable for each user to have a set of tables that they own. These tables usually contain a subset of data found in other tables or personal settings for applications. A front-end application usually manages the creation of these tables and handles moving data into and out of them. This prevents the user from having to manage the permissions.

Object and statement permissions are the important finale in a security setup that starts with identifying the security mode and creating logins and users. Identifying and creating object permissions is an important job for a system administrator and is covered in depth on the exam.

Lab

Questions

1. A database user named John creates a table called Inventory and needs to provide user Jennifer with access to the table. John performs the correct `Grant` statement. What command does Jennifer need to use to select all rows from the table?

   A. `Select * from Inventory`

   B. `Select * from John.Inventory`

   C. `Select * from John..Inventory`

   D. `Select * from John(Inventory)`

2. A database user named Sam needs to provide Janice, the database owner, with permanent access to his table. Janice is not the system administrator. What does he need to do?

   A. Nothing. Database owners automatically have access to all data.

   B. Tell Janice to use the `Setuser` command to access his data.

   C. Grant the dbo `Select` permission for the table.

   D. Perform a select and copy and paste the results into an electronic mail message to Janice.

3. Josie, the system administrator, needs to enable her assistant Dave to dump a database. She only wants to give Dave the minimum amount of access required. How can she do this?

   A. Alias Dave's login to the database owner in the database.

   B. Add Dave to the Backup Operators group in Windows NT.

   C. The `Dump Database` permission is not transferable, so Dave can't perform this operation.

   D. Create a user for Dave in the database. Grant that user the capability to execute the `DUMP DATABASE` command.

4. Norm wants to enable Cliff to grant permissions on his database table, Beverages, so Cliff can grant other users access to select data from the table and so Cliff only has select access. What statement should Norm execute?

8

A. Grant Select on Beverages to Cliff with grant option

B. Grant Select on Beverages to Cliff

C. Grant All on Beverages to Cliff with grant option

D. Grant Select on Beverages to Cliff, Public with grant option

5. After further consideration, Norm decides it was irresponsible to enable Cliff to even select data from the Beverages table. How can he undo this permission?

A. Revoke Select on Beverages to Cliff

B. Revoke Select on Beverages from Cliff

C. Revoke all on Beverages from Cliff with cascade

D. Revoke Select on Beverages from public

6. Amy creates a table called Contacts and creates a view on the Contacts table called vContactNames. She grants Bob the capability to select from vContactNames. Bob likes the vContactNames view but thinks it has too many columns, so he creates a view called vContactFirstNames. Charlie needs the data in vContactFirstNames for a project he's working on, so Bob grants him access to vContactFirstNames. Will Charlie be able to see any data in vContactFirstNames?

A. Yes. He has permissions to the view.

B. No. Amy didn't give Bob permission to create a view based on her view.

C. Yes. Bob should check with Amy first, however, because it is her table.

D. No. Amy didn't provide Charlie with access to the base view.

7. Josie creates a table called Weather and grants access to the group Public. She then builds a view based on that table called vLocalWeather, and she grants select permission to Kim. Kim builds a view on vLocalWeather called vLocalTemperature and grants permission to Linda. Will Linda be able to use the view?

A. Yes. The base table Weather has permissions granted to public.

B. No. Linda does not have select permission on the view vLocalWeather.

C. Yes. Linda has permission to view vLocalWeather.

D. No. Linda does not have permission to the base table Weather.

8. Which of the following is a privilege granted only to the system administrator?

   A. `Create Database`

   B. `Drop Database`

   C. `Dump Database`

   D. `Disk Init`

9. In a database with user ownership of tables, how can the database owner modify data in a table without getting the table owner involved?

   A. The database owner can directly access any table in the database, so no special steps are required.

   B. Use the `sp_changetableowner` procedure to change table ownership to the database owner.

   C. Select the data from the user's table, modify it, and insert it back.

   D. Use the `Setuser` command to impersonate the user and then make the changes.

10. While designing a database, the database owner is trying to decide who will own the tables: the database owner or individual users. Which two of the following are points to consider when making this decision?

    A. Databases with single object owners require less tracking of object ownership and permissions by the database owner.

    B. Databases with multiple object owners require users to understand object permissions and ownership. Therefore, they require more user training.

    C. Databases with a single object owner have less-complex ownership chains.

    D. Databases with multiple object owners have less-complex ownership chains.

Exercises

The following exercises make a few key assumptions:

- Your server is in standard security mode.

- You don't have a database called Perms, as mentioned in the tutorials earlier in this chapter. If you do have one, remove it before you begin these exercises.

8

- The only login accounts these exercises use are sa, User1, User2, and Admin. If you have any logins with these names, you can leave them, but just be aware they are used here.

- Each of these exercises depends on the one(s) before it. For best results, perform these exercises completely and in order.

1. Granting and Revoking Permissions

In this exercise, you'll set up a database called Perms and set up logins and users to access that database.

This exercise helps to address the following certification exam objectives:

- Identify system administrator functionality
- Grant and revoke permissions

1. Start the SQL Enterprise Manager. Remember, all activity in the SQL Enterprise Manager is performed as the system administrator because that's how you registered the server when you configured the SQL Enterprise Manager. Expand the server on which you want to work.

2. Right-click the Devices folder and choose New Device. Create a new device called PermsDev that is 5MB in size.

3. Right-click the Logins folder and choose New Login. Create a login called Admin. Click in the Permit column of the Master row to create a user for Admin in the Master database. Click the Add button to create the user and click Close to close the window.

4. Expand the Databases folder, right-click Master, and choose Edit. Click the Permissions tab and check the box under Create DB for the user Admin. This enables the user Admin to create a database. Click OK to commit the change.

5. Start ISQL/W and connect to the server as Admin. Create the database Perms on the device PermsDev as a 5MB database with no external log device:

```
create database Perms on PermsDev = 5
```

SQL Server enables Admin to create the database. The response from SQL Server after a bit of grinding on the hard disk is CREATE DATABASE: allocating 2560 pages on disk 'permsdev'.

6. In the Query window, choose Perms from the DB drop-down box in the toolbar. It might be necessary to choose <Refresh> and then choose Perms. Enter the following query and execute it:

```
Select User_Name()
```

This returns the name of the current user (in this case, dbo). Note that the current login, Admin, was automatically mapped to the dbo because the Admin login created the database. Congratulations, you've made a database.

7. Go to the SQL Enterprise Manager, right-click the Databases folder, and choose Refresh. Create logins for User1 and User2 with both of them allowed in the Perms database. Because the SQL Enterprise Manager uses the sa login, it still can create logins and users in the new database—even though the system administrator did not create the Perms database.

8. Because the Admin user does not need to create any more databases, right-click Master and choose Edit. On the Permissions tab, revoke Admin's permissions to the `Create Database` command.

In this exercise, you successfully created a database that is not owned by the system administrator. It doesn't matter, however, because the system administrator can get into anything he wants, regardless of permissions. You also extended permissions for `Create Database` and then revoked them.

2. Analyzing Ownership Chains

Now you get to look at ownership chains. In this exercise, you'll create a broken ownership chain that doesn't work and then fix it. In the process, you'll be granting and revoking statement permissions. As promised, this ownership chain uses stored procedures rather than views because the tutorial used an example with views.

 Note   This exercise helps to address the following certification exam objectives:
- Grant and revoke permissions
- Predict the outcome of a broken ownership chain

1. If one isn't open already, open an ISQL/W window and log in to the server as Admin. Remember, Admin is a database owner that is not the system administrator. Select the Perms database.

8

2. Execute the following command to create a table:

```
Create Table Food (FoodName char(30))
```

SQL Server creates the table. By default, the table has no permissions granted on it or data in it. Execute the following commands to add some data:

```
Insert into Food values ("Spaghetti")
Insert into Food values ("Lasagna")
Insert into Food values ("Pizza")
Insert into Food values ("BBQ")
```

3. Create a stored procedure to return all the food in the table:

```
Create Procedure sp_GetFood as
Select * from Food
```

4. Execute the query so that you can see what it is supposed to look like. Grant User1 permission to execute the query, as follows:

```
Grant execute on sp_GetFood to User1
```

5. Start another ISQL/W window that is connected to the same server as User1. Have User1 execute the stored procedure, and you'll see the contents of the Food table. Next, have User1 attempt to directly select data from the Food table, as follows:

```
Select * from Food
```

User1 receives this error: SELECT permission denied on object Food, database perms, owner dbo. Even though User1 can get data from the table using sp_GetFood, User1 cannot pull data directly from the source table.

6. User1 likes the sp_GetFood query but wants to add some information. Run the following to create a stored procedure in the User1 window:

```
                create procedure sp_MyGetFood as
begin
     print "Food Name courtesy of DBO"
     exec sp_GetFood
end
```

You'll receive this error message: CREATE PROCEDURE permission denied, database perms, owner dbo. You need to go to the window where Admin is connected and grant User1 permission, as follows:

```
Grant Create Procedure to User1
```

Execute the create procedure again for User1 and the procedure is created. Grant Execute permission on the procedure to User2.

7. Log in as User2. What will happen when User2 attempts to execute the stored procedure sp_MyGetFood? Write down what you think will happen and then attempt to run the procedure user1.sp_MyGetFood. The following is the entire returned message:

```
Food Name courtesy of DBO
Msg 229, Level 14, State 1
EXECUTE permission denied on object sp_GetFood, database perms, owner
dbo
```

You can see that the print statement executed fine, but the stored procedure call did not work. How can you fix this problem?

8. In the ISQL/W window for Admin, grant execute permission on sp_GetFood to User2. User2 then can execute the stored procedure.

Answers to Questions

1. **B**   Because John and Jennifer are two different database users, they need to specify the username in the table name part of the select. The syntax is database.user.object, so the answer John.Inventory works.

2. **B**   Only the system administrator can access data in tables without being granted permission. Setuser provides Janice with the capability to select data from the table. She'll have to re-execute SetUser each time she wants to access the data, however, so this is not a permanent solution.

3. **D**   Choice A works, but it provides Dave with more responsibility than he can be trusted with. Choice B doesn't do anything to SQL Server. Choice C just isn't true.

4. **A**   Choice B grants Select access to Cliff without granting him the capability to give permission to anyone else. Choice C grants All access to Cliff, which he could then pass on to everyone else. Choice D results in a syntax error because with grant option cannot be assigned to a group.

5. **C**   The with cascade option must be used to ensure that anyone Cliff granted access to will be removed from the permission list for the table.

6. **D**   Follow the ownership chain and remember that the permissions are checked when the owner changes. Charlie has permissions to Bob's view, so Bob's table isn't checked. Charlie does not have permissions to Amy's view, so he can't select data from it.

7. **B**   The ownership chain principle states that objects are checked all the way down, and views are checked first whenever ownership changes. Linda has access to Kim's view, and Kim has access to Josie's view, but Linda doesn't have access to Josie's view. The permissions fail at that point.

8. **D**   Because the other three options all involve databases—and database owners own databases—they have the capability to perform those operations.

9. **D** Setuser enables the dbo to modify table data belonging to any user in the database.

10. **B, C** Object permissions must be tracked carefully in a single-owner database. Multiple-owner databases force users to track permissions and ownership, which makes choice A invalid. Choice D is incorrect because, if there are multiple owners of objects, the ownership chain will be considerably more complex than Single Owner models.

8

This chapter introduces SQL Server tasks, events, and alerts. The following are some key facts you'll learn in this chapter:

- The SQLExecutive service runs the task engine, processes alerts, and handles the notification of operators. If the SQLExecutive isn't running, none of these features will work.

- The SQLExecutive service is an independent service and runs with a user context just like any other service in Windows NT.

- The msdb database contains all the details used by the SQLExecutive service to track alerts, schedule tasks, and schedule events.

- The SQLExecutive service monitors the Windows NT Event Log and starts alert processing based on events that are logged to this database. If the event log is not working or is full, the alert process will not work. If a particular event that happens in SQL Server is not logged to the Windows NT Event Log, then it cannot be acted—by the SQLExecutive service.

- Scheduled tasks can be either CmdExec jobs, which are Windows NT command shell jobs, or T-SQL jobs—Transact-SQL that is run in SQL Server. All CmdExec jobs are run in the user context of the SQLExecutive service. All Transact-SQL jobs are run as the sa.

Day 9

Scheduling Events and Creating Alerts

This chapter examines how SQL Server schedules tasks and notifies you of problems. The task and alert processing in SQL Server is one of the great achievements of the whole 6.x release of SQL Server. It can make your servers much easier to manage.

Objectives

This chapter covers the following Microsoft material:

- Identify the role of the msdb database.
- Identify the role of the SQL Executive service.
- Identify conceptual relationships between the Scheduler service, the msdb database, and the Windows NT Event Log.
- Set up alerts.
- Schedule tasks.

9.1. Events, Alerts, and Tasks

This chapter examines the role of the SQL Executive Windows NT service. This service has the following main responsibilities:

- Monitoring the Windows NT Event Log and handling specified events, called *alerts*
- Monitoring the clock to determine whether it is time to run specified jobs, called *tasks*
- Monitoring and managing replication

This chapter examines tasks and alerts. Day 12, "SQL Server Replication," discusses replication. The SQL Executive service uses the msdb database to handle alerts, tasks, and replication. All the configuration information for the preceding responsibilities is stored in the msdb database, just as all the startup information for SQL Server is stored in the Master database.

9.1.1. Setting Up and Monitoring Tasks

Tasks are added to the SQL Enterprise Manager using the New Task window, shown in Figure 9.1. A *task* is a job that can be run by the SQL Executive service. Tasks can be scheduled or can be executed on demand. Scheduled tasks are configured to start at a specific time every day, week, or month. On-demand tasks must be executed, either by you or by an alert. Alerts are discussed further in the section "Event Log Monitoring and Alert Handling" later in this chapter.

Figure 9.1.

The New Task window, showing the default settings for the different options you can set.

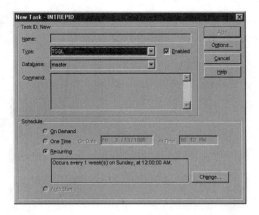

Of the following five types of tasks, only the first two are covered in this chapter:

- *CmdExec.* Tasks of this type start a Windows NT command shell and then execute your command in that shell. This means your commands can use Windows NT shell functions such as `copy`, `del`, `dir`, and `cd`. Enter the command to execute in the Command box.
- *TSQL.* Tasks of this type are Transact-SQL commands or queries.
- *Distribution, Log Reader, and Sync.* These types of tasks are used by replication processes, which are covered on Day 12.

Many common tasks that are time-consuming can be scheduled, such as database creation or backup. When moving through the SQL Enterprise Manager interface (especially on Day 10, "Backing Up and Managing SQL Server Data," which covers backups), you'll notice a Schedule Now button in windows. This button enables the current task to be scheduled to run at a later time and represents another entry point into task scheduling.

The command portion of a TSQL or CmdExec task can be no more than 256 characters. This can be very limiting to these command types. For CmdExec tasks, you can get around this by using a batch file. For TSQL statements, you can write the TSQL command into a text file and execute it with the ISQL program. ISQL is a command-line version of the ISQL/W program used to check out user accounts. It provides a query interface to SQL Server. Because ISQL is a program run at the command prompt, to schedule a long TSQL job, you need to create a CmdExec job that runs ISQL with the correct parameters. The following are the normal parameters:

```
isql -Usa -P -n -i <input file> -o <output file>
```

These parameters mean the following:

- `-Usa`—Log in as user *sa.*
- `-P`—The password. If you use integrated security, you still have to provide a `-P` option, but you can leave the password blank. Otherwise, you need to immediately follow the `-P` option with a password.
- `-n`—Supress line numbering in the output file.
- `-i`—The input file is a set of Transact-SQL statements.
- `-o`—The output file is the output from running the Transact-SQL statements.

Sometimes it's a good idea to use this method even when the Transact-SQL isn't larger than the size that can be run inside the task manager. Keep in mind that after the task is complete, the only status recorded in the task history is that of the last statement in the batch. Even that is cut off if it's too long. By using ISQL, you can specify an output file, so you can go through the results at your leisure.

> **Note**
>
> A couple pointers can help you use ISQL in batch mode. First, for any SQL Server command-line utility, assume that all the parameters are case sensitive. With some utilities they are; with some they aren't. Second, always use an output file, or you won't know how the task completed.

The SQL Server scheduler has an incredibly flexible scheduling system, as shown in Figure 9.2. The scheduler enables you to set up tasks to execute either once or as recurring events. Recurring tasks can execute daily, weekly, or monthly. You can choose to execute a monthly task on a specific date in the month or on a given day of the week, such as the last Sunday of the month. Weekly tasks can execute multiple times during the week; for example, a task can be run every other Monday, Wednesday, and Friday. When a task's chosen day arrives, it can execute either once at a specified time or repeatedly throughout the day at user-provided intervals.

Figure 9.2.

The options for scheduling a weekly task are very flexible. Notice that a weekly task can be run more than once a week.

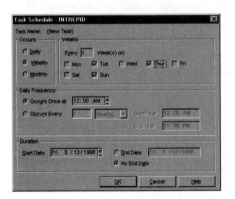

SQL Server also enables you to set up an operator to be notified of whether a job is successful. Operators are discussed in the section "Event Log Monitoring and Alert Handling" later in this chapter. It's usually a good idea to initially set a task to notify upon either success or failure. When it seems to be working correctly, you can set the task to notify only upon failure.

Unfortunately, the SQL Executive has an unusual viewpoint on what constitutes success and failure for CmdExec jobs. A CmdExec job is successful unless the process returns a nonzero exit code. If you're using ISQL via a CmdExec task and ISQL runs the job completely through, ISQL returns zero. As far as the SQL Executive is concerned, everything ran fine. The ISQL script could have failed disastrously, but as long as ISQL was able to find and execute the input file, it is considered a success. To resolve this problem, use logged events and alerts as outlined in the next section.

When creating tasks, it usually helps to create them as on-demand tasks, test them, and then activate the scheduling. This enables you to iron out any problems before the script runs and fails in the middle of the night and you receive a page at 3 a.m. from SQL Executive because your job failed. Also, keep in mind that the default setting for a task is to run as a recurring event every Sunday night. If you had to guess the default, you'd probably have guessed the tasks run on demand. Now you know to change a task's setting so that you won't have any surprises when you walk into the office on Monday morning.

The following tutorial shows you how to set up a task and see how it works.

In this tutorial, you set up a task, test it, schedule it, and monitor the results.

1. Start the SQL Enterprise Manager and expand the server you're working with.

2. Choose Server | Scheduled Tasks to open the Manage Scheduled Tasks window.

3. Choose File | New Task or click the sparkling clock on the toolbar. This opens the New Task dialog box.

4. Enter a name for the task. Keep in mind that the names are displayed in alphabetical order. If you name the tasks carefully, you can group them together. Call this task `Test`.

5. Change the type of task to CmdExec and type the following command into the Command box:

```
net send "Hello" <User> Say, divide
```

Substitute your network logon for `<User>`.

6. Choose On Demand in the Schedule box and then click ADD to create the task.

7. Choose File | Run Task or click the clock with the triangle on the toolbar. You'll see the message `Task 'Test' started successfully. When the task finishes executing, its completion status can be viewed in the 'Task History' dialog`. Click OK.

8. By the time you finish reading that message, the task is complete. Click the Refresh button on the toolbar to show the status of the task. Task windows don't automatically refresh; you always have to use the Refresh button to update your screen.

9. Double-click your task and then click the History button. You'll see how long the task took to run and what output was produced. Click Close.

10. Now that you know the task executes correctly, you can schedule it. Choose Recurring and then click the Change button. Make the event run daily, every minute, starting in 5 minutes, for 15 minutes, as shown in Figure 9.3. Click OK to accept the scheduling.

Figure 9.3.

This is how the scheduling window should look in step 10 if you happen to execute the job at 8 p.m. The times on the screen will vary, depending on when you run this job.

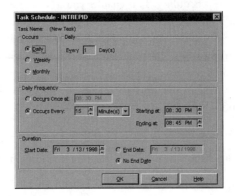

11. Click Options and choose to be notified of success or failure in the Windows NT Event Log. Click OK.

12. Go grab a beverage, surf the Web, pet the dog, or find something else to do for 20 minutes until the tasks finish.

13. Open the Event Log and check your server to make sure the jobs ran. You should see one event for each time the job ran. You also should receive some messages from the server if the Messenger service is running.

Keep in mind that tasks are run with the Windows NT account of the SQL Executive service. Day 2, "Installing SQL Server," showed you how to configure the SQL Executive service to log on with different login accounts. If you want a task to communicate with another server, you need to make sure the SQL Executive is logged on using an account with sufficient permissions for that interaction.

9.1.2. Event Log Monitoring and Alert Handling

SQL Server logs many messages into the Windows NT Event Log. These messages range from routine startup information to bulletins about corrupt databases. To understand alerts, an understanding of messages and events is necessary.

All the messages you receive from SQL Server are stored in a table called sysmessages in the Master database. Each message has a number and a severity level. Severity levels increase as the number increases. Informational messages, for example, have a severity level of 10; fatal errors have severity levels of 19 and higher. Some messages are logged into the Windows NT Event Log in addition to being displayed to the user. Messages marked by SQL Server as needing to be logged will be logged—you can't change that. Messages not logged into the Windows NT Event Log can forcefully be logged in if you change their status using Server | Messages in the SQL Enterprise Manager.

You also can create your own messages. Microsoft has promised that it will never create system standard-error messages above message number 50,000. This means that you can create your own system error messages starting with that number. Because 50,000 is a normal integer type, you still are able to define billions of messages.

In SQL Server, the term *alert* is used to denote an action or a series of actions that respond to an event. An alert is triggered by the SQL Executive service whenever certain events are entered into the Windows NT Event Log. The sysalerts table in the msdb database stores a list of events that cause alerts. An alert can cause the following actions:

- Send an SNMP trap. If your environment uses management software such as HP OpenView, you can set up Windows NT and SQL Server to send traps to an SNMP console to enable the console to handle notifications.
- Execute a task. If the event is a full transaction log, for example, a task to dump the transaction log can be executed.
- Send an email to an operator.
- Send a page to an operator.

You need to know two things to set up an alert. First, you need to know what event triggers the alert. Second, you need to know what you want SQL Server to do when the event occurs. An *alert* is an action that takes place in response to an event. One option is to notify the active operators. An *operator* is a combination of an email address and a pager email address, as shown in Figure 9.4. Operators can be set up on shifts, and different operators can be notified for different errors. If a database administrator is responsible for a particular database on the server, for example, you can set up all alerts for that particular database so that, when the alert occurs, the administrator is emailed during the day but paged after working hours.

Figure 9.4.

These options are available when you create an operator.

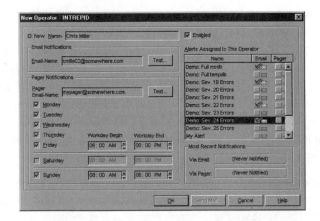

Note

For any event, alert, or task processing to occur, the SQL Executive service must be started. You can start this service in SQL Enterprise Manager by right-clicking the SQL Executive object and choosing Start, or you can start it in Control Panel | Services. Some exercises require the Windows NT Messenger service, which can be started from Control Panel | Services.

To make the event and message process even easier, the SQL Enterprise Manager includes a graphical interface for searching and modifying which events are logged. This can, in turn, cause alerts. The following tutorial shows you how to set up a SQL Server error message so that it causes an event to occur.

In this tutorial, you select a message to log itself on the Windows NT Event Log. This tutorial assumes you're sitting at a Windows NT workstation or server.

1. Start the SQL Enterprise Manager and expand the server you're working with.

2. Choose Server | Messages. This opens the Manage SQL Server Messages dialog box.

3. In the Message Text Contains box, type Version and then click the Find button. Several events will display.

4. Choose the first event, which is Error 1 Severity 10, Version Date of Last Upgrade: 10/11/90. This is an unused event that works nicely for tracking down problems with event and alert handling. This message never displays unless you direct it to.

5. Double-click the event. This opens the Edit Message dialog box. Enable the Always Write to Windows NT Eventlog check box and then click OK. You're now back to the Manage SQL Server Messages dialog box.

6. The event now contains a check mark in the Logged column. Click Close.

7. Choose Tools | SQL Query Tool from the dialog box. Execute the following query:

```
raiserror (1, 10, 1)
```

The `raiserror` command manually causes error messages. The arguments are message number, state, and severity. This example shows message 1, state 10 (informational), and state 1 (no impact). This command returns Version `Date of last upgrade: 10/11/90`.

8. Start the Windows NT Event Viewer in Start | Programs | Administrative Tools (Common). Choose Log | Application. If you're administrating the server remotely, you need to choose Log | Select Computer and enter the name of the computer.

9. Read the top event, which is event 17060 from MSSQLServer. It should have the same message in it.

Follow the preceding steps to cause events to occur. You can also use the Manage SQL Server Messages dialog box to create new messages. The Lab exercises at the end of this chapter show you how to do this.

After creating the event, you can create targets for the alerts, called *operators*. It's not required for an alert to notify an operator, so if you don't want to use operators, you don't have to. An operator is essentially two email addresses (one for a pager and one for regular email) and a schedule. The schedule determines who should be notified and how the notification should take place, depending on what time of day it is. To effectively use operators, SQLMail must be set up. You learned how to do this on Day 1, "Introduction to SQL Server."

In this tutorial, you learn how to set up an operator. You'll use the operator later when you set up an alert.

1. Start the SQL Enterprise Manager and expand the server with which you're working.

2. Choose Server | Alerts/Operators to open the Manage Alerts and Operators dialog box. Click the Operators tab.

3. Choose File | New Operator or click the sparkling fireman's hat on the toolbar.

4. Enter a name for the operator. This is just a friendly name you'll use later to set up alerts.

5. Enter an email address in the Email-Name box and then click the Test button to test email. If you don't have SQLMail configured, don't click the Test button.

6. Enter a pager email address in the Pager Email-Name box. You can also schedule when the operator will be paged in the Pager Notifications frame.

7. Click OK to create the operator and close the dialog box.

Now that you've created an operator, take a look at how to use the operator in an event.

The New Alert dialog box has four parts, as shown in Figure 9.5. The Alert Definition frame specifies which event causes a particular alert. You can search for an alert by clicking the ... button, which opens the Manage SQL Server Messages dialog box.

Figure 9.5.

Use the New Alert dialog box to set up alerts.

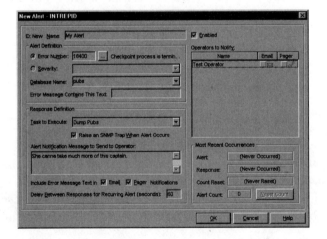

The Response Definition section enables you to describe what should happen when an event occurs. The options are to raise an SNMP trap, execute a task, or send an email or page to an operator. In the Delay Between Responses for Recurring Alert (Seconds) dialog box, some events are logged tens or hundreds of times. The `Cannot allocate space for object` error, for example, occurs each time a transaction attempts to add data to a database when the database is full. To reduce the number of emails or pages being sent, set the delay to approximately 90 seconds. The Operators to Notify section details which operators should be notified when this event occurs. The Most Recent Occurrences section shows the last time this event was triggered.

In this tutorial, you set up an alert. This alert is triggered on the event you set up in the preceding tutorial, message 1, with a severity of 10.

1. Start the SQL Enterprise Manager and expand the server you're working with.

2. Choose Server | Alerts/Operators. This opens the Manage Alerts and Operators dialog box.

3. Choose File | New Alert to open the New Alert dialog box. In the Name: dialog box, enter `Test Alert`.

4. Click the Error Number: option and enter 1 in the box. An error message displays, stating the version date of the last upgrade.

5. In the Task to Execute dialog box, choose New Task. The New Task dialog box opens. Create a CmdExec task that sends a message to you using the following command line:

```
net send <user> Test alert from SQL Server!
```

Substitute your username for *<user>*.

6. In the Operators to Notify box, check the boxes next to the operator you created in the preceding tutorial, if you want the operator to be paged or emailed when the event occurs. Click OK to create the alert.

7. Open a SQL Query window and perform the same `raiserror` command as before:

```
Raiserror (1, 10, 1)
```

Assuming the messenger service is started on the local workstation, you should receive the message fairly quickly. The net send command works well for alerts that occur during the work day. If you set up an operator in step 6, the operator should receive the notifications you specified.

You can set up some important options to help manage your alerts in the Alert Engine Options dialog box, shown in Figure 9.6. You can open this dialog box by choosing File | Alert Engine Options. What happens if there's a failure to carry out an alert? The fail-safe operator is notified. The fail-safe operator is one of the operators notified when an alert fails in its execution. How can an alert fail? If the alert causes a database dump and the database is offline.

9

Figure 9.6.

The Alert Engine Options dialog box can help you manage alerts such as the fail-safe operator.

Event forwarding is another helpful feature for alerts and events. When many SQL Servers are networked together, the alert part of the SQL Executive can be set up so that all events are forwarded to one server. This means that you can set up all the alerts that you use on one server and then set up all the notifications and operators on another server. This helps reduce the headaches of managing servers. You also can set up an individual server to handle some alerts and to forward other alerts. This is accomplished in the Alert Engine Options dialog box.

The last item in the Alert Engine Options dialog box is the configuration for Pager Email. You can specify how the pager service should receive email and how that email should be set up.

9.2. The msdb Database

The msdb database is used by the SQL Executive to carry out its tasks. This database contains the schedules for tasks that need to run, the names and addresses of the operators, and the actions that need to occur when alerts happen. The msdb database also tracks backups and replication tasks.

Some maintenance is involved with the msdb database. In particular, the task engine logs should be cleared periodically to prevent the database from becoming full. Database size should be monitored because certain tables—such as sysbackupdetail and sysbackuphistory, which track the backups—tend to grow larger as the server gets older.

The sysmessages table contains information about every message that SQL Server returns. It also contains a field that determines whether each message is logged in to the Windows NT Event Log. This means that it is used by SQL Server, not the SQL Executive service. Because it is primarily a SQL Server table, it is stored in the Master database. It is still critical to know how the SQL Executive operates, however.

9.3. How the SQL Executive Works

The SQL Executive service is a multithreaded service. Think of it as one service that contains many separate services. Each of the alert, event log reader, task scheduler, and replication threads runs independently, and they all run with the same user context—that of the SQL Executive user. The process uses a nominal (by today's standards) 2.5MB–3MB of RAM. In addition to its other duties, the SQL Executive also monitors SQL Server and handles restarting the service if it stops unexpectedly. This can be configured by right-clicking the SQL Executive and choosing Configure.

9

Lab

The following are questions to help you prepare for the exam. The Lab exercises that follow are designed to provide a more in-depth understanding of how this all fits together.

Questions

1. The administrator is having problems getting a task to copy the backup dump file from the SQL Server to another server. The SQL Executive is set to use the local system account, and both machines are in the same domain. The task history shows Access is denied messages. The administrator can copy files to the other server manually with no difficulties. How can the administrator fix the problem?

   A. Add the LocalSystem account to the other computer's administrators group.

   B. Change the SQL Executive service startup so that it can interact with the desktop.

   C. Add the SQL Executive account sqlexec to the server operators group.

   D. Change the SQL Executive service startup so that it logs on with a user account that has access to write to the share on the other computer.

2. After setting up tasks to complete database maintenance and alerts and operators to monitor the database, the administrator is concerned about saving this configuration information. What should the administrator back up to preserve his settings?

   A. The Master database

   B. The Windows NT Registry

   C. The msdb database

   D. The msdb and Master databases

3. The administrator sets up her assistant, Dave, to receive email from 9 a.m. to 5 p.m. daily whenever database problems occur. Dave never receives any email, even though some database problems are logged in to the Windows NT Event Log. What could be causing this problem?

A. SQLMail isn't configured on the server.

B. The SQL Executive service isn't running.

C. The electronic mail server isn't operational.

D. All of the above.

4. The administrator notices that her alert to dump the database's transaction log when it becomes full does not always work. How can she arrange to receive email notification when this alert fails?

A. Set up the task to notify upon failure.

B. Set up a fail-safe operator.

C. Change options for the task to notify when the transaction log is dumped.

D. All of the above.

5. The administrator configures Server B to perform event forwarding so that all events on Server B will be forwarded to Server A. The events, however, are not being forwarded at all. Which of the following could be the problem?

A. The SQL Executive service isn't running on Server B.

B. The SQL Executive service isn't running on Server A.

C. The events are all being handled on Server B, so Server B doesn't forward the events.

D. A and C.

6. For an alert to fire, which of the following must occur?

A. An event must be logged to the SQL Server error log in \mssql\log\errorlog.

B. The alert must be defined to fire on a given message.

C. The message must log an event to the Windows NT Event Log.

D. Both B and C.

7. For a task to run successfully, which of the following conditions must be met?

A. The SQL Executive service must be running.

B. SQLMail must be configured.

C. The Windows NT Scheduler must be running.

D. Both A and C.

8. Which of the following are accomplished by the SQL Executive? (Select all that apply.)

    A. Restarting SQL Server if it stops unexpectedly

    B. Executing tasks

    C. Monitoring the Event Log

    D. Invoking alerts

9. Which of the following are stored in the msdb database? (Select all that apply.)

    A. Task setup information and history

    B. Alert setup information and history

    C. Messages that cause events

    D. Backup history

10. The administrator is having a problem. When a database fills up, she is being notified by email tens and hundreds of times. How can she eliminate this problem?

    A. Establish a waiting period between duplicate alerts.

    B. She can't; she needs to live with it.

    C. Use Inbox rules to delete incoming messages that are repeats.

    D. Use paging instead of email.

Exercises

1. Scheduling a Database Backup

 Note This exercise helps to address the following certification exam objective:
- Schedule tasks.

In this exercise, you schedule a database backup. Don't worry about the syntax of the Transact-SQL used here; it is explained on Day 12. The reason you're skipping ahead is because the most common use for the task scheduler is backups. You probably need to see how to set one up. This one is set up as a Transact-SQL job.

1. Start the SQL Enterprise Manager and expand the database that you want to work on.

2. Choose Server | Scheduled Tasks. This opens the Manage Scheduled Tasks window.

3. Choose File | New Task to open the New Task window. In the Name box, enter Backup Pubs. Verify that Type is set to TSQL and choose On Demand for scheduling. Enter the following command in the Command box:

```
dump database pubs to disk = "c:\mssql\backup\pubs.dat"
```

9

4. Click the Add button to add the task. This returns you to the Manage Scheduled Tasks window.

5. Select the task you just built and choose File | Run Task. When asked whether you are sure you want to start the task, click Yes. You'll be informed that the task started successfully. Click OK.

6. By the time you get through the dialog boxes, the task probably is completed. Click the Refresh button on the toolbar or choose File | Refresh to refresh the task's status. It now should show Successful.

7. Double-click the event and schedule it as a one-time event to occur in 5 minutes. Click the Options button in the Edit Task window. Set up the task to write an event to the Windows NT Event Log upon success or failure.

8. Wait for the event to run and then check the Event Log. You can also check a task's history by double-clicking the task and choosing History.

9. Follow these steps to create and schedule a task. This is a common process, so make sure you're comfortable with the task before you run it.

2. Setting Up a User-Defined Event and Alert

This exercise helps to address the following certification exam objective:
- Set up alerts.

In this exercise, you set up your own message to fire. You then set up an alert to start a task based on your message. Finally, you try out the whole chain to make sure it all works.

1. Start the SQL Enterprise Manager and expand the server you want to work on.

2. Choose Server | Messages. This opens the Manage SQL Server Messages dialog box.

3. Click the New button at the bottom of the window. This opens the New Message dialog box. It automatically generates an error number greater than 50,000. Leave the severity at 10 and enter a new message in the Message Text box. Enable the Always Write This Event to the Windows NT Event Log check box and then choose OK. Close the Manage SQL Server Messages window.

4. Open a SQL Query window and use the `raiserror` command to force your error to occur:

```
raiserror (50001, 10, 1)
```

5. Open the Windows NT Event Viewer and view the Application Log on your server. There should be an event logged by source MSSqlServer in the Server category. Double-click this event to see your error message: `Error : 50001, Severity: 10, State: 1 User Defined Message Test`.

6. Choose Server | Alerts/Operators in the SQL Enterprise Manager. Then choose File | New Alert. Set the alert name to My Alert. Trigger the alert on Error Number 50001 by choosing Error Number and entering `50001`.

7. In the Task to Execute drop-down box, choose New Task. This opens the New Task dialog box. In the Name box, enter `New Name`. Set Type to CmdExec and enter the following:

```
Net Send Administrator "Alert fired"
```

Substitute your username or computer name for `Administrator`, if necessary. Then click Add to create the task.

8. Click OK to create the new alert.

9. If you still have the SQL Query window open, execute the query again. Otherwise, open a SQL Query window and use the `raiserror` command to force your error to occur:

```
raiserror (50001, 10, 1)
```

10. You should receive a message fairly quickly.

Answers to Questions

1. **D**   None of the other options alleviate the permissions problem. This is a common problem with tasks and the SQL Executive.

2. **D**   The msdb database contains the alerts, operators, and tasks; the Master database contains the logged messages.

3. **D**   Any of these problems can stop electronic mail delivery.

4. **A**   A fail-safe operator works only if the alert itself fails, which is not the problem. The task associated with the alert is failing, so notification at that stage is most effective.

5. **D**   Option B doesn't work because the events forward to Server A's Event Log regardless of whether Server A is running the SQL Executive.

6. **D**   This is the classic definition of an alert trigger.

7. **A**   Task scheduling doesn't rely on the Windows NT scheduler. SQLMail needs to be running only if you want to be notified upon failure or success.

8. **A, B, C, D**   The SQL Executive performs all these tasks and replication.

9. **A, B, D**   Message status is stored in the master.sysmessages table.

10. **A**   By establishing a waiting period between alerts, the administrator can dramatically reduce the amount of mail she receives.

9

TEST DAY
FAST FACTS

The following are some key facts you'll learn in this chapter:

- You should back up your databases frequently to ensure recoverability in the case of catastrophic failure.

- The frequency of your backups depends on the amount of data change in your databases. A database that changes frequently should be backed up more often than a database updated infrequently.

- SQL Server provides two ways to back up databases. A *full database dump* provides an exact copy of everything in the database. A *transaction log backup* backs up everything in the database that has changed since it last was backed up.

- You can dump data to several types of devices, including tape drives, disk drives, networked file servers, and named pipes.

- You should make backups of the system databases—in particular the Master, msdb, and model databases—whenever you make changes.

- Database dumps can be set to run at off-peak hours using the scheduling features built into the SQL Enterprise Manager.

- You should run DBCC checks against a database after backing it up to make sure the database is in a consistent state.

Day 10

Backing Up and Managing SQL Server Data

There are many reasons for SQL administrators to perform backups and no good reasons not to. The most important reason to perform backups is for disaster recovery. No one wants to have a crashed database without a recent backup. It can boil down to whether you'll have a job after a catastrophic failure.

Objectives

This chapter covers the following material:

- Identify the best uses for the dumping command and the loading command in managing data.
- Identify the functionality of dynamic backup.
- Identify how automatic recover works.
- Perform a database dump.
- Perform a striped backup.
- Create a dump device.
- Dump a transaction log.
- Identify the best uses for bcp when managing data.

10.1. Why You Should Back Up

You should already realize the importance of the data in your database and the importance of backing that data up. Disaster recovery is the most important reason you should back up your databases regularly. Having backups enables you to get production databases back online quickly and efficiently after the server has crashed. In addition to disaster recovery, backups also are useful for the following reasons:

- Accidental or malicious updates or deletion of data
- Natural disasters such as fires, floods, or tornadoes
- Theft or destruction of equipment
- Transportation of data from one machine to another
- Permanent archival of data

10.1.1. When and Where to Back Up

You now should realize the importance of backing up the data in your databases. The next step is to decide when and how often to perform these backups. SQL Server provides many efficient and reliable ways to back up your data, most of which have little impact on users.

To determine when to back up, you need to decide what the acceptable loss is. *Acceptable loss* is defined as the amount of data that can be lost without having an extremely detrimental impact on the business. In online transaction processing (OLTP) environments, in which an hour's worth of data loss can result in millions of dollars of lost business, there is no acceptable loss.

The other factor in determining the frequency of backups is the degree to which the data has changed. If the data in your database does not change frequently, it is safe to back it up only after changes have been made. If your database is updated daily, you should make backups daily.

A frequently used backup strategy is the grandfather/father/son, or generational, backup scheme. In this strategy, a monthly backup is made either the first or the last day of the month. This is the grandfather generation. It should be kept offsite and should be retained indefinitely. The father generation is a weekly backup. It also should be kept offsite and should be retained for a specific period of time, such as a year. The son generation is a daily backup that should be retained for a month before overwriting. This generation of backup tapes should be kept onsite in a safe place, such as a fire-proof safe.

In addition to frequency, the following factors also can influence your backup strategy:

- What medium (disk or tape) will you back up to?
- What time of day will backups run?
- Where will backups be stored?
- How long will you keep the backups?
- How will backups be verified?
- If the system administrator is not available, is there someone else who can change tapes and make sure that backups are running properly?

Your backups should not be stored on the same machine as the data itself. For performance reasons, you often dump data to the local machine's drives because it is much faster than dumping to tape. Afterwards, it is imperative for you to copy that data through the network to another server or to copy it to tape. Another option for your backup tapes is offsite storage. This can be as simple as taking the tapes home with you or as complex as having an offsite storage facility pick up the tapes on a daily basis.

10.1.2. What to Back Up

SQL Server provides two ways to back up your databases. First, you can dump the database. This is a full backup of all data and objects within the database. Second, you can dump just the transaction log. A transaction log dump only records changes made after the prior transaction log dump. A good backup scheme contains a combination of full database dumps and incremental transaction log dumps.

 Note

Many people believe full backups aren't productive due to the length of time they can take to complete. With the recent advances in both size and speed of tape drives, however, a daily full backup can be achieved with little problem. You should experiment with your backup equipment to determine the best mix of full backups and transaction log dumps.

10

10.2. Types of Dump Devices

 As you read this section, you'll notice that the terms *dump device* and *backup device* are used interchangeably. This is because Microsoft documentation uses the term *dump device*, and the SQL Enterprise Manager uses the term *backup device*.

A *dump device* is a location in which SQL Server can store backup copies of databases or transaction logs. Dump devices can be disk files on the local machine, disk files on remote servers, tapes, floppy disks, or named pipes. When you create a dump device, you give it both a logical name and a physical name. The logical name can have up to 30 characters and must follow the SQL Server naming conventions for identifiers. The physical name is a file system name that includes the path or the universal naming convention (UNC) for network devices. If the share resides on a server called BackupServ, for example, the UNC is similar to \\BackupServ\BackupShare. Table 10.1 provides examples of logical and physical names for the different types of dump devices.

Table 10.1. Sample logical and physical names for dump devices.

Type of device	Logical Name	Physical Name
Local disk	DB_DUMP_DISK	D:\BACKUPS\DBDUMP01.DAT
Network disk	TL_DUMP_SQLBACK	\\SQLBACK\BACKUPS\TLDUMP.DAT
Tape	TAPE_BACKUP	\\.\TAPE0
Floppy disk	DISKETTEDUMPA	A:\SQLTABLE.DAT
Named pipe	NP_DUMP	\\SQLBACK\PIPE\SQL\DUMP
Null	DISKDUMP	NUL

10.2.1. Disk Dump Devices

Disk dump devices can reside either on the local machine or on a networked server. The advantage of using a disk dump device to back up your database is that the backup process is extremely fast. When using a disk device on the local machine, it is important to copy the backup device to tape or to a network server to protect it from disk crashes. When using a disk device on a network share, you first must check to see whether the service account under which SQL Server is running has the correct permissions to write to the machine.

10.2.2. Tape Dump Devices

SQL Server currently supports only local tape devices. SQL Server 6.5 does not support networked tape drives. Before SQL Server can recognize a tape drive, it first must be installed using Windows NT. When you create a tape device in SQL Server, you must specify the physical name Windows NT assigned it. The first tape drive installed in the computer is assigned the name \\.\TAPE0. Other drives installed are given incremental names.

> It is important to note that the format of a SQL Server tape is incompatible with the Windows NT Backup program. Do not attempt to use a tape that has been formatted with SQL Server in conjunction with the Windows NT Backup program. Doing so causes the Windows NT Backup program to lock up and become a nonkillable process. To use the Windows NT Backup program, you must then restart the server.

10

10.2.3. Floppy Disk Dump Devices

When SQL Server is installed, it creates two floppy disk dump devices, DISKETTE-DUMPA and DISKETTEDUMPB. Floppy disk devices are present for backwards compatibility with previous releases of the software. To make a backup to a floppy disk dump device, you must use the console utility and initiate the dump using ISQL. You cannot use the SQL Enterprise Manager to dump to a floppy disk dump device.

10.2.4. Named Pipe Dump Devices

Microsoft provides named pipe dump devices as a way for third-party software vendors to back up and restore SQL Server. Named pipe dump devices cannot be created or administered using the SQL Enterprise Manager. To back up to a named pipe, you must provide the name of the pipe when you invoke the dump command.

10.2.5. NULL Dump Devices

When SQL Server is installed, it creates a special device called DISKDUMP. Backing up to the DISKDUMP device sends data to the NULL device on the computer. This does not save the data, and you cannot restore data that has been sent to it.

10.3. Creating Dump Devices

Before making backups of your databases, you first must create devices to which you can send data. You can add dump devices from the Database Backup/Restore dialog box in the SQL Enterprise Manager or from the Server Manager window itself.

This tutorial shows you how to create a dump device using the SQL Enterprise Manager. To complete this exercise, the server on which you are creating the device must be registered in the SQL Enterprise Manager.

1. From the Server Manager window in the SQL Enterprise Manager, select a server, right-click the Backup Devices folder, and choose New Backup Device. The New Backup Device dialog box opens.

   Another way to open the New Backup Device dialog box is to select the server in the Server Manager window of the SQL Enterprise Manager. Choose Tools | Backup/Restore. From the Database Backup/Restore dialog box, choose the New button in the Backup Devices frame. The New Backup Device dialog box opens, as shown in Figure 10.1.

Figure 10.1.

The New Backup Device dialog box enables you to create new disk and tape dump devices.

2. In the device Name box, enter a name for the device. This is the name you should specify when backing up to the device. The name can have up to 30 characters; names longer than 30 characters are truncated.

   The following are the naming conventions for dump devices:

   ■ The first character of an identifier can be any letter or the underscore symbol (_).

   ■ Characters following the first character can be any letter, any number, the underscore symbol (_), the pound sign (#), or the dollar sign ($).

   ■ Embedded spaces are not allowed by default.

3. In the device Location box, enter the path to the physical location where you want the file to reside. This should be the full path and filename or, in the case

of a network dump device, the universal naming convention (UNC) location of the file.

If you do not know the full path of the location where you are going to store the file, click the button with the ellipsis (...). This opens a window that enables you to browse for the folder (see Figure 10.2).

Figure 10.2.

You can explore and find the path of the location where you want to store the backup device.

4. Select the type of device you want to create. A *disk backup device* is a device that resides on the local hard drive or on a network share. A *tape backup device* is a tape drive that resides on the local machine.

5. If you want to create a tape device, you can select Skip Headers. This option enables you to force SQL Server to ignore the ANSI header written to the tape.

   The ANSI header provides information about what is stored on the tape. Skipping headers enables SQL Server to overwrite tapes that have not yet expired.

6. Click the Create button to complete the operation. After adding the device, you can now perform backups to it. A file that corresponds to a file system device does not show up until you perform a backup to it.

When adding backup devices, you also can use the `sp_addumpdevice` system stored procedure. This stored procedure can add disk, tape, and floppy disk dump devices. The following is the syntax of the `sp_addumpdevice` stored procedure:

```
sp_addumpdevice {'disk' ¦ 'diskette' ¦ 'tape'}, 'logical_name',
'physical_name', { noskip ¦ skip }
```

The `'disk' ¦ 'diskette' ¦ 'tape'` option enables you to select the type of dump device to create. Use `'disk'` to create a local or network disk device. Use `'diskette'` to create a dump device on a 3 1/2-inch or 5 1/4-inch floppy drive. Use `'tape'` to specify any Windows NT-supported tape drive as a backup device.

`logical_name` is the name you use to reference the device when performing backups and restores. The name must follow the naming conventions previously listed in this chapter.

`physical_name` is the physical location where the backup device is stored on the local drive or network share. If you are creating a tape device, remember that devices are named by Windows NT and are sequential starting with zero. For example, the first tape device on a server is \\.\TAPE0.

The `noskip ¦ skip` option enables you to choose whether the ANSI headers on the tape are skipped (`skip`) or read (`noskip`).

10.4. Managing Dump Devices

You can get information about the dump devices on your SQL Server in several ways. You can list the dump devices on the machine and the backups contained on an individual device.

10.4.1. Listing Dump Devices

You can list the dump devices on the SQL Server in two ways. You can use the SQL Enterprise Manager, or you can use stored procedures to list all the devices on the machine.

This tutorial shows you how to display all the dump devices on a machine using the SQL Enterprise Manager.

1. From the Server Manager window, select a server and connect to it.
2. Go to the Backup Devices folder and click the plus sign next to it. The folder expands to show you a list of all the dump devices on the machine, as shown in Figure 10.3.

Figure 10.3.

By expanding the Backup Devices folder in the Server Manager window, you can view a list of all the dump devices on the machine.

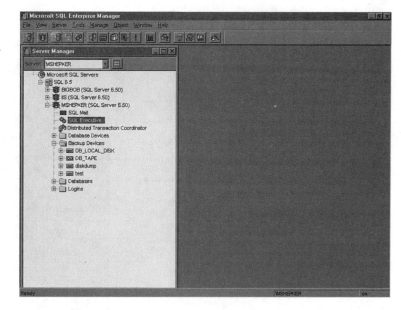

The other option is to use the `sp_helpdevice` system stored procedure. This stored procedure returns information about every device on the machine, not just the dump devices. The stored procedure returns, among other things, the logical name and the physical location of the device.

10.4.2. Viewing Information About Dump Devices

If you perform either multiple backups to the same device or backups to different devices, you need to be able to see which dumps have been stored on which dump devices. You can accomplish this within the Server Manager window of the SQL Enterprise Manager. Use either the Database Backup/Restore dialog box or the LOAD command.

This tutorial shows you one way to display information about which backups have been made to a device:

1. From the Server Manager window, select a server and connect to it.

2. Go to the Backup Devices folder and click the plus sign next to it. The folder expands to show you a list of all the dump devices on the machine.

3. Click the plus sign next to the name of the dump device you want to investigate. If you have backed up to it, it expands to show you which dumps are stored on it (see Figure 10.4). This provides information about the type of

backup performed, the date the backup was started, and the size of the backup.

Figure 10.4.

You can view information about which backups are stored on which dump devices in the Server Manager window in the SQL Enterprise Manager.

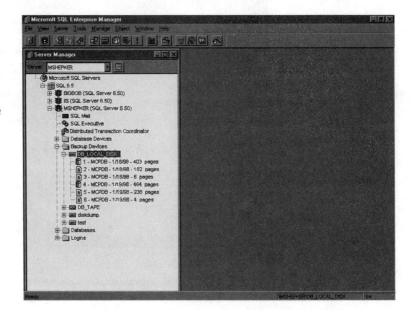

You can view more detailed information about which backups are contained on a backup device in the Database Backup/Restore dialog box. This provides the same information as the Server Manager, plus information about when the backup completed and the sequence number of the backup.

This tutorial shows you how to display information about database dumps using the Database Backup/Restore dialog box:

1. From the Server Manager window, select a server and connect to it.

2. Go to the Databases folder and click the plus sign next to it. The folder expands to display a list of all the databases on the server.

3. Right-click a database and choose Backup/Restore. This displays the Database Backup/Restore dialog box, as shown in Figure 10.5.

4. Choose the dump device you want information from and click the Info button. This displays the Backup Device Information dialog box, as shown in Figure 10.6.

Figure 10.5.

The Database Backup/Restore dialog box displays a list of dump devices from which you can get information.

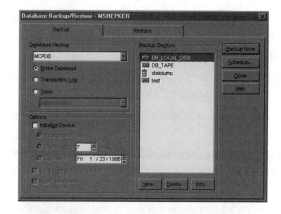

Figure 10.6.

The Backup Device Information dialog box displays all the dumps contained on a device.

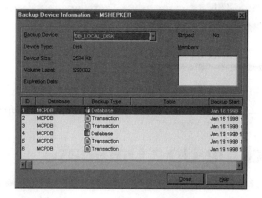

10

5. Click the Close button to exit the Backup Device Information dialog box.

You also can view detailed information about a dump device using ISQL/W. You just start ISQL/W, type the following in the query window, and execute it:

```
LOAD HEADERONLY FROM dumpdevicename
```

In the preceding, *dumpdevicename* is the name of the dump device from which you are trying to get information.

10.4.3. Dropping a Dump Device

At times, you will need to drop a dump device. SQL Server provides several ways to drop dump devices you no longer want to use. All data stored on a dump device is lost when you drop the device.

1. Within the Server Manager, select the server you want and connect to it.

2. Click the plus sign next to the Backup Devices folder. The folder displays a list of all dump devices on the machine.

3. Right-click the dump device you want to drop; the Delete Backup Device dialog box opens. Click the Delete button.

4. A confirmation box opens. Click the Delete button to confirm deletion of the device.

5. Finally, you must delete the operating system file from the hard drive. You can use either Explorer or the del command from the command prompt.

The other option when dropping a dump device is to use the sp_dropdevice system stored procedure. This stored procedure drops the dump device from the system catalog and deletes the operating system file. The following is the syntax of the command:

```
sp_dropdevice logical_name [, DELFILE]
```

In the preceding, logical_name is the name of the device you want to delete. If you specify the DELFILE option, the stored procedure deletes the operating system file.

10.5. Backing Up a Database

You can use either the SQL Enterprise Manager or the DUMP command in ISQL/W to back up your databases. Using the SQL Enterprise Manager, you can schedule backups to take place any time during the day or night. SQL Server backups are dynamic. This means that they can be made while users are using the database. You should perform backups when the database is not being heavily updated, however, because the backup process can slow the system down. A *dump* is a static picture of the data in the database at the time the dump statement is executed.

When you perform backups, you can back up either the entire database or just the transaction log. Dumping only the transaction log takes less space and time than dumping the entire database. Dumping the transaction log periodically during the day provides up-to-the-minute recoverability of a crashed database.

You should maintain regular backups of all databases, including the following:

- The Master database
- The msdb database
- The model database

■ All user databases

■ The distribution database (if the server is configured as a replication distribution server)

1. In the Server Manager window, select the server containing the database you want to back up and connect to it.

2. From the Tools menu, select Database Backup/Restore or right-click the database you are going to back up and choose Backup/Restore. Either of these methods displays the Database Backup/Restore dialog box, as shown in Figure 10.7.

Figure 10.7.

You can set various options for backing up your databases in the Database Backup/Restore dialog box.

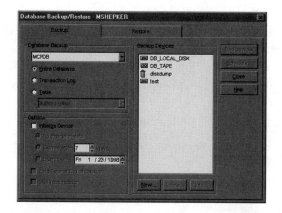

10

3. In the upper-left corner, choose the database you want to back up from the drop-down box.

4. Select what you want to back up from the available options. If you choose the Entire Database option, all the database objects, the data, and the transaction log are backed up. If you choose Transaction Log, only the transaction log is backed up. If you choose Table, you can pick an individual table to back up.

5. Under Backup Devices, choose the device to which you are going to back up. If you are performing a striped backup (a backup to multiple devices), you can hold down the Ctrl key to select multiple devices. You also can click New to create a new device to which to back up.

6. Under Options, select Initialize Device if you want to overwrite everything currently on the dump device. Otherwise, the backup appends what is already on the tape.

If you initialize the device, you then can set an expiration date for the tape. This expiration date is written to the ANSI header of the tape. The tape cannot be overwritten until the date you specify.

If you are using a tape dump device, you can choose to rewind and eject the tape after completing the backup cycle. If you are appending multiple dumps to the same tape, you need to make sure that this option is cleared. You can also choose to skip the header on the tape. This enables you to back up to a tape with an expiration date.

7. You can choose either Backup Now or Schedule. Scheduling the backup enables you to set the task to run when the database is not in use. You also can set it up as a reoccurring task.

When backing up the database, you also have the option to use ISQL/W and to back up the database using the DUMP command. This command can be used in a script activated with the Windows NT command scheduler. You can run other commands before and after the backup. The following is the complete syntax of the DUMP command:

Dumping a database

```
DUMP DATABASE {dbname ¦ @dbname_var}
     TO dump_device [, dump_device2 [..., dump_device32]]
[WITH options
     [[,] STATS [ = percentage]]]
```

Dumping a transaction log

```
DUMP TRANSACTION {dbname ¦ @dbname_var}
     [TO dump_device [, dump_device2 [..., dump_device32]]]
[WITH {TRUNCATE_ONLY ¦ NO_LOG ¦ NO_TRUNCATE}{options}]
```

In the preceding syntaxes, *dump_device* is

```
{dump_device_name ¦ @dump_device_namevar}
¦ {DISK ¦ TAPE ¦ FLOPPY ¦ PIPE} =
     {'temp_dump_device' ¦ @temp_dump_device_var}}
[VOLUME = {volid ¦ @volid_var}]
```

and *options* is

```
[[,] {UNLOAD ¦ NOUNLOAD}]
[[,] {INIT ¦ NOINIT}]
[[,] {SKIP ¦ NOSKIP}]
[[,] {{EXPIREDATE = {date ¦ @date_var}}
     ¦ {RETAINDAYS = {days ¦ @days_var}}]
```

This looks complicated until you break it down into the parts you use most. When dumping a database or just the transaction log, you are required to supply the database name and a dump device. When dumping the transaction log, however, if you do not supply a dump device name, you can supply the TRUNCATE_ONLY or NO_LOG option to eliminate the unused portion of the transaction log without backing it up.

The following are other options you can supply that are pretty straightforward:

- The UNLOAD ¦ NOUNLOAD option enables you to instruct SQL Server to rewind and eject the tape at the end of the backup process. This option only is available if you back up to a tape device.

- The INIT ¦ NOINIT option enables you to specify whether any previous data on the device should be erased.

- The SKIP ¦ NOSKIP option enables you to load or not load the ANSI header on the tape. This option only is available if you back up to a tape device.

- The EXPIREDATE and RETAINDAYS options enable you to specify either a date for the backup device to expire or the number of days that the data on the device should be retained.

10

10.6. Scheduling Backups

To make sure that all your pertinent databases and transaction logs are backed up frequently, you can schedule your backups to occur at regular intervals using the SQL Enterprise Manager. Recurring backups can occur on an hourly, daily, weekly, or monthly basis.

1. Define the backup you want to schedule, as previously described in this chapter. Click the Schedule button. You are prompted to supply a volume label. Do so and then click the OK button. The Schedule Backup dialog box opens, as shown in Figure 10.8.

Figure 10.8.

The Schedule Backup dialog box enables you to schedule backups to occur at a later time or on a regular basis.

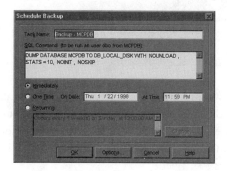

2. Choose the One Time option. Set the time and date at which you want it to occur or click the Recurring button.

3. If you choose to set up a recurring backup, click the Change button. This displays the Task Schedule dialog box, as shown in Figure 10.9.

Figure 10.9.

The Task Schedule dialog box enables you to set up a task to occur on a regular basis.

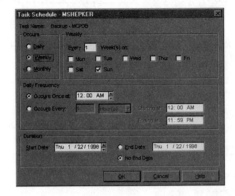

4. In the Task Schedule dialog box, you can set dates, times, and frequencies for your databases to be backed up. It also enables you to set up a date interval during which the task will run. After you have scheduled your backup, click OK to close the Task Schedule dialog box.

5. If you click the Options button, the TSQL Task Options dialog box opens, as shown in Figure 10.10.

Figure 10.10.

The TSQL Task Options dialog box enables you to set notification options and the number of times the task should retry in case of failure.

6. In the Notifications section of the TSQL Task Options dialog box, you can choose to email an operator or write an event to the Windows NT Application log upon success or failure of a task. In the Retries section, you can set the number of times SQL Server attempts to retry the task in the event of a

failure. After choosing your options, click OK to close the TSQL Task Options dialog box.

7. Click OK in the Schedule Backup dialog box to finish scheduling the backup and then close the Database Backup/Restore dialog box.

10.7. Running DBCCs in Conjunction with Backups

The Database Consistency Checker (DBCC) checks the physical and logical consistency of a database. It is recommended that you run the following DBCCs in conjunction with your backups:

```
DBCC CHECKDB
DBCC NEWALLOC
DBCC TEXTALLOC
DBCC CHECKCATALOG
```

You can run these checks before or after the dump takes place. Because activity can occur in the database during the backup process, the best option is to run the DBCCs after the backup process has completed. This ensures that the database you backed up is consistent. On larger databases, these commands can take a long time to run. When this is the case, you might want to run the DBCCs with the NO_INDEX option. This causes the DBCC to check only the data and the clustered index pages. This reduces the amount of time it takes to run.

10.8. Backing Up the System Databases

As with user databases, you should make periodic backups of certain system databases—specifically, the Master and msdb databases. You also should back up the distribution database if your server is set up to participate in the replication process.

10.8.1. Backing Up the Master Database

The Master database contains information about the configuration of the SQL Server and all the other databases on the server. You should make frequent backups of this database, especially after making any configuration changes to the SQL Server or the databases contained on it. You should dump the database after any of the following:

- Using the CREATE or ALTER statement on a database
- Using the DBCC SHRINKDB command
- Adding or dropping logins or changing security permissions for users
- Creating, dropping, or resizing database or dump devices

10.8.2. Backing Up the msdb Database

The msdb database is used by the SQL Executive. This database is a storage area for all scheduled tasks and the history of those tasks. The database changes whenever you add or modify tasks, add or modify automatic backup tasks, or change alerts. By default, the Truncate Log On Checkpoint option is turned on when SQL Server is installed. To perform transaction log dumps, you must turn this option off. You can back up this database as you would any user database.

10.8.3. Backing Up the distribution Database

If SQL Server is set up to participate as a remote distribution server or as a publisher/distributor in the replication process, a database will be dedicated to the distribution process. By default, the database's name is distribution, but this can be changed when setting up replication. The distribution database holds all transactions waiting to be replicated and then forwards them on subscription servers. You can back up the distribution database as you would any user database. The distribution database should be dumped frequently.

10.9. Transaction Logging

SQL Server uses the transaction log to keep its databases consistent. The transaction log records any insertions, updates, and deletions in the database. It also records a certain amount of housekeeping data about changes in indexes, allocation of data pages, and extent allocation.

When a transaction begins, a row is written to the transaction log informing SQL Server that the transaction has begun. The transaction log is a write-ahead log. This means that, before any actual data is modified, a record is written to the transaction log. When a transaction has completed, a commit transaction row is written to the log. These begin and end records enable SQL Server to outline a completed transaction.

> **Warning**
>
> SQL Server must be able to write begin, modification, and end rows to the disk to keep the database consistent. The use of a write-caching disk controller can make it look as though a record has been written when it hasn't. This can result in 605 errors and database corruption. If you have a controller with write-caching features, turn them off for database consistency.

If SQL Server fails while the database is being updated, the final commit transaction record is not written to the log. When SQL Server is back online, it performs the Automatic Recovery process. The Automatic Recovery process goes through the transaction log one row at a time to make sure that all transactions have completed. If a commit transaction record is not found, the transaction is rolled back, and all changes made during that transaction are undone. If a commit transaction record is found but the pages were not flushed from the data cache to the disk, the transaction is rolled forward, and the changes are written to the disk.

10

> **Warning**
>
> If the Truncate Log on Checkpoint or Select Into/Bulk Copy options are turned on in a database, you cannot perform transaction log dumps. You have to perform full database dumps to back up these databases.

10.10. The Checkpoint Process

To speed up the Automatic Recovery process, SQL Server performs a process called *checkpoint*. During this process, SQL Server writes all pages that have been changed to disk. After the process finishes, it writes a record to the transaction log. This identifying point tells SQL Server that all completed transactions were guaranteed to have been written to the disk.

There are two types of checkpoints: user initiated and automatic. A *user-initiated checkpoint* is issued by the database owner. An *automatic checkpoint* is issued by SQL Server and is based on the amount of system activity and the recovery interval value in the sysconfigs table. The recovery interval determines the amount of time it should take the server to recover after a failure.

Databases are checkpointed at two other times. When you use the sp_dboption stored procedure to change a database, it automatically is checkpointed. When you issue the shutdown command, SQL Server automatically checkpoints all databases on the server.

10.11. SQL Transfer Manager

SQL Server provides an easy way to transfer data from any Microsoft or non-Microsoft SQL database into a Microsoft SQL Server—use the SQL Transfer Manager. The SQL Transfer Manager transfers all objects and data from one server to another. Because data tapes from one processor architecture cannot always be transferred to another, the SQL Transfer Manager provides an easy way to transfer data from different processor architectures.

The Database/Object Transfer dialog box enables you to move data from one SQL Server Database to another. You can use this dialog box to transfer all objects and data in a database or selected data only.

1. In the Server Manager window, select the server containing the database you want to transfer and connect to it.

2. Click the plus sign next to the Databases folder to expand it. Right-click the database and choose the Transfer option. This displays the Database/Object Transfer dialog box, as shown in Figure 10.11.

Figure 10.11.

The Database/Object Transfer dialog box provides an easy way to transfer data from one SQL Server to another.

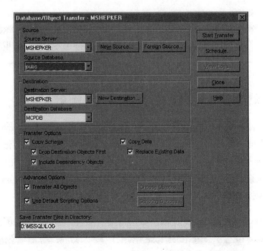

3. In the Source section, the Source Server and Source Database boxes already should be filled in for you. If you want to change these, choose a new registered server from the drop-down box or click the New Source button and register a new server. If you are going to transfer data from a non-Microsoft SQL Server, click the Foreign Source button and supply the Server Name, Login, and Password required to log on to the server.

4. In the Destination section, click the drop-down box to choose the server to which you are going to transfer (if it has already been registered) or click the New Destination button and register a new server. After you have selected the server to which you are going to transfer, select the Destination Database. This database must already reside on the destination server. If a database does not already exist on the destination server, you must create one before performing the transfer.

5. In the Transfer Options section, choose the options that reflect your needs. To copy only the physical structures of the database—such as tables, triggers, and stored procedures—choose the Copy Schema option. To copy data to a database that contains the same structures, choose the Copy Data option. By default, all options are set.

6. In the Advanced Options section, you can select individual objects or choose to Transfer All Objects. You also can choose the scripting options you need. The default options automatically create scripts that re-create the destination database table triggers, table DRI, table bindings, nonclustered and clustered indexes, and owner-qualified objects from the source database. The default security options re-create users and groups, logins, and object and statement permissions.

7. In the Save Transfer Files in Directory box, enter the path to the location where you want the SQL Transfer Manager to store the scripts it creates during the transfer process.

8. You can schedule the transfer to occur at a later date or time by clicking the Schedule button, or you can start the transfer immediately by clicking the Start Transfer button.

9. After the scripting process finishes, you are told whether the transfer process was completed successfully. If everything was completed properly, it is a good idea to back up the new database before allowing users to start using it.

10.12. The Bulk Copy Program

The bulk copy program, or bcp utility, is a command-line program that copies SQL Server data to and from operating system files. bcp frequently is used to copy data into or out of a SQL Server from other databases, spreadsheets, or applications. SQL Server can accept data in any format as long as the field separator—the characters that separate the columns and rows—can be defined. A user must have SELECT permissions on a table to export data out of it and must have INSERT permissions to import data into it. The following is the full syntax of the bcp command:

```
usage: bcp dbtable {in | out} datafile
       [-m maxerrors] [-f formatfile] [-e errfile]
       [-F firstrow] [-L lastrow] [-b batchsize]
       [-n native type] [-c character type] [-q quoted identifier]
       [-t field terminator] [-r row terminator]
       [-i inputfile] [-o outfile] [-a packetsize]
       [-E explicit identity] [-U username] [-P password]
       [-S server] [-v version] [-T trusted connection]
```

When loading information into a database, speed is often an important consideration. You can speed up bcps into a database by running what is called a *fast* bcp. The following steps are required to perform a fast bcp:

1. On the database into which you are going to be performing the bcp, turn on the Select Into/Bulk Copy database option. You can do this using the sp_dboption stored procedure or from the Options tab of the Edit Database dialog box.

2. Drop the indexes in the destination table.

3. Perform the bcp operation. When you perform a fast bcp operation, the actual inserts into the table are not logged; only the changes in database allocation are logged.

4. After the bcp operation is complete, re-create the indexes and perform an immediate backup of the database. The database cannot recover from a catastrophic failure because all the insertions into the database were not logged.

Backing up databases frequently is important so that, should the unthinkable occur, you can recover as much data as possible in the shortest amount of time. Microsoft provides many tools for you to use in managing your data. It is important to remember to use these tools to keep your databases in good condition.

Lab

Questions

1. What are the reasons you should back up your SQL Server data? (Select all that apply.)

   A. Disaster recovery

   B. Historical archival of data

   C. Transferring from one processor architecture to another

   D. Transferring from one server to another

2. What types of dump devices can you create, dump data to, and then restore the data? (Select all that apply.)

   A. Tape devices

   B. NULL devices

   C. Named pipe devices

   D. Local disk devices

3. You are the administrator of a SQL Server that contains two user databases. Values in one database are loaded using a fast bcp procedure every weekend. On Monday morning when you try to back up the transaction log, you receive an error. How can you fix this?

   A. You cannot fix this error. You must stop the SQL Server service and back up the physical devices.

   B. Turn off the Select Into/Bulk Copy option on Monday morning and perform a full backup of the database. Perform transaction log dumps when you need them. Turn the Select Into/Bulk Copy option back on before the weekend.

   C. Perform a full backup of the database.

   D. Perform a DUMP TRANSACTION WITH NO_LOG.

4. You are the administrator of a SQL Server, and you have just installed a new database. You want to create a new network disk dump device and the share \\BACKUPSERV\SQLDATA to which to back it up. What command should you use in ISQL to accomplish this?

A. `DISK DUMPDEVCE INIT`

B. `sp_addumpdevice 'disk', 'DUMPDEVICE_NETWORK',`
`'\\BACKUPSERV\SQLDATA\DUMPDEVICE_NETWORK.DAT'`

C. `sp_addumpdevice 'network', 'DUMPDEVICE_NETWORK',`
`'\\BACKUPSERV\SQLDATA\DUMPDEVICE_NETWORK.DAT'`

D. `DISK INIT`

5. You have just received a new Alpha AXP server that you are going to use to upgrade your current SQL Server. The current server is a Pentium 120. Both machines have 4-mm DAT tape drives in them. How would you transfer the data from the old server to the new one?

A. Use the `DUMP` command to dump the data to the new server.

B. `DUMP` the database to tape on the old server and restore the database using that tape on the new server.

C. Use the SQL Transfer Manager to re-create the database schema and transfer the data.

D. Re-create the database schema by hand and then use `bcp` to move the data.

6. SQL Server backups are dynamic backups. As a system administrator, what does this mean to you?

A. You do not have to plan your backups; SQL Server does them automatically for you.

B. You can back up the database while users are using it with little impact on performance.

C. The backup and restoration process happens as necessary without user intervention.

D. Dynamic backup is the transaction logging process, and that process is constantly running.

7. You are the administrator of a SQL Server that contains an online-transaction processing database. The database operates on a 24×7 basis. Full database dumps to tape take approximately 4 hours to perform; transaction log dumps to tape take approximately 20 minutes.

Primary objective: To create a database backup scheme that allows less than an hour of data loss.

Secondary objectives: To allow the database to be restored until a certain point in time. To allow users to continue to work in an efficient manner during peak usage times.

Proposed solution: Perform a full backup of the database four times a day.

A. The proposed solution meets the primary and both the secondary objectives.

B. The proposed solution meets the primary and one of the secondary objectives.

C. The proposed solution meets only the primary objective.

D. The proposed solution does not meet the primary objective.

8. You are the administrator of a SQL Server that contains an online-transaction processing database. The database operates on a 24×7 basis. Full database dumps to tape take approximately 4 hours to perform; transaction log dumps to tape take approximately 20 minutes.

Primary objective: To create a database backup scheme that allows less than an hour of data loss.

Secondary objectives: To allow the database to be restored until a certain point in time. To allow users to continue to work in an efficient manner during peak usage times.

Proposed solution: Perform a full backup of the database during off-peak hours. Dump the transaction log to tape every hour.

A. The proposed solution meets the primary and both the secondary objectives.

B. The proposed solution meets the primary and one of the secondary objectives.

C. The proposed solution meets only the primary objective.

D. The proposed solution does not meet the primary objective.

9. You are the administrator of a SQL Server that contains an online-transaction processing database. The database operates on a 24×7 basis. Full database dumps to tape take approximately 4 hours to perform; transaction log dumps to tape take approximately 20 minutes.

Primary objective: To create a database backup scheme that allows less than an hour of data loss.

Secondary objectives: To allow the database to be restored until a certain point in time. To allow users to continue to work in an efficient manner during peak usage times.

Proposed solution: Perform a full backup of the database during off-peak hours. Dump the transaction log to disk every hour.

A. The proposed solution meets the primary and both the secondary objectives.

B. The proposed solution meets the primary and one of the secondary objectives.

C. The proposed solution meets only the primary objective.

D. The proposed solution does not meet the primary objective.

10. Which command do you use to back up a database?

A. DUMP DATABASE

B. sp_backupdb

C. BACKUP DATABASE

D. BACKUP DB

Exercises

1. Creating a Backup Device

 Note

This exercise helps to address the following certification exam objective:

■ Create a dump device

This exercise shows you how to create a disk backup device using the SQL Enterprise Manager. This exercise should take approximately 10 minutes to complete:

1. Open the SQL Enterprise Manager and connect to the SQL Server on which you will be creating the backup device.

2. Click the plus sign next to the Backup Devices folder to expand it. This lists all the backup devices on the server.

3. Right-click the folder and choose the New Backup Device option. This opens the New Backup Device dialog box.

4. In the Name field, enter TEST_BACKUP.

5. Leave the default location as it is.

6. Make sure that the Disk Backup Device option is chosen and click the Create button.

This creates a backup device you can use to back up databases. Until the first time you back up a database to the device, there will be no physical file on the disk.

2. Backing Up a Database and Its Transaction Log

Note — This exercise helps to address the following certification exam objective:
- Perform a database dump

10

This exercise shows you how to back up the pubs database to the device you created in the preceding exercise. This exercise should take approximately 15 minutes to complete:

1. Open the SQL Enterprise Manager and connect to the SQL Server on which you created the TEST_BACKUP device.

2. Click the plus sign next to the Databases folder to expand it. This lists all databases on the server.

3. Right-click the pubs database and choose the Backup/Restore option. This displays the Database Backup/Restore dialog box.

4. In the Backup Devices section, choose the TEST_BACKUP device you created in the first exercise.

5. Check the Initialize Device option. This causes any previous backups to be deleted from the device.

6. Click the Backup Now button.

7. After the database has finished backing up, close the Database Backup/Restore dialog box.

After performing a backup to the new backup device, make sure that a physical file is on the disk.

Answers to Questions

1. **A, B, D**   Backing up SQL Server does not work to transfer from one processor architecture to another. To do this, you must use the SQL Transfer Manager.

2. **A, D**   You can only create tape and disk devices. Although you can back up and restore to a named pipe, this requires third-party backup software and an actual device is not created. Dumping to the NULL device makes the data nonrecoverable.

3. **B**   You cannot back up the transaction log because of the fast bcp. When you perform a fast BCP, the inserts into the database are not logged; only the expansion of the database is logged. Because you cannot recover with that, you must perform a full database backup to ensure recoverability.

4. **B**   You create a network disk dump device using ISQL; you use the sp_adddumpdevice with the disk option. The DISK INIT command creates a database device, not a dump device.

5. **C**   When transferring from one processor architecture to another, it is simplest to use the SQL Transfer Manager. Transferring a dump on tape does not work. Re-creating the schema and copying the data out of the old server and into the new takes too much time.

6. **B**   SQL Server dynamic backups provide a way to back up the database while users are in it.

7. **D**   Backing up the database four times a day does not allow for less than an hour of downtime.

8. **B**   Performing a full database backup nightly and performing hourly transaction log dumps provide the greatest amount of recoverability. Backing up to tape, however, does not allow users to continue working efficiently while the dumps are performed due to the amount of time it can take.

9. **A**   Performing a full database backup nightly and performing hourly transaction log dumps provide the greatest amount of data redundancy. Dumping the transaction log to disk allows users to continue to work efficiently.

10. **A**   The correct command for backing up a database is DUMP DATABASE.

- Restoring a database is the process of loading the database's most recent backup and then applying the transaction logs to re-create the database as it was until the point of failure.

- Point-in-time recovery enables you to restore a database up to a certain point in time. This option only works with transaction log dumps.

- SQL Server's automatic recovery process provides a built-in way to keep the database consistent. The process cancels any transactions that had not completed at the time of failure.

- Users cannot access any database being recovered until the automatic recovery process has finished.

- There are two basic causes that would make you have to restore user databases: data corruption or media failure.

- When restoring transaction log dumps, you have to restore them in the order they were made.

- When re-creating a database, you need to create and expand it in the same steps as the original.

- If the Master database crashes and you have a good backup, rebuild the database exactly like the original and then restore it.

Day 11

Restoring SQL Server Data

In the event of a database failure, you need to recover both the actual structure of the database and the database's data as close to the point of failure as possible. If you have a current database backup and transaction logs, you can restore the database until the point of failure. Restoring a database is the process of loading the most recent backup and then applying the transaction log dumps. If current backups are not present, you must attempt to extract the data from the corrupt database and then re-create the database. This is why it's extremely important to back up your databases.

Objectives

This chapter covers the following material:

- Restore a corrupted database.
- Re-create a lost device.
- Load a database dump.

11.1. An Overview of the Restore Process

Restoring a database is the process of loading a backup or dump of the database and then applying the transaction logs to re-create it. After applying the transaction logs, the database will be back as it was prior to the last transaction log dump.

If the device on which the database resides experiences media failure, you must re-create the devices, rebuild the database, and then restore the data. If the database contains corrupt or incorrect data as the result of malicious or unintentional inserts, updates, or deletes, you can restore the database to how it was before the data corruption took place.

Users cannot go into the database being restored during the restoration process. All the data in a database is replaced when the database is restored. When a database is restored after a media failure, you first must drop the database and the devices it resided on. You then must re-create the devices and the database itself. If you create the database using the FOR LOAD option, it saves time during the creation process. Before users can begin using the database again, you must turn the DBO USE ONLY option off.

When restoring transaction log dumps, you should keep in mind several key factors. First, transaction logs must be loaded in the same order as they were dumped. When the log is dumped, SQL Server places a time stamp in the file. When you start the restore process, SQL Server checks the time stamps to make sure that the sequence is correct. The changes in the transaction log are then re-executed. All other transactions are rolled back.

Transaction logs can be restored to a specific time and date. This is called *point-in-time recovery*. All transactions after that time are rolled back. Point-in-time recovery only applies to transaction log dumps; it cannot be used with table or full-database restores.

11.2. Automatic Recovery

Before venturing further into restoring user backups, you need to learn about the automatic recovery feature of SQL Server. Automatic recovery occurs every time SQL Server is started. It is designed to check and see whether any recovery needs to take place.

As mentioned in Day 10, "Backing Up and Managing SQL Server," not all changes to the database are written at the time they are made. Changed data is stored in cache and is written to the disk during the checkpoint process, which occurs about every 60 seconds. If the system crashes or loses power before a checkpoint has occurred, the automatic recovery process examines the transaction log to determine whether all transactions have been completed.

When a transaction begins—and before any actual data is modified—a row is written to the transaction log showing the beginning of the transaction. All changes made are then logged to the transaction log. When the transaction has completed, an end transaction row is written to the log. The begin and end records are how SQL Server delineates the beginning and the end of a transaction.

The automatic recovery process examines the transaction logs of each database. The process searches for the begin and end records of transactions and compares them to the data in the database. Transactions that had not been completed at the time of the system crash are canceled (rolled back). When both begin and end transaction records are found in the transaction log, the transactions are re-executed (rolled forward).

The automatic recovery process begins with the Master database and then moves to the model database. SQL Server uses the model database as a template when new databases are created. After the model database has been recovered, the automatic recovery process clears tempdb of all objects. The tempdb database is where SQL Server formats query results and creates temporary tables and other temporary working storage needs. The msdb database is recovered next, followed by the pubs database. The msdb database is where SQL Server stores information about scheduled tasks and the completion of those tasks. The pubs database is a small database that can be used for testing and experimentation. If the server is set up as a distribution server, the distribution database is recovered next. User databases are recovered after all system databases have been recovered. Users can log in to the server after the system databases have been recovered. They cannot use any user database, however, until it has completed recovery.

The automatic recovery process cannot be turned off, but two configuration options can affect it. During the automatic recovery process, databases being recovered are grayed out in the SQL Enterprise Manager with the word *Recovering* next to them. The Recovery Flags option determines what information SQL Server displays during the recovery process. The Recovery Interval option controls the maximum amount of time SQL Server should take to recover the database. The value you specify here is used by SQL Server to determine the frequency of the checkpoint process. These options can be set using either the SQL Enterprise Manager or the sp_configure stored procedure.

11

11.3. Recovering User Databases

All SQL administrators have to recover user databases at some point. There are two basic reasons you would have to restore a user database. The first reason is if the data in the database becomes corrupt somehow. Database corruption can be caused by a system glitch or by a user accidentally firing off an insert, update, or delete that drastically changes the data. The other reason you might need to restore a user database is if you experience media failure of some kind. Of the two, restoring because of data corruption is much easier.

11.3.1. Restoring User Databases

When restoring user databases, it is important to restore the database and the transaction logs in the same order they were made. SQL Server keeps track of the date stamps on database and transaction log dumps and prevents you from restoring them out of order. It can be quite frustrating, however, if you are missing a tape or they are out of order.

When database corruption occurs, it is important to find out what happened before you allow users back into the database. This can help prevent it from happening again. For more information, go to Day 14, "Troubleshooting SQL Server." The following tutorial shows you how to restore a user database.

After you discover how your database has been corrupted, you need to restore the database so that people can begin to use it again.

1. From the Server Manager window in the SQL Enterprise Manager, select a server and connect to it.

2. From the Tools menu, select the Database Backup/Restore option. This opens the Database Backup/Restore dialog box shown in Figure 11.1. Select the Restore tab.

3. From the Database drop-down box, choose the database you want to back up.

4. From the Restore option area, choose the type of restore you are going to perform.

   Choosing the Database and/or Transaction Logs option enables you to perform a full database restore and to apply the transaction logs automatically.

   Choosing the Single Table option enables you to restore a single table from one of the full database backups. You should not rely on restoring single tables to provide data backup security. If you restore a table referenced by a foreign key or with columns derived from other tables, you can end up with an inconsistent database.

Figure 11.1.

In the Database Backup/Restore dialog box, you can choose to restore a database, its log, or a single table within the database.

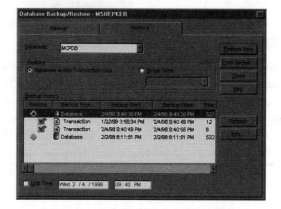

5. In the Backup History section, choose a database backup to restore. When you choose a full database backup, the transaction logs since the last backup automatically are chosen. When you run the restore, the transaction logs automatically are applied.

6. If you want to recover the database until a certain point in time, you can click the Until Time check box and enter a time to which to restore. Point-in-time recovery only applies to transaction logs, not to full database or table backups.

7. After you have selected all the dumps to restore, click the Restore Now button. If you backed up to a disk device, SQL Server automatically looks to that device for the backups. If you backed up to a tape device, you are prompted to insert the tape that contains the backup in question.

The other option you have when restoring a database is to use the LOAD command from ISQL. Using the LOAD command, you can restore full databases, transaction logs, or single tables. The following is the syntax of the LOAD command:

Loading a database

```
LOAD DATABASE dbname
     FROM dump_device [, dump_device2 [..., dump_device32]]
[WITH options
     [[,] STATS [ = percentage]]]
```

Loading a transaction log

```
LOAD TRANSACTION dbname
     FROM dump_device [, dump_device2 [..., dump_device32]]
[WITH options]
```

Loading a table

```
LOAD TABLE [[database.]owner.]table_name
     FROM dump_device [, dump_device2 [..., dump_device32]]
[WITH options]
```

11.3.2. Recovering User Databases After Media Failure

You need to follow several steps when recovering user databases after media failure. First and foremost, you should back up everything you can if the database is accessible. This is especially important if you can access the transaction log. If you can get a dump of the transaction log, you can restore the database to the point of failure. You also should stop SQL Server and, if possible, make backups of the physical devices. You should gather as much information as possible about the database (or databases) on the disks that failed. This includes information about the size of the devices, the size of the database, and the order in which the database was created and expanded.

The first step is to drop both the corrupt database and the devices it resides on and then re-create the database devices. The following tutorial walks you through this process.

The first step in re-creating a corrupt database is to drop and re-create the devices it resides on. These steps assume no users are in the database or any other database on the server.

1. Open the SQL Enterprise Manager and connect to the server that contains the database you are going to repair.

2. Choose the Database Devices option from the Manage menu. This displays a list of all the devices on the server. Double-click the devices you are going to be re-creating. This opens the Edit Database Device dialog box shown in Figure 11.2. Note the size of each device in question.

Figure 11.2.

The Edit Database Device dialog box tells you where a database device resides on disk and provides the size of the device.

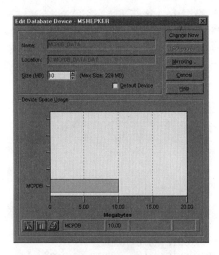

3. Stop the SQL Server service by starting the SQL Service Manager in the Microsoft SQL Server 6.5 program group (see Figure 11.3). Choose the MSSQLServer service and double-click the stop section of the stoplight. Close the SQL Service Manager.

Figure 11.3.

The SQL Service Manager provides a GUI interface for controlling the SQL Server services.

4. From the command line, start SQL Server by typing the following:

```
sqlservr /c /dmaster_device /m
```

In the preceding, *master_device* is the physical path and name for the master device.

5. Drop each database on the damaged device. You can use either the SQL Enterprise Manager or the DBCC DBREPAIR statement. The following is the syntax of that statement:

```
DBCC DBREPAIR (database_name, DROPDB)
```

In the preceding, *database_name* is the name of the database you are going to drop.

6. Drop the lost device using the sp_dropdevice stored procedure. The following is the syntax of that command:

```
sp_dropdevice logical_name, delfile
```

In the preceding, *logical_name* is the name of the device as listed in the sysdevices table in the Master database. The delfile option specifies that the physical device should be deleted if possible.

7. Execute a CHECKPOINT. This ensures that all changes you made have been written to disk.

8. Stop SQL Server and then restart it in normal mode.

9. Re-create the devices you just dropped using the DISK INIT statement. Use the sizes of the original devices in step 2. The following is the syntax of the DISK INIT statement:

```
DISK INIT NAME = 'logical_name', PHYSNAME = 'physical_name', VDEVNO =
➥virtual_device_number, SIZE = number_of_2K_block
```

11

In the preceding, *logical_name* is the logical name of the device you are going to create. The *physical_name* is the path and name of the device on disk.

The *virtual_device_number* is a number from 0 through 255; numbers 0, 126, and 127 are reserved. To choose a virtual device number, run the sp_helpdevice stored procedure. From the results, you can pick a number not listed in the device_number column.

The size is the number of 2KB blocks the device comprises. If you are going to create a 20MB device, for example, use 10240 for the number of blocks.

After you have re-created the devices your database resided on, the next step is to re-create the databases that resided on the devices. To restore the databases, you must re-create the database in the same way it was originally created. Every time you expand or shrink a database, you should keep a record of exactly what you did. If you restore an expanded database onto a new database created as one large segment, you do not get any errors at first. Nevertheless, the database becomes corrupt in time and stops functioning. If you do not have this information, you can extract it from the Master database.

You need to gather information about the corrupt databases so that you can re-create them in the same way they were created. You then need to restore the previously backed up database.

1. You can gather information about how the database was created by running the following query in ISQL:

```
USE master
GO
SELECT 'Type' =
        CASE segmap
                WHEN 3 THEN 'Data'
                WHEN 4 THEN 'Log'
        END,
        'Size' = (size * 2) / 1024
FROM sysusages
WHERE dbid =
        (SELECT dbid FROM sysdatabases
        WHERE name = 'MCPDB')
GO
```

In the preceding, MCPDB is the name of the database you are going to be re-creating. When you re-create the database, you need to assign the blocks of space in the same order and size.

2. Examine the output of the query. The order of the rows is the same as how the database was expanded. The size is listed in megabytes. The following is the output:

```
Type Size
---- -----------
Data 10
Log  3
Data 5
Data 5
Log  5
```

3. Next, you need to re-create the database using the CREATE DATABASE statement. The following is the syntax of the CREATE DATABASE statement:

```
CREATE DATABASE database_name
     [ON {DEFAULT ¦ database_device} [= size]
     [, database_device [= size]]...]
[LOG ON database_device [= size]
     [, database_device [= size]]...]
[FOR LOAD]
```

The FOR LOAD option prevents anyone from using the database between the CREATE DATABASE and LOAD statements. When a database is created with FOR LOAD, SQL Server makes sure that only the database can use the database. After the database has been loaded, you can change the database option using the sp_dboption stored procedure.

4. Because the database was expanded several times after the initial creation, you need to use the ALTER DATABASE statement to expand the database again. The following is the syntax of the ALTER DATABASE statement:

```
ALTER DATABASE database_name
[ON {DEFAULT ¦ database_device} [= size]
[, database_device [= size]]...]
[FOR LOAD]
```

You can use sp_logdevice to allocate log space on a device not currently in use by the database. You need to do this immediately after you run the ALTER DATABASE statement. The following is the syntax of the command:

```
sp_logdevice dbname, database_device
```

5. Restore the database and transaction logs using either the LOAD DATABASE statement or the SQL Enterprise Manager.

Two new stored procedures have been included in SQL Server 6.5 that can greatly ease the task of rebuilding a database after media failure. The two stored procedures are sp_coalesce_fragments and sp_help_revdatabase.

The sp_coalesce_fragments stored procedure takes any contiguous fragments that are on the same device and collapses them into a single fragment. The output of the sp_coalesce_fragments stored procedure tells you the number of fragments that were reduced. Before you begin to re-create a database, you first should run the sp_coalesce_fragments stored procedure. The following is the syntax of the command:

sp_coalesce_fragments *database_name*

The sp_help_revdatabase stored procedure creates a CREATE DATABASE and ALTER DATABASE script that enables you to re-create the database exactly as it was initially created. Any time you create or expand a database, you should run this stored procedure so that, if you ever need the information, it will be there. The following is the syntax of the command:

sp_help_revdatabase *database_name*

The following is an example of the output from sp_help_revdatabase:

```
/********1*********2*********3*********4*********5*********6**
Reverse generated at 1998/02/01   19:48:54:270
Server / Database / Default sortorder ID :
MSHEPKER / MCPDB / 50
DBName                          FromLPage   ToLPage    segmap
------------------------------- ----------- -          ------
MCPDB                           0           5119       3
MCPDB                           5120        6655       4
MCPDB                           6656        11775      3
MCPDB                           11776       14335      4
@@version:  Microsoft SQL Server  6.50 - 6.50.201 (Intel X86)
********1*********2*********3*********4*********5*********6**/
go
USE master
go
----------------- Space and Log allocations  --------------
CREATE  Database  MCPDB
       on  MCPDB_DATA  =   10  -- 5120  of two Kb pages
go
ALTER   Database  MCPDB
       on  MCPDB_LOG  =  3  -- 1536  of two Kb pages
go
EXECute sp_logdevice MCPDB ,MCPDB_LOG
go
ALTER   Database  MCPDB
       on  MCPDB_DATA_EXP1  =   10  -- 5120  of two Kb pages
go
ALTER   Database  MCPDB
       on  MCBPD_LOG_EXP1  =  5  -- 2560  of two Kb pages
go
EXECute sp_logdevice MCPDB ,MCBPD_LOG_EXP1
go
------------------- DB Options  ------------------
EXECute sp_dboption  MCPDB ,'ANSI null default'
                           , false
EXECute sp_dboption  MCPDB ,'dbo use only'
                           , false
EXECute sp_dboption  MCPDB ,'no chkpt on recovery'
```

```
                              , false
/***
EXECute sp_dboption  MCPDB ,'offline'
                              , false
***/
/***
EXECute sp_dboption  MCPDB ,'published'
                              , false
***/
EXECute sp_dboption  MCPDB ,'read only'
                              , false
EXECute sp_dboption  MCPDB ,'select into/bulkcopy'
                              , TRUE
EXECute sp_dboption  MCPDB ,'single user'
                              , false
/***
EXECute sp_dboption  MCPDB ,'subscribed'
                              , false
***/
EXECute sp_dboption  MCPDB ,'trunc. log on chkpt.'
                              , false
go
------------------ sa  is  dbo --------------------
go
```

After generating this script, you just need to open it up and run it in ISQL.

11.4. Recovering System Databases

Most SQL Server functions are controlled by system databases. It is imperative to have good backups of all the system databases so that, if the need ever arises, you can restore them as necessary. The system databases you should be most concerned with are the Master, msdb, and model databases.

11.4.1. Restoring the Master Database with a Good Backup

The Master database controls most of SQL Server's activity. A corruption or loss of the Master database can be devastating. A damaged Master database makes itself known in several ways. SQL Server might not start, segmentation or I/O errors (or both) might develop, or you might receive error reports from a DBCC.

Recovering a damaged Master database is different from recovering a user database. You first must re-create the Master database using SQL Setup and then restore it from a known good backup. The following tutorial shows you how to re-create and restore the Master database.

Recovering the Master database when you have a known good backup requires that you first re-create the Master database and then restore from backup.

1. Start the SQL Server setup program either from the SQL Server installation CD, from the BINN directory in the MSSQL installation directory, or from the SQL Server 6.5 program group. After the setup program has started, click the Continue button.

2. In the SQL Server 6.5 Setup—Options dialog box, choose the Rebuild Master Database option and click the Continue button (see Figure 11.4).

Figure 11.4.

The SQL Server 6.5 Setup—Options dialog box.

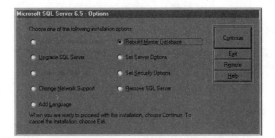

3. In the Rebuild Master Database dialog box, you are asked whether you want to rebuild the Master database. Click the Resume button.

4. In the SQL Server 6.5 Rebuild Options dialog box, choose the Character Set and Sort Order used when you originally set up the server (see Figure 11.5). If you do not choose the Sort Order used when you set up the original server, you cannot restore the Master database. Click the Continue button.

Figure 11.5.

The SQL Server 6.5 Rebuild Options dialog box.

5. For the SQL Server Installation Path, choose the original path to the location where you installed SQL Server.

6. For the Rebuild Master Device, enter the size of the original Master database and click the Continue button.

7. When SQL Server finishes rebuilding the Master database, start the MSSQLServer service, open the SQL Enterprise Manager, and connect to the server.

8. Add a dump device that corresponds to the type and name of the device on which your last backup of the master device resides.

9. Stop SQL Server and restart it from the command line by typing the following:

```
sqlservr /c /dmaster_device /m
```

In the preceding, *master_device* is the path and name of the master device. This starts SQL Server in single user mode, which enables you to make updates to system tables.

10. Restore the Master database from the most recent backup. After the Master database has been restored, the SQL Server service automatically stops.

11. Restart the SQL Server service and reapply any changes made since the most recent backup.

12. Restore the msdb database or re-create all the tasks and alerts you had. You must do this because the process of rebuilding the Master database destroys and rebuilds the msdb database.

11.4.2. Recovering the Master Database Without a Valid Backup

It is possible to re-create the Master database even if you do not have a valid backup of it. Using the DISK INIT and DISK REFIT statements, you can recover and rebuild all pertinent information about the other databases. For this to work, the following statements must be true:

- The media is where the master device fails, or there is physical corruption or deletion of the master device.
- The backup copy of the master device is corrupt or does not exist.
- The data for all other databases exists and is intact.
- You know the virtual device number for all the devices that resided on the server.

The following tutorial shows you how to use the DISK REINIT and DISK REFIT statements to rebuild the Master database.

1. Start the SQL Server setup program either from the SQL Server installation CD or from the BINN directory in the MSSQL installation directory. After the setup program has started, click the Continue button.

2. In the SQL Server 6.5 Setup—Options dialog box, choose the Rebuild Master Database option and click the Continue button.

3. In the Rebuild Master Database dialog box, you are asked whether you want to rebuild the Master database. Click the Resume button.

4. In the SQL Server 6.5 Rebuild Options dialog box, choose the Character Set and Sort Order used when you originally set up the server. Click the Continue button.

5. For the SQL Server Installation Path, choose the original path to the location where you installed SQL Server.

6. For the Rebuild Master Device, enter the size of the original Master database and click the Continue button.

7. Stop SQL Server and restart it from the command line by typing the following:

```
sqlservr /c /dmaster_device /m
```

In the preceding, `master_device` is the path and name of the master device. This starts SQL Server in single user mode, which enables you to make updates to system tables.

8. Use the `DISK REINIT` statement to reinitialize each device. The `DISK REINIT` statement puts an entry into the sysdevices table for each device. You should execute it once for each device. The following is the syntax for the statement:

```
DISK REINIT
    NAME = 'logical_name',
    PHYSNAME = 'physical_name',
    VDEVNO = virtual_device_number,
    SIZE = number_of_2K_blocks
```

It is important that you give the `DISK REINIT` statement the correct information about the sizes of the devices. If the correct information is not provided, you can corrupt your data permanently. SQL Server warns you about potential problems if it can find them, but be sure to run the suggested DBCCs after issuing `DISK REINIT` and `DISK REFIT`.

9. Immediately after executing the `DISK REINIT` statement, you must run the `DISK REFIT` statement to rebuild the entries in the sysusages and sysdatabases tables. This re-creates all the entries entered by the `CREATE DATABASE` and `ALTER DATABASE` statements.

10. Stop SQL Server and restart in normal mode.

11.4.3. Restoring the msdb Database

During the Master database's rebuild process, the msdb database is dropped and rebuilt. This results in the loss of all scheduling information. After the Master database has been rebuilt, you must restore the msdb database. If a current backup of msdb does not exist, you must re-create all scheduled tasks by hand. The following tutorial shows you how to restore the msdb database.

1. If you expanded the original msdb database, allocate more space to the msdb database.

2. Restore msdb from the most recent backup, if it exists.

3. Apply all transaction log dumps performed after the most recent backup.

4. Re-create any scheduled tasks that were created after the last transaction log backups.

11.5. Final Thoughts

Restoring a database always is easier when you have complete information about the database and how it was created. If you keep your information consistent, you can re-create and rebuild your databases much quicker. Every time you do anything to your database, you should write it down and keep it handy in case of database failure.

Before you automatically restore a failed database, it is important that you research the reason behind the failure. If the database became corrupt due to media failure, you need to replace the failed media. If the database corruption was due to user problems, you need to educate the user about what happened and how to avoid it in the future.

11

Lab

Questions

1. As the administrator of a SQL Server, you need to restore a database in which the data has become corrupt. You suspect the cause was a user running an unqualified delete statement against a table. In the time since the database stopped working, you have performed a transaction log dump. What can you do to solve this problem?

    A. Restore the most recent backup and then apply all transaction logs made after the backup.

    B. Apply the transaction logs since the last backup.

    C. Restore from the most recent backup and then have the users re-create the data lost after the backup.

    D. Restore from the most recent backup and then apply the transaction logs until the point of failure.

2. You are attempting to start the MSSQLServer service, and you find the server does not start properly. When examining the Windows NT event log, you find the server is failing to start due to a problem with the master device. What is the first thing you should do?

    A. Check to see whether the master data device is still in place and that no other process, such as third-party backup software, is using or accessing the device.

    B. Restart the SQL Server and everything will function properly.

    C. Replace the hard drive and reinstall SQL Server to fix this error.

    D. Run the DISK REINIT statement to reinitialize the master device.

3. You have determined that the machine on which the SQL Server resides has suffered a hard drive crash. The only database affected was a user database called MCPDB. The database originally was created as a 150MB database with a 25MB log. After a couple months, you expanded the database by 50MB. You have replaced the hard drive. What do you need to do to re-create the database?

    A. Reinstall SQL Server and restore the database from backup.

    B. Create a 200MB data device and a 25MB log device. Restore the database from the most recent backup.

C. Create a 150MB database with a 25MB device. Use the ALTER DATABASE command to expand the database by another 50MB and then restore the database from the most recent backup.

D. Use the DISK REINIT and DISK REFIT commands to re-create the database devices.

4. The Master database has crashed on the SQL Server. The only device affected was the Master database device, and you do not have a good backup. What steps must you take to re-create the databases on the server?

A. Rebuild the Master database and re-create the database devices using the DISK INIT statement.

B. Rebuild the Master database using the SQL Setup program. Then use the DISK REINIT and DISK REFIT statements to re-create the databases.

C. Restore the database from whatever backup you have. Then re-create the database devices and restore the other databases from the most recent backups.

D. Reinstall SQL Server and restore the user database from backup.

5. You have just rebuilt and restored the Master database after a disk crash. After a couple days, you notice the scheduled backups that had been running previously are no longer running. What is the most likely cause of the problem?

A. The Master database has become corrupt. You need to go through the steps to re-create it.

B. The msdb database was dropped and re-created during the rebuild of the Master database. You must restore the msdb database from the most recent backup.

C. The SQL Executive service is not running.

D. You forgot to install the msdb database. You must reinstall SQL Server.

6. You are in the process of restoring a user database that crashed because a user accidentally dropped several objects in the database. When you attempt to apply transaction logs, you get errors. What is the most likely reason for the errors?

A. The user dropped the syslogs table.

B. The database was not corrupted by the user; media failure actually caused the problem.

11

C. You cannot restore transaction logs to repair a database.

D. You are attempting to restore the transaction logs out of order.

7. You have just rebooted your SQL Server after performing routine maintenance. Several users have informed you that they cannot access the user
   database DATAREPOS. What is the most likely reason the users cannot access
   the database?

   A. The database has crashed and must be restored from backup.

   B. The database is being recovered.

   C. The users are trying to log in to the server using the incorrect username
      and password.

   D. The DBO Use Only option is turned on.

8. You are attempting to recover the Master database on a SQL Server. You have
   a current backup. You have rebuilt the Master database using the SQL Setup
   program, but you receive errors when you attempt to restore from backup.
   What is the most likely reason you are getting these errors?

   A. You re-created the Master database using the incorrect sort order or
      character set.

   B. Someone is using the Master database.

   C. The backup you made of the Master database is corrupt.

   D. You are not using the correct process to restore the Master database.

9. What happens to users that are in a database when you restore it?

   A. All user connections are dropped, and any transactions are rolled back.

   B. All user connections are dropped, but state information is maintained so
      that they can restart exactly where they left off.

   C. All user connections are maintained.

   D. You cannot restore a database when users are in it.

10. When restoring transaction log dumps, you can perform point-in-time recov-
    ery of databases. What does this mean?

    A. Point-in-time recovery means you can recover a database until the cur-
       rent time.

B. Point-in-time recovery means transaction logs can be restored through a date and time you specify. Transactions committed after that date and time are rolled back.

C. Point-in-time recovery means you can recover an interval of days from a transaction log backup.

D. Every restoration of a transaction log dump is a point-in-time recovery.

Exercises

1. Restoring a Database

> **Note**
>
> This exercise helps to address the following certification exam objective:
> ■ Restore a corrupted database.

This exercise shows you how to restore the pubs database from the backup you made in Day 10. This exercise should take approximately 15 minutes to complete:

1. From the Server Manager window in the SQL Enterprise Manager, select a server and connect to it.

2. From the Tools menu, select the Database Backup/Restore option. This opens the Database Backup/Restore dialog box. Select the Restore tab.

3. From the Database drop-down box, choose the pubs database.

4. From the Restore option area, choose the Database option.

5. In the Backup History section, choose the backup you made in Day 10.

6. After you have selected the dump, click the Restore Now button. SQL Server automatically looks to the disk device for the backups and restores the dump.

2. Recovering the Master Database with a Good Backup

> **Note**
>
> This exercise helps to address the following certification exam objective:
> ■ Re-create a lost device.

This exercise shows you how to re-create and restore the Master database after it has been lost. This exercise takes approximately 30 minutes to complete.

> **Warning**
>
> This exercise should only be performed on a backup server. If not performed correctly, dropping and rebuilding the Master database can result in the loss of all user databases on the server.

1. From the SQL Enterprise Manager, choose the server you will be working with and connect to it.

2. Create a backup device and back up the Master database to it.

3. From the Server menu, choose Error Log. This opens the SQL Server Error Log. Look through the error log to find the default sort order and the default character set. Make note of these.

4. Open the SQL Server Service Manager and stop the MSSQLServer service.

5. Open Windows NT Explorer and go to the directory in which the Master database device resides. This most likely is C:\MSSQL\DATA.

6. Rename the master.dat to master.bak.

7. Open the SQL Server Service Manager and try to start the MSSQLServer service. It does not start. An error stating that the file could not be found is added to the Application log in the Windows NT Event viewer.

8. Start the SQL Server setup program either from the SQL Server installation CD, from the BINN directory in the MSSQL installation directory, or from the SQL Server 6.5 program group. After the setup program has started, click the Continue button.

9. In the SQL Server 6.5 Setup—Options dialog box, choose the Rebuild Master Database option and click the Continue button.

10. In the Rebuild Master Database dialog box, you are asked whether you want to rebuild the Master database. Click the Resume button.

11. In the SQL Server 6.5 Rebuild Options dialog box, choose the Character Set and Sort Order you wrote down in step 3. If you don't choose the same Sort Order used when you set up the original server, you cannot restore the Master database. Click the Continue button.

12. For the SQL Server Installation Path, choose the original path to the location where you installed SQL Server.

13. For the Rebuild Master Device, enter the size of the original Master database and click the Continue button.

14. When SQL Server finishes rebuilding the Master database, start the MSSQLServer service, open up the SQL Enterprise Manager, and connect to the server.

15. Add a dump device that corresponds to the backup you made in step 2.

16. Stop SQL Server and restart it from the command line by typing the following:

```
sqlservr /c /dmaster_device /m
```

In the preceding, *master_device* is the path and name of the master device. This starts SQL Server in single user mode, which enables you to make updates to system tables.

17. Restore the Master database from the most recent backup. After the Master database has been restored, the SQL Server service automatically stops.

18. Restart the SQL Server service. Any user databases that were on the server before you renamed the device are now available.

Answers to Questions

1. **D**   Restoring transaction logs until the point of failure enables you to re-create the database if you know approximately what time the failure happened.

2. **A**   The first step in troubleshooting errors with the master device is to check whether the device still exists and that SQL Server can gain exclusive use of it.

3. **C**   You have to re-create and expand the database in exactly the same order as it was originally created.

4. **B**   When re-creating the Master database without a good backup, you must re-create the database using the SQL Server Setup program and then use the DISK REINIT and DISK REFIT commands to rebuild the user databases.

5. **B**   The msdb database, which controls scheduled tasks, is dropped and rebuilt during the rebuild process of the Master database.

6. **D**   When restoring transaction logs, you must restore them in the same order as they were made.

7. **B**   After the SQL Server service is started, all databases go through the automatic recovery process. Users cannot access databases being recovered.

8. **A**   When you rebuild the Master database, you have to specify a character set and a sort order. If you specify a different sort order from the one used in the original Master database, you cannot restore.

9. **D**   You cannot restore a database when users are in it.

10. **B**   Point-in-time recovery means transaction logs can be restored using a date and time you specify. Transactions committed after that date and time are rolled back.

11

TEST DAY
FAST FACTS

The following are some key facts
you'll learn in this chapter:

● SQL Server replication is a
  powerful, built-in feature
  that enables data from a single server to be sent to
  multiple servers.

● SQL Server replication uses
  a publisher/subscriber
  metaphor.

● Three distinct server roles
  are involved in SQL Server
  replication: publication, distribution, and subscription.

● Replicated data always
  should be treated as read-
  only.

● After replication is set up,
  the published database and
  the subscription database
  are synchronized. This
  ensures that the schema and
  data on the publishing
  server are the same as on
  the subscription servers.

● SQL Server replication is
  transaction log based.

● Several scenarios can be
  used to solve different business applications.

Day 12

SQL Server Replication

In the business world, information needs to be in the
right place at the right time. Information in the form of
books and papers can be difficult to share. With the
advent of computers and, more importantly, computer
networks, sharing information has become easier than
ever. Microsoft provides a powerful tool with SQL Server
to assist in the sharing and movement of data from one
area of a computer network to another. This tool is SQL
Server replication.

Objectives

This chapter covers the following material:

- Identify prerequisites for replication
- Identify the appropriate replication scenario to use
- Configure the servers used for setting up replication
- Set up various replication scenarios
- Implement replication
- Schedule a replication event
- Recognize the situations in which you must perform manual synchronization
- Identify the system tables used in replication
- Resolve setup problems
- Resolve fault-tolerance problems and recovery problems

12.1. Replication Definition and Process Overview

Before setting up and running SQL Server replication, you need to understand what replication is and how it works. *Replication* is the process of moving data from one database to another. You can set this up in several different ways, and there are different ways to make it work in your business.

12.1.1. The Benefits of SQL Server Replication

Setting up SQL Server replication has several benefits. Data can be delivered to different locations to eliminate network traffic and unnecessary loads on a single server. You can, for example, move all or some of the information from an online transaction processing database over to a different server to provide report generation. Another benefit is that data can be moved from a single server to several other servers to increase availability and to decentralize data. You can create a mirror of your main database on another server so that, if the main server crashes, users can switch to the other server and continue to work with little downtime or data loss. Using SQL Server, replication can move data in both these situations.

12.1.2. An Overview of Distributed Data

The process of sharing and moving data often is referred to as *distributed data*. Two models are available to you in the distributed data process. In some applications, such as online transaction processing and inventory-control systems, data needs to be synchronized at all times. This model is known as *tight consistency*. In other applications, such as decisions-support systems and report-generation engines, 100 percent data synchronization is not as important. This is known as *loose consistency*.

SQL Server implements tight-consistency data distribution in the form of two-phase commits. A *two-phase commit* makes sure that a transaction is committed on all servers; otherwise, the transaction is rolled back on all servers. This ensures that all data on all servers is 100 percent in sync at all times. One of the main drawbacks of tight consistency is that it requires a high-speed LAN to work. The two-phase commit is not actually part of SQL Server replication and is not covered in this chapter. Two-phase commits are implemented using the distributed transaction coordinator.

Loose consistency is implemented in SQL Server through replication. Replication enables data to be updated on all servers, but the process is not a simultaneous one. The result is *real-enough time data*. There is a lag between the time that data is updated on the main server and the replicated data. Unlike the two-phase consistency model, replication works over LANs and WANs as well as slow or fast links.

12.2. Characteristics of Replication

The following characteristics make SQL Server replication a reliable option for distributing data:

- When describing various parts of replication, SQL Server uses a publisher/subscriber metaphor.

- Three distinct server roles are involved in SQL Server replication: publication, distribution, and subscription. These roles are not exclusive of each other, and any server can perform one or all of them at any point.

- Data sent to the subscription server is treated as read-only.

- After replication is set up, the published database and the subscription database are synchronized. This ensures that the schema and data contained on the publishing server are the same as on the subscription servers.

- SQL Server replication is a transaction log–based process. Any transaction to be replicated is read from the source database's transaction log and then applied to the source database.

- When setting up SQL Server replication, a specialized database is created. Transactions are stored in this specialized database before they are sent out to the destination database.

- Replicated data can be controlled by choosing specific columns, rows, tables, or full databases to be replicated.

12.2.1. The Publisher/Subscriber Metaphor

The following SQL Server replication terminology comes from the publisher/subscriber metaphor:

- The basic unit of replication is an article. An *article* is data from a table marked for replication.

- A *publication* is a group of tables or articles to which other servers can subscribe. A publication must contain at least one article.

12

- The server making publications available is called the *publishing server* or *publisher*. This server is where the original database is stored.
- The server that uses the publications made available on a publishing server is called the *subscription server* or *subscriber*. A subscriber can subscribe to some or all of the publications on the publishing server and can use some or all of the articles in a subscription.

12.2.2. Server Roles in Replication

A SQL Server can play three separate roles in the replication process. A server can play any of these roles at once but not in the same scenario. A publisher, for example, cannot subscribe to its own publication. Table 12.1 outlines the roles a server can play.

Table 12.1. Roles a server can play in the replication process.

Server Role	Description
Publication server	The publication server contains the published databases. It makes data from the published databases available for subscription and sends updates to the distribution server.
Distribution server	The distribution server can be the same server as the publication server, or it can reside on a different server. This server contains the distribution database. This database, also called the store-and-forward database, holds changes that were forwarded from the publication database and then forwards them to the subscription servers. A single distribution server can be used to support several publication servers.
Subscription server	The subscription server contains a copy of the database being distributed. Any changes made to the distributed database are sent and applied to the copy. The subscription database should be treated as read-only but not marked as read-only. If the database is marked read-only, changes made to the distributed database are not applied to the subscription database.

12.2.3. The Synchronization Process

The synchronization process is performed with every new subscriber to a publication. The synchronization process happens only one time for each new subscriber. It makes sure that the database schema and data are exact replicas on both servers. After the initial synchronization, all updates are made using replication.

When a new server subscribes to a publication, synchronization is performed. When synchronization begins, a copy of the table schema is copied to a file with an .sch extension. This file contains all information necessary to create the table and any indexes on the table, if requested. Next, a copy is made of the data in the table to be synchronized and is written to a file with a .tmp extension. The data file is a BCF, or bulk copy file. Both files are stored in the temporary working directory, which by default is \MSSQL\REPLDATA, on the distribution server.

After the synchronization process has started and the data files have been created, any INSERTs, UPDATEs, and DELETEs are stored in the distribution database. These changes are not replicated to the subscription database until the synchronization process is complete.

When the synchronization process starts, only new subscribers are affected. Subscribers that already have been synchronized and have been receiving modifications are unaffected. The synchronization set is applied to all servers waiting for initial synchronization. After the schema and data have been re-created, all transactions stored in the distribution server are sent to the subscriber.

Four options are available for synchronization. The options are listed in Table 12.2.

Table 12.2. Types of synchronization available.

Synchronization Type	Description
Automatic synchronization	Automatic synchronization is initiated by SQL Server on a scheduled basis. The process automatically creates the synchronization set and sends it to the distribution server. No user intervention is required. Because automatic synchronization occurs on a scheduled basis and requires a large amount of server resources, it is best to schedule the event as infrequently as possible and during off-peak times.
Manual synchronization	Manual synchronization is initiated and carried out by the user. As with automatic synchronization, the publication server creates a schema script and the data file and stores it in the working directory of the distribution server. The files are then applied to

continues

12

Table 12.2. continued

Synchronization Type	Description
	the subscription server by the user. The user must inform SQL Server when synchronization is complete. Manual synchronization is useful when replicating across a slow WAN link. The synchronization set can be sent on a tape or other physical media to the location where the subscription database is.
No synchronization	When setting up synchronization, you can specify that SQL Server should not synchronize the published database with the destination. This assumes all tables already are synchronized. This option is intended for advanced users that are going to implement a custom replication solution.
Scheduled table refresh	Scheduled table refresh is another available option when setting up a subscription. In effect, the synchronization process is repeated at regular intervals. Standard replication of INSERTs, UPDATEs, and DELETEs is not provided to the subscribers. Scheduled table refresh is useful when you need to refresh the data on a subscriber at regularly scheduled intervals.

12.2.4. The Log Reader Process

After the initial synchronization has taken place, SQL Server uses log-based replication to move transactions from the publication server to the subscription server. As mentioned on Day 10, "Backing Up and Managing SQL Server Data," all actions that modify data in a database are logged to the transaction log in that database. Not only is this log used in the automatic recovery process, but it also is used in the replication process.

When an article is created for publication and the subscription is activated, all entries about that article are marked in the transaction log. For each publication in a database, a log reader process reads the transaction log and looks for any marked transactions. When the log reader process finds a change in the log, it reads the changes and converts them to SQL statements that correspond to the action taken in the article. The SQL statements then are stored in a table on the distribution server. The distribution server then reads the changes and runs them on the subscription server.

Because replication is based on the transaction log, this causes several changes in the way the transaction log works. During normal processing, any transaction that has been successfully completed or rolled back is marked inactive. When performing replication, completed transactions are not marked inactive until the log reader process has read them and sent them to the distribution server. One of the major changes in the transaction log occurs when the Truncate Log on Checkpoint database option is turned on. With this option on, SQL Server truncates the transaction log every time a checkpoint is performed, which can be as often as every several seconds. The inactive portion of the log is not truncated until the log reader process has read the transaction.

Another change is made in nonlogged processes. Truncating a table, for example, and fast bulk copying into a table are nonlogged processes. In tables marked for publication, you cannot perform nonlogged operations unless you turn off replication on that table.

12.2.5. What Can and Can't Be Published

When setting up replication, it is important to know what you can and cannot publish. One of the advances of SQL Server 6.5 from SQL Server 6.0 is that you are able to publish text/image columns. The following is a list of what you can publish:

- You can publish entire databases by selecting all tables when setting up a publication.
- You can publish a subset of tables in a database.
- You can publish single tables in a database.
- You can publish a horizontal subset of rows in the published table, as shown in Figure 12.1. The subscribing servers receive only the subset of rows.
- You can publish a vertical subset of columns in the original table, as shown in Figure 12.2. The subscribing server receives only the subset of rows.
- You can publish a horizontally and vertically partitioned article, as shown in Figure 12.3. The subscription server receives only a subset of rows and columns.

The following is a list of what cannot be published:

- User tables without a primary key cannot be published.
- The model, msdb, and tempdb databases and all system tables in the Master database cannot be published.
- Timestamp columns cannot be published. When timestamp columns are chosen for publication, they are converted to binary(8) before they are sent.

12

Figure 12.1.

When an article is horizontally partitioned, the subscribing servers receive only a subset of the rows in the original table.

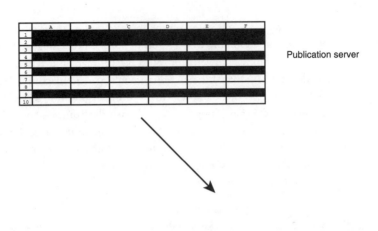

Publication server

Subscription server

Figure 12.2.

When an article is vertically partitioned, the subscribing servers receive only a subset of the columns in the original table.

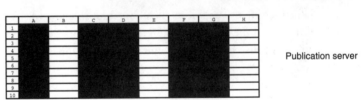

Publication server

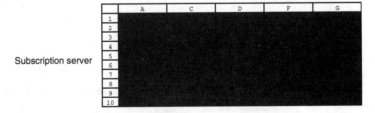

Subscription server

Figure 12.3.

In a horizontally and vertically partitioned article, the subscribing server receives a subset of rows and columns.

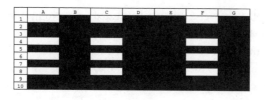

Publication server

Subscription server

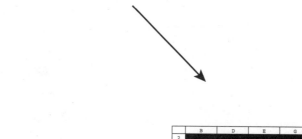

12.3. Identify and Set Up Replication Scenarios

You can choose from several scenarios when setting up replication. You can do specific things with each scenario. The following are the different replication scenarios:

- Central publisher
- Central publisher with a remote distributor
- Publishing subscriber
- Central publisher
- Central subscriber
- Multiple publishers of a single table

12.3.1. Central Publisher

The central publisher replication scenario, shown in Figure 12.4, is the most commonly used scenario. In this scenario, one server functions as both publisher and distributor. The publisher/distributor services any number of subscribers. The data

12

sent to the subscriber server should be treated as read-only and should not be updated. This is because replication is a one-way process. Data moves only from the publisher to the subscriber. When data is updated on the subscriber, the changes are not reflected on the publication server. If there is a need to update data, the user should connect to the publication server and update the data there. The changes are then replicated down to the subscription servers. The central publisher scenario is the default scenario for SQL Server replication.

Figure 12.4.

The central publisher scenario is the simplest and most frequently used scenario.

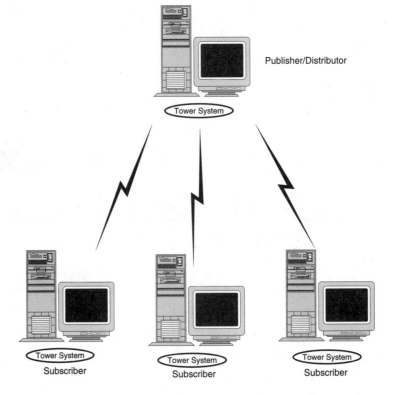

The central publisher scenario can be used in the following situations:

- When creating a copy of a database for ad hoc queries and report generation
- When sending out a copy of a master price list to remote locations

■ When maintaining a local copy of an online transaction processing database during communications outages

12.3.2. Central Publisher with Remote Distributor

The central publisher with remote distributor scenario, shown in Figure 12.5, is similar to the central publisher subscriber and can be used in the same situations. The major difference is that a second server is brought in to perform the role of distributor. This is useful when you need to free the publishing server from having to perform the distribution task. A single distributor server can distribute changes for several publishers. The publisher and distributor need to be connected to each other through a reliable, high-speed data link.

Figure 12.5.

The central publisher with remote distributor scenario is used when the task of replication needs to be removed from the publishing server.

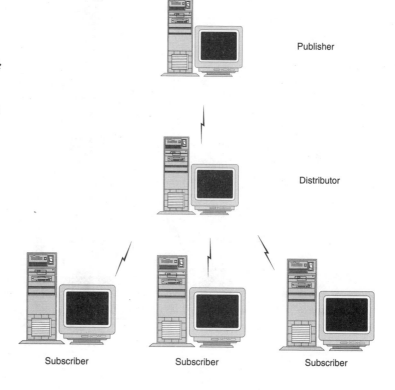

Publisher

Distributor

Subscriber   Subscriber   Subscriber

12

12.3.3. Publishing Subscriber

In the publishing subscriber scenario, shown in Figure 12.6, the distribution server acts as both a subscriber to the original database and a publisher of the local copy. This scenario works best when there is a slow or expensive network link between the primary server and the rest of the subscribers. ABC Corp's main office is in San Diego, for example, and has several branch offices in Japan. Instead of replicating changes to all the branch offices in Japan, ABC Corp chooses to send all updates to a server in Tokyo. The server in Tokyo then replicates updates to all other subscriber servers in Japan. The major benefit of this scenario is a reduction in network traffic and communication costs.

Figure 12.6.

The publishing subscriber scenario is used when you need to replicate across a slow or expensive WAN link.

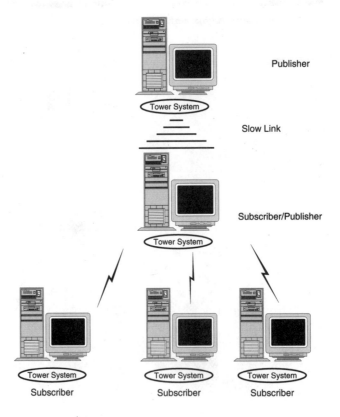

Publisher

Slow Link

Subscriber/Publisher

Subscriber   Subscriber   Subscriber

12.3.4. Central Subscriber

In the central subscriber scenario, shown in Figure 12.7, several publishers replicate data to a single, central subscriber. You should use this scenario when you need to provide a central location that has all the data from the remote locations. When you implement this scenario, you need to take several precautions to make sure that all data remains synchronized and is not overwritten. Before implementing this scenario, you need to perform the following tasks:

1. Create a column that contains a unique identifier for the data replicated from each site. Use this identifier to partition the rows.

2. Add the column that contains the unique identifier to the primary key.

3. Perform a manual synchronization of the table.

Figure 12.7.

When using the central subscriber scenario, several publishers send data to a single, central subscriber.

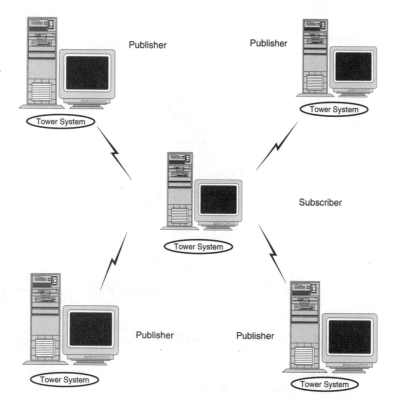

12

12.3.5. Multiple Publishers of a Single Table

In the multiple publishers of a single table scenario, shown in Figure 12.8, a single, horizontally partitioned table is maintained on every server participating in the scenario. Each server publishes a particular set of rows and subscribes to the rows published by all other servers. When implementing this scenario, make sure that all sites remain synchronized. The most frequently used applications of this system are regional order-processing systems and reservation-tracking systems. Also make sure that only local users can update local data. This can be implemented through stored procedures, restrictive views, or a CHECK constraint.

Figure 12.8.

In the multiple publishers of a single table scenario, a single, horizontally partitioned table is maintained by every server.

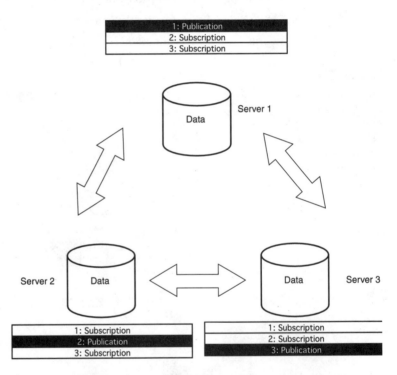

12.4. Configuring Servers for Replication

When setting up SQL Server replication, you must perform several tasks to make sure that everything works as planned. The following is a list of what must be completed:

- Make sure that there's an adequate amount of memory on the distribution server. The distribution server must have at least 32MB of RAM available with at least 16MB dedicated to SQL Server. The publication and subscription servers only need 16MB. If your replication scenario requires the distribution database to reside on the publication server, the publication server must have 32MB of RAM.

■ Make sure that the working directory on the distribution server is available to the publication server. This, by default, is \MSSQL\REPLDATA.

■ Use one character set on all servers. If you want all query results on all servers to remain the same, you also should use the same sort order, although this is not required.

■ Register all servers participating in the replication scenario using the SQL Enterprise Manager.

■ Make sure that the default network library is Named Pipes or Multi-Protocol. Replication can be set up to run on servers using any security mode. Despite the security mode, the distribution server connects to the subscription servers using a trusted connection. Use the SQL client configuration utility to set the distribution server to use the Named Pipes or Multi-Protocol network library.

■ When setting up replication between servers that reside in different domains, you must establish a trust relationship between the domains.

■ Make sure that there's enough disk space for the destination databases.

■ Make sure that there's enough disk space for the transaction log on the publication database. Remember that, during replication, the oldest transactions are not purged from the publication database until they have been sent to the distribution database.

■ Create a user account to be used for the SQL Executive service. This account should be a part of the Administrator group and should be granted permission to Log On as a Service. When setting up this account, the User Cannot Change Password and Password Never Expires options should be set.

■ Increase the number of user connections available on both the publisher and subscription servers. On the publishing server, increase the number of user connections by the number of databases to be enabled for publishing. On the subscription server, increase the number of user connections by the number of subscription databases.

■ Make sure that all tables to be published have a declared primary key.

12

12.5. Setting Up Replication

This section outlines the steps you need to take to create a replication scenario. The following steps are required to set up replication:

1. Install or select a distribution database.

2. Set up options for the publishing server.

3. Set up options for the subscribing server.

4. Create and manage publications.

5. Create and manage subscriptions.

12.5.1. Installing a Distribution Database

When setting up a replication scenario, you need to either choose an existing distribution server or set up a new one for use by your publication server. The following tutorial shows you how to set up a new distribution database and options for the publishing server.

A key component in any replication scenario is the distribution database. These steps assume you have chosen to use a local distribution database.

1. Start the SQL Enterprise Manager and select the server you will be using as the publication server.

2. From the Server menu, choose Replication Configuration and then click Install Publishing. At this point, if your server is not configured correctly, you receive one of two errors. The first possible message indicates that SQL Server has not been configured with enough memory. To fix this, allocate more memory to SQL Server. The second possible message indicates that replication must run under a Windows NT user account other than the LocalSystem account. To fix this, you must right-click the SQL Executive and choose Configure SQL Executive. If everything is set correctly, the Install Replication Publishing dialog box opens, as shown in Figure 12.9.

3. Make sure that Local—Install New Local Distribution Database is chosen.

4. In the Database Name box, type `distribution`.

5. In the Data Device drop-down box, select New. You are prompted to create a new data device. The minimum recommended size for this device is 30MB. This size can be expanded if necessary.

Figure 12.9.

You can choose to install a new local distribution database or to connect to an existing one.

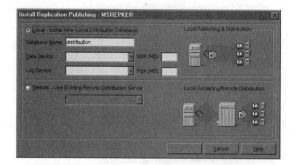

6. In the Log Device drop-down box, select New. You are prompted to create a new log device. The minimum recommended size for this device is 15MB. This size can be expanded if necessary.

7. Click OK to complete the installation of the distribution database and close the Install Replication Publishing dialog box.

8. When installation of the distribution database is complete, you are asked whether you want to install publishing databases and subscribers at this time. Click Yes and the Replication—Publishing dialog box opens, as shown in Figure 12.10.

Figure 12.10.

You can choose which servers to publish to and which databases to publish.

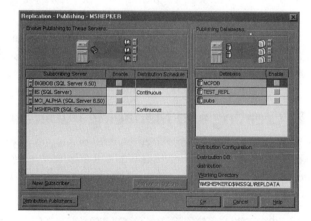

12

9. In the Enable Publishing to These Servers area of the Replication—Publishing dialog box, you can choose any server registered in the SQL Enterprise Manager.

10. After enabling replication to a server, the Distribution Options button becomes active. If you click it, the Distribution Options dialog box opens, as shown in Figure 12.11.

Figure 12.11.

You can configure how changes are sent to subscribers.

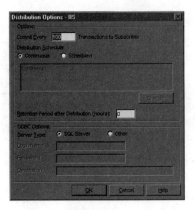

11. In the Distribution Options dialog box, you can set up and configure how frequently changes are sent to subscriber databases. By default, the subscription server receives every 100 transactions made on the publishing server. You also can designate specific days and times for distribution by clicking the Scheduled option and choosing the Change button.

12. After making changes in the Distribution Options dialog box, click OK to commit the changes.

13. Repeat steps 9 through 12 to configure other servers to act as subscription servers.

14. In the Publishing Databases area, you can select which user databases will be available for publication on your server. Only user databases can be chosen for publication. When you are finished setting up publication servers and published databases, click OK to commit the changes.

12.5.2. Creating and Managing Publications

After creating a distribution database, you need to create publications that are available for subscription. After you create publications, other servers can connect to the publication server and receive changes. The following tutorial shows you how to set up a publication.

Before a subscription server can connect to your publisher and begin receiving changes to published databases, you must set up publications.

1. Start the SQL Enterprise Manager and connect to the publishing server on which you want to create a new publication.

2. From the Manage menu, click Replication and then Publications. The Manage Publications dialog box opens, as shown in Figure 12.12.

MESSAGE

Date .... Time ....

To ....

WHILE YOU WERE OUT

984-9101

From ....

TELEPHONE ....

Telephoned		Please call	
Called to see you		Will call again	
Wants to see you		Returned your call	

MESSAGE .... *St Josephs Prest* ....

3261 Henry

Clark Park

Operator.. URGENT ☐

46-501 pink
46-502 yellow

Hilroy

which you enabled replication in the previous
Edit Publications dialog box opens, as shown

dbo.authors
dbo.employee
dbo.jobs
dbo.pub_info
dbo.publishers
dbo.sales
dbo.stores
dbo.titleauthor
dbo.titles

Add >
< Remove

4. In the Publication Title box, enter the name of the publication. This is a required field.

5. In the Description box, enter a short description of the publication. This is not a required field.

6. In the Replication Frequency area, choose either Transaction Based or Scheduled Table Refresh. If you will be performing standard log-based replication, choose Transaction Based. If you are planning to refresh the entire contents of the table—including schema and data—choose Scheduled Table Refresh.

12

7. In the Articles in Publication area of the Articles tab, you can choose which tables or articles are going to be available to anyone that subscribes to the publication.

8. If you need to horizontally or vertically partition an article, select that article and click the Edit button. The Manage Article dialog box opens, as shown in Figure 12.14. In this dialog box, you can choose specific columns to replicate (vertical partitioning) and can provide a restriction clause that will choose specific rows in the table (horizontal partitioning).

Figure 12.14.

You can horizontally and vertically partition a table using the Manage Article dialog box.

9. When you have completed editing the article, press the OK button to return to the Edit Publications dialog box. In the Synchronization tab, you can choose the initial synchronization method. The default option is Bulk Copy Data—Native Format. This option only works for replication between SQL Servers. If you will be replicating data to ODBC data sources, you must choose Bulk Copy Data—Character Format. You also can change the default synchronization schedule.

10. In the Security tab, you can choose whether to provide Restricted or Unrestricted subscription security. If you need to make sure that only certain servers can access the publication, choose the Restrict option and then choose the servers with access.

11. After you have completed defining the publication, click the Add button to create the publication.

12.5.3. Setup Options for the Subscribing Server

When setting up subscription options, you need to determine which servers can replicate to the server you have and which destination databases can subscribe to publications. The following tutorial shows you how to set up options for subscription servers:

1. Open the SQL Enterprise Manager and connect to the subscribing server.

2. From the Server menu, choose Replication Configuration and then click Subscribing. The Replication—Subscribing dialog box opens, as shown in Figure 12.15.

Figure 12.15.

In the Replication—Subscribing dialog box, you can enable subscription from the specified server and can choose the destination databases for subscriptions.

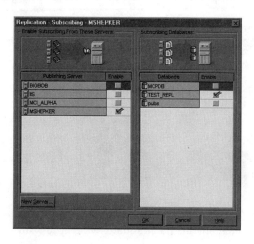

3. In the Enable Subscribing From These Servers area, you can choose the servers from which you will be publishing.

4. In the Subscribing Databases area, you can choose where the data from the subscription databases should go.

12.5.4. Setting Up Subscriptions

Before a subscription server can receive data from a publication server, it must subscribe to articles or publications. This can be accomplished by performing either a push subscription or a pull subscription.

A *pull subscription* is set up and managed by the subscription server. The subscription server pulls the publication down from the publication server. The biggest advantage is that pull subscriptions enable system administrators of the subscription servers to

12

choose what publications they receive. With pull subscriptions, publishing and subscribing are separate acts. They are not necessarily performed by the same user.

The following tutorial shows you how to set up a pull subscription.

A pull subscription is set up and administered by the subscription server. Before setting up a pull subscription, you should create the destination database on the subscribing server.

1. Open the SQL Enterprise Manager and connect to the subscription server.
2. From the Manage menu, choose Replication and then Subscriptions. The Manage Subscriptions dialog box opens, as shown in Figure 12.16.

Figure 12.16.

In the Manage Subscriptions dialog box, you can choose the server and publications to which you subscribe.

3. Click the plus sign next to the server and then the plus sign next to the database containing the publication to which you want to subscribe.
4. Highlight the publication to which you want to subscribe and click the Subscribe button. The Subscription Options dialog box opens, as shown in Figure 12.17.

Figure 12.17.

In the Subscription Options dialog box, you can choose which database the replicated data goes into and how the initial synchronization process takes place.

5. In the Database area, you can choose a preexisting database to replicate into or you can create a new database.

6. In the Sync Method area, you can choose how synchronization takes place. If you want SQL Server to automatically synchronize the subscription for you, choose Data Synchronization Automatically Applied. If you want to synchronize data by hand, choose Data Synchronization Manually Applied by Operator. If you already have set up synchronization, choose No Data Synchronization.

7. After you have set up your subscriptions, click OK to activate them.

A *push subscription* is created and managed by the publication server. The publication server pushes the publication down to the subscription server. The advantage of push subscriptions is that all administration takes place in a central location. Publishing and subscribing can be done at the same time, and many subscribers can be set up at once.

The following tutorial shows you how to set up a push subscription.

A push subscription is set up and administered on the publication server. Before setting up a pull subscription, you should create the destination database on the subscription server. This assumes you already have created a subscription and are now setting it up to be pushed to subscribers.

1. Open the SQL Enterprise Manager and connect to the publication server.

2. From the Manage menu, choose Replication and then click Publications. The Manage Publications dialog box opens, as shown in Figure 12.18.

12

Figure 12.18.

In the Manage Publications dialog box, you can either create a new publication or edit an existing one to set it up for a push subscription.

3. Choose an existing publication and click the Change button, or create a new publication following the instructions previously outlined. In the Edit Publications dialog box, click the Subscribers button. The Publication Subscribers dialog box opens, as shown in Figure 12.19.

Figure 12.19.

The Publication Subscribers dialog box.

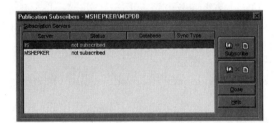

4. Choose the server to which you will push the subscription and click the Subscribe button. The Subscription Options dialog box opens, as shown in Figure 12.20.

Figure 12.20.

In the Subscription Options dialog box, you can set up the options you will use in a push subscription.

5. In the Database area, enter the name of a preexisting database to replicate into or create a new database.

6. In the Sync Method area, you can choose how synchronization takes place. If you want SQL Server to automatically synchronize the subscription for you, choose Data Synchronization Automatically Applied. If you want to synchronize the data by hand, choose Data Synchronization Manually Applied by Operator. If you already have set up synchronization, choose No Data Synchronization.

7. After you have set up your subscriptions, click OK to activate them.

12.6. Identify System Tables Used in Replication

Replication relies on several system tables. These tables track the status of publications and the changes sent to the subscriptions. Table 12.3 lists table names, the server on which each table resides, and a description of what each table does.

Table 12.3. System tables.

Table Name	Server	Description
MSjobs	Distribution	Contains one row for each job scheduled for distribution.
MSjob_commands	Distribution	Contains a row for each command distributed to the subscribers. There is at least one record per job listed in the MSjobs table.
MSjob_subscriptions	Distribution	Contains one row for each article to which a subscriber subscribes.
MSlast_job_info	Subscription	Contains a row that designates the last job successfully replicated to the subscriber.
MSsubscriber_info	Distribution	Contains one row for each subscriber to any publication.
MSsubscriber_jobs	Distribution	Contains one row for every transaction sent to every subscriber. If you have one command generating five rows in the MSjob_commands table and if you have five subscribers, there are 25 rows in this table.
MSsubscriber_status	Distribution	Contains information about the last set of commands sent to each subscriber.
sysarticles	Publication	Contains one row for each article published on the server.
syspublications	Publication	Contains a row for each publication published on the server.
syssubscriptions	Publication	Contains a row that associates articles with subscription servers expecting to receive data.

12

12.7. Troubleshooting Replication

SQL Server is designed to work with as little user interaction as possible. After you set up your publications and subscriptions, you rarely should have to intervene. Nevertheless, you need to know how to fix the following situations:

■ No subscription servers are receiving changes.

■ One subscription server of many is not receiving changes.

■ The transaction log on the publishing database is filling up or is completely full.

12.7.1. No Subscription Servers Are Receiving Changes

After you have set up replication and synchronization has taken place, your subscription server should begin receiving changes from the publication server. If no changes are sent, there are two places you can look: the log reader task or the distribution task. Before you can troubleshoot one or the other, however, you must discover which one is not working. To accomplish this, you need to examine the MSjob_commands table in the distribution database. You can do this by running the following SQL statement:

```
SELECT command FROM MSjob_commands
```

If the changes you made to the published tables are not contained in the results set, the problem is the log reader task. Otherwise, the problem is the distribution task. The following tutorial shows you how to troubleshoot the log reader task:

1. Start the SQL Enterprise Manager and connect to the distribution server.

2. From the Server menu, choose Scheduled Tasks. The Manage Tasks window opens. Double-click the log reader task to open the Edit Task dialog box, as shown in Figure 20.21.

3. In the Schedule area, choose Recurring and then select the Change button.

4. In the Task Schedule dialog box, set the log reader task to run daily at one-minute intervals and then click OK.

5. Choose OK to close the Edit Task dialog box.

6. Stop and restart the SQL Executive service. This activates the changes you made to the scheduling of the replication task.

7. Examine the Task History of the log reader task and look for any errors. Look up the errors in SQL Server Books Online.

Figure 12.21.

In the Edit Task dialog box, you can choose how frequently tasks run.

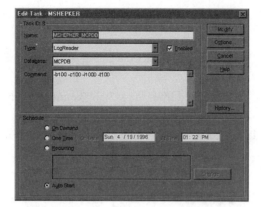

When troubleshooting the distribution task, you must realize that a single transaction probably is causing the problem. The following tutorial shows you how to troubleshoot the distribution task:

1. Start the SQL Enterprise Manager and connect to the distribution server.

2. From the Server menu, choose Scheduled Tasks. The Manage Tasks window opens. Double-click the distribution task to open the Edit Task dialog box, as shown in Figure 12.22.

Figure 12.22.

When troubleshooting the distribution task, concentrate on the -c option of the command.

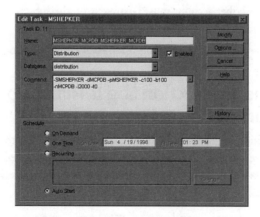

12

3. In the Command section of the task, change the -c parameter to -c1. This causes the distribution task to commit every transaction. The distribution task fails on the command causing the problems.

When you know where the distribution task is failing, you have the following three options:

- Use SQL statements to correct the failing command within the MSjob_ commands table.
- Remove the command from the MSjobs_commands table by running the `sp_Mskill_job` stored procedure.
- Manually correct and apply the transaction to all servers and then remove the command using the `sp_Mskill_job` stored procedure.

12.7.2. One Server of Many Isn't Receiving Changes

If only one server in a replication scenario is not receiving changes, there still might be a problem with the distribution task. Troubleshoot the distribution task as described in the preceding section. If the distribution task is still running properly, you must investigate and correct the following:

- Is the subscription database available? If it has become unavailable, that server stops receiving changes.
- Is the subscription server available? Is the MSSQLServer service still running?
- Has the replication login been removed from the subscription server? The repl_subscriber account must be present on the subscription server for successful replication to take place.
- Is the subscription server waiting for manual subscription to take place?

12.7.3. The Transaction Log Is Filling Up or Is Completely Full

If the transaction log in the publishing database is filling up, there might a problem with the log reader task. Troubleshoot it as previously described. The other option is that, during the initial planning phase, you neglected to make the transaction log large enough.

If the transaction log is completely full, you cannot dump it as you normally would. You have three options to fix this problem. First, you can expand the transaction log. This provides more space for transactions to take place before the log reader process marks them as replicated. Second, you can increase the frequency of the cleanup tasks. This enables them to clear the log more frequently.

The third option is to remove nonreplicated transactions from the transaction log using the `sp_repldone` stored procedure with the following options:

```
sp_repldone 0, 0, NULL, 0, 0, 1
```

This marks all transactions as replicated. You then can dump the transaction log using the following command:

```
DUMP TRANSACTION database_name WITH NO_LOG
```

In the preceding, *database_name* is the name of the published database. At this point, you should stop all subscriptions and resubscribe so that full synchronization can take place.

12.8. Final Thoughts

Replication is a powerful feature in SQL Server that can be used in many business situations. Companies can use it for anything from roll-up reporting to relieving the main server from ad hoc queries and reporting. Replication is the best solution for moving data from server to server in a quick and efficient manner.

12

Lab

Questions

1. You need to replicate data from a heavily updated online transaction processing database to several other servers. Which replication scenario fits this best?

   A. Publishing subscriber

   B. Subscribing publisher

   C. Central publisher using remote distributor

   D. Central subscriber

2. When using replication, where are the working files stored on the distribution server?

   A. \MSSQL\DATA

   B. \MSSQL\REPLTEMP

   C. \MSSQL\REPLDATA

   D. \MSSQL\REPLICATION

3. You are setting up a replication article based on a subset of rows within a table. What is this called?

   A. Vertical partitioning

   B. Horizontal partitioning

   C. Row-based replication

   D. Cross-section replication

4. When using SQL Server replication, how should the replicated data be treated?

   A. The data can be updated and sent back to the publishing database.

   B. The data can be updated, but the changes are not sent back to the publishing database.

   C. The subscribing database should be marked read-only.

   D. The subscribing database should be treated as read-only but should not be marked read-only.

5. What is a subscription configured from the publishing server called?

   A. A push subscription

   B. A pull subscription

   C. A push-pull subscription

   D. A pull-push subscription

6. What is the purpose of the log reader process?

   A. It moves data from the publishing server to the subscriber servers.

   B. It moves data from the subscribing server to the publishing server.

   C. It moves data from the publishing server to the distribution server.

   D. It reads the changes made on the subscribing server and rolls them up to the publishing server.

7. Which of the following databases can be published?

   A. msdb

   B. Master

   C. model

   D. pubs

8. Which consistency model is SQL Server replication considered to be?

   A. Tight consistency

   B. Loose consistency

   C. Real-enough time consistency

   D. Real-time consistency

9. What must you have on all tables to be replicated?

   A. A foreign key

   B. An identity column

   C. A primary key

   D. A replication-enabled key

12

10. You are the administrator of a SQL Server and are planning to set up replication for your company. The main server is in Boston, and you will be replicating to several servers in Europe. What replication scenario is the best in this situation?

    A. Central publisher

    B. Central publisher with a remote distributor

    C. Publishing subscriber

    D. Central publisher

Exercises

Note All exercises in this section require you to have access to multiple SQL Servers to set up replication. Both servers should be registered in the SQL Enterprise Manager.

1. Setting Up and Installing a Distribution Database

Note This exercise helps to address the following certification exam objective:
- Configure servers for replication

This exercise shows you how to set up and install a distribution database. This exercise should take about 25 minutes to complete:

1. Start the SQL Enterprise Manager and select the server you will be using as the publication server.

2. From the Server menu, choose Replication Configuration and then click Install Publishing.

3. Make sure that Local—Install New Local Distribution Database is chosen.

4. In the Database Name box, type `distribution`.

5. In the Data Device drop-down box, select New. You are prompted to create a new data device. The minimum recommended size for this device is 30MB. This size can be expanded if necessary. For this exercise, make the size of this device 30MB.

6. In the Log Device drop-down box, select New. You are prompted to create a new log device. The minimum recommended size for this device is 15MB. This size can be expanded if necessary. For this exercise, make the size of this device 15MB.

7. Click OK to complete the installation of the distribution database and close the Install Replication Publishing dialog box.

8. When the installation of the distribution database is finished, you are asked whether you want to install publishing databases and subscribers at this time.

12

9. In the Enable Publishing to These Servers area of the Replication—Publishing dialog box, you can choose the server that acts as the subscription server.

10. After enabling replication to a server, the Distribution Options button becomes active.

11. In the Distribution Options dialog box, you can configure how frequently changes should be sent to subscriber databases.

12. After making changes in the Distribution Dialog box, click OK to commit the changes.

13. In the Publishing Databases area, you can select the pubs database for publication. Only user databases can be chosen for publication. When you are finished setting up publication servers and published databases, click OK to commit the changes.

2. Creating and Managing Publications

Note

This exercise helps to address the following certification exam objective:
- Implement replication

This exercise shows you how to create a publication using the pubs database. This exercise should take about 20 minutes to complete:

1. Start the SQL Enterprise Manager and connect to the publishing server you set up in the preceding exercise.

2. From the Manage menu, click Replication and then Publications.

3. Choose the pubs database on which you enabled replication in the preceding exercise and then click the New button.

4. In the Publication Title box, enter TEST for the name of the publication.

5. In the Description box, enter a short description of the publication.

6. In the Replication Frequency area, choose Transaction Based.

7. In the Articles in Publication area of the Articles tab, choose All Tables.

8. In the Synchronization tab, choose Bulk Copy Data—Native Format. This option only works for replication between SQL Servers.

9. Click Add to create the publication.

3. Setting Up the Subscription Server

This exercise helps to address the following certification exam objective:
- Configure servers for replication

This exercise shows you how to set up the subscription server. Before completing this exercise, create a database with a 10MB data segment and a 5MB log segment. This acts as the destination database. This exercise should take about 10 minutes to complete:

1. Open the SQL Enterprise Manager and connect to the subscribing server.
2. From the Server menu, choose Replication Configuration and then click Subscribing.
3. In the Enable Subscribing From These Servers area, choose the publication server.
4. In the Subscribing Databases area, choose the database you previously created as the destination.

4. Setting Up a Pull Subscription

This exercise helps to address the following certification exam objective:
- Implement replication

This exercise shows you how to set up a pull subscription. This exercise should take approximately 25 minutes to complete:

1. Open the SQL Enterprise Manager and connect to the subscription server you previously set up.
2. From the Manage menu, choose Replication and then Subscriptions.
3. Click the plus sign next to the publication server and then the plus sign next to the pubs database.
4. Highlight the TEST publication and click the Subscribe button.
5. In the Database area, choose the database you previously created and set up.

12

6. In the Sync Method area, choose Data Synchronization Automatically Applied.

7. Click OK and to activate the subscription.

8. After about 10 minutes, you should see database elements and data show up in the destination database.

Answers to Questions

1. **C**   On a heavily updated online transaction processing server, you should remove any extraneous processing from the server using the central publisher with a remote distributor.

2. **C**   The temporary directory on the distribution server is \MSSQL\ REPLDATA.

3. **B**   Replication based on a subset of rows in a table is horizontal partitioning.

4. **D**   Replicated data should be treated a read-only but should not be marked read-only.

5. **A**   A subscription set up from the publication server is called a push sub-scription.

6. **C**   The log reader process reads data from the publication server and moves it to the distribution server.

7. **D**   Only the pubs database can be published because system databases cannot be published.

8. **B**   SQL Server replication is considered to be loose consistency.

9. **C**   All replicated tables must contain a primary key.

10. **C**   When replicating across a slow or expensive WAN link, you should use the publishing subscriber scenario.

Day 13

Tuning and Optimizing SQL Server

In this chapter, you'll start to learn about performance tuning for SQL Server. Performance tuning takes a long time to learn and requires lots of experience to do it correctly. This chapter provides the foundation of how performance tuning works so that you can start building this experience.

Objectives

This chapter covers the following material:

- Identify the benefits of installing the tempdb database in RAM
- Configure the number of worker threads
- Select the appropriate settings for read ahead
- Select the appropriate settings for locks
- Monitor log size
- Tune and monitor physical and logical I/O
- Tune and monitor memory use
- Set database options
- Update statistics

13.1. Introduction to Performance Tuning

SQL Server performance tuning involves monitoring processes, making changes, and then checking to see whether the changes provide the desired results. When tuning a car's engine, you know it needs a tune-up if it runs rough or is hard to start. You make the necessary modifications, such as adjusting ignition timing or changing the spark plugs, and then you start the car and drive it a while to make sure that you've corrected the problem. Similarly, you need to monitor how well SQL Server runs, make changes as necessary, and then monitor the changes.

Compared to other database engines, such as Oracle's database server products, SQL Server is easy to tune and optimize. The main reason for this is SQL Server's integration with Windows NT, specifically with the Performance Monitor. The Performance Monitor provides the capability to see how the server uses memory, processor, and disk resources. Using the Windows NT Performance Monitor and other tools discussed in this chapter makes tuning SQL Server significantly less complicated.

13.2. Monitoring Performance

Two principal tools are used to monitor the performance of SQL Server. The Windows NT Performance Monitor provides lots of information about SQL Server, such as how often the cache is used, how many users are connected, and how many locks are used. The Windows NT Performance Monitor doesn't, however, provide the capability to see what objects are in cache or how big these objects are. To find out what's going on inside the cache, you need to use DBCC MEMUSAGE, which is covered later in this chapter.

13.2.1. The Performance Monitor

The Windows NT Performance Monitor provides an integrated look at all the application and operating-system performance statistics. This includes the capability to monitor nearly all facets of the operating system as well as many aspects of SQL Server. The Performance Monitor is used to monitor objects, and a specific object can have one or more counters associated with it. If you are monitoring the processor, for example, one of the counters represents the percentage of processor time used. A counter can have multiple instances, such as when a computer has multiple processors. When this chapter takes you through monitoring the SQL Server Cache Hit Ratio, this means you should add the SQL Server object's Cache Hit Ratio counter. The following tutorial shows you how the Performance Monitor works.

This tutorial shows you how to start the Windows NT Performance Monitor to monitor a specific counter. In this example, you set up to watch the Processor % Processor Time and SQL Server Cache Hit Ratio. This tutorial should only be run under Windows NT because it uses the Performance Monitor utility, which is not available in Windows 95.

1. Start the Performance Monitor by clicking Start | Programs | Administrative Tools | Performance Monitor. An empty Performance Monitor window opens.

2. Choose Edit | Add to Chart or click the plus sign on the toolbar. This opens the Add to Chart dialog box, as shown in Figure 13.1.

Figure 13.1.

The Windows NT Performance Monitor shows the percentage of processor time in the chart in the background.

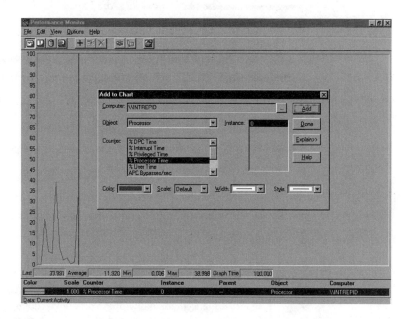

3. In the Computer field, enter the name of the SQL Server you want to monitor and click in the Object window. There might be a brief delay while the Performance Monitor locates a remote computer and loads its counter information.

4. In the Object drop-down box, choose Processor. The default counter for the Processor object is % Processor Time. Click the Explain button to see an explanation of the counter. In this case, the explanation reads as follows:

13

Processor Time is expressed as a percentage of the elapsed time that a processor is busy executing a non-Idle thread. It can be viewed as the fraction of the time spent doing useful work. Each processor is assigned an Idle thread in the Idle process which consumes those unproductive processor cycles not used by any other threads.

Essentially, % Processor Time represents the time Windows NT spends executing threads that aren't part of the Idle process. Click the Add button to add the counter to the chart.

5. In the Object drop-down box, choose SQLServer; in the Counter drop-down box, choose Cache Hit Ratio. Click the Explain button to view the explanation. Click the Add button to add the Cache Hit Ratio to your chart. Then click the Close button to close the dialog box.

6. Beneath the chart is a list of the counters on the chart, in this case % Processor Time and Cache Hit Ratio. Between this list and the chart are the last, average, minimum, and maximum values for the currently highlighted item in the list. To highlight the current counter in the chart, press the back-space key. This turns the currently selected item on the chart to white, making it easier to see.

Throughout the rest of the book, you'll see references to various objects and counters. Now you know how to view them. The process is the same for every object and counter. You'll only encounter differences when viewing processor time statistics on computers with multiple processors. In this case, you need to choose an instance of the processor to monitor.

 Note

There is one more catch to using the Performance Monitor. As a performance enhancement, many of the disk drive counters available in the Performance Monitor are turned off by default. Turning them on results in a 1 to 2 percent performance hit and requires a reboot of the server. For the exercises in this book, you should enable disk performance counters. This can be done by executing the following command at a Windows NT command line, *not* in a SQL Query window:

```
diskperf -y
```

The `diskperf` command then returns the following message:

```
Disk Performance counters on this system are now set to
start at boot.
This change will take effect after the system is restarted.
```

Restart the system before viewing any disk statistics. If you view the Performance Monitor and all the disk statistics are at zero percent, you know `diskperf` needs to be turned on.

SQL Server provides seven different objects to monitor and has several different counters for each object. Table 13.1 describes some of the most commonly monitored counters.

Table 13.1. Commonly monitored counters.

Object	Counter	Description
SQL Server	Cache Hit Ratio	The number of pages SQL Server needs that come from cache divided by the total number of pages SQL Server needs. This number optimally should be over 98 percent.
SQL Server	RA—Slots Used	The number of slots currently in use by the Read Ahead (RA) process.
SQL Server	I/O—Outstanding Reads	The number of physical reads that need to be done.
SQL Server	I/O—Outstanding Writes	The number of physical writes pending.
SQL Server	User Connections	The number of user connections currently in use. Use this to determine whether you need to add more user connections to your server.
SQL Server —Locks	Total Locks	The total number of locks currently in use. Use this to determine whether you need to add more locks to your server.
SQL Server —Locks	Users Blocked	The current number of user queries waiting for a resource currently in use.
SQL Server —Log	Log Space Used %	The current amount of log space in use for a given database. Choose which database to monitor from the Instances list.

13

continues

Table 13.1. continued

Object	Counter	Description
SQL Server —Procedure Cache	Procedure Cache Used %	The percentage of the procedure cache currently in use. Use this to determine whether SQL Server is using the procedure cache it has available and whether you can reallocate some of that cache to normal data cache.

Table 13.1 does not provide an exhaustive list of available counters. It only contains the most commonly monitored counters, which are discussed later in this chapter.

You also can use the Performance Monitor to watch for threshold values and to send alerts. This can be done by choosing View | Alert and adding an alert to the Performance Monitor. Alerts are added in much the same way as for monitoring, except a base value is added. If this base value is exceeded, you can run a program to correct the problem, or you can notify people using a Net Send command. These alerts should not be confused with the SQL Server alerts handled by the SQL Executive. Microsoft recommends using this alert system to monitor database log size. If the log size exceeds a certain amount, you can dump the log. Microsoft even puts a question about this on the test. The following tutorial shows you how to set up an alert and how to use Net Send in the alert.

This tutorial shows you how to use the Performance Monitor to set up an alert for processor time. You can substitute any Performance Monitor counter here, including SQL Server log size.

1. Start the Performance Monitor and choose View | Alert.
2. Choose Edit | Add Alert or click the plus sign on the toolbar to add an alert. The Add Alert dialog box opens.
3. Choose the Processor object and choose % Processor Time as the counter. In the Alert If frame, choose Under and enter 5, as shown in Figure 13.2. You will be alerted if processor utilization falls under 5 percent. Note that this has already happened once in the figure.

Figure 13.2.

*These settings cause
an alert if processor
utilization falls
below 5 percent.*

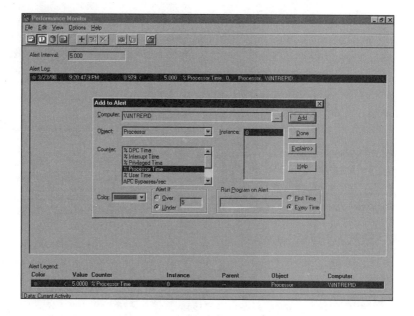

4. Click the Add button to add the alert. Then click Done to close the dialog box.

5. Don't do anything, including move the mouse or type. Alerts should start popping up.

6. Double-click the alert. In the Run Program on Alert box, enter the following:

```
Net Send Administrator "ALERT-Processor time below minimum"
```

7. As soon as you receive an alert, you might want to shut it off by choosing the alert, choosing Edit | Edit Alert Entry, deleting the command line, and choosing OK.

Follow these steps to add an alert. You can add an alert for any counter you can find in the Performance Monitor, and you can start any program you want when the alert happens.

13

 Note

Don't trust this alert in real life; it doesn't always work. It is covered here because it might be on the exam. If you decide to use it, be sure to adjust the polling interval by changing the value in the Alert Interval box to a high number (such as 300 to check every five minutes).

Now that you know how to use the Performance Monitor, you need to learn how to use another important tool—the DBCC MEMUSAGE command. The Performance Monitor can tell you how much cache you have and what percentage of it is being used, but it can't tell you what is in the cache. For that you need DBCC MEMUSAGE.

13.2.2. Using DBCC MEMUSAGE

The DBCC MEMUSAGE command is used to find out what your SQL Server is caching and how much of it is in cache. You can use this statement to monitor what is going in and coming out of cache and to determine whether your server has enough memory. The command takes no parameters and is executed at any SQL Server Query window. The following is some sample output, after which is an explanation of how to read it:

```
Memory Usage:

                         Meg.       2K Blk      Bytes

    Configured Memory: 16.0000       8192     16777216
           Code size:  1.7166        879      1800000
    Static Structures:  0.2473        127       259328
              Locks:  0.2861        147       300000
        Open Objects:  0.1144         59       120000
      Open Databases:  0.0031          2         3220
   User Context Areas:  0.7505        385       787002
          Page Cache:  8.9232       4569      9356608
        Proc Headers:  0.2148        110       225212
      Proc Cache Bufs:  3.6074       1847      3782656


Buffer Cache, Top 20:

      DB Id     Object Id    Index Id    2K Buffers

          1             5          0          132
          1             3          0           41
          1             1          0           21
          1             6          1            3
          2             2          0            3
          1            45        255            2
          1     704005539          1            2
          2            99          0            2
          4             2          0            2


Procedure Cache, Top 20:
```

```
Procedure Name: sp_MSdbuserprofile
Database Id: 1
Object Id: 1449056198
Version: 1
Uid: 1
Type: stored procedure
Number of trees: 0
Size of trees: 0.000000 Mb, 0.000000 bytes, 0 pages
Number of plans: 2
Size of plans: 0.171600 Mb, 179936.000000 bytes, 90 pages


Procedure Name: sp_helpdistributor
Database Id: 1
Object Id: 1372531923
Version: 1
Uid: 1
Type: stored procedure
Number of trees: 0
Size of trees: 0.000000 Mb, 0.000000 bytes, 0 pages
Number of plans: 2
Size of plans: 0.042969 Mb, 45056.000000 bytes, 24 pages


Procedure Name: sp_server_info
Database Id: 1
Object Id: 361052322
Version: 1
Uid: 1
Type: stored procedure
Number of trees: 0
Size of trees: 0.000000 Mb, 0.000000 bytes, 0 pages
Number of plans: 2
Size of plans: 0.006332 Mb, 6640.000000 bytes, 4 pages
```

This is not the complete report, which would run more than 10 pages. This report contains three sections. The first section is a summary of how SQL Server is configured and how memory is partitioned for different uses. The second section lists the top 20 objects in cache and tells how big they are. The third section lists the top 20 stored procedures in cache and how big they are.

The only section that needs interpretation is the list of objects and how much of each object is in cache. Unfortunately, rather than a convenient list of database and object names, you are presented with a list of database and object ID numbers. How can you translate these into something you can recognize? Fortunately, two Transact-SQL functions can return that data for you. The following tutorial shows you how.

13

This tutorial shows you how to translate database and object ID numbers into database and object names so that you can understand a DBCC MEMUSAGE report:

1. Open a SQL Query window. Enter the command DBCC MEMUSAGE and execute it.

2. Scroll down the report to the Buffer Cache-Top 20 section. Note the database ID for the top item in the list.

3. Choose File | New to open a new connection to the server. Enter Select db_Name(<ID>), substituting the database ID for <ID>, and then execute the query. The database name is returned.

4. In the query results from DBCC MEMUSAGE, highlight and copy an object ID using Edit | Copy.

5. In a Query window, execute Select object_name(<ID>), pasting in the ID you copied from the report in place of <ID>. This returns the object name.

Use these steps to translate DBCC MEMUSAGE output into data that you can actually use.

Now you're familiar with the tools to monitor your server, so you can diagnose performance problems. The next section shows you how to resolve these performance problems by changing configuration details and by performing maintenance.

13.3. Configuring for Performance

SQL Server is a configurable database management system. In this section, you'll learn how to configure SQL Server, and then you'll look at specific things to change to fully configure SQL Server and to resolve common performance problems.

13.3.1. Changing Configuration Options

This tutorial shows you how to set SQL Server options using sp_configure and the SQL Enterprise Manager. You'll use this procedure throughout the chapter to modify different settings.

1. Start the SQL Enterprise Manager and connect to the server with which you want to work.

2. Open a Query window using Tools | SQL Query Tool.

3. Execute the following query:

```
sp_configure
```

This returns a list of all the configuration options along with maximum, minimum, new, and existing values. Scroll down to the show advanced options line to see whether that option is turned on.

4. Assuming it isn't turned on, execute the following query to turn it on:

```
sp_configure "show advanced options", 1
```

5. After executing this query, you need to run the following query to make the change take effect:

```
reconfigure
```

It is important to run reconfigure after running sp_configure. If you don't, the changes made with sp_configure will not take effect.

6. Run sp_configure again and make sure that the option actually changed. Unlike most options, this one does not require you to reboot.

7. Close the Query window.

8. Choose Server | SQL Server | Configure. This opens the Server Configuration/Options dialog box. Choose the Configuration tab.

9. Note that this tab essentially looks the same as the query output from sp_configure. The five columns show Configuration, Minimum, Maximum, Running, and Current values.

10. To make a change, choose the row containing the setting you want to change and click in the Current column of that row. Enter the desired new value and click OK.

13.3.2. Configuring Memory Options

SQL Server provides two different options for handling memory. One option is the amount of memory available overall for use by SQL Server; the other is whether tempdb is stored completely in memory.

SQL Server works differently from other programs you've worked with in the past in that it statically allocates memory from the operating system. If you use Microsoft Word, for example, Word allocates memory as it needs memory. As your document grows, it requests more memory from the operating system. If you add graphics, Word requests more memory to hold the picture. SQL Server, however, must be told up front how much memory to grab. Based on that request, it decides how much memory to use for caching.

13

The amount of memory used by SQL Server is determined by the memory value set using the sp_configure stored procedure. The sp_configure stored procedure is used to change options in SQL Server. After running sp_configure, you must run the reconfigure command for the changes to take effect. For any option that affects allocation of memory, SQL Server must be stopped and restarted.

SQL Server setup sets the memory option based on the amount of memory available on your server. If your server has less than 32MB of RAM, SQL Server is configured to use 8MB of RAM. If you have more than 32MB of RAM, SQL Server configures itself with 16MB of RAM.

If a server is used only for SQL Server, a simple formula is used to determine how much memory SQL Server should have and how much should be left for Windows NT. For a server with 80MB of memory or less, Windows NT and SQL Server each gets half the memory. For a server with more than 80MB of RAM, Windows NT gets 40MB, and SQL Server gets the rest. If a server has 128MB of RAM, for example, the best configuration is to give SQL Server 88MB, leaving Windows NT with 40MB.

When setting the memory option, the amount of memory given to SQL Server is measured in 2KB pages, just like on Day 2 when you were building devices. To provide SQL Server with 88MB of RAM, you need to set the memory option to 45,056, which is 88 times 1,024 divided by 2 or (if you're quick at math) 88 times 512.

> **Note** Here's a helpful test-taking hint: Exam questions requiring you to figure out how many 2KB pages to use are set up so that you can make a quick estimate. They won't try to trick you by having four choices that all differ by one or two pages. If you can make a quick estimate that 32MB is going to result in 16,000 or so pages (divide by two, multiply by 1,000), that's usually good enough to choose the correct answer.

How does SQL Server use that memory? The memory you assign to SQL server can be divided into roughly three segments. The first segment is overhead. Overhead includes SQL Server executable code, the structures SQL Server uses to manage itself, and memory for storing user and lock information.

The next segment is data cache memory, which should be the largest memory segment. The third segment is procedure cache, which is memory space made available for stored procedures, stored procedure plans, and cursors. Procedure cache size is set as a percentage of the data cache size, and it defaults to 30 percent. To determine how much memory is used by each segment, run DBCC MEMUSAGE and read through the summary at the top of the report.

One key indicator that you might need more RAM is if the number one object in cache as reported by DBCC MEMUSAGE changes frequently, especially if it alternates back and forth between a few objects. This indicates that SQL Server does not have enough memory to cache all the objects, so it is cycling through which objects belong in cache.

13.3.3. Storing tempdb in RAM

SQL Server includes an option to store the tempdb database in memory at all times. For databases that make extensive use of tempdb, this can provide performance improvement. If the TempDB in RAM configuration setting is set to zero, tempdb is stored on disk. If the setting is not zero, the number specifies the number of megabytes tempdb should be in RAM. The TempDB in RAM setting can be found in the SQL Server configuration window previously discussed. TempDB in RAM adds to the amount of memory reserved by SQL Server. If the server has 128MB of RAM (88MB of which goes to SQL Server) and if TempDB in RAM is set to 5, Windows NT only gets 35MB of RAM (128–88–5 = 35).

This option is best used when tempdb is used frequently but the amount of data in tempdb is small. If tempdb needs to be large, placing tempdb in RAM means less memory is available for caching data. This can be even more detrimental to performance.

The biggest advantage of having tempdb in RAM is that all the overhead of transaction logging also is done in RAM, so the performance of queries in tempdb is very good. On the other hand, tempdb usually is used for sorting data. It would probably be better to use other methods, such as clustered indexes, to speed sorting.

As with any other option, you need to monitor the server, make the change, and then monitor the server again. Compare the baseline data with the experimental data and decide whether the performance tradeoffs benefit or hinder performance.

13

13.3.4. Users, Locks, and Open Objects

Another key to managing memory is handling locks, open objects, and user connections. These three SQL Server options in sp_configure can be set and tuned to optimize memory use. *Locks* is the number of simultaneous locks that can be used in the database at the same time. Each lock uses 32 bytes of memory. The default is 5,000 locks, or 160,000 bytes of memory. In most cases, this is an adequate number of locks. If you run out of locks, however, you can increase this number. Monitor the number of locks in use with the Performance Monitor counter SQL Server—Locks Total Locks. This shows you how many locks are in use at any given time, so you can see if you are approaching your maximum value.

Open objects is the number of objects SQL Server can use simultaneously. Objects in this context refer to tables, views, stored procedures, triggers, defaults, or rules. Each open object requires 70 bytes of memory. The default is 500 open objects, so your server starts out using 35,000 bytes to track open objects. Unfortunately, the Performance Monitor doesn't have a counter to track the number of open objects, so you have to guess to a certain extent. It's a good idea to count the number of objects on the server and add 15 percent as a contingency.

One of the more confusing memory values is called *user connections*. User connections has absolutely nothing to do with product licensing. This number should be set to the number of simultaneous user connections you expect the database to have plus 10 or 20 percent. Each user connection uses 37KB. The default is 15 user connections, so 555KB of SQL Server memory is used to track user connections. User connections is difficult to set because some applications require only one connection and others use multiple connections. This value is one you'll have to monitor until you are comfortable with the utilization of user connections on your server. User connections can be tracked using the Performance Monitor. An exercise at the end of this chapter shows you how to monitor user connections.

When setting these options, keep in mind that you are imposing limits to SQL Server. On a production server, RAM is cheap compared to the productivity lost when one of these values is set too low and users can't work. Set the options to a level you believe to be the maximum and then add 15 to 25 percent just to be safe.

13.3.5. Worker Threads

SQL Server uses a threaded process model to handle incoming connections. This means each incoming connection is assigned to a thread that handles all the incoming requests for that connection. By default, there are 255 maximum worker threads. This means SQL Server creates a new thread for each of 255 user connections. When connection 256 is established, threads automatically begin handling multiple connections using a process called *thread pooling*.

By watching the SQL Server Net-Command Queue Length, you can monitor how many commands that have been sent to threads are waiting to be processed because all the threads are busy. If this number stays high, you should increase the Max Worker Threads configuration option. The default for this option is 255; the maximum is 1,024. After increasing the number of worker threads, be sure to monitor the percentage of processor time to make sure that threads have enough processor time available to execute instructions. This option requires the server to be restarted before it takes effect.

13.3.6. Read Ahead Options

SQL Server 6 introduced the concept of read ahead. *Read ahead* is a predictive disk-reading system. When a query is reading a lot of data not in cache, read ahead starts up and begins reading sequential data into cache before the thread actually requests the data. This improves performance by increasing the cache hit ratio and making maximum use of disk time.

Read ahead generally is used either when text and image data is being retrieved or by DBCC commands that scan tables, such as DBCC CHECKDB() or DBCC CHECKTABLE(). In these cases, read ahead is helpful because data is being read sequentially.

The only non-advanced read ahead option is RA worker threads. According to Microsoft in the Administrative Companion section of Books Online, this number should be set to equal the number of user connections. In reality, however, the default number usually remains unchanged unless logged events state that a user connection requested read ahead and no threads were available.

SQL Server also provides advanced options for tuning read ahead. You can view these options by setting Show Advanced Options in sp_configure to 1 and then using reconfigure. The following are the advanced options for read ahead:

13

- *RA Cache Hit Limit.* The number of cache hits that should occur before read ahead is canceled. The read ahead cancels because it's likely that the data the connection is looking for already is in cache. The default of 255 cache hits should not need to be changed.

- *RA Cache Miss Limit.* The number of cache misses that should occur in a sequential read before read ahead is started. The default of 255 cache misses should not need to be changed.

- *RA Delay.* The amount of time in milliseconds between when the read ahead starts and when it is expected to deliver data. This enables read ahead to get started reading ahead. The default of 15 milliseconds can be decreased for extremely fast I/O subsystems or increased for extremely slow ones.

- *RA Pre-fetches.* The number of extents ahead of the connection that read ahead can get before it goes idle. The default is 3 extents. An extent is four pages.

- *RA Slots Per Thread.* The number of read ahead tasks that a single read-ahead thread can process simultaneously. The default is 5.

The number of RA slots per thread multiplied by the number of RA worker threads equals the number of simultaneous requests the RA system can handle. If the number of requests exceeds what can be handled, an event is logged in the Windows NT event log and in the SQL Server error log.

13.4. Setting Database Options

In addition to the serverwide options that are set with sp_configure, there are other options for each database. These options determine how different parts of the database work and provide the administrator with the ability to cut databases off from user access so that maintenance can be performed. These options are as follows:

- *Select Into/Bulk Copy.* If turned on, this option allows certain operations to be performed without logging each individual row. These operations are the Select Into operation, used to copy a table into a new table, and Bulk Copy, which is much faster. Keep in mind that whereas the individual row operations aren't logged, the allocations of extents are logged, so if the server goes down in the middle of the operation, the operation is still rolled back.

- *Columns Null by Default.* If turned on, this option affects new tables that are created in the database. Each column defaults to allowing null values.
- *No Checkpoint on Recovery.* If turned on, this option makes a database completely read-only. Normally, when a server starts, it writes a checkpoint record into the transaction log. Turning this option on prevents this from happening.
- *Truncate Log on Checkpoint.* If this option is turned on, all the inactive transactions are removed from the transaction log every time a checkpoint occurs. Additionally, all transaction log backup and recovery is disabled.
- *Single User.* This enables only one user to access the database. However, that one user isn't restricted to the sa or dbo, so any user who gets to the database first is the only user allowed. This disables all locking in the database; because there's only one user in the database, there's no reason to lock anything.
- *DBO Use Only.* If this option is turned on, only the database owners will be allowed in the database.
- *Read Only.* If this option is turned on, the database is read-only. There's no locking performed in a read-only database, and there are no checkpoints except on recovery.

Each of these options is turned off by default, and for normal databases in production, you should leave them turned off. Truncate Log on Checkpoint must be on in the Master database.

To set these options, simply double-click the database in SQL Enterprise Manager and choose the Options tab. Changes take effect as soon as you click OK. In a Query window, use the command `sp_dboption`, which takes three arguments—the database name, the option name, and either `true` or `false`. See the following example:

```
sp_dboption "trunc. Log on chkpt.", "true"
```

This turns on Truncate Log on Checkpoint. This is the only option that is abbreviated.

13

13.5. Performance Tuning Through Maintenance

If your car starts running rough, you know it needs to go in for a tune-up. To ensure maximum performance, SQL Server needs regular maintenance just like your car. One of the most important maintenance jobs that impacts performance is Update Statistics. The Update Statistics command changes how SQL Server looks at indexes and has a huge impact on which indexes are used to perform queries.

When an index is created for a table, SQL Server generates summary information about the usefulness of the index. This helps SQL Server to quickly determine whether that index should be used for a given query. The degree of usability of an index is determined by how many rows a given value returns. An index on sex that has two values (male or female), for example, is totally useless because on average it returns half the rows in the table. This does not help you locate a particular row, especially if there are thousands of rows in the table. An index on last names, however, returns very few rows and is a much more acceptable index than sex.

Index statistics can become out-of-date in a couple different ways. First, if the distribution of a table changes significantly, a previously useless index can become very useful. The following is an example:

1. A table is preloaded with data of all the records in which the last names are Smith and Jones.

2. An index is created on last names.

3. The remainder of the table is loaded.

In this case, the distribution statistics on the index are poor because, at the time the index was created, only two values were in the table. This results in the index never being used, even though it's a good index for certain queries.

Data being added to a table also can result in bad distribution statistics. When a significant amount of data is changed or added in a table, SQL Server eventually decides that its distribution statistics are suspect, and it quits using certain indexes on that table. At this point, the administrator will receive lots of phone calls related to poor performance and lockups.

The solution to both problems is to run Update Statistics on a regular basis. It doesn't take long and often is implemented as a scheduled job after a backup is conducted.

The Update Statistics command takes one or two parameters. The first parameter is the name of the table; the second parameter, which is optional, is the name of the index. If the index is not specified, Update Statistics works on all indexes on the specified table. The following example updates the statistics for the authors table:

```
Update Statistics authors
```

This runs quickly, but it should be run after hours or during periods of low user activity. It consumes lots of processor time and is blocked by users attempting to write data to the table.

13.6. I/O Performance Tuning

It takes a long time to read a page of data from disk into memory. Even with a fast disk subsystem, times can range in the single-digit milliseconds. SQL Server takes every step it can to avoid accessing the disk drive because accessing memory is thousands of times faster. Remember that memory speeds are measured in billionths of seconds, and disk access is measured in thousands. That's a factor of a million in performance of media.

When it's unavoidable, however, SQL Server does its best to make sure that any disk access it performs is done as quickly and efficiently as possible. There are many steps you can take to improve the throughput of the disk subsystem that also help SQL Server.

The first step is to monitor the physical I/O. This can be done by turning on the disk performance counters and by using the Windows NT Performance Monitor to measure Physical Disk % Disk Time, Disk Read Bytes/sec, and Disk Byte Writes/sec. When % Disk Time is at 100 percent, the amount of disk bandwidth can be determined by looking at the amount of data read from and written to the drive.

Another step in monitoring—at least to determine whether there are performance problems—is to monitor SQL Server I/O Outstanding Reads and I/O Outstanding Writes. If these two counters are above zero for any length of time, there are at least some threads waiting for the disk to read or write data. You might want to consider increasing your disk throughput.

A number of hardware and software solutions can be used to increase disk throughput. On the hardware side, use hardware-based RAID controllers to control the disk drives. RAID level 5, striping with parity, is the most commonly used RAID system.

13

Hardware-based RAID, in addition to providing nice fault tolerance, also equalizes traffic across multiple devices. This enables each device to independently seek and read the data users are waiting on.

If you don't want to implement hardware RAID, Windows NT comes with a software RAID implementation. It can improve performance the same way but with more processor overhead. This still improves fault tolerance and can improve performance because it has the capability to seek on multiple drives simultaneously.

If you have I/O Outstanding Writes, either the checkpoint process or the transaction log is attempting to write data to the disk. To minimize the time necessary for writing to the transaction log, consider putting the transaction log on a disk by itself. If the transaction log is the only item on the disk, there is no seek activity because the transaction log isn't read in normal operations. This means the disk head always is positioned in the correct place for the next write. The disk doesn't have to seek the correct place to write the next log record before doing so. This improves performance writing to the transaction log. If you also are using a RAID system for your data, you might want to consider using hardware mirroring for the transaction log to improve fault tolerance.

If the main problem is I/O Outstanding Reads, consider adding more memory to the server. This increases the cache size and the cache hit ratio. Another possibility is to reorganize the database so that data is more compact and the indexes are better. This makes the memory you already have more useful.

Lab

Questions

1. Which of the following commands sets SQL Server to the maximum recommended amount of memory on a computer with 128MB of RAM?

   A. `sp_dboption "master", "memory", 128`

   B. `sp_configure "memory", 88`

   C. `sp_configure "memory", 45056`

   D. `DBCC MEMUSAGE(128)`

2. Users are complaining to the administrator that the server suddenly is running slowly when querying certain large tables. These tables are modified heavily by the users. Which of the following is the best solution to try first?

   A. Add memory to the server.

   B. Modify memory configuration options.

   C. Upgrade to a RAID level 3 disk controller.

   D. Run `Update Statistics` on the table.

3. An administrator shuts his server down, adds more memory, and then brings the server back up. Unfortunately, his SQL Server isn't performing any better. What is the likely cause of this problem?

   A. The memory isn't fast enough for SQL Server.

   B. SQL Server can't handle more than 16MB of memory.

   C. SQL Server needs to be configured to use the additional memory.

   D. The memory is defective.

4. Which of the following situations causes thread pooling?

   A. Multiple users in contention for the same object.

   B. The number of user connections exceeds the value of max worker threads.

   C. The amount of SQL Server memory is set too low.

   D. The number of logins in use exceeds the value of max worker threads.

5. Which two of the following types of queries are most likely to use read ahead?

   A. `DBCC CHECKTABLE()`

   B. Reading every record in an entire table using a nonclustered index

13

    C. Pulling the entire value stored in a text datatype

    D. `DBCC MEMUSAGE`

6. Where does the memory for the TempDB in RAM option come from?

    A. The procedure cache

    B. The data cache

    C. Outside the amount of memory allocated to SQL Server in the Memory option

    D. Inside the tempdb portion of memory allocated to SQL Server using the Memory option

7. Which of the following tools can be used to monitor log size and to warn before the log fills up?

    A. The SQL Executive Alert system

    B. `DBCC LOGUSAGE()`

    C. `DBCC SQLPERF(LOGSTATS)`

    D. The Windows NT Performance Monitor

8. Wendy is trying to monitor the physical drive usage on her Windows NT Server using the Performance Monitor. It always shows zero, however, no matter which counter she chooses or how busy the server is. What's wrong?

    A. The server has so much memory it never writes to disk.

    B. The cache hit ratio is at 100 percent, so there is no disk activity.

    C. The performance counters for disk performance are disabled.

    D. The Physical Disk counters don't work on logical drives.

9. Ronald notices that his SQL Server is running slow and appears to be reading and writing data a lot. After checking the Performance Monitor, his cache hit ratio is at 99 percent. There are no outstanding reads, but there are a large number of outstanding writes. What should Ronald do to speed up his server?

    A. Add memory

    B. Add drive space

    C. Increase disk throughput with striping

    D. Isolate the transaction log onto its own physical disk

10. John has a problem with SQL Server performance when his users are querying pictures and other binary data from the database. What options should John examine and change?

    A. Read-ahead options

    B. Memory options

    C. Open-object options

    D. Locks options

13

Exercises

1. Monitoring the Number of User Connections and the Cache Hit Ratio

This exercise helps to address the following certification exam objective:

- Tune and monitor memory use

This exercise shows you how to monitor the number of user connections currently in use and the cache hit ratio. This exercise assumes you have free reign to start and stop the server so that you can see how cache hit ratio is affected.

1. Start the Performance Monitor by clicking Start | Programs | Administrative Tools | Performance Monitor. An empty Performance Monitor window opens.

2. Choose Edit | Add to Chart or click the plus sign on the toolbar. This opens the Add to Chart dialog box.

3. In the Computer field, enter the name of the SQL Server you want to monitor and click in the Object window. There might be a brief delay while the Performance Monitor locates a remote computer and loads its counter information.

4. In the Object drop-down box, choose SQL Server. In the Counter box, choose Cache Hit Ratio and click Add. Choose User Connections in the Counter box and click Add. Click Done.

5. Note the number of user connections. Start a SQL Query window and execute the query sp_who. Note that when you opened the SQL Query window, the number of connections increased. If you count the number of connections, you can verify that the Performance Monitor is telling the truth. Don't just go by the last SPID reported by sp_who. You should actually count the processes because not all SPIDs are in use.

6. Stop and restart SQL Server. Note that the cache hit ratio is very low when SQL Server restarts. Perform some queries, such as `Select * from authors`, in the pubs database. If you execute the same query repeatedly, you can pump the cache hit ratio up to 100 percent.

2. Using `sp_configure` to Change the Memory Option

 Note This exercise helps to address the following certification exam objective:

■ Set database options

This exercise shows you how to change the memory option of SQL Server to the optimal number for your installation. You'll also take a look at `config_value` and `run_value`.

1. Open a SQL Query window.

2. You first need to find out what the memory option is currently set to. Execute the following query:

`sp_configure`

3. Scroll through the output to the `memory` line and read the currently configured value for memory in the `config_value` column (the next-to-last column). Also read the current running value for memory in the `run_value` column (the last column). The value in `config_value` is the currently configured value; it's the value that will be used the next time SQL Server is started. The value in `run_value` is the value currently in use. To verify this, you change the value in the next step.

4. Execute the following query:

`sp_configure "memory", 16384`

Run `sp_configure` with no parameters. Note that the value in the `config_value` column is 16384, but the value in `run_value` has not changed.

5. Stop and restart SQL Server. Reopen the Query window if necessary and execute `sp_configure`. Note that the 16384 value is still the `config_value`, and the `run_value` has not changed. Why didn't it work? It didn't work because you didn't run `reconfigure`. Options don't change unless you execute `reconfigure`. Use `sp_configure` to set the database option back to what it should be, execute `reconfigure`, and then stop and restart the server.

13

Answers to Questions

1. **C**   Remember to allow 40MB for SQL Server, which leaves 88MB of RAM. The syntax calls for the number of pages—not the number of megabytes—and 88 pages is not nearly enough.

2. **D**   Always run Update Statistics first. It's cheaper than the other solutions and doesn't require any downtime.

3. **C**   SQL Server does not automatically detect new memory and take it over. It has to be configured to use new memory.

4. **B**   Option D is incorrect because SQL Server doesn't care how many different logins are in use. It's only interested in the total number of user connections.

5. **A, C**   Option B does not cause sequential reads, and option D doesn't read data from any user tables.

6. **C**   Memory for tempdb comes from outside what's allocated to SQL Server. Options A and B, which are within SQL Server, won't work. The region of memory described in option D doesn't exist.

7. **D**   The SQL Server alert system warns you after the log fills up, which isn't very helpful. Options B and C are bogus commands.

8. **C**   Although not strictly a SQL Server question, it's very likely one like this will show up on the exam. Even if there's an infinite amount of disk activity and the cache hit ratio is at 100 percent, transaction log records will be written, checkpoints will happen, and there is some paging on the biggest servers. The counters will never be all zero and reading correctly, so they must be disabled.

9. **D**   On servers with a high transaction volume, putting the transaction log on its own physical disk reduces the amount of disk time required by the transaction log writer.

10. **A**   Read ahead is used when text and image data is read from disk.

TEST DAY
FAST FACTS

The following are some key facts you'll learn in this chapter:

- Troubleshooting SQL Server databases is a methodical process that should be followed every time you experience problems.

- Before attempting to fix anything, it is best to clearly understand what caused the error and the correct ways to fix it. Some attempts to fix an error, when used at an inappropriate time, can cause more harm than good.

- SQL Server error messages are identified with a unique error number. You can use this number to find more information about the error.

- SQL Server logs error messages to the SQL Server error log and the Windows NT application log.

- The Database Consistency Checker (DBCC) can be used to identify errors within a database.

- The DBCC also can be used to monitor statistics within databases.

- The transaction logging process is an internal SQL Server process used to keep databases consistent.

- Always use preventative maintenance and frequent backups to make sure that your databases are online as much as possible.

Day 14

Troubleshooting SQL Server

Every SQL Server administrator has to fix a broken database at some point. It can be very frustrating and stressful because users and management want to know exactly when it will be done. It is very important that you keep calm during this crisis.

Troubleshooting is a systematic process that cannot be completely taught. After learning the basic steps of troubleshooting, you must rely on intuition and experience to figure out what step to take next and when to contact the experts for help. A successful troubleshooter is able to balance the need for a functional database with a few hours of data loss. In other words, it is not always the best idea to keep a database offline for three days to correct three hours of lost data.

Objectives

This chapter covers the following material:

- Locate information relevant to diagnosing a problem.
- Resolve network error messages.
- Check object integrity.
- Investigate a database that is marked suspect.
- Cancel a sleeping process.

14.1. Finding the Facts

Most often, reports of database errors come from database users. The first step after a problem is reported is to verify there actually is a problem. Users often report any error that comes across their screens, even if the error was a direct result of their own actions. This does not mean everything users report should be suspect. Instead, you need to take what the user tells you and pare it down.

Imagine, for example, you receive a call from Joe in accounting. Joe tells you he is trying to update the employee database, and it is failing. He explains that he and several other people have been making updates all morning, and they have all begun to fail in the last few minutes. The error message says it has something to do with the transaction log.

Without the exact text of the message in front of you, there is no way you can discern the complete nature of the problem. You should, however, be able to glean several things from this account. First, Joe (and perhaps others in the accounting department) is having problems updating the employee database. Second, the problems relate in some way to the transaction log. Anything else mentioned during the conversation, although seemingly pertinent, is not important to fix the problem at hand.

14.1.1. Identify the Problem

The next logical step is to see whether you can replicate the problem yourself. In this case, you should open the same application used in the accounting department, perform the same operations, and see if you get the same errors. The only problem is that some developers do not give you the errors SQL Server is returning. Developers often use their own error codes and text to explain an error. These codes might not provide the same information as SQL Server.

To eliminate this problem, the best way to investigate is to start ISQL/W and perform operations against the database. If you can perform SELECT, INSERT, UPDATE, and DELETE against a database, your users should be able to as well. In Joe's case, when you perform INSERT, UPDATE, or DELETE, you get the error shown in Figure 14.1.

Luckily, in this case, the error tells you exactly what the problem is and how to fix it.

Figure 14.1.

With a full transaction log, you get an 1105 error when you run any logged transaction against the database.

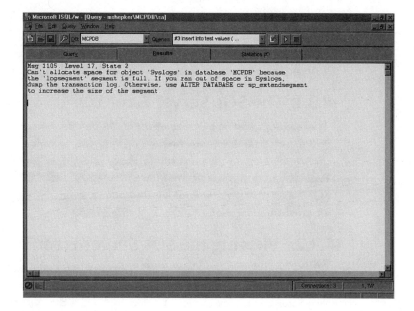

14.1.2. Attempt a Fix

After discovering the exact nature of the problem, your next step should be to try and fix it. In this case, the fix is quite simple. You should dump the transaction log, and the users should be able to continue their work. This is not a difficult problem to troubleshoot, and most SQL administrators run into it more than once. In other situations, you might need to try several different remedies before you find a fix that works.

14.2. Document Everything

As a SQL administrator, you should keep a log of all changes you make to the databases and the server. This step is one of the most frequently overlooked. Every time you make any kind of change to the database, you should write it down. This enables you to backtrack if you make a mistake while trying to troubleshoot a problem. Your log also can help if the same errors occur again in the future. If you know what fixed a problem the last time, you can try that solution first to see if it works again. This log, if well kept, also is an invaluable resource in the event of a catastrophic failure in which databases must be rebuilt. This one step does not take very long, and it can save a great deal of time in the long run.

14

14.3. SQL Server Information Sources

This section discusses some of the informational sources you can turn to while troubleshooting a SQL database.

14.3.1. The SQL Server Error Log

The error log is where SQL Server writes startup information, error messages, and informational messages that occur during everyday operation. This file is a text file that can be viewed with a text editor. The location of the file is determined in the Registry, and the default path for the error log is C:\MSSQL\LOGS\ERRORLOG. SQL Server creates a new error log every time it restarts. The previous six error logs are saved with extensions numbered .1 through .6.

14.3.2. Viewing the SQL Server Error Log

When attempting to troubleshoot SQL Server, you often need to view the error log. The easiest way to do this is within the SQL Enterprise Manager. Click Server and then Error Log to view the log. The log displayed is the most current one. To view any of the past six error logs, click the drop-down box at the top of the window. Figure 14.2 shows an example of the SQL Server error log.

Figure 14.2.

You can select any of the past six error logs from the drop-down box at the top of the window.

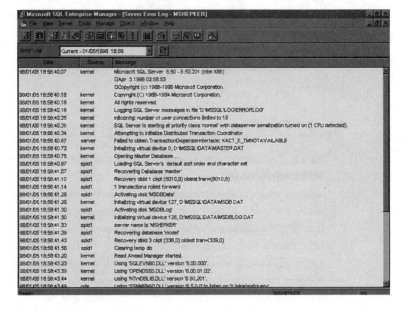

14.3.3. SQL Server Error Messages

When SQL Server encounters an error, it writes a message to the error log, sends a message to the user, or both, depending on the severity level of the error. Every SQL Server error message contains the following information:

- A unique number that identifies the message
- A number that identifies the severity level of the error
- A number that identifies the source of the error
- An informational message that describes the error and sometimes provides steps to fix it

All error messages are stored in the sysmessages table in the Master database. To view a complete list of all messages, run the query in Listing 14.1.

Listing 14.1. Getting a listing of all SQL Server error messages.

```
use master
go
select * from sysmessages
go
```

Every SQL Server error message contains a severity level that indicates the type of problem and how bad that problem can be. Error messages can be divided into two distinct categories: nonfatal errors and fatal errors.

Nonfatal Errors

Nonfatal errors have a severity level of 0 or 10 through 18. Nonfatal errors often are user-correctable errors. These errors do not cause the SQL Server connection to be dropped. Table 14.1 shows examples of nonfatal errors.

Table 14.1. Nonfatal SQL Server errors.

Severity Level	Definition	Example
0 or 10	These messages are not errors. They are informational messages that do not require any user correction.	Msg 2528, Level 10, State 1. DBCC execution completed. If DBCC printed error messages, see your system administrator.

continues

14

Table 14.1. continued

Severity Level	Definition	Example
11 through 16	These errors are user correctable. Most often, they are due to syntax or logic errors in SQL statements.	`Msg 109, Level 15, State 1. There are more columns in the INSERT statement than values specified in the VALUES clause. The number of values in the VALUES clause must match the number of columns.`
17	Indicates that SQL Server has run out of some resource. This can be a physical resources, such as disk space, or configurable resources, such as locks.	`Msg 1105, Level 17, State 1. Cannot allocate space for object Syslogs in database PUBS because the syslogs segment is full. If you run out of space in Syslogs, dump the transaction log. Otherwise, use ALTER DATABASE or sp_extendsegment to increase the size of the segment.`
18	Indicates that an internal error has kept SQL Server from completing the statement, but the connection to the server is not terminated.	`Msg 1521, Level 18, State 1. Sort failed because a table in tempdb that is used for the processing of the query had a bad data page count. Tempdb should not have been damaged.`

Fatal Errors

Fatal errors have a severity level of 19 or greater. When a fatal error occurs, the user's connection to SQL Server is terminated. Correcting these errors often requires that the database be taken offline and the SQL Administrator perform corrective actions. Table 14.2 shows examples of fatal errors.

Table 14.2. Fatal SQL Server errors.

Severity Level	Definition	Example
19	These errors indicate that a nonconfigurable internal limit has been reached. These errors rarely happen.	Msg 422, Level 19, State 1. Too many nested expressions or logical operators to compile. Try splitting the query or limiting ANDs and ORs.
20	These indicate that the error was in the current process. They affect only the current process, and the database probably was not damaged.	Msg 405, Level 20, State 1. Cannot route query results—query internal representation corrupted.
21	These errors indicate that a problem has occurred, affecting all processes in the current database. There was likely no corruption in the database, though.	Msg 611, Level 21, State 1. Attempt made to end a transaction that is idle or in the middle of an update.
22	These indicate that the integrity of a table is suspect. Level 22 errors are rare.	Msg 904, Level 22, State 1. Unable to find Master database row in sysdatabases. Cannot open Master database.

continues

14

Table 14.2. continued

Severity Level	Definition	Example
23	These messages indicate that the integrity of an entire database is suspect. These errors are rare.	Msg 277, Level 23, State 1. A transaction that began in this stored procedure that did updates in tempdb is still active. This causes corruption in tempdb that exists until the server is rebooted. All BEGIN TRANs and END TRANs must have matching COMMITs and ROLLBACKs.
24	These messages indicate a media failure of some sort. It might be necessary to replace hardware and reload the database.	Msg 902, Level 24, State 1. Hardware error detected reading logical page 24145, virtual page 340782 in database PUBS.
25	These messages indicate a system error of some sort that is internal to SQL Server.	Msg 3508, Level 25, State 1. Attempt to set PUBS database to single user mode failed because the usage count is 2. Make sure no users are currently using this database and rerun CHECKPOINT.

It is important to investigate all fatal errors. This often involves taking the database offline and running diagnostics. Some fatal errors that occur do not reappear during diagnostics. It is better to investigate errors when you first find them, before they get any worse.

14.4. The Windows NT Event Log

Another valuable source for SQL Server information is the Windows NT application log. Not only does it contain information about SQL Server, but it also contains information about Windows NT Server and any other application running on the server. This can be especially useful if an outside event or series of events is affecting SQL Server.

When viewing the Windows NT event log, it often is difficult to discern what information comes from SQL Server. To alleviate this problem, you can filter the source of the event information. In the Event Viewer application, choose View and then Filter Events. In the source box, click the drop-down box and choose MSSQLServer. This filters the events to show only those related to SQL Server. You can filter the events further by selecting a category from which to view information.

14.5. DBCC and Trace Flags

The Database Consistency Checker (DBCC) is the tool most frequently used to diagnose and repair database errors. You can use the DBCC command with a few, select trace flags to help you troubleshoot.

SQL Server 6.5 has a certain amount of functionality and error recording that is necessary for everyday operation. At times, however, a SQL administrator needs to either get more information about what is going on or turn on functionality that was present in previous versions of the software. Trace flags enable administrators to do this.

 Warning

> Trace flags are not a supported part of SQL Server. This means Microsoft might not include them in future releases of SQL Server, and Microsoft support people might not be able to help you with them. Even so, they should be a great help in troubleshooting your databases.

14.5.1. Setting Trace Flags

You can set trace flags in three ways: using the DBCC command, using the -T option when starting SQL Server from the command line, and during setup. Most trace flags should be used only for short periods of time. They can result in degraded system performance and increased error log size.

14

DBCC TRACEON

The easiest way to turn on trace flags is to use the DBCC TRACEON command. Using this method, trace flags can be turned on and off at any time without having to down the server. This is especially useful when you are troubleshooting problems that occur during certain times of the day. The following is the syntax for the command:

```
DBCC TRACEON (FLAG1, FLAG2, ...)
```

Turning off trace flags uses the same convention, as follows:

```
DBCC TRACEOFF (FLAG1, FLAG2, ...)
```

To check whether individual trace flags are turned on, use the following syntax:

```
DBCC TRACESTATUS (FLAG1, FLAG2, ...)
```

To check the status of all active trace flags, you can run the preceding command with the -1 option, as follows:

```
DBCC TRACESTATUS`(-1)
```

Setting Trace Flags at the Command Line

If you need trace flags in effect as soon as SQL Server starts, you can start them at the command line using the -T option. The following is an example:

```
sqlservr -dc:\mssql\data\master.dat -ec:\mssql\log\errorlog -T3609
```

The trace flag parameter is case sensitive. If you start SQL Server using -t rather than -T, you start not only the trace flags, but other, internal traces as well. Trace flags activated this way are in effect for all user connections to the server.

Setting Trace Flags in Server Options

The third option for trace flags is to set them in the Server Configuration dialog box in the Enterprise Manager. Click the Parameters button on the Server Options tab and add the trace flags with a -T, as shown in Figure 14.3. When trace flags are set this way, they are active as soon as the server comes online, and they affect all connections to the server.

Figure 14.3.

Add the trace flags with a -T.

14.5.2. Informational Trace Flags

There are a number of Microsoft undocumented trace flags. You should use them only under the supervision of your primary support provider. The following are some of the more useful and informational trace flags:

Flag	Description
302	This flag provides information about the use of the statistics page and what SQL Server estimates to be the physical and logical cost for using the indexes. Trace flag 302 should be used in conjunction with trace flag 310.
310	This flag prints information about the join order. When used in conjunction with flag 302, it returns information similar to the SET SHOWPLAN ON command.
1200	This flag returns lock information, including the type of lock requested and the spid of the user that requested it.
1201	This flag returns information about the types of locks participating in a deadlock at the time it happens. It also provides the spids of the users affected and the command running at the time.
1202	This flag returns detailed information about the commands running when a deadlock occurs. This flag is especially useful when used in conjunction with trace flag 1204.
4030	This flag prints both a byte and an ASCII representation of the receive buffer. This is useful when you need to see exactly what the client is sending to the server.
4031	This flag prints both a byte and an ASCII representation of the send buffer. The send buffer is what the server sends back to the client.
4032	This flag prints only the ASCII contents of the receive buffer. This flag commonly is used in place of trace flag 4030 when trace speed is important.

14

14.5.3. Compatibility and Behavior-Changing Trace Flags

The other main type of trace flags modifies SQL Server operations. These changes usually emulate behaviors present in previous versions of SQL Server. They are provided for backwards compatibility with client applications. Because Microsoft does not support trace flags, they might change in future releases. You should use them as a temporary fix while client applications are being retooled to take better advantage of the new features in SQL Server.

Flag	Description
107	This flag causes SQL Server to interpret a number containing a decimal point as a float instead of a decimal.
110	This flag disables the ANSI SELECT feature, which is new in SQL Server 6.5. This feature disallows duplicate column names in SELECT and UPDATE statements. The following SELECT statement, for example, causes an error in SQL Server 6.5 without having trace flag 110 set: `SELECT * FROM authors, authors`
204	This flag enables you to use non-ANSI standard features of SQL Server 6.5 for backward compatibility. This turns on the following features: ■ It enables queries containing aggregate functions or GROUP BY clauses to contain items in the SELECT clause and not in the aggregate or GROUP BY. ■ It enables SELECT DISTINCT queries to contain sort columns in the ORDER BY clause that are not in the SELECT list. ■ It causes SQL Server to ignore the trailing blanks in a statement containing a LIKE clause.
237	This flag enables users who have SELECT permissions on a table to create a new table that references the first table. In SQL Server 6.5, a user must have REFERENCES permissions to do this.
246	In SQL Server 6.5, column names must be explicitly provided when performing SELECT INTO and CREATE VIEW queries. If a column is created using an aggregate or mathematical function, for example, SQL Server returns an error. This flag suppresses this error.
3608	This flag causes SQL Server to skip automatic recovery of all databases except the Master database.

Flag	Description
4022	This flag causes SQL Server to skip the execution of all startup stored procedures. This is especially useful if a stored procedure is causing SQL Server to hang during startup.

14.5.4. Special Trace Flags

Three special trace flags can be used in conjunction with any of the preceding trace flags. The following control output of information from the traces and who is affected by them:

Flag	Description
-1	This flag indicates that trace flags should be set for all current client connections. This affects only the current connections to the server, not connections made after the command has been issued. This flag is not necessary when setting the trace from the command line or from server options because these methods automatically affect all connections to the server.
3604	This flag redirects informational messages from DBCC commands and traces to the client machine. When running DBCC commands without trace flag 3604, you often receive no other information except the following: DBCC execution completed. If DBCC printed error messages, see your Systems Administrator.
3605	This flag indicates that informational messages should be redirected to the error log. This enables you to watch a sequence of events that might be causing problems rather than single errors that might not show the big picture.

14.6. The Database Consistency Checker

The DBCC command originally was intended to do what the name implies—check the consistency of the database. Over time, however, the DBCC command has become a catch-all for many useful functions.

14

There are a limited number of supported DBCC commands. The following is a list of the supported commands:

```
DBCC {
     CHECKALLOC [(database_name [, NOINDEX])] |
     CHECKCATALOG [(database_name)] |
     CHECKTABLE (table_name [, NOINDEX | index_id]) |
     CHECKDB [(database_name [, NOINDEX])] |
     CHECKIDENT [(table_name)] |
     DBREPAIR (database_name, DROPDB [, NOINIT]) |
     dllname (FREE) |
     INPUTBUFFER (spid) |
     MEMUSAGE |
     NEWALLOC [(database_name [, NOINDEX])] |
     OPENTRAN ({database_name} | {database_id})
          [WITH TABLERESULTS] |
     OUTPUTBUFFER (spid) |
     PERFMON |
     PINTABLE (database_id, table_id) |
     SHOW_STATISTICS (table_name, index_name) |
     SHOWCONTIG (table_id, [index_id]) |
     SHRINKDB (database_name [, new_size [, 'MASTEROVERRIDE']]) |
     SQLPERF ({IOSTATS | LRUSTATS | NETSTATS | RASTATS [, CLEAR]} | {THREADS} |
{LOGSPACE}) |
     TEXTALL [({database_name | database_id}[, FULL | FAST])] |
     TEXTALLOC [({table_name | table_id}[, FULL | FAST])] |
     TRACEOFF (trace#) |
     TRACEON (trace#) |
     TRACESTATUS (trace# [, trace#...]) |
     UNPINTABLE (database_id, table_id) |
     UPDATEUSAGE ({0 | database_name} [, table_name [, index_id]]) |
     USEROPTIONS}
[WITH NO_INFOMSGS]
```

Sometimes the DBCC command requires the database name; other times it requires the database ID. You can obtain the database ID from either viewing the SQL Server error log or running the query in Listing 14.2. Substitute the name of the database for *dbname* in the SELECT statement.

Listing 14.2. Getting the database ID for use in many of the DBCC commands.

```
USE dbname
GO
SELECT DB_ID
GO
```

14.6.1. DBCC Permissions

Permission to run the DBCC varies by command. The more far-reaching the command, the more permission is required to run it. Permission to execute the

DBCC command cannot be transferred to other users. The following are some general rules for using DBCC commands:

- Commands that affect individual objects, such as CHECKTABLE, can be run by the object owner, the database owner, or the system administrator.

- Commands that affect an entire database, such as CHECKDB and NEWALLOC, can be run by the database owner or the system administrator.

- Any other DBCC command, such as TRACEON and TRACEOFF, only can be run by the system administrator.

14.6.2. Using the DBCC Command

The DBCC command is a great tool to help you isolate and repair problems within your database. In addition to the supported DBCC commands, many others are undocumented by Microsoft. If you come across any of the undocumented commands, use them with caution and only after discussing it with your primary support provider. When repairing an error, some commands can cause problems for your database due to other underlying problems. The following section discusses some of the more frequently used DBCC functions.

Warning

Be careful when using and experimenting with DBCC commands. Not all DBCCs are supported features of SQL Server. This means Microsoft might not include them in future releases of SQL Server.

CHECKDB

If you only have time to run one DBCC on your database, you should run CHECKDB. CHECKDB performs a comprehensive check of all tables in the database for the following:

- It makes sure that all data pages are properly linked. Data pages in SQL Server are in a double-linked list. This means page 1 in the list points to page 2 in the list, and page 2 points back to page 1.

- It makes sure that all index pages are properly linked.

- It makes sure that all indexes are in the correct sort order.

- It makes sure that the row offsets are reasonable. The row offset specifies where on a data page the row resides.

- It makes sure that the data on each data page is readable and in logical form.

14

The following is the syntax of the CHECKDB command:

```
DBCC CHECKDB [(database_name [, NOINDEX])] [WITH NO_INFOMSGS]
```

If you leave out the *database_name*, CHECKDB checks the database you are currently using. The NOINDEX option provides quick execution of CHECKDB, but its check is not as complete. NOINDEX checks the clustered index and data only on user-defined tables. If a clustered index is not present, only the data is checked. The NOINDEX option does not affect the way CHECKDB handles system tables. When checking system tables, clustered indexes, nonclustered indexes, and data are checked. If you specify the WITH NO_INFOMSGS option, the command runs without returning informational messages.

The normal output of a CHECKDB run on the pubs database looks similar to the following:

```
Checking pubs
Checking 1
The total number of data pages in this table is 4.
Table has 69 data rows.
Checking 2
The total number of data pages in this table is 4.
Table has 49 data rows.
Checking 3
The total number of data pages in this table is 10.
Table has 277 data rows.
.
.
.
Checking 688005482
The total number of data pages in this table is 1.
The total number of TEXT/IMAGE pages in this table is 62.
Table has 8 data rows.
Checking 752005710
The total number of data pages in this table is 2.
Table has 43 data rows.
DBCC execution completed. If DBCC printed error messages,
see your System Administrator.
```

On large databases, the output of CHECKDB can be quite long. The easiest way to look for errors is, after CHECKDB has finished running, choose Edit, choose Find, and type Msg in the Find box. If it comes back without finding anything, your database is clean. Otherwise, you need to start investigating what the message tells you. You most likely do not need to worry about messages with severity levels less that 16.

CHECKTABLE

The CHECKTABLE command performs all the same functions as the CHECKDB command, just to individual tables. This is useful when you suspect problems with a single table and do not have time to run CHECKDB. The following is the syntax of the CHECKTABLE command:

```
DBCC CHECKTABLE (table_name [, NOINDEX ¦ index_id]) [WITH NO_INFOMSGS]
```

The `table_name` option must be supplied for this command to work. If you only want to check one index for corruption, you can supply the `index_id` of that index. To get the `index_id`, run the query in Listing 14.3. Replace `dbname` with the name of the database the table resides in and replace `indname` with the name of the index you want to investigate.

Listing 14.3. This SQL query enables you to get the index ID for use in the CHECKTABLE command.

```
use dbname
go
select indid from sysindexes where name = 'indname'
go
```

CHECKCATALOG

The CHECKCATALOG function checks for consistency in the system tables. The system tables do not have foreign keys, so it is up to SQL Server itself to keep track of their consistency. It is rare to find problems with the system tables. When it happens, however, the results can be catastrophic. The following is the syntax of the CHECK-CATALOG command:

```
DBCC CHECKCATALOG [(database_name)][ WITH NO_INFOMSGS]
```

NEWALLOC

The NEWALLOC command verifies all the extents in the database. It is called NEWALLOC because it replaces the CHECKALLOC command. During creation and deletion of objects in the database, SQL Server has to allocate and deallocate space for each object. Each object is allocated a 16KB unit of disk space called an *extent*. As objects grow, SQL Server allocates another extent for its use. NEWALLOC makes sure that all extents are properly allocated or deallocated. The following is the syntax of the NEWALLOC command:

```
DBCC NEWALLOC [(database_name [, NOINDEX])][ WITH NO_INFOMSGS]
```

If you run the NEWALLOC command without the NO_INFOMSGS option, you will see the first message shown in Figure 14.4.

14

Figure 14.4.

When running NEWALLOC, *SQL Server reports an error if the database is not in single user mode.*

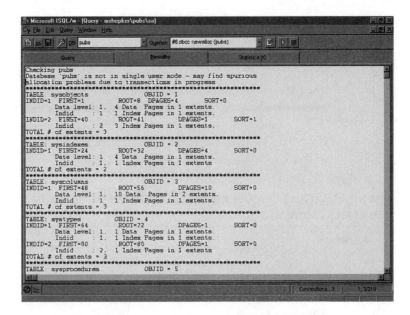

This error is normal if the database is not in single user mode. It rarely is possible for the SQL administrator to bring the server down long enough to perform this check, so you might end up with errors. The most common error returned when running NEWALLOC in an active database is error 2540. If you do not suspect problems in your database and you get this error from NEWALLOC, it most likely is nothing to worry about.

TEXTALL and TEXTALLOC

For databases that contain columns of text or image datatypes, it is important to run the TEXTALL or TEXTALLOC command on the individual tables or the entire database. The TEXTALLOC command is run on single tables. It checks the allocation of the text and image columns and makes sure that the pages are linked. The TEXTALL command is run on an entire database. It selects tables that contain columns of text or image datatypes and then runs TEXTALLOC on them. The following is the syntax of the two commands:

```
TEXTALL [({database_name ¦ database_id}[, FULL ¦ FAST])]

TEXTALLOC [({table_name ¦ table_id}[, FULL ¦ FAST])]
```

Two options control the speed at which the TEXTALLOC takes place. The FULL option checks all allocation pages in the database. It also checks the linkage of text chains and makes sure that the pages in the chains are linked. The FAST option does not provide an allocation report, but it does check the text chains and linkages.

14.6.3. Other DBCC Commands

So far, you have learned about DBCC functions that isolate possible errors in a database. Next you will deal with DBCC commands that enable you to look for possible degradations in overall system performance and then enable you to correct them.

SHOW_STATISTICS

One of the most important jobs of a SQL administrator is to keep the database running quickly. Developers add indexes to their tables to speed the performance of SELECTs made against the tables. SQL Server keeps statistics about the selectivity of those indexes and then uses those statistics to make decisions in query processing. Unfortunately, SQL Server does not always keep these statistics updated. After a great deal of information has been added or the table had been truncated and reloaded, it is a good idea to run SHOW_STATISTICS to check the selectivity of the indexes in the table. The following is the syntax of the SHOW_STATISTICS command:

```
DBCC SHOW_STATISTICS (table_name, index_name)
```

The output of the SHOW_STATISTICS command looks something like Figure 14.5. This was run on the clustered index on the authors table in the pubs database.

Figure 14.5.

The results of SHOW_STATISTICS *provide valuable information about the selectivity of your indexes.*

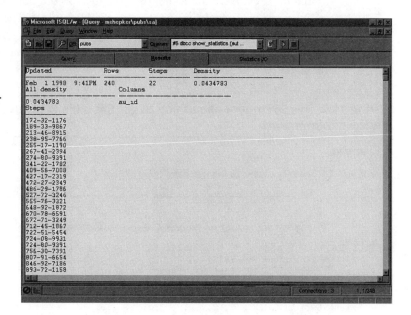

14

The most important bit of information to get out of this report is the density number. This is the number SQL Server uses to determine the selectivity of the index. You can multiply the number of rows by the density number to determine the selectivity. The lower the number, the more likely it is SQL Server will use the index. In this case, the clustered index should have a selectivity of 1. The statistics are off, however, giving you a selectivity of about 10. This causes SQL Server to perform a table scan instead of using the index. To correct this problem, you can run the following:

UPDATE STATISTICS (*tablename*)

You need to substitute the name of your table for *tablename*. This updates all the statistics to the most current values to ensure that the correct indexes are chosen.

SHOWCONTIG

The SHOWCONTIG command scans the table you specify for fragmentation. Table fragmentation occurs when INSERTs, UPDATEs, and DELETEs are made against tables. In time, the order of the pages becomes so disorganized that read-ahead cache can do little to keep up with the physical reads required to get the information off the disk. The following is the syntax of the SHOWCONTIG command:

DBCC SHOWCONTIG (*table_id*, [*index_id*])

To run the SHOWCONTIG command, you need to know the table ID of the table you are interested in. To find out, run the query in Listing 14.4. The index ID is not required to run this command; it defaults to index ID 0 or 1. Replace *dbname* with the name of the database the table resides in and replace *tbl_name* with the name of the table you want to investigate.

Listing 14.4. This SQL query allows you to get the table id for use in the SHOWCONTIG command.

```
use dbname
go
select id from sysobjects where name = 'tbl_name'
go
```

The following output of SHOWCONTIG contains several valuable pieces of information:

```
DBCC SHOWCONTIG scanning 'testtable' table...
[SHOW_CONTIG - SCAN ANALYSIS]
Table: 'testtable' (1625056825)   Indid: 0   dbid:1
TABLE level scan performed.
- Pages Scanned...............................: 68
- Extent Switches.............................: 8
```

```
- Avg. Pages per Extent........................: 7.6
- Scan Density [Best Count:Actual Count].......: 100.00% [9:9]
- Avg. Bytes free per page.....................: 51.2
- Avg. Page density (full).....................: 97.46%
- Overflow Pages...............................: 67
- Avg. Bytes free per Overflow page............: 52.0
- Avg. Overflow Page density...................: 97.4%
- Disconnected Overflow Pages..................: 0
```

The first number you need to pay attention to is the Scan Density. The optimal number for this is 100. The Best Count is the ideal number of extent changes if everything is contiguously linked. The Actual Count is the actual number of extents the table extends across.

To correct fragmented tables, you need to drop and then rebuild the indexes on the table. For a simple table, this is not a problem. For tables that contain a primary key, you must drop the foreign keys that reference it and then drop the primary key. For large and complex databases, this can be a long and arduous task. With the release of SQL Server 6.5, Microsoft provides an easier way to perform this task.

DBREINDEX

The DBREINDEX command can rebuild either one or all of the indexes in a table. There are two major advances in using the DBREINDEX command rather than manually dropping and re-creating the indexes. First, indexes that enforce PRIMARY KEY or UNIQUE constraints can be re-created without dropping and re-creating the constraints. Second, indexes can be re-created without having to know anything about the structure of the table. The following is the syntax of the DBREINDEX command:

```
DBCC DBREINDEX ([table_name [, index_name [, fillfactor [, {SORTED_DATA ¦
➥SORTED_DATA_REORG}]]]]) [WITH NOINFOMSGS]
```

You must specify the table_name for this command to work. If you only want to rebuild a single index in a table, you can specify it (index_name). To rebuild all indexes, you can specify ' '.

UPDATEUSAGE

The UPDATEUSAGE command corrects inaccuracies in the sysindexes table. These inaccuracies can result in incorrect values when viewing database information in the Enterprise Manager and when running the sp_spaceused stored procedure. SQL Server does not automatically keep track of this information, so when you view the size of your database in the Enterprise Manager, it might not be accurate. The following is the syntax of UPDATEUSAGE:

```
DBCC UPDATEUSAGE ({0 ¦ database_name} [, table_name [, index_id]])
```

14

If you use 0 in the place of the *database_name*, UPDATEUSAGE checks the current database. UPDATEUSAGE can take a long time to run and can result in a degradation of system performance. It only should be run if you suspect inaccuracies or during off hours.

MEMUSAGE

The MEMUSAGE command provides a detailed report about how SQL Server uses memory. MEMUSAGE returns the following three reports:

- How memory was allocated to SQL Server at startup
- How much memory is used by the 20 largest objects in the data cache
- How much memory is used by the top 12 items in the procedure cache including stored procedures, triggers, rules, and defaults

The first section of MEMUSAGE details how memory is allocated to the various items is SQL Server. Configured Memory tells you how much memory is allocated to SQL Server as a whole. The other lines provide a breakdown of the other allocations. The following is a sample first section:

	Meg.	2K Blks	Bytes
Configured Memory:	16.0000	8192	16777216
Code size:	1.7166	879	1800000
Static Structures:	0.2472	127	259232
Locks:	0.2861	147	300000
Open Objects:	0.1144	59	120000
Open Databases:	0.0031	2	3220
User Context Areas:	0.7505	385	787002
Page Cache:	8.8639	4539	9294432
Proc Headers:	0.2134	110	223748
Proc Cache Bufs:	3.5840	1835	3758080

The second section provides a breakdown of the top 20 items in the data cache. This information is particularly useful after SQL Server has been running for some time. The more frequently accessed objects are in the data cache. The database IDs and the object IDs of the associated objects are listed. This gives you a chance to explore which objects are used most in your database. The following is a sample second section:

```
Buffer Cache, Top 20:
```

DB Id	Object Id	Index Id	2K Buffers
1	5	0	2178
1	6	0	892
1	36	0	101

1	1625056825	0	68
1	5	1	67
5	688005482	255	62
1	1625056825	2	50
1	3	0	41
1	99	0	34
1	36	2	31
5	5	0	22
1	12	0	15
1	6	1	12
1	688005482	0	12
5	3	0	10
1	1	0	9
1	688005482	2	8
2	3	0	8
1	1	2	6

14.7. Fixing Corrupt Databases

After you have located problems in your database, the next step is to decide what to do about it. This always is a difficult decision to make; often, it is out of the hands of the SQL administrator. Management and users sometimes have a hand in making this decision. You often have to weigh the amount of time the database already has been offline against the time it would be offline for repairs. Sometimes restoring from a known good backup is your only option.

14.7.1. User Tables

All data that is important to your day-to-day operations is stored in user tables. Even so, user tables are easier to repair than system tables.

The first step in repairing a user table is to make a backup of the database in its current state. You need this as a record of what was wrong with the database before you started making changes to it. You also can use this backup to restore the database if you make changes that do not fix it.

The next step is to figure out exactly where the corruption is located. If the corrupted object is an index, you might be able to take care of it by dropping and re-creating the index. If the corruption is within the table itself, you need to drop and re-create the table. This is more difficult without an index.

The biggest problem when re-creating a table is the data. Ideally, you can restore a table and all the data from backup. This is not always an option, however. You might have to extract the data from the failed table or re-create the data. If there has not been much activity in the database, it might be easier for your users to re-create the data by hand. Otherwise, you might have to use the bcp utility to get it out.

14

After you have rebuilt the tables, you need to run DBCC checks against it again. If everything checks out, make another backup and allow the users back into the database. This is the acid test of whether it is working.

14.7.2. System Tables

System tables are more difficult to repair than user tables because you cannot drop them. This is a difficult situation to be in, and there is little you can do to fix it.

The first step in repairing a system table is to make a backup of the database. As with corrupted user tables, you need this as a record of the database's state when you started troubleshooting.

The next step is to call your primary support provider or Microsoft's technical support lines. As previously mentioned, a number of undocumented DBCC commands and trace flags might be able to help you repair your database.

Next you need to restore a previous backup and run a DBCC against it. System table corruption has a way of hanging around for quite some time before making itself evident. If you are running DBCCs on a daily basis, you might have caught the corruption on the day it occurred. If you don't run DBCCs daily, don't be surprised if your previous backups also are corrupt.

As a last resort, you can bcp all the data out of your user tables. After all the data is out, you should drop the database and the devices it resides on and completely re-create the database. When the database creation is done, you can bcp all the data back in.

14.8. Preventative Maintenance

So far, this chapter has focused on what you should do after you suspect database errors. Although this is important information, you also can do a number of things to minimize errors and, when they do occur, to recover from them quickly.

It is impossible to overemphasize the importance of making daily backups of production databases. You always should have a backup scheme in case something catastrophic happens. Many SQL administrators have lost sleep trying to repair a database that could have been fixed quickly if there had been current backups.

If you can, it is important to run DBCCs against your databases frequently. In a 7×24×365 production situation, this can be difficult to do. You should try to find at least one time during the week to run a DBCC CHECKDB. The best time is late at night after you have run your backup. That way, you know whether the database you have on tape is consistent.

You also should document everything you do to your database. It might seem to be an extra, inconsequential step during day-to-day operation, but this documentation is invaluable during troubleshooting.

14.9. Investigating Suspect Databases

As a database administrator, one of the worst feelings that you will ever have is after you reboot the server and a database comes up marked as suspect. Databases are marked suspect during the automatic recovery process because the transaction log is corrupt or because the target tables are corrupt.

When troubleshooting this problem, it is important to figure out why a database has been marked suspect. Some reasons that databases can be marked suspect are as follows:

- SQL Server cannot open the database device files because they do not exist, because they are being used by another process, or due to device failure.
- An error occurs when SQL Server reads the transaction log of the database being recovered, due to a structural error in the transaction log, or due to a disk error.
- An error occurs when SQL server attempts to write a transaction that was successfully completed in the transaction log, but cannot write the transaction because of a write error on the data device.

Often you can look in the SQL Server error log to learn why a database was marked suspect. With this information, you can determine whether you can simply fix the error and reset the database status or whether you need to restore from backup.

If the database has been marked suspect because a device was in use when SQL Server was started or because a device has been moved, the fix is simple. The first step is to either move the database device back to where it was before or to stop the process that is currently using it. When the devices have been moved back, you must reset the database status flag, which can be performed by running the following in the SQL Query tool:

```
USE master
GO
sp_configure "allow updates", 1
```

14

```
RECONFIGURE WITH OVERRIDE
GO
UPDATE sysdatabases
SET status = status - 256
WHERE name = 'dbname'
GO
sp_configure "allow updates", 0
RECONFIGURE WITH OVERRIDE
GO
```

dbname is the name of the database that is marked suspect. After you have performed the preceding, you need to restart the SQL Server service.

If the database has been marked suspect due to disk errors or device problems, you need to drop and re-create the database and then restore from a clean backup. After you finish restoring, you need to investigate why the database became corrupt in the first place.

14.10. Other Common Problems

In the daily operation of a database, several problems occur more frequently than others. Sometimes they are difficult to troubleshoot; other times they are quite simple. This section discusses some of the more common problems and their solutions.

14.10.1. A Full Transaction Log

Every operation in SQL Server is logged in the transaction log. This functionality enables SQL Server to roll back, or cancel, transactions that have not been completed. This provides a stable environment for a database, but it can be frustrating when the transaction log fills up. A full transaction log usually is seen as error 1105, as follows:

```
Can't allocate space for object syslogs in database dbname because the
logsegment is full. If you ran out of space in syslogs, dump the transaction
log. Otherwise use ALTER DATABASE or sp_extendsegment to increase the size
of the segment.
```

If the transaction log is completely full, DUMP TRANSACTION WITH TRUNCATE_ONLY will fail because SQL Server cannot write a checkpoint record to the transaction log. The only option you have is to dump the log WITH NO_LOG. The following is the syntax for dumping the transaction log:

```
DUMP TRANSACTION WITH NO_LOG
```

After this finishes, you need to back up the database as soon as possible because you have lost that extra measure of redundancy.

14.10.2. Connection Problems

Trying to troubleshoot connection problems can be an extremely difficult process. Several variables need to be checked.

The first step is to determine whether the problem lies with a single client or multiple clients. If everyone is having the same problem, the problem most likely is SQL Server or the networking hardware between the client and the server.

If a single client is having a problem, the next step is to investigate the network on that client. You have various options, depending on the network protocol you use to connect to SQL Server. The following sections discuss troubleshooting named pipes and TCP/IP.

Named Pipes

If you are using named pipes to connect to the server, you first should determine whether you can connect to the IPC$ share of the SQL Server. You can do this entering the following at the command line:

```
net use \\ServerName\IPC$
```

If you can connect to the IPC$ share, yet you still cannot connect to the SQL Server, you can use the `makepipe` and `readpipe` commands to test the connection. The `makepipe` command creates a named pipe on the server and listens for connections. This command can be run only on Windows NT machines. The `readpipe` command connects to the named pipe, sends data to it, and then reads it back again.

The first step is to create the named pipe on the server. To do this, execute `makepipe` at the command prompt. If the server successfully creates the pipe, you should receive the following message:

```
Making PIPE:\\.\pipe\abc

read to write delay (seconds):0


Waiting for Client to Connect...
```

At the client workstation, go back and enter the `readpipe` command. It is found in the \MSSQL\BIN directory on DOS and Windows clients and in the \MSSQL\BINN directory on Windows NT machines. The following is the syntax of the command:

```
readpipe /Sservername /Dstring
```

14

In the preceding, *servername* is the name of the server to which you are connecting, and *string* is the text you want to send to the server. If you omit the string, `readpipe` by default sends the text `shutdown` to the named pipe listening on the server. If it is successful, you receive the following information:

```
SvrName:\\servername
PIPE    :\\servername\pipe\abc
DATA    :shutdown
Data Sent: 1 :shutdown
Data Read: 1 :shutdown
```

If your results are different from those shown above, yet all other clients can connect to the server, check the physical connections to the network and try again.

TCP/IP

When using TCP/IP to connect to the SQL Server, you can make sure that the connection is open by using the `ping` utility. If the IP address of the SQL Server is `10.1.1.152`, you would type the following at the command prompt:

```
ping 10.1.1.151
```

If the network connection is alive, you should receive the following output:

```
Reply from 10.1.1.151: bytes=32 time<10ms TTL=128
```

If you are using DNS or WINS for name resolution, you can substitute the name of the server for the IP address.

Blocking

When more than one user accesses a database at the same time, SQL Server uses locking to make sure that the two users' actions do not interfere with each other. *Locking* stops one user from using the same resources as another. A *block* occurs when one user has a lock on a resource that another user is attempting to access. If the first user does not relinquish its lock quickly, it effectively locks up the second user. You can use the `sp_who` stored procedure within ISQL/W to find users that are blocking:

```
spid   status      loginame hostname   blk   dbname      cmd
------ ----------- -------- ---------- ----- ----------- ------------------
1      sleeping    sa                  0     master      MIRROR HANDLER
2      sleeping    sa                  0     master      LAZY WRITER
3      sleeping    sa                  0     master      CHECKPOINT SLEEP
4      sleeping    sa                  0     master      RA MANAGER
10     sleeping    Jack     12-102     0     pubs        AWAITING COMMAND
11     runnable    Larry    07-468     10    pubs        SELECT
```

In this example, there is a number in the blk column of spid 11. This indicates that spid 10 is blocking spid 11. Transactions should complete quickly and should rarely block. In some circumstances, however, you need to use the KILL command to clear up the block. The following is the syntax of the KILL command:

```
KILL spid
```

In the preceding, you substitute the spid of the user connection you are going to terminate. The spid of the user is the number listed in the first column before the username. This terminates the user connection and clears up the blocks. You need to investigate why the blocks are taking place, however, and how to alleviate them in the future.

14.11. Other Sources of Information

In addition to SQL Server Books Online, several other sources of information are available to help you troubleshoot databases. Some of these resources are free and some are not, but they all will be useful to you at one time or another.

14.11.1. An Online Knowledge Base

If you have access to the Internet, the most extensive source of frequently updated information is Microsoft's Online Support site. It is located at http://www.microsoft.com/KB. You can search the entire site for bug notices, fixes, and tips.

14.11.2. Microsoft's Newsgroups

Microsoft also makes many newsgroups available to the general public. You can find them by pointing your newsreader to msnews.microsoft.com. There are hundreds of groups you can post to and ask questions. Remember, people who respond to your posts might not always know the correct answer to your questions. In other words, take their advice with a grain of salt.

14.11.3. TechNet and MSDN

Both TechNet and the Microsoft Developers Network (MSDN) library contain articles, white papers, and knowledge bases for nearly all Microsoft's products. The MSDN library is updated and sent out on a quarterly basis, and TechNet is updated monthly. Although both are excellent resources, TechNet is more for administrators. You will find a great deal of useful information there.

14

14.11.4. Technical Support

When your resources have run out, you can call Microsoft's technical support. Although the people at Microsoft technical support might not always have the answers, they do have one advantage over all other resources—access to the people that wrote the software. They can help you implement many undocumented fixes and features in SQL Server that normally are unavailable to you.

14.12. Conclusion

This chapter has discussed the troubleshooting process for SQL Server. It is important to remember to narrow the focus of your search and to take your time looking for the answer. The SQL Server error log and the Windows NT application event log are resources you should use to isolate the problem. Do not make snap decisions and make sure that everything is taken care of before reopening the database to users.

After you discover the exact nature of the problem, you can use many of the commands in this chapter to isolate it and repair it. This chapter also described various sources of support and information that you can use to help solve problems.

Lab

Questions

1. You are the administrator of a SQL Server. You suspect users are encountering errors. Where can you look to see whether any errors are occurring?

   A. The Windows NT system event log

   B. The Windows NT application event log

   C. The SQL Server error log

   D. The syserrors table in the Master database

2. How many archived copies of the SQL Server error log are kept?

   A. 4

   B. 6

   C. 8

   D It is user configurable.

3. You are the administrator of a SQL Server that resides on a TCP/IP network. Users are complaining that they cannot connect to the server. What utility should you use to troubleshoot this?

   A. makepipe

   B. readpipe

   C. TCPTest

   D. ping

4. You perform an sp_who in the SQL Query window, and you notice one user is blocking another. What information do you need to use the KILL command to cancel the user's process?

   A. The IP address of the user's computer

   B. The user's login name

   C. The user's process ID

   D. The text of the command that the user is running

14

5. You need to cancel a blocking user's process. How do you do this?

    A. `KILL` the user's spid in the SQL Query tool.

    B. Run the `sp_cancel` procedure in the SQL Query tool.

    C. Shut off the user's computer.

    D. You cannot cancel a sleeping process.

6. What protocol do you troubleshoot using the `makepipe` and `readpipe` utilities?

    A. TCP/IP

    B. DecNet sockets

    C. AppleTalk ASDP

    D. Named pipes

7. How do you fix a completely full transaction log?

    A. Expand the transaction log.

    B. Run a `DUMP TRANSACTION dbname WITH NO_LOG`.

    C. Run the `sp_dumplog` stored procedure.

    D. Nothing. The transaction log will clear itself.

8. You suspect there is corruption in a table containing a text/image column. How can you check this table?

    A. `DBCC CHECKTABLE`

    B. `DBCC CHECKDB`

    C. `DBCC TEXTALLOC`

    D. `DBCC TEXTALL`

9. What happens to a user's connection to the SQL Server when a fatal error occurs?

    A. The user's connection is dropped, and all open transactions are rolled back.

    B. The user's connection is dropped, and all open transactions are rolled forward.

C. The user's connection and state information are saved to the Master database, and the connection is dropped. The user then can reconnect to the server and pick up where he left off.

D. The user's connection stays the same. SQL Server relies on the client application to handle the error.

10. In the Windows NT event log, which section contains information about SQL Server?

A. The application log

B. The system log

C. The SQL Server log

D. The security log

14

Exercises

1. Exploring the SQL Server Error Log

This exercise helps to address the following certification exam objective:
- Locate information relevant to diagnosing a problem

In this exercise, you explore the current SQL Server error log. This exercise takes about 15 minutes to complete:

1. Start the SQL Enterprise Manager and connect to the server you will be investigating.
2. Expand the server you want to work with by clicking the plus sign to the left of the server name.
3. From the Server menu, choose Error Log.
4. The window contains the text of the error log. The top of the window contains a drop-down box with the word Current followed by a date and a time. The date and time represent the last time an event was written to the error log. You can choose any of the past six error logs from the drop-down box.
5. Read the startup messages in the error log file.
6. Scroll down to the message that says Recovery Complete. This message indicates that SQL Server has finished the automatic recovery sequence and is almost finished with its startup routine.
7. The next few lines in the error log show the character set and sort order used. This information is important to know if the Master database needs to be recovered.
8. Close the Error Log window.

2. Stopping a User Process in ISQL/W

This exercise helps to address the following certification exam objective:
- Cancel a sleeping process

This exercise shows you how to find and stop a blocking process. It should take about 15 minutes to complete:

1. Open ISQL/W and connect to the server on which you will be performing this exercise.

2. Choose the pubs database from the DB drop-down box.

3. In the Query window, enter the following and execute it:

```
BEGIN TRAN
GO
UPDATE authors SET au_fname = 'Annie' WHERE au_id = '427-17-2319'
GO
```

4. Open a second Query window by clicking the New Query button. Enter the following and execute it:

```
BEGIN TRAN
GO
DELETE FROM authors WHERE au_id = '427-17-2319'
GO
```

Note that the globe stays spinning in the Queries drop-down box.

5. Open another Query window by clicking the New Query button. Enter the following and execute it:

```
sp_who
```

Note that there is a number in the blk column of one process.

6. Use that number to execute the KILL command in the Query window by entering the following:

```
KILL spid_number
```

7. Click the Queries drop-down box. Note that the globe no longer is next to the second query. This indicates that the process has completed.

8. Go to the second Query window and enter the following and execute it:

```
ROLLBACK
```

This cancels the delete statement you originally ran.

Answers to Questions

1. **B, C**   Information about SQL Server is stored in the Windows NT application log and the SQL Server error log.

2. **B**   SQL Server keeps 6 archived copies of the error log.

3. **D**   Use the ping utility to begin the troubleshooting process on a TCP/IP network.

14

4. **C**   To kill a user's process, you need to process the ID of the user.

5. **A**   Use the `KILL` command in the SQL Query tool to stop a sleeping process.

6. **D**   Troubleshoot the named pipes protocol using the `makepipe` and `readpipe` utilities.

7. **B**   Dump the transaction log with the `NO_LOG` option.

8. **C**   To check the text/image allocations in a single table, use `DBCC TEXTALLOC`.

9. **A**   When a fatal error occurs, the user's connection drops, and all open transactions are rolled back.

10. **A**   Information about SQL Server is stored in the Windows NT application log.

Appendix A

Practice Exam

The Microsoft SQL Server 6.5 System Administration exam, at the time of this writing, consists of 61 questions and has a 90-minute time limit. The passing score is 707 of 1000. On average, you should spend just over one minute per question.

The exam is computer-administered and consists of a number of multiple-choice, situational, and pick-the-best-answer questions. It is possible that some questions might contain *exhibits*, which are either diagrams or screen captures from the SQL Enterprise Manager. Unlike many other Microsoft exams, however, this is not common.

Situational questions present a scenario and a proposed solution. It is up to you to carefully read the situation and the proposed solution to determine how valid it is. Make sure that you carefully read both the problem and the proposed solution to make sure that you have a thorough understanding of what is being done and whether it makes sense. It might be worthwhile to spend more time on these questions than other multiple-choice questions.

Because of the wordiness of the exam, you might find there is not enough time to answer all the questions. If you find yourself stuck on a particular question, mark it and go on to the next one. You can always go back to the marked questions and look at them again to figure out the answer. Also, as you move forward, another question might refer to something that helps you answer the question on which you were stumped.

The speed at which you move through the questions—and the feeling of whether there is enough time to complete the exam—is directly proportional to your preparation prior to the exam. There is no substitute for actually working with Microsoft SQL Server and encountering some of the problems presented on the exam. This is not to say you need to become a total expert on SQL Server prior to the exam, but you should feel comfortable with the command-line syntax, stored procedures, and features of the product. This goes a long way in helping you pass the exam the first time you take it.

The exam tests your knowledge of the following 12 areas of SQL Server:

- *Server installation and upgrade.* This section contains questions on the installation and configuration of SQL Server. It covers upgrade issues from SQL Server 4.2x to 6.5.

- *Integration of SQL Server with other applications and technologies.* Questions tend to focus on the integration of SQL Server with Windows NT.

- *Enterprisewide database administration.* This section deals with the configuration and administration of servers in the enterprise.

- *Managing database storage.* Topics in this section include the creation of devices and databases.

- *Managing user accounts.* In this section, you are tested on the creation of login IDs, database users, and groups.

- *Managing permissions.* Areas covered in this section include granting and revoking permissions and implementing various methods of secure access to data.

- *Server alert processing and task scheduling.* The SQL Executive service, the Scheduler, alerts, tasks, and the msdb database are tested in this section.

- *Managing data.* In this section, you are tested on how to use bcp, the SQL Transfer Manager, and other similar tools to manage data. You also will encounter questions about backing up and restoring databases and transaction logs.

- *Replication.* This section asks questions about replication scenarios and how to use replication.

- *Connectivity and network support.* This section contains questions about support for network clients and various network protocols used by SQL Server. Some questions about extended procedures also might be asked.

- *Tuning and monitoring.* This section focuses on configuration issues pertaining to the tempdb database, worker threads, memory, and so on. Expect questions about tuning and monitoring physical and logical I/O, and memory usage.

- *Troubleshooting.* In this section, you are tested on problem determination and resolution, recovery from lost devices and databases, problematic replication, and other issues.

Practice Exam

1. You have been hired by XYZ Inc. to install and configure Microsoft SQL Server. XYZ Inc. has a multiple-master domain model, and all domains have PDCs, BDCs, and member servers. All servers have sufficient capacity to install and run Microsoft SQL Server. Where should you place Microsoft SQL Server?

   A. PDC in a resource domain

   B. BDC in a master domain

   C. Member server in a master domain

   D. Member server in a resource domain

2. You are the database administrator of a large organization with Microsoft SQL Server and Sybase databases. Your company has offices in the United States, Canada, the United Kingdom, and France. You need to be able to store data in Microsoft SQL Server in the users' native languages at the various offices. You also need to maintain compatibility with your Sybase servers. All clients are using either Windows NT- or Windows-based workstations. Which character set should you choose?

   A. Code Page 850 (Multilingual)

   B. ISO 8859-1 (ANSI or Latin 1)

   C. Code Page 437 (US English)

   D. No character set satisfies all requirements

3. Which of the following requires you to rebuild your data if it is changed after your databases and tables are built? (Select all that apply.)

   A. SQL Executive logon account

   B. Licensing mode

   C. Sort order

   D. SQL Server security mode

   E. Character set

4. Your company recently migrated a database to Microsoft SQL Server. The database will be accessed by clients running on an existing Novell network, a Microsoft Windows NT domain, and several UNIX machines. Management wants to minimize the number of user logins accessing the database from the

Windows NT domain. It also wants to maintain the capability of UNIX and Novell users to access the database. Which Microsoft SQL Server security mode should you choose for this environment?

   A. Standard security

   B. Integrated security

   C. Mixed security

   D. None of the above

5. You need to create a database with a total size of 30MB. The database will use 20MB of disk space for the data segment and 10MB of disk space for the log segment. Which of the following SQL statements creates the device(s) to be used by this database? (Select all that apply.)

   A.
```
DISK INIT NAME='MyDatabase', PHYSNAME=
'C:\MSSQL\DATA\MyDatabase.DAT', SIZE=30, VDEVNO=10
```

   B.
```
DISK INIT NAME='MyDatabaseData', PHYSNAME=
'C:\MSSQL\DATA\MyDatabaseData.DAT', SIZE=10240, VEDVNO=10

DISK INIT NAME='MyDatabaseLog', PHYSNAME=
'C:\MSSQL\DATA\MyDatabaseLog.DAT', SIZE=5120, VEDVNO=15
```

   C.
```
DISK INIT NAME='MyDatabaseData', PHYSNAME=
'C:\MSSQL\DATA\MyDatabaseData.DAT', SIZE=20, VEDVNO=10

DISK INIT NAME='MyDatabaseLog', PHYSNAME=
'C:\MSSQL\DATA\MyDatabaseLog.DAT', SIZE=10, VEDVNO=15
```

   D.
```
DISK INIT NAME='MyDatabase', PHYSNAME=
'C:\MSSQL\DATA\MyDatabase.DAT', SIZE=15360, VDEVNO=10
```

   E. None of the above

6. You want to change the configuration of your Microsoft SQL Server. You want to use integrated security and connect to SQL Server from Windows NT Workstation and Windows 95 clients. Your SQL Server is installed on a Windows NT member server and has TCP/IP, NWLink IPX/SPX, and NetBEUI installed in Control Panel/Networking. Which of the following SQL Server network protocols support your configuration? (Select the two correct answers.)

   A. TCP/IP Sockets

   B. Multi-Protocol

    C. Named Pipes

    D. NWLink IPX/SPX

    E. NetBEUI

7. Which of the following Microsoft SQL Server database objects can be used to enforce data integrity? (Select all that apply.)

    A. Indexes

    B. Constraints

    C. Rules

    D. Tables

    E. Defaults

    F. Triggers

8. As the database administrator for Acme United Ltd., you are charged with installing Microsoft SQL Server on a new machine. Acme United Ltd. uses replication between its various sites, and this new server will act as a distribution server for your site. What is the minimum amount of memory required to install Microsoft SQL Server on this new machine?

    A. 16MB

    B. 64MB

    C. 32MB

    D. 12MB

9. You have set up Microsoft SQL Server to send and respond to email messages. Which of the following stored procedures should you use for SQL Server to respond to mail sent to it?

    A. xp_answermail

    B. sp_sendmail

    C. sp_processmail

    D. xp_processmail

    E. sp_getmail

10. You are deciding on ways to automate some of the administration of your Microsoft SQL Server. You have decided you want daily backups of transaction logs performed every night at 2 a.m. You also want a full-database backup

to take place every Sunday at 1 a.m. You do not want to bring the server down to perform backups because users access databases on the server 24 hours a day. What are three ways you can have SQL Server perform your backup tasks automatically without affecting users' capabilities to access the server?

A. Use `sp_createtask` to create your backup task and use `sp_scheduletask` to schedule your tasks.

B. Use the Database Maintenance Wizard.

C. Use the Windows NT AT scheduler to start Windows NT Backup to back up your transaction logs and database.

D. Use the Task Manager in the SQL Enterprise Manager to create two tasks and to schedule them at the required times.

E. Use `sp_addtask` to add and schedule the backups.

11. You are the database administrator of United Systems Inc., a company with offices throughout North America. Your organization has adopted Microsoft BackOffice as a standard platform for file and print, application, and other network services. You have been asked to install Microsoft SQL Server in the organization. Your network administrator informs you that United Systems Inc. uses a single-master domain model with all user accounts controlled by head-office MIS staff. You ask him to correctly configure the Windows NT domain user account that will be used by the SQL Executive service to start up. What characteristics of the user account should he set? (Select all that apply.)

A. Must change password at next logon

B. Password never expires

C. User cannot change password

D. All logon hours allowed

E. Has the right to Log On as a Batch Job

12. To view the startup information of Microsoft SQL Server on your Windows NT machine, which Registry key should you look at in REGEDT32?

A. `HKEY_LOCAL_MACHINE`

B. `HKEY_CURRENT_USER`

C. `HKEY_LOCAL_USER`

D. `HKEY_CLASSES_ROOT`

E. `HKEY_SERVICE_SOFTWARE`

13. Which of the following components are not part of the SQL Server Distributed Management Framework (SQL-DMF)? (Select the two correct answers.)

    A. SQL Enterprise Manager

    B. ISQL/W

    C. SQL Security Manager

    D. SQL Server Distributed Management Objects

    E. SQL Executive

14. Which of the following Microsoft SQL Server utilities should you use to enable or disable SQL Server's capability to interface with the Windows NT Performance Monitor? (Select all that apply.)

    A. SQL Enterprise Manager

    B. SQL Client Configuration utility

    C. SQL Trace

    D. SQL Setup

    E. SQL Service Manager

15. You are a developer of a sophisticated call-tracking application that uses Microsoft SQL Server to store its database and to provide high-performance transaction processing for your clients. You want to reduce the learning curve of your users by integrating management of SQL Server within your application. Which Microsoft SQL Server Distributed Management Framework component do you need to interface with to provide this capability within your application?

    A. SQL Executive

    B. SQL Server Distributed Management Objects

    C. SQL Server Engine

    D. SQL Enterprise Manager

    E. None of the above

16. Which of the following Microsoft SQL Server services must be started for your users to have access to databases and data? (Select all that apply.)

    A. SQLExecutive

    B. SQLMail

A

    C. MSDTC

    D. MSSQLServer

17. Which of the following is *not* a Microsoft SQL Server system database?

    A. Master

    B. pubs

    C. tempdb

    D. msdb

    E. model

18. You have a database called CustomerDB on your SQL Server with the following storage structure: 20MB for data and log on device DataDev01. You want to separate the log from the data segment and create a new 5MB device called LogDev01. Which of the following Microsoft SQL Server commands can you use to accomplish this task?

    A. `sp_movelog CustomerDB,LogDev01`

    B. `ALTER DATABASE CustomerDB ON LogDev01=5`
       `EXEC xp_logdevice CustomerDB, LogDev01`

    C. `ALTER DATABASE CustomerDB ON LogDev01=2560`
       `EXEC sp_logdevice CustomerDB, LogDev01`

    D. `xp_movelog CustomerDB, LogDev01`

    E. `ALTER DATABASE CustomerDB ON LogDev01=5`
       `EXEC sp_logdevice CustomerDB, LogDev01`

The next three questions outline a scenario for which you are provided a proposed solution. You should read each question and decide whether the proposed solution works and to what extent. Then choose the best answer.

19. Your database has lost one of the devices holding your data segment as a result of a hard drive failure. You want to make sure that minimal data loss occurs, and you decide to perform the following steps to recover your database:

    1. Back up the current transaction log using `DUMP TRANSACTION WITH NO_TRUNCATE` to save all changes up to the point of failure.

    2. Use the SQL Enterprise Manager to drop the database and associated devices.

3. Replace the failed hard drive and reformat it with Windows NT Disk Administrator.

4. Re-create your devices and database in the SQL Enterprise Manager with the same names and characteristics as before the failure.

5. Restore your database and transaction logs in the proper order using LOAD DATABASE and LOAD TRANSACTION.

This solution

A. Is an outstanding solution that works.

B. Is an acceptable solution that works.

C. Appears to be an outstanding solution but does not work.

D. Does not appear to be a valid solution and does not work.

20. Your database has lost one of the devices holding your data segment as a result of a hard drive failure. You want to make sure that minimal data loss occurs, and you decide to perform the following steps to recover your database:

1. Back up the current transaction log using DUMP TRANSACTION WITH NO_TRUNCATE to save all changes up to the point of failure.

2. Use the stored procedure sp_dbremove with the DROPDEV parameter to drop the database and associated devices.

3. Replace the failed hard drive and reformat it with Windows NT Disk Administrator.

4. Re-create your devices and database in the SQL Enterprise Manager with the same names and characteristics as before the failure.

5. Restore your database and transaction logs in the proper order using LOAD DATABASE and LOAD TRANSACTION.

This solution

A. Is an outstanding solution that works.

B. Is an acceptable solution that works.

C. Appears to be an outstanding solution but does not work.

D. Does not appear to be a valid solution and does not work.

21. Your database has lost one of the devices holding your data segment as a result of a hard drive failure. You want to make sure that minimal data loss occurs, and you decide to perform the following steps to recover your database:

1. Back up the current transaction log using DUMP TRANSACTION WITH NO_TRUNCATE to save all changes up to the point of failure.

2. Use sp_dbremove to drop the database and associated objects.

3. Use sp_dropdevice with the DELFILE parameter to drop all the devices.

4. Replace the failed hard drive and reformat it with Windows NT Disk Administrator the SQL Enterprise Manager with the same names and characteristics as before the failure.

5. Restore your database and transaction logs in the proper order using LOAD DATABASE and LOAD TRANSACTION.

This solution

A. Is an outstanding solution that works.

B. Is an acceptable solution that works.

C. Appears to be an outstanding solution but does not work.

D. Does not appear to be a valid solution and does not work.

22. You have configured your Microsoft SQL Server to use integrated security. What further task should you perform to enable your Windows NT users to access the SQL Server?

A. Create SQL Server user accounts using sp_adduser.

B. Use the SQL Security Manager to specify which Windows NT users and groups have access to SQL Server.

C. Create SQL Server login IDs using sp_addlogin.

D. Do nothing.

23. You decide to review the users and logins currently created in SQL Server. You notice that a user account exists in a database not in use by any of the individuals accessing that database. You decide to drop the user by executing the sp_dropuser stored procedure, but this fails. Which of the following is a possible reason why you were unable to drop the user?

A. The user currently is accessing the database.

B. The user has been flagged persistent.

C. The user is a member of the group PUBLIC and cannot be deleted.

D. The user owns database objects.

E. The user is a member of the group OWNERS and cannot be deleted.

24. As the database administrator for Acme United Ltd., you have been charged with installing Microsoft SQL Server on a new machine. Acme United Ltd. uses replication between its various sites, and this new server will act as a distribution server for your site. This machine has 32MB of RAM installed. You need to configure Microsoft SQL Server to request 16MB of memory from the operating system when it starts up. Which of the following commands accomplishes this?

    A. `sp_configure 'memory', 16384`

    B. `sp_configure 'memory', 8192`

    C. `sp_configure 'memory', 16384000`

    D. None of the above

25. You are a database administrator of a Microsoft SQL Server within a small software company. All the members of your research and development department have administrator privileges on your Windows NT domain so that they can test their software on any workstation in the organization. You use integrated security and have not created mappings between Windows NT user accounts and SQL Server logins for all members of the R&D department. Which of the following statements is true?

    A. Members of R&D have access to the SQL Server only if they have been configured in the SQL Security Manager.

    B. Members of R&D always access the SQL Server as system administrator.

    C. All users in the company, including R&D, have the same access to SQL Server.

    D. Members of R&D do not have access to SQL Server.

    E. Members of R&D who have not been configured in the SQL Security Manager should access SQL Server as guest.

26. When creating a SQL Server database user account, information about the account is stored in

    A. The sysusers table in the Master database

    B. The sysusers table in the database where the user account was created

    C. The syslogins table in the database where the user account was created

    D. The syslogins table in the Master database

A

E. The Windows NT Security Accounts Database on the machine where SQL Server is installed

F. A hidden table that cannot be accessed manually

27. Your company has recently migrated a database to Microsoft SQL Server. Clients include Windows NT and Windows 95 machines connecting to a Windows NT domain, Novell NetWare clients connecting to several NetWare servers, and a few UNIX workstations. You want to make sure that users from all environments can access Microsoft SQL Server. Which network protocol support should you install for Microsoft SQL Server? (Select all that apply.)

   A. Named Pipes

   B. NWLink IPX/SPX

   C. Banyan Vines

   D. DEC Net Sockets

   E. TCP/IP Sockets

28. When creating Windows NT groups to map to SQL Server groups when using integrated security, you should do which two of the following:

   A. Use valid SQL Server characters.

   B. Make sure that group names have fewer than 64 characters.

   C. Use the SQL Security Manager to create the groups.

   D. Use the Windows NT User Manager to create the groups in SQL Server.

   E. Make sure that a user appears in only one group.

29. You need to assign permissions to users and groups for proper access to your sales information database. The security needs are as follows:

   ■ The SalesManager database user should have all permissions on the Leads table.

   ■ The SalesPeople group should have update permissions on the Leads table.

   ■ All other users should have read permissions on the Leads table.

   You decide to issue the following commands to assign permissions to the Leads table:

```
GRANT SELECT ON Leads TO ALL
GRANT ALL ON Leads TO SalesManager
GRANT UPDATE ON Leads TO SalesPeople
```

The proposed solution (choose the best answer)

    A. Is an outstanding solution that works.

    B. Is an acceptable solution that works.

    C. Appears to be an outstanding solution but does not work.

    D. Does not appear to be a valid solution and does not work.

30. You need to create a database that has a total size of 30MB. The database will use 20MB of disk space for the data segment and 10MB of disk space for the log segment. Which of the following SQL statements results in a database with the appropriate characteristics? (Select all that apply.)

    A. `CREATE DATABASE MyDb ON MyDataDevice=20`
       `ALTER DATABASE MyDb ON MyLogDevice=10`
       `sp_logdevice MyDb, MyLogDevice`

    B. `CREATE DATABASE MyDb ON MyDataDevice=10240 LOG ON`
       `MyLogDevice=5120`

    C. `CREATE DATABASE MyDb ON MyDataDevice=20 LOG ON`
       `MyLogDevice=10`

    D. `CREATE DATABASE MyDb ON MyDataDevice=20, MyLogDevice=10`
       `LOG ON MyLogDevice`

    E. `CREATE DATABASE MyDb ON MyDataDevice=10240`
       `ALTER DATABASE MyDb ON MyLogDevice=5120`
       `sp_logdevice MyDb, MyLogDevice`

31. You need to assign permissions to users and groups for proper access to your sales information database. The security needs are as follows:

    ■ The SalesManager database user should have all permissions on the Leads table.

    ■ The SalesPeople group should have update permissions on the Leads table.

    ■ All other users should have read permissions on the Leads table.

You decide to issue the following commands to assign permissions to the Leads table:

```
GRANT SELECT ON Leads TO PUBLIC
GRANT UPDATE ON Leads TO SalesPeople
GRANT ALL ON Leads TO SalesManager
```

The proposed solution (choose the best answer)

A. Is an outstanding solution that works.

B. Is an acceptable solution that works.

C. Appears to be an outstanding solution but does not work.

D. Does not appear to be a valid solution and does not work.

32. Which of the following commands enables you to check the consistency of tables within your database containing text or image columns?

A. sp_checktext

B. DBCC TEXTALL

C. DBCC CHECKDB

D. sp_checkdb

E. DBCC NEWALLOC

33. You are the database administrator of a large database used for order entry by your company. The database, called Orders, currently takes more than 20 hours to back up to a single tape device. You have decided to add two more tape devices to speed up the backup process. Which of the following SQL Server commands should you use to speed up your backup of the Orders database?

A. DUMP DATABASE Orders TO Tape1, Tape2, Tape3

B. BACKUP DATABASE Orders TO Tape1, Tape2, Tape3

C. sp_dbbackup ('Orders','Tape1, Tape2, Tape3')

D. LOAD DATABASE Orders TO Tape1, Tape2, Tape3

E. BACKUP DATABASE Orders TO (Tape1, Tape2, Tape3)

34. You need to assign permissions to users and groups for proper access to your sales information database. The security needs are as follows:

- The SalesManager database user should have all permissions on the Leads table.
- The SalesPeople group should have update permissions on the Leads table.
- All other users should have read permissions on the Leads table.

You decide to issue the following commands to assign permissions to the Leads table:

```
GRANT ALL ON Leads TO PUBLIC
GRANT ALL ON Leads TO SalesManager
REVOKE INSERT, DELETE ON Leads FROM SalesPeople
REVOKE INSERT, UPDATE, DELETE ON Leads FROM PUBLIC
```

The proposed solution (choose the best answer)

    A. Is an outstanding solution that works.

    B. Is an acceptable solution that works.

    C. Appears to be an outstanding solution but does not work.

    D. Does not appear to be a valid solution and does not work.

35. After executing which of the following commands is it recommended that you back up the Master database? (Select all that apply.)

    A. sp_dropuser

    B. sp_addlogin

    C. sp_adduser

    D. sp_configure

    E. sp_dropserver

36. You are the database administrator for Microstuff Incorporated. You installed Microsoft SQL Server in your organization some time ago. You are now concerned that recovery time might become an issue in the event of a disk drive failure because current tape backups require about six hours to complete. Several servers on the network have large amounts of disk space available, and you have a free 9GB hard disk on your current SQL Server. Your database currently resides on two 4GB hard disks on your server.

To reduce the impact of a hard drive failure on your database, you decide to perform the following:

> Use Windows NT disk mirroring to mirror each of the 4GB disk partitions on which your database resides to the new 9GB drive on your server.

The proposed solution (choose the best answer)

A. Is an outstanding solution that works.

B. Is an acceptable solution that works.

C. Appears to be an outstanding solution but does not work.

D. Does not appear to be a valid solution and does not work.

37. You are the database administrator for Microstuff Incorporated. You installed Microsoft SQL Server in your organization some time ago. You are now concerned that recovery time might become an issue in the event of a disk drive failure because current tape backups require about six hours to complete. Several servers on the network have large amounts of disk space available, and you have a free 9GB hard disk on your current SQL Server. Your database currently resides on two 4GB hard disks on your server.

To reduce the impact of a hard drive failure on your database, you decide to perform the following:

> For each SQL Server database device, issue the DISK MIRROR command to mirror the device to a remote server on the network.

The proposed solution (choose the best answer)

A. Is an outstanding solution that works.

B. Is an acceptable solution that works.

C. Appears to be an outstanding solution but does not work.

D. Does not appear to be a valid solution and does not work.

38. You are the database administrator for Microstuff Incorporated. You installed Microsoft SQL Server in your organization some time ago. You are now concerned that recovery time might become an issue in the event of a disk drive failure because current tape backups require about six hours to complete. Several servers on the network have large amounts of disk space available, and you have a free 9GB hard disk on your current SQL Server. Your database currently resides on two 4GB hard disks on your server.

To reduce the impact of a hard drive failure on your database, you decide to perform the following:

For each SQL Server database device, issue the DISK MIRROR command to mirror the device to the 9GB hard disk on your server.

The proposed solution (choose the best answer)

A. Is an outstanding solution that works.

B. Is an acceptable solution that works.

C. Appears to be an outstanding solution but does not work.

D. Does not appear to be a valid solution and does not work.

39. What command enables you to verify that you can connect to a SQL Server's named pipe?

A. `ping \\SQLServer`

B. `net use \\SQLServer`

C. `net use \\SQLServer\IPC$`

D. `show pipe \\SQLServer`

E. `net use \\SQLServer\Pipe`

40. DBCC MEMUSAGE can be used to determine which of the following? (Select all that apply.)

A. The amount of memory used by the 20 largest objects in the procedure cache

B. The amount of memory used by each user connecting to SQL Server

C. The amount of memory allocated to SQL Server at startup

D. The amount of memory reserved by SQL Server to perform backups

E. The amount of memory used by the 20 largest objects in the buffer cache

41. You are the database administrator for Microstuff Incorporated. The Orders database is experiencing a rapid increase in the number of transactions as year-end approaches. You want to make sure that the transaction log for the database does not grow past 80 percent. You decide to monitor its usage in real time. Which of the following enables you to do this?

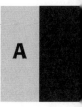

A. SQL Server Alert Manager

B. Windows NT Performance Monitor

C. The sp_checklog stored procedure

D. SQL Trace

E. SQL Executive

42. When using SQL Server replication, where are database constraints and triggers enforced?

A. The publishing server

B. The subscribing server

C. The trigger server

D. The distribution server

E. All servers taking part in replication

43. Which of the following can be used as a publishing server SQL Server replication? (Select the two correct answers.)

A. Microsoft SQL Server 6.5

B. Oracle

C. Microsoft SQL Server 6.0

D. Microsoft Access

E. Sybase

44. When replicating from a Microsoft SQL Server 6.5 server to a Microsoft SQL Server 6.0 server, the subscribing Microsoft SQL Server 6.0 server will be treated as a

A. Microsoft SQL Server 6.0 server.

B. Microsoft SQL Server 6.5 server.

C. ODBC data source.

D. You cannot replicate from SQL Server 6.5 to 6.0.

45. Which of the following are supported synchronization methods when using Microsoft SQL Server replication? (Select all that apply.)

A. Scheduled table refresh

B. Manual synchronization

    C. Automatic synchronization

    D. Trigger-based synchronization

    E. No synchronization

46. You have configured events within SQL Server to be written to the Windows NT application event log. An alert has been configured for an error severity code, and another alert has been configured to fire on an error number. If the severity code of the error and the severity code for the event match, which alert fires?

    A. Only the error number alert fires.

    B. Only the severity code alert fires.

    C. The error number alert runs first followed by the severity code alert.

    D. The severity code alert runs first followed by the error number alert.

    E. Neither alert fires.

47. You have configured an Alerts Management Server to handle alerts for events occurring on a number of busy SQL Server machines. If you have an alert defined both locally on a SQL Server machine and on the Alerts Management Server, where does the alert run?

    A. On the Alerts Management Server.

    B. On both the Alerts Management Server and the local SQL Server.

    C. On the local SQL Server only.

    D. The alert will not run.

48. Which of the following commands exports the Customers table from the Orders database of a Intel-based Microsoft SQL Server in a format compatible for importing into a Microsoft SQL Server running on an Alpha-based Windows NT server?

    A. `bcp Orders..Customers in Customer.txt /n /t "~" /r \n /U SA /a 4096 /m 1000 /e errors.out`

    B. `B. bcp Orders..Customers out Customer.txt /c /t "~" /r \n /U SA /a 4096 /m 1000 /e errors.out`

    C. `export Orders..Customers out Customer.txt -alpha`

    D. `export Orders..Customers Customer.txt -from Intel  -to Alpha`

    E. `bcp Orders..Customers out Customer.txt /n /t "~" /r \n /U SA /a 4096 /m 1000 /e errors.out`

49. You are the database administrator of Really Big Inc., and you have been charged with upgrading your Microsoft SQL Server 6.0 database to SQL Server 6.5. Your current server is an Intel-based dual-Pentium machine with 128MB of RAM. The new server you are migrating your database to is an Alpha-based quad-CPU system. Which of the following tools can you use to transfer your data to your new server? (Select the two correct answers.)

    A. The SQL Transfer Manager in SQL Enterprise Manager.

    B. SQL Server DUMP and LOAD commands.

    C. The bcp utility in native mode.

    D. The bcp utility in character mode.

    E. This upgrade cannot be performed.

50. What items are displayed in the Current Activity windows in the SQL Enterprise Manager? (Select all that apply.)

    A. The currently executing stored procedures

    B. The locks currently being applied to database objects

    C. The current users accessing the database and the objects they are referencing

    D. The currently executing alerts

    E. The list of currently running processes

    F. The size of the database transaction log

51. To get current information about the space occupied by the transaction log in your Orders database, which command should you issue?

    A. DBCC SPACEUSED ('Orders', LOG)

    B. sp_logspace Orders

    C. xp_logspace Orders

    D. sp_spaceused syslogs

    E. sp_spaceused logspace

52. Which command should you use to create a SQL script that properly re-creates your database and devices in the same order and with the same structure as before any media failure?

    A. sp_recreatedb

    B. sp_dbrebuild

    C. `sp_help_rebuild_db`

    D. `sp_help_revdatabase`

    E. `sp_genscript DBREBUILD`

53. Microsoft SQL Server automatic recovery (select the three correct answers)

    A. Cannot be configured.

    B. Cannot be turned off.

    C. Makes sure that completed transactions are rolled forward.

    D. Makes sure that incomplete transactions are rolled forward.

    E. Recovers the user databases first.

    F. Recovers the Master database first.

54. You reconfigure your Microsoft SQL Server and accidentally set the memory configuration parameter to a value too high for your current hardware to support. Your SQL Server attempts to start, but it fails after many minutes of busy disk activity. Without adding more memory to your Windows NT machine, how can you start SQL Server to reconfigure the memory setting to an acceptable value?

    A. Start SQL Server from the command prompt using the syntax `sqlservr -c -m -dC:\MSSQL\DATA\MASTER.DAT`.

    B. From the Services section of the Windows NT Control Panel, set the MSSQLServer service to start manually and then restart the service.

    C. From the Services section of the Windows NT Control Panel, set the SQLExecutive service to start manually and then restart the service.

    D. Start SQL Server from the command prompt using the syntax `sqlservr -f -m -dC:\MSSQL\DATA\MASTER.DAT`.

    E. You must add more memory to Windows NT to solve this problem.

55. When upgrading a database from SQL Server 4.21 to SQL Server 6.5, which steps should you take to make sure that your upgrade runs smoothly? (Select the two correct answers.)

    A. Run UPGRADE.EXE to perform the upgrade.

    B. Create the database with a data segment and a transaction log segment larger than the size of the original.

A

C. Create the database with the exact same segment structure as the original database.

D. Run the sp_dbupgrade script to perform the upgrade.

E. Run the CHKUPG65.EXE utility after loading to check for any keyword conflicts.

F. Run the CHKUPG65.EXE utility before loading to check for any keyword conflicts.

56. You are the database administrator for a large insurance company. Management has decided to equip all salespeople with a notebook computer running SQL Workstation 6.5 and a custom-designed application. This application will access data that is updated periodically by sending a CD-ROM to each salesperson. You are responsible for creating the master copy of the database to be sent to each salesperson. Which conditions must be met so that your database can safely be distributed to the salespeople via CD-ROM? (Select the two correct answers.)

A. The system administrator is the database owner.

B. All objects must be owned by the dbo.

C. You will use CREATE DATABASE to create the master.

D. Permissions must be set prior to copying the database to the CD-ROM.

E. Each salesperson must have a login ID in your database.

57. You want to monitor your SQL Server in Performance Monitor and track the average value of an order entered in your Orders database in real time. How should you accomplish this?

A. Create a user-defined counter in Performance Monitor for the SQL Server object.

B. Create the sp_user_counter1 stored procedure in your database to track the average value of an order.

C. Modify the sp_user_counter1 stored procedure in your database to track the average value of an order.

D. Modify the sp_user_counter1 stored procedure in the Master database to track the average value of an order.

E. It is not possible to create or monitor user-defined counters in Performance Monitor or SQL Server.

58. A situation in SQL Server in which a user wants to modify a record on a page that is heavily accessed for read by other users is called a

    A. Deadlock

    B. Write lock

    C. Blocking lock

    D. Livelock

    E. Shared lock

59. You are the database administrator of a busy order-entry database running on SQL Server. You notice that on Friday afternoons your sales managers regularly run reports to look at the week's volume of orders. This slows down the speed of new orders entered by the order-entry clerks. To alleviate this situation, you decide to perform the following:

    1. Configure a second Microsoft SQL Server on another Windows NT machine.

    2. Configure the order-entry SQL Server to publish the entire database to your new SQL Server machine using SQL Server replication.

    3. Configure the sales managers' client software to use the replicated copy of the database when running reports.

    The proposed solution (choose the best answer)

    A. Is an outstanding solution that works.

    B. Is an acceptable solution that works.

    C. Appears to be an outstanding solution but does not work.

    D. Does not appear to be a valid solution and does not work.

60. What is the default Net-Library installed when you set up SQL Server on your Windows NT machine?

    A. TCP/IP

    B. Multi-Protocol

    C. NWLink IPX/SPX

    D. Named Pipes

    E. Banyan Vines

61. Maria needs to run a stored procedure called `sp_updateClient`, which updates records in the Client table in the Orders database. She has been granted `EXECUTE` permissions to the `sp_updateClient` stored procedure by David, who is the dbo for that object. The Client table is owned by Tim, who has granted Maria `SELECT` and `INSERT` permissions on the Client table. Which of the following is true:

   A. Maria is able to update any record in the Client table using the `sp_updateClient` stored procedure.

   B. Maria cannot update any record in the Client table using the `sp_updateClient` stored procedure.

   C. Maria is prompted for a password when updating any record in the Client table using the `sp_updateClient` stored procedure.

   D. None of the above.

Answers

1. **D**   A member server in a resource domain. In general, placement of an application of any sort is not recommended on a domain controller. This is because domain controllers are required to perform other resource-intensive tasks, such as authentication of users, domain accounts synchronization, pass-through authentication, and others. These can impact the performance of Microsoft SQL Server, and as such, options A and B are not good candidates for installing Microsoft SQL Server.

   Microsoft SQL Server is best installed on a member server in a resource domain (option D). Although it can be installed on a member server in a master domain (option C), it generally is preferred that application servers be located closest to where the greatest number of users will be making use of them. This typically is a resource domain with a trust relationship to the master domain. In general, master domains are used solely for the creation and maintenance of user accounts and global groups. As such, they contain few, if any, member servers.

2. **B**   Although your initial thought might be to use Code Page 850—Multilingual (option A), this does not satisfy one of the stated requirements—compatibility with Sybase. Code Page 437 (option C) does not provide international character support for French characters (the only other

language needed because both Canada and France use French). The correct answer is B because the ISO 8859-1, or ANSI, character set provides support for the required languages and provides compatibility with Sybase databases. This also is the default character set for Microsoft SQL Server 6.5 and should be used in most cases.

3. **C, E**   Sort order and character set. When installing Microsoft SQL Server, you are prompted to choose a character set and sort order that must remain constant for the life of the SQL Server. All databases and all data should use the same character set and sort order. Changing either of these requires that all databases and data be rebuilt.

Changing the Licensing mode (such as going from Per Server to Per Seat) does not affect the data in any way. Changing the SQL Server security mode from standard to mixed or integrated does not affect the data in any way. It might, however, limit the users that can attach to the server.

Changing the SQL Executive logon account does not prevent SQL Server from starting or prevent users from accessing data. It might inhibit replication, however, if all instances of SQL Server do not share the same SQL Executive logon account.

4. **C**   Because of the requirement that the number of logins by users should be minimized while maintaining existing Novell and UNIX users, the security mode should be mixed. In the mixed security mode, existing Windows NT users and groups can be exported to SQL Server using the Security Manager. Users from Novell and UNIX environments can be created within SQL Server and can access the database by specifying a username and password for the server.

Standard security requires all users to provide a SQL Server username and password in addition to the NT domain username and password. Integrated security enables only Windows NT domain-based users to have access to the servers. This eliminates the capability of Novell and UNIX users to connect.

5. **B**   When creating disk devices for SQL Server, the size of the device must be specified in 2KB pages. This means options B and D are possible answers to satisfy the requirement that the final size of the devices in either case be 30MB. The correct answer, however, is B because you need to separate the data segment of 20MB from the log segment of 10MB. To keep the log

A

separate from the database, it is necessary to use at least two devices. Creating one device 30MB in size, as in option D, does not satisfy the requirements presented.

6. **B, C**   When configuring Microsoft SQL Server for integrated security, Multi-Protocol or Named Pipes (or both) must be installed. This is because these are the only two protocols provided by SQL Server that can make use of Microsoft Networking Inter-Process Communication (IPC) mechanisms required by integrated security.

TCP/IP Sockets (option A) and NWLink IPX/SPX (option D) are not correct because they are not used for integrated security. These are required if you want to support clients using network protocols connecting to SQL Server in either standard or mixed security modes.

NetBEUI (option E) is not a protocol supported by SQL Server. It is only used by Windows NT for network communication—it is not an option when selecting SQL Server network protocols.

7. **B, C, E, F**   Defaults enable you to specify a default value to be inserted into a column if no value is specified at the time the row is added. Rules specify the conditions that must be met by data being entered into a column for the row to be saved.

Constraints enable you to specify data conditions either for an individual column or for a table as a whole. An example of a constraint is a primary key used to uniquely identify a row within a table. No other row can have the same value, or the constraint is violated and the affecting row is not added or updated.

Triggers can be used when you have complex conditions that must be verified to ensure that the data makes logical sense. When an employee's salary is updated, for example, you need to make sure that it's not less than the original salary or an unacceptably large increase. You can create a trigger that compares the old and new salary values to check these conditions.

When taking the Microsoft SQL Server Administration exam, be prepared to field at least one, if not several, questions dealing with database implementation issues.

8. **C**   32MB. Microsoft SQL Server requires a minimum of 16MB on a Windows NT Server. For a SQL Server acting as a distribution server in a replication scenario, the minimum memory is 32MB. 64MB is a better

amount of memory to use in this case, but it's more than the minimum required and, as such, also is incorrect.

9. **C** `sp_processmail`. SQL Server does not have stored procedures called `xp_answermail`, `sp_getmail`, or `xp_processmail`. There also is no stored procedure called `sp_sendmail`, although the extended stored procedure `xp_sendmail` can be used to tell SQL Server to send a message.

10. **B, D, E** You can use the Database Maintenance Wizard in Microsoft SQL Server to schedule backups and other maintenance activities at required times. This creates tasks in the SQL Server Task Manager that call SQLMAINT.EXE with the appropriate parameters to perform the backups.

    You also can manually schedule the backup tasks in the Task Manager within the SQL Enterprise Manager to perform transaction log and database backups at the required times. This involves a few more steps but enables automation of the backup process.

    It is not possible to use Windows NT Backup to perform online backups of SQL Server databases. To use Windows NT Backup, the Microsoft SQL Server must be stopped, and the device files must be accessible to the Windows NT Backup.

    There are no Microsoft SQL Server stored procedures called `sp_createtask` and `sp_scheduletask`, although the stored procedure `sp_addtask` can be used to manually add a task and to schedule its execution.

11. **B, C, D** The SQL Executive service account must have a password that never expires because the SQL Executive service is not be able to respond to the Windows NT request to change a password. The user account also must be able to log on to Windows NT any time during the day or night in case the machine resets and the SQL Executive service needs to restart.

    The SQL Executive service account needs to have the Log On as a Service right on the Windows NT Server machine where Microsoft SQL Server is installed. It also should be a member of the Administrators group on that machine. Another way to make it a member of the Administrators group is to add this account to the Windows NT domain's Domain Admins global group. Make sure that this group is a member of the local machine's Administrators group.

12. **A** `HKEY_LOCAL_MACHINE\Software\Microsoft\MSSQLServer`. Other information can be found at
`HKEY_LOCAL_MACHINE\System\CurrentControlSet\Services\MSSQLServer` and
`HKEY_LOCAL_MACHINE\System\CurrentControlSet\Services\SQLExecutive`.

    Options C and E are incorrect because these keys do not exist in Windows NT. `HKEY_CLASSES_ROOT` contains information about OLE mappings and other registered components of Windows NT. `HKEY_CURRENT_USER` contains information about the current and default user characteristics. Neither of these contain information about startup parameters for SQL Server.

13. **B, C** The SQL Enterprise Manager, SQL Server Engine, SQL Executive service, and SQL Distributed Management Objects (SQL-DMO) all are part of the Distributed Management Framework. In addition, OLE Automation is considered part of SQL-DMF because you can use OLE within your application to manage SQL Server.

14. **D** SQL Setup. Although it is possible to change the mode (either Direct Response or On-Demand) SQL Server uses to interface with the Performance Monitor in the SQL Enterprise Manager, the capability to turn integration on or off is not available in this utility. (It's grayed out.) Neither the Client Configuration utility nor SQL Trace nor SQL Service Manager has any capability to determine how SQL Server interfaces with the Performance Monitor. SQL Setup is the only tool that enables you to modify this particular server option.

15. **B** SQL Server Distributed Management Objects (SQL-DMO). SQL-DMO exposes interfaces for all SQL Server management functions to any OLE-compliant application. Therefore, through the use of OLE within your application, it *is* possible to manage SQL server functions.

16. **D** MSSQLServer. For users to be able to access data and databases within your SQL Server, only the MSSQLServer service needs to be started. For tasks, scheduled events, and replication to take place, however, the SQLExecutive service also must be running. The Microsoft Distributed Transaction Coordinator (MSDTC) service needs to be running only if your server is part of a distributed network of SQL Servers participating in distributed transaction and using the two-phase commit protocol. SQLMail is needed only if you have configured SQL Server to send and receive mail, for which the MSSQLServer and SQLExecutive services also should be running.

17. **B** pubs. The pubs database is installed so that you and Microsoft Technical Support can diagnose problems with your SQL Server. It is not required for normal operation of Microsoft SQL Server, and it can be dropped without affecting the overall configuration of the server.

Master, model, tempdb, and msdb are all systems databases. Master stores information about all databases, SQL Server configuration, and login IDs for the server. The model database is the model used to create new databases on the server. The tempdb database is a temporary storage area used when performing sorts or other temporary operations. It is reset every time you restart SQL Server. The msdb database stores information about scheduled tasks, operators, alerts, events, backups, and restores.

18. **E** Although options B, C, and E all look quite similar, the correct syntax is found in option E. In option B, the name of the stored procedure to move the transaction log is incorrectly specified as xp_logdevice. In option C, the size to alter the database by is specified in 2KB pages. This is incorrect—database sizes always are specified in megabytes.

Options A and D refer to nonexistent procedures in SQL Server—xp_movelog and sp_movelog.

Another way to expand the database and allocate a separate transaction log is to use the SQL Enterprise Manager to modify the database by specifying a 5MB segment for the transaction log within the dialog box.

19. **C** Appears to be an outstanding solution but does not work. When dropping devices using the SQL Enterprise Manager, SQL Server does not delete the underlying operating system files. When re-creating your device (in particular the log device you backed up), you will receive an error from SQL Server informing you that it could not create the operating system file. This is because the old file is still around and SQL Server cannot overwrite any operating system files when creating a database device.

20. **C** Appears to be an outstanding solution but does not work. Dropping databases using the sp_dbremove stored procedure and the DROPDEV parameter (as with the SQL Enterprise Manager) does not delete the underlying operating system files. When re-creating your devices (in particular the log device you backed up), you will receive an error from SQL Server informing you that it could not create the operating system file. This is because the old file is still

around and SQL Server cannot overwrite any operating system files when creating a database device.

21. **A** This is an outstanding solution that does work. The stored procedure sp_dbremove removes any entries for the database from the sysdatabases and sysusages tables in the Master database. Using the stored procedure sp_dropdevice with the DELFILE parameter ensures that the operating system files associated with any devices still around also are removed. This enables the re-creation of the devices and the database without any errors.

22. **B** The mapping of the Windows NT users and groups that have access to Microsoft SQL Server while using integrated security is accomplished through the SQL Security Manager. The stored procedures sp_addlogin and sp_adduser are used when adding logins to SQL Server and mapping logins to database users, respectively, in either standard or mixed security modes.

23. **D** The user owns objects. It is not possible to drop a database user that owns a database object such as a table, view, stored procedure, and so on. To drop this user, you must first drop the associated objects belonging to the user and then drop the user.

Membership in any group does not prevent a user from being dropped. Therefore, options C and E are not correct. Because the question stated that this user was not being used by any of the individuals accessing the database, option A also is incorrect. There is no way to flag a user account as persistent in Microsoft SQL Server, so option B is a bogus answer.

24. **B** When specifying memory to be used by Microsoft SQL Server, the value given to sp_configure is in 2KB pages. The correct answer is B because 8,192 times 2KB is 16MB of memory. Option A allocates 32MB of memory (16,384×2KB) to SQL Server in this machine, which does not provide sufficient RAM for other operating system functions and causes Windows NT to perform excessive paging. Option C is above the maximum setting for memory (1,048,576) and results in an error.

25. **B** All members of R&D access SQL Server as the system administrator. By default, any member of the Windows NT group Administrators is given system administrator privileges and connects to SQL Server as the login ID sa

when using a trusted connection. Because you are using integrated security, all connections to SQL Server are trusted. This gives anyone in R&D the capability to connect to SQL Server as the system administrator.

26. **B** The sysusers table in the database where the user account was created. SQL Server database users are specific to an individual database. This enables certain individuals to connect to SQL Server but to access only the specific databases permitted by the system administrator. Login IDs, on the other hand, enable an individual to connect to the SQL Server without a user account set up in a database. The Login ID only enables the individual to access databases in which a guest user has been created.

27. **A, B, E** Named Pipes, NWLink IPX/SPX, and TCP/IP Sockets. By default, NetWare client machines use the IPX/SPX protocol for communication with the NetWare LAN. For them to connect to SQL Server, therefore, you need to install NWLink IPX/SPX protocol. UNIX workstations generally use TCP/IP for LAN-based communication; support for this protocol also should be installed. You are not informed of the protocol used by Windows 95 and Windows NT clients to connect to their domain, but neither Banyan Vines nor DEC Net Sockets are common in Windows NT. The only other possible choice is Named Pipes, which is a common protocol on Microsoft networks.

28. **A, E** When creating Windows NT groups to be exported to SQL Server using the SQL Security Manager, you should use only valid SQL Server characters. You also should make sure that a user appears in only one group. This is because SQL Server enables a user to be a member of the group PUBLIC and one other group in each database. Putting a user in two groups mapping to the same database causes an error and does not enable the user to get added to the database.

You also should make sure that group names, including the domain separator, have no more than 30 characters. This is the maximum length of a group name in Microsoft SQL Server.

In general, when using integrated security, Microsoft SQL Server rules always should be followed when creating Windows NT groups to be exported to SQL Server through the Security Manager.

Options C and D are incorrect because it is not possible to create groups in the SQL Security Manager. It also is not possible to create groups in SQL Server from the User Manager.

A

29. **D** The solution does not work because the first statement, GRANT SELECT ON Leads TO ALL, is not valid within SQL Server. The other GRANT statements succeed.

30. **A, C** The simplest way to create a database and assign the data and log segments to appropriate devices is indicated by option C. This option creates a 20MB data segment on MyDataDevice and tells SQL Server to allocate a 10MB log segment on MyLogDevice.

Because the amount of space to allocate to a database and to log on a device always is specified in megabytes, options B and E do not satisfy the requirements.

Option D is not correct syntax because the LOG ON component of the CREATE DATABASE command requires that a device name and size be specified. The first part of the statement (CREATE DATABASE MyDb ON MyDataDevice=20, MyLogDevice=10) is valid, however. It allocates 20MB to the database on MyDataDevice and 10MB on MyLogDevice without specifically putting a separate log segment on any of the devices.

When looking at option A, you might think it is a long-winded way of allocating space to a database on a device, and it might very well be. This, however, satisfies the requirement of a 20MB data segment and a 10MB log segment. It is important to note that sp_logdevice always must follow any ALTER DATABASE statement in which you are moving a log from one device to another—in this case, from the same device as the database (MyDataDevice) to a new device (MyLogDevice) to which the database was altered.

31. **A** This is an outstanding solution. When assigning permissions to SQL Server groups and users, they first go to PUBLIC, then individual groups, and finally individual users. The proper method has been followed in this case, and only the required permissions have been assigned. This ensures that users do not get any permissions they should not have.

32. **B** DBCC TEXTALL. DBCC TEXTALL checks the allocation of text and image columns in all tables in a database. DBCC CHECKDB makes sure that all tables and indexes are allocated correctly. DBCC NEWALLOC makes sure that all pages in a database are properly allocated and accounted for. There are no SQL Server stored procedures called sp_checkdb or sp_checktext.

33. **A**   The DUMP DATABASE statement tells SQL Server to back up a database to a backup device. It is possible within SQL Server to specify more than one backup, or dump, device by separating the defined devices with commas. These devices must be created within SQL Server using either the SQL Enterprise Manager or the sp_addumpdevice stored procedure.

    BACKUP DATABASE is not valid syntax in SQL Server. The LOAD DATABASE command restores a database or transaction log backup, in which case the presented syntax is incorrect. There is no SQL Server stored procedure called sp_dbbackup.

34. **B**   This is an acceptable solution and provides the desired results. It also, however, assigns too many permissions to other users on the system. Furthermore, it requires more commands than necessary to be issued to accomplish the results.

35. **B, D, E**   Each command makes a change to the tables in the Master database. It is recommended that Master be backed up every time it changes. Adding a login ID using sp_addlogin, reconfiguring the server using sp_configure, and dropping a known remote server using sp_dropserver modify the syslogins, sysconfigures, and sysservers tables in the Master database. For this reason, the Master database should be backed up after issuing any of these commands.

    The stored procedures sp_adduser and sp_dropuser modify the sysusers table in the database where the user is added or dropped. Because these two commands do not modify the Master database, they do not require you to back up Master but rather the database where the user resides.

36. **A**   This is an outstanding solution. It is always more efficient to mirror disk devices at the Windows NT level than to use SQL Server device mirroring. In this manner, Windows NT ensures that all writes to the database also are copied to the new 9GB drive. In the event of a disk failure, SQL Server continues to operate without any discernible indication of a problem.

37. **D**   This solution does not work. It is not possible to mirror SQL Server database devices to a remote machine on a Windows NT network. All database devices for SQL Server must exist on the same machine as the SQL Server itself.

38. **B**   This is an acceptable solution. SQL Server device mirroring ensures that all writes to the primary database device also are copied to the mirror device. This process requires SQL Server itself to manage the two write operations. It is not as efficient as using Windows NT disk mirroring.

39. **C**   If you receive the response `Command completed successfully`, you have correctly established a connection to the machine. If you still have problems connecting to Microsoft SQL Server, you should use the `makepipe` and `readpipe` utilities to test the named pipe connection.

40. **A, C, E**   `DBCC MEMUSAGE` can be used to display the amount of memory allocated to SQL Server at startup and the memory used by the 20 largest objects in the data buffer cache and procedure cache.

41. **B**   The Windows NT Performance Monitor enables you to monitor the usage of a transaction log in real time. This can be done by looking at the SQL Server Object, Log Space Used (%) parameter for the Orders database.

42. **A**   The publishing server. The publishing server is where the data originates; therefore, it is the best place to enforce triggers and other constraints. It is impossible to guarantee that any other tables required to enforce triggers are always available on servers other than where the data originates. There is no such thing as a trigger server.

43. **A, C**   Microsoft SQL Server 6.0 and 6.5 servers. SQL Server replication enables SQL Server data to be replicated to any ODBC data source, including Oracle, Microsoft Access, Sybase, xBASE, and others. The publishing server must be a Microsoft SQL Server 6.x server.

44. **C**   Microsoft SQL Server 6.5 replication treats a subscription server running Microsoft SQL Server 6.0 as an ODBC data source. It therefore is necessary to configure an ODBC data source name (DSN) for the SQL Server 6.0 server on the publishing server machine.

45. **A, B, C, E**   SQL Server supports automatic synchronization, which is initiated and controlled by SQL Server but can be scheduled during periods of low activity. Manual synchronization is initiated by the user and can be

applied to the subscriber using tape or another medium. Scheduled table refresh provides the capability to periodically update a subscriber database's table with current data from the publisher. No synchronization is self-explanatory. There is no such thing as trigger-based synchronization.

46. **A**   When an alert has been configured for both an error number and a severity code that matches the error number, only the most specific alert fires. This prevents SQL Server from unnecessarily firing alerts when a more precise set of conditions has been defined.

47. **C**   When SQL Server processes alerts, it processes alerts on the local server first. Any events not handled locally are forwarded to the Alerts Management Server.

48. **B**   The bcp utility can be used to export individual tables in both SQL Server native format (which must be used on the same hardware platform as the data's source) and in character format (which can be used on any SQL Server platform). The bcp command-line switches /c and /n specify whether to export in character or native format, respectively. When transferring from an Intel- to an Alpha-based platform, the /c switch must be used. There is no export utility in SQL Server.

49. **A, D**   The SQL Transfer Manager can be used to transfer data from any SQL Server to any other SQL Server (or ODBC data source), regardless of the originating and target platforms. This is the easiest way to upgrade your server.

    The bcp utility also can be used to transfer data from one server to another if it is run in character mode. This is because native format files are specific to the platform on which they were created. Although bcp enables you to transfer data, it does not enable you to transfer other database objects.

    SQL Server DUMP and LOAD cannot be used in this example because SQL Server backups are specific to the platform on which they were created.

50. **B, C, E**   The Current Activity windows in the SQL Enterprise Manager show User Activity (the current user connections, objects, and locks), Detail Activity (a list of processes, their statuses, locks, and commands that active users are running), and Object Locks (a list of database objects currently locked and the kinds of locks applied).

51. **D** The sp_spaceused stored procedure can be used to find current database space-usage information. The table syslogs is the transaction log for any database. Querying the space used by the syslogs table provides information about the size of the transaction log. To get a 100-percent accurate figure on the space utilization within the database by any database object, the @updateusage=true optional parameter should be used with sp_spaceused. This runs the DBCC UPDATEUSAGE stored procedure on the object whose space utilization is being checked and provides a more accurate picture.

52. **D** The SQL Server stored procedure sp_help_revdatabase can be used to generate a SQL script. You can use this script to later rebuild your database and devices with the exact same structure and sizes as before any media failure. It takes information from the sysdatabases, sysusages, and sysdevices tables in the Master database to reverse-engineer the structure of any database.

53. **B, C, F** SQL Server automatic recovery is a feature that makes sure that database consistency is maintained after a catastrophic failure such as a crash or power failure. It cannot be turned off, and it ensures that any committed transactions in the transaction log are rolled forward. Incomplete transactions are rolled back.

    The database recovery order starts with the Master database, followed by the model, tempdb, msdb, pubs, distribution, and user databases.

    The characteristics of automatic recovery can be configured using the recovery flags and recovery internal configuration parameters. These parameters govern how much information is displayed during recovery and how frequently a checkpoint occurs during the automatic recovery process.

54. **D** Starting Microsoft SQL Server from a command prompt with the -f parameter forces SQL Server to start independent of Windows NT and in its minimal configuration mode. In this mode, the memory configuration parameter is reset to the default value of 4,096 pages. SQL Server is running in this mode, which enables you to connect to the server using ISQL/W or the SQL Enterprise Manager. You then can use either sp_configure or the Configure item after right-clicking the server name in the Enterprise Manager to change the memory setting.

55. **C, E** When upgrading a database from SQL Server 4.21 to SQL Server 6.5, it is necessary to re-create the database on the SQL Server 6.5 server with the

exact same segment structure as the original 4.21 database. Because the upgrade process makes use of the DUMP and LOAD commands to upgrade the database, it is treated as a backup and restore of sorts. When performing a restore, it is necessary to follow the same order of CREATE DATABASE, ALTER DATABASE, and other sequences. This ensures that the restore/LOAD performs correctly as the segment structure is stored with the backup.

After successfully loading the database into SQL Server 6.5, the CHUPG65.EXE utility should be run to check for any potential problems with the upgraded database. Potential problems include keyword conflicts between database objects and new keywords in SQL Server 6.5, no data in the text column of the syscomments table for database objects in the upgraded database, or the database status being set to read-only. These conditions need to be corrected prior to making the database available to users. After, it also might be necessary to modify the client application, but that's a different topic.

56. **A, B** When creating a database to be distributed to other sites or users, the database cannot be created by the CREATE DATABASE statement. It needs to be created using the sp_create_removable stored procedure, which initializes the database structure so that it can later be replicated on CD-ROM or any removable media.

For the sp_certify_removable stored procedure to certify that a database is removable and to properly configure the database and devices to later distribute, the system administrator must be the owner of the database (the dbo), all objects must be owned by dbo, and no permissions can be set on objects. This is true because sa is the only known login ID on all SQL Server databases. Other logins and users can exist on the target server, but this cannot be guaranteed. Therefore, the sp_certify_removable stored procedure does not enable other users or permissions to be configured.

There is no requirement for each salesperson to have a login ID on your master server. Each salesperson will be accessing the database on his own SQL Server, which is installed on his notebook as part of the SQL Workstation package.

57. **D** SQL Server 6.5 has 10 empty stored procedures in the Master database called sp_user_counter1 to sp_user_counter10. These can be modified to track specific application-related information with the Performance Monitor.

In the Performance Monitor, they appear under the SQL Server object as User Counter 1 to User Counter 10. This makes it possible to track the average value of an order.

58. **D** Livelock. In a livelock situation, many users consistently are reading a page on which a user wants to modify a record. This is detected automatically by SQL Server, and further read requests are suspended until the user makes the change—a process called lock queuing. Following the change, users once again can read the page.

    A write lock is applied to a page when a user makes a change to a record on it, thereby blocking all other users until the change completes. This is also sometimes referred to as a blocking lock.

    A shared lock, or read lock, is applied to a page when a user reads a record contained on that page. At this point, no updates can be made to data on that page until the lock is cleared.

59. **A** By configuring SQL Server replication and having the new server subscribe to the original database in its entirety, you will have a copy of the data in the original system. By configuring the sales managers' clients to use the replicated data instead of working on the original order entry system, you don't slow down the order-entry process, and you enable the sales managers to get the necessary reports printed.

60. **D** Named Pipes. Other protocols can be selected and installed using SQL Setup.

61. **B** The stored procedure and the underlying object are not owned by the same user, so SQL Server checks permissions every time a referenced object's ownership changes because it executes the stored procedure. Because Maria has been given SELECT and INSERT permissions on the Client table by Tim, she can add or read data in the table but cannot update the data using either the UPDATE command or the sp_updateClient stored procedure. This situation is called a broken ownership chain and can be avoided by making sure that all objects within a database are owned by the dbo.

Index

Symbols

16-bit client utilities, installing, 70
32-bit client utilities, installing, 69-70

A

accounts, 180
    adding, 188
Add Alert dialog box, 364
Add to Chart dialog box, 361
Alert Engine Options dialog box, 259
Alert Manager, 23
alerts, 255
    actions, 255
    management, 259
    operators, 255-257
        creating, 257-258
    processor time, 364-365
    setting up, 255, 259, 265-266
aliases, 204
    adding
        Enterprise Manager, 204-205
        sp_addalias stored procedure, 204
    dropping, 206
        Enterprise Manager, 206
        sp_dropalias stored procedure, 206
    sysalternates table, 213
allocation pages, 146
allocation units, 148
ALTER DATABASE statement, 160, 307

ANSI-92, SQL Server support, 13
AppleTalk ADSP network library, 60
architecture, 18
    distributed management framework,
        18-20
        back end, 19, 23-24
        front end, 19-21
        SQL Server Object Library, 19-23
articles, replication, 323
    nonpublishable, 327
    publishable, 327
automatic recovery, 300
    checkpoints, 287
    model database, 301
    msdb database, 301
    pubs database, 301
    tempdb database, 301
    user databases, 301
automatic synchronization, 325

B

back-end architecture, 19, 23-24
    Distributed Transaction Manager service,
        24
    SQL Executive service, 23-24
        Alert Manager, 23
        Event Manager, 23
        Replication Manager, 23
        Task Manager, 23
    SQL Server service, 23
BackOffice, integration with, 14
Backup Device Information dialog box,
    278
backup devices, *see* dump devices
backups, 270-271, 280-283, 295
    checkpoints, 287
    configuring NT Server for, 53
    DBCCs, running with, 285